MEASURING ACCOUNTABILITY IN PUBLIC GOVERNANCE REGIMES

Government accountability is generally accepted to be an essential feature of modern democratic society; while others might turn a blind eye to corruption and wrongdoing, those who value accountability would instead shine a bright light on it. In this context, it is common to hear claims of accountability 'deficit' (a particular mechanism or area is lacking in accountability) and 'overload' (a particular mechanism or area over-delivers on accountability). Despite the frequency of references to these concepts, their precise content remains undeveloped. This book offers an explanation, as well as a framework for future exploration, of these concepts. It highlights the difficulty of defining a benchmark that might be used to measure the amount of accountability in a particular situation, and also the challenge of mapping out accountability mechanisms as a system. While difficult, if accountability is indeed a foundational concept underpinning our system of government, there is merit in meeting these challenges head-on.

ELLEN ROCK is a lecturer in the Faculty of Law at the University of Technology Sydney. Her research interests include government account-ability and liability, and she has published widely on these topics in leading law journals and edited collections. She is also co-author of *Government Liability: Principles and Remedies* (2019).

T0384519

MEASURING ACCOUNTABILITY IN PUBLIC GOVERNANCE REGIMES

ELLEN ROCK

University of Technology Sydney

CAMBRIDGE
UNIVERSITY PRESS

University Printing House, Cambridge CB2 8BS, United Kingdom

One Liberty Plaza, 20th Floor, New York, NY 10006, USA

477 Williamstown Road, Port Melbourne, VIC 3207, Australia

314-321, 3rd Floor, Plot 3, Splendor Forum, Jasola District Centre, New Delhi - 110025, India

103 Penang Road, #05-06/07, Visioncrest Commercial, Singapore 238467

Cambridge University Press is part of the University of Cambridge.

It furthers the University's mission by disseminating knowledge in the pursuit of
education, learning and research at the highest international levels of excellence.

www.cambridge.org
Information on this title: www.cambridge.org/9781108814126
DOI: 10.1017/9781108886154

© Ellen Rock 2020

First published 2020
First paperback edition 2022

A catalogue record for this publication is available from the British Library

Library of Congress Cataloging in Publication data
Names: Rock, Ellen, 1984– author.
Title: Measuring accountability in public governance regimes / Ellen Rock,
University of Technology Sydney.
Description: Cambridge, United Kingdom ; New York, NY : Cambridge University Press, 2020. |
Based on author's thesis (doctoral - Australian National University, 2018) issued under title:
Accountability Deficits and Overloads: A Missing Framework. | Includes bibliographical
references and index.
Identifiers: LCCN 2020013859 (print) | LCCN 2020013860 (ebook) | ISBN 9781108840484
(hardback) | ISBN 9781108814126 (paperback) | ISBN 9781108886154 (epub)
Subjects: LCSH: Administrative law. | Public administration–Auditing. | Government
accountability. | Government accountability–Australia.
Classification: LCC K3400 .R63 2020 (print) | LCC K3400 (ebook) | DDC 352.8/8–dc23
LC record available at https://lccn.loc.gov/2020013859
LC ebook record available at https://lccn.loc.gov/2020013860

ISBN 978-1-108-84048-4 Hardback
ISBN 978-1-108-81412-6 Paperback

For Charlie and Penny

CONTENTS

vii

FOREWORD

When, around the turn of the twentieth century, the term 'accountability'
became commonplace in discussions of public governance, its meaning –
as is often the way with buzzwords – was far from clear. Public accountability was understood in a mechanistic sense rather than as a principle
or value: it was a *process* designed to exact an account of their doings
from public figures. Colin Scott identified three essential accountability
questions: Who is to be held accountable? To whom? And what for?[1] He
should perhaps have added 'How'?

Since those early days, use of the word has proliferated. It is used in a
myriad of different ways and situations: in a political context to express
the relationship between governors and governed, in a managerial context to exert hierarchical control over public servants, in a legal context as
a substitute for responsibility or liability, to name only a few. The term
now possesses a normative meaning as a principle or 'cultural keyword'
that is the *sine qua non* of democratic government.[2] Academic studies
have multiplied inside the disciplines of law, political science and public
administration and the concept has crossed national boundaries into the
worlds of European and international studies. A *Handbook of Accountability* exists, which attempts to collect, consolidate and integrate the
various standpoints. Yet to Matthew Flinders, the concept appears to be
'in some ways more nebulous, contested and vague than it has ever
been'.[3]

Ellen Rock's ambitious study attacks the problem of imprecision head
on. She does not seek the El Dorado of a single, all-encompassing

---

[1] Colin Scott, 'Accountability in the Regulatory State' (2000) 27 *Journal of Legal Studies* 38.
[2] Melvin Dubnick, 'Accountability and Ethics: Reconsidering the Relationships' (2003) 6
International Journal of Organization Theory and Behaviour 405.
[3] Matthew Flinders, 'The Future and Relevance of Accountability Studies' in Mark Bovens,
Robert E Goodin and Thomas Schillemans (eds.), *The Oxford Handbook of Public
Accountability* (Oxford University Press, 2014) 661, 661.

meaning for accountability or a single paradigmatic procedure. Instead she takes as her starting point the challenge of treating accountability as a measureable commodity, employing the concepts of accountability 'deficit' and 'overload'. The latter of these concepts is beginning to find its way into the literature as a counterweight or perhaps a corrective to the 'implicit normative implication' that accountability is a public good that we cannot get too much of, a viewpoint that, the *Oxford Handbook* editors suggest, has been over-emphasised.[4] It is beginning to be said that 'the accountability pendulum has swung so far in the direction of answering cries of deficit, that we have inadvertently caused a new style of accountability problem. Government officials have become so overwhelmed by – or enraptured with – complying with accountability mechanisms that accountability is being undermined by the very processes designed to support it.' Rock therefore notes the emergence of 'two distinct camps: those calling for increased accountability by expanding the number, reach, or "bite" of accountability mechanisms, and those calling for a reduction in the number, reach or bite of accountability mechanisms.' If, as the managerial school has always insisted, accountability deficits encourage maladministration, then arguably accountability overload has the same effect.

The proper balance between these two camps is the problem that Rock sets out to tackle. She embarks on the ambitious task of establishing a quantum of 'enough' accountability, which could stand as a 'benchmark' in debates over 'too much' and 'not enough'. This she does by varying the three accountability questions to read: 'Who *should* be held accountable?', 'To whom *should* they be accountable?' and 'For what?' Equally important is the fourth question of *how*. This not only reopens the perennial debate over legal and political accountability and which has the greater legitimacy, but also opens the question of whether, as most members of the general public seem to think, accountability requires a punitive element. We are all familiar with the strident calls for 'heads to roll' that follow every disaster, scandal or public inquiry.

What Rock provides is a very detailed exploration of these questions, structured around five different rationales or objectives for accountability that she characterises as transparency, control, redress, desert and deterrence. Against these rationales, Rock measures mechanisms for

---

[4] Mark Bovens and Thomas Schillemans, 'Meaningful Accountability' in Mark Bovens, Robert E Goodin and Thomas Schillemans (eds.), *The Oxford Handbook of Public Accountability* (Oxford University Press, 2014) 673, 676.

accountability, such as ombudsman investigations or criminal and civil liability. Some machinery scores more highly on one rationale than others: legal liability is, for example, strong on transparency and desert; ombudsman investigations, on the other hand, are low on transparency and desert but, because they are less punitive, may be higher on redress and deterrence. This finding leads Rock to undertake a further evaluation. She situates each accountability mechanism in a wider system of accountability to see whether any shortfall identified can be redressed by other mechanisms.

At the end of the day, Rock concludes pragmatically that the search for an umbrella concept of accountability is likely to prove impossible; 'horses for courses' is likely to be a better approach. 'If we adopt a variety of (potentially competing) rationales for accountability, we must in turn accept that accountability must be supported via a range of mechanisms.' Without undertaking an analysis of the accountability system as a whole, perhaps through a series of case studies, it will not be possible to identify accountability deficits and overloads. Clearly, much work remains to be done in the scientific exploration of accountability. This enjoyable book, however, provides a valuable set of stepping stones towards rationalisation.

Carol Harlow
Emeritus Professor of Law
London School of Economics

ACKNOWLEDGEMENTS

I owe my thanks to a large number of people, without whom this book could certainly not have been written. Many colleagues have offered their advice, guidance and support at numerous points throughout this process, including Tracey Booth, Nina Boughey, Brett Heino, Leighton McDonald, Brian Opeskin and Amanda Sapienza. My work has also been generously supported by colleagues at the conferences where I have presented this research, including the *Unity of Public Law* conference hosted by the University of Cambridge in September 2016, and the *Frontiers of Public Law* and *Obligations IX* conferences hosted by the University of Melbourne in July 2018.

I would particularly like to thank those who have generously devoted their time to reviewing and commenting on drafts of various chapters, including Mark Aronson, Mark Lunney, Anita Stuhmcke and Greg Weeks. Their insightful comments and suggestions have been very much appreciated and have greatly improved this book in many ways. I also owe my thanks to Mark Bovens, Carol Harlow and Richard Mulgan, who examined the thesis on which this book is based. Their thoughtful commentary has proved invaluable in preparing this work for publication, and I thank them for taking the time to engage so thoroughly with my ideas. I would especially like to thank Carol for kindly writing the Foreword which appears in this book.

My greatest debt of gratitude is owed to my supervisor, Peter Cane. It is no exaggeration to say that this book would not have been written without his constant support and guidance during my PhD candidature and beyond. Early on, Peter encouraged me to 'chart a course out to sea' in my research and promised that he would let me know if I managed to venture too far from land. At Peter's encouragement I have embraced the challenges and uncertainties of the topics explored in this book, and I am grateful for his ever-insightful advice and tireless efforts on my behalf.

Thanks go also to my wonderful family and friends for their unwavering support. I would like to thank my parents Robyn and Peter, who have always encouraged me to pursue the things I care about. I would also like to thank my wonderful parents-in-law Kerry, Rob, Bill, Sue and Kerry for their generous support (and free childcare). I would like to thank my children, Charlie and Penny, for their love and patience in the lengthy writing process that has taken me away from them more often than I would like. Finally, I would like to thank my husband, Tom, for his steadfast support in this project and always. Over the past few years he has learned far more about government accountability than he ever cared to know, and it is not an overstatement to say that I could not have done this without him.

The content of this book is accurate to 1 July 2019.

This research has been generously funded by an Australian Government Research Training Program (RTP) Scholarship.

TABLE OF CASES

TABLE OF STATUTES

~

Introduction

The concept of accountability features frequently in discussions about public governance, denoting the values of equity, democracy and justice. Rising from near anonymity, accountability has come to be regarded as the '*über*-concept of the twenty-first century'.[1] Notwithstanding our apparent willingness to jump on the accountability bandwagon, the precise metes and bounds of the concept remain contested. The literature abounds with definitions of accountability and descriptions of the essential features of accountability mechanisms. Far from assisting in clarification, the never-ending efforts at defining accountability leave us with many more questions than answers. Is accountability a normative concept, or should it be defined mechanically? Is it only about making government operations transparent, or does it also entail some form of response to what is discovered? Rather than seeking to answer these questions by contributing yet a further definition of accountability, this book builds on the existing literature positioning accountability as central to securing the legitimacy of government.[2] Where a government is accountable to its citizens, they are more likely to accept its legitimacy; conversely where a government is viewed as unaccountable, legitimacy is eroded.

Given the lofty status that has been afforded to the concept of accountability, it is perhaps unsurprising that many have turned their attention to concerns about a lack of accountability. Where there are accountability deficits, maladministration and malfeasance are rife. Politicians and

---

[1] Matthew Flinders, 'The Future and Relevance of Accountability Studies' in Mark Bovens, Robert Goodin and Thomas Schillemans (eds.), *The Oxford Handbook of Public Accountability* (Oxford University Press, 2014) 661, 661.

[2] Frederick Barnard, *Democratic Legitimacy: Plural Values and Political Power* (McGill-Queen's University Press, 2001) xi; Mark Bovens, Deirdre Curtin and Paul 't Hart, 'Studying the Real World of EU Accountability: Framework and Design' in Mark Bovens, Deirdre Curtin and Paul 't Hart (eds.), *The Real World of EU Accountability: What Deficit?* (Oxford University Press, 2010) 31, 53.

1

public servants alike are engaged in graft and corruption, and secret deals are done with corporate fat-cats behind closed doors. Government decision-makers are inefficient, uninterested or abusing their powers, and citizens who lose out are left to fend for themselves. Under this lens of accountability deficits, 'every man ought to be supposed to be a knave',[3] and the call for increased accountability is concerned with putting in place checks and controls to prevent our officials from yielding to their avarice. While it is difficult to pinpoint or articulate the nature of an 'accountability deficit', it appears to contain a temporal element. Deficit claims frequently accompany a perceived change or shift in the status quo, and calls for increased accountability represent a reaction to that shift. So, for instance, the changing size and structure of the executive branch is associated with a contraction in the reach and effectiveness of responsible government as an accountability mechanism. Suggestions to combat this deficit have focused attention on the expansion of existing mechanisms (e.g. the growth of judicial review),[4] and the introduction of new mechanisms (e.g. merits review tribunals and ombudsmen regimes).

Alongside our continued efforts to identify and correct areas of potential accountability deficit, the past two decades have seen the emergence of a new breed of accountability concern: the accountability 'overload'. It is said that the accountability pendulum has swung so far in the direction of answering cries of deficit, that we have inadvertently caused a new style of accountability problem. Government officials have become so overwhelmed by – or enraptured with – complying with accountability mechanisms that accountability is being undermined by the very processes designed to support it. Officials are said to be conflicted or paralysed in selecting which accountability demands to respond to, or engaging in practices of 'gaming the system' to improve results as measured by a particular mechanism. They might also be hindered in the development of new and innovative practices by rigid accountability standards, or simply be so overburdened by compliance regimes that their primary functions are neglected.

---

[3] David Hume, 'Of the Independency of Parliament' in Eugene F Miller (ed.), *Essays, Moral, Political, and Literary* (Liberty Fund, 1987) 42, 42.

[4] *Hot Holdings Pty Ltd v Creasy* (2002) 210 CLR 438, 467 [93] (Kirby J): 'It is not coincidental that this growth in administrative law remedies has occurred at a time when the theory of ministerial responsibility, as an effective means of ensuring public service accountability, has been widely perceived as having serious weaknesses and immunities.'

We thus see the development of two distinct camps: those calling for increased accountability by expanding the number, reach or 'bite' of accountability mechanisms, and those calling for a reduction in the number, reach or bite of accountability mechanisms. Both camps view their task as one of 'fixing' accountability as it applies in the context of public governance. In deciding which direction we ought to go, it is critical that we are careful in deciding whether there is, in fact, an accountability deficit or overload that needs to be addressed. These claims of deficit, on the one hand, and overload, on the other, suggest that there is a middle ground for which we ought to aim; too far either side will not only fail to correct an existing problem, but may produce an unintended new problem. Accordingly, the proper diagnosis of accountability deficits and overloads is critical to the identification of an appropriate cure.

But correctly identifying potential accountability deficits and overloads is not only relevant to the goal of curing these problems. It is also critical as a perception issue; *misconceptions* about deficits and overloads may pose just as great a problem as *genuine* accountability deficits and overloads. If (as I accept) accountability makes an important contribution to the legitimacy of government, public perception about lack of accountability may pose as significant a threat to legitimacy as academic thoughts on the topic. In other words, a perceived accountability deficit may be as problematic as a real one. Similarly, misconceptions about the existence of accountability overloads may be as damaging to an official's performance as an actual overload; an official who believes that they are subject to a range of competing accountability priorities may be paralysed by that perceived overload in just the same manner as an official who is actually subject to competing accountability priorities. If perceived deficits and overloads pose a threat to legitimacy and performance, the issue may be one not of 'fixing' the applicable accountability mechanisms, but rather of correcting the misconception through education and reinforcement of the effectiveness of the existing regime. Again, proper diagnosis is critical to the application of the correct treatment.

With this in mind, this book seeks to articulate the concepts of accountability deficits and overloads within the context of public governance. Despite the popularity of these concepts, the existing literature tends to gloss over the detail of their content. Claims of deficit and overload are often made in a generalised manner that focuses more on a perceived shift in the status quo than on articulating what has been lost. So, for example, those who identify an accountability deficit in the gradual diminution of responsible government often focus on the nature of that change (e.g. the changing shape and size of the executive branch). In focusing on that shift, we are left to infer that accountability was in the past effectively supported through that now diminished mechanism. Similarly, those who identify a deficit in the outsourcing of public functions to private contractors often focus on the missing source of accountability (e.g. the inability to seek judicial review of the decisions of private bodies). In turn, we are left to infer that accountability was in the past effectively supported through the now circumvented mechanism of judicial review. Claims of accountability overload are similarly framed, in focusing on the overlapping quantity of mechanisms and remedies that are said to produce undesired effects.

The argument drawn out in this book is that in the hunt for accountability deficits and overloads, we need to explicitly unpack two key steps in logic. The first is to define a 'benchmark' of accountability, which would enable us to articulate what 'enough' (and, in turn, 'not enough' and 'too much') accountability might look like. The second is in locating the particular mechanism under scrutiny within a wider system of accountability mechanisms. Without the former, we cannot explain how it is that a mechanism either falls short of, or exceeds, our accountability expectations. Without the latter, we cannot say that this shortfall or excess is not ameliorated by other mechanisms within the wider system. If the concepts of accountability deficit and overload are indeed as important as we are led to believe, then there is merit in seeking to address these two gaps in the literature. What this book in fact demonstrates, however, is that these gaps are not so much a matter of inadvertence as a reflection of some of the core difficulties in defining government accountability more generally.

Taking the first of these two points, the task of defining an accountability benchmark is one that leads us into some particularly difficult areas of legal philosophy. To craft a benchmark that represents an 'ideal amount' of government accountability, we would need to be able to move beyond the mechanistic understanding of accountability widely adhered to in the literature, an understanding that analyses accountability mechanisms within the rubric of *who* is accountable *to whom, for what* and *how*?[5] Instead of asking simply 'who is held accountable?', we instead need to be able to offer an answer to the question 'who *should* be held

---

[5] See, e.g., Mark Bovens, 'Analysing and Assessing Accountability: A Conceptual Framework' (2007) 13 *European Law Journal* 447, 454–55; Richard Mulgan, *Holding Power to*

accountable?'. Instead of 'to whom are they accountable?', we must decide 'to whom *should* they be accountable?'. Instead of 'for what are they held accountable?', we must ask 'for what *should* they be held accountable?'. Instead of 'how are they held accountable?', we must ask 'how *should* they be held accountable?'. If we were able to answer these questions, we could move beyond a mechanical definition of accountability, and into the more nuanced territory of articulating what we *expect* of that mechanism. The answers we identify in response to those questions would then provide us with a tool to measure a given mechanism and to determine whether it falls short of expectations (accountability deficit) or overperforms in respect of those expectations (accountability overload).

The difficulty, I suggest, is that answering these questions is no small task. Taking one of the more simple questions, *who should be held accountable*, we are confronted by some complex decisions that we must make about our conceptualisation of 'the government'. Would our accountability benchmark be shaped by reference to an understanding of the government as a corporate entity, or as a collection of individuals? Our answer to this question will shape our accountability benchmark and tell us whether accountability would demand that the government be made to answer as a whole, or whether responsibility should instead sheet home to individual officials. Only after we have confronted, and answered, this question can we move on to assess whether a particular mechanism satisfies or departs from that benchmark. Of course, deciding on the proper conceptualisation of the government is not a simple choice, harking back to the centuries-old debate reflected in the theories of Blackstone, on the one hand, and Dicey on the other.[6] If we are to offer an answer to the question of *who should be held accountable*, we first need to engage with and resolve this debate. Similar difficulties are confronted in answering the questions of *to whom* should the

---

Account: Accountability in Modern Democracies (Palgrave Macmillan, 2003) 22–23; Jerry Mashaw, 'Accountability and Institutional Design: Some Thoughts on the Grammar of Governance' in Michael Dowdle (ed.), *Public Accountability: Designs, Dilemmas and Experiences* (Cambridge University Press, 2006) 115, 118; Mark Philp, 'Delimiting Democratic Accountability' (2009) 57 *Political Studies* 28, 42; Colin Scott, 'Accountability in the Regulatory State' (2000) 27 *Journal of Law and Society* 38, 41; Ruth Grant and Robert Keohane, 'Accountability and Abuses of Power in World Politics' (2005) 99(1) *American Political Science Review* 29.

[6] Janet McLean, *Searching for the State in British Legal Thought: Competing Conceptions of the Public Sphere* (Cambridge University Press, 2012) ch 1.

government be accountable, *for what* and *how?* We see, therefore, that defining a benchmark of accountability is not simply a matter of plugging a small hole in the literature, but one that draws us into difficult territory that has exercised academic minds throughout history, and continues to do so.

This book suggests that one way of tackling the task of articulating a benchmark of accountability is to move beyond the generalised goal of holding the government 'accountable', and to articulate our underlying purpose in doing so. The literature often tends to gloss over the broader question of *why* it is that we seek to hold the government accountable.[7] This omission is not so critical in a mechanistic analysis, which focuses on exploring the way in which a given mechanism operates. Once we move into the territory of seeking to define a benchmark of accountability, however, this difficulty can no longer be avoided. In order to say *who should be held accountable*, we need to consider what our purpose in targeting that agent might be. Similarly, in order to say *to whom* they should be accountable, *for what* and *how*, we must turn our attention to what it is we are hoping to achieve. Though not always at the forefront of analysis, the accountability literature points to a range of potential rationales or goals for accountability. These include the facilitation of transparency, control, redress, desert and deterrence.

Adopting these five potential rationales, we can then seek to give shape to our accountability benchmark by considering what answer to each question best supports each rationale. So, for instance, in asking *how* accountability should be achieved, the transparency rationale might lead us to look to procedures capable of compelling the production of information, the control rationale might lead us to look for regulatory orders, the redress rationale for reparative remedies, the desert rationale for punitive sanctions and the deterrence rationale for the approach most likely to facilitate change going forward. In asking *who* should be held accountable, the rationales of transparency and control might suggest that we adopt a broad approach in order to reduce the possibility that the exercise of public power will be shielded from scrutiny or that its misdirected exercise be immune from review and redirection. The desert rationale, in contrast, might suggest that we adopt a much narrower approach, one that focuses on identification of the party most responsible for the wrongdoing in question. The redress rationale might direct us to

---

[7] Mark Bovens, Thomas Schillemans and Paul 't Hart, 'Does Public Accountability Work? An Assessment Tool' (2008) 86 *Public Administration* 225, 230.

look for the party with the greatest capacity to restore a victim, whereas the deterrence rationale might suggest we look for the party with the greatest capacity to facilitate positive change. We would reach similarly disparate answers to our remaining questions of *to whom* and *for what* the government should be held accountable.

A further point of difficulty is that even if we can accept that there are a range of possible rationales for accountability, it does not follow that we must all choose to subscribe to the *same set* of rationales. The goals of accountability might validly differ as between contexts, jurisdictions and possibly even by reference to the preferences of the individual commentator. Given the anomalous nature of accountability, is certainly possible (and even probable) that people will choose to prioritise different goals within their benchmark, or might identify further goals not considered in this book. All of this means that attempting to define a single universal 'ideal' benchmark is an inherently idealistic challenge. This book cannot hope to propose a universal benchmark that will be appropriate to every context and will appeal to every reader. Rather, the point being made here is that if we wish to have meaningful discussions about accountability deficits and overloads, it is imperative that we each reveal the benchmark that we are using, even if we disagree with those proposed by others. We need not necessarily deploy the *same* benchmark, but we must be able to clearly articulate our own.

Assuming that it was possible to settle on the rationale(s) we would choose to assign to accountability, we might then be able to create a standard by which we could measure a given accountability mechanism. So, for example, if we adopt desert as our guiding rationale, we might define our benchmark such that accountability would be said to demand that an *individual official* would be accountable to a *defined prosecutor* for their *deliberate wrongdoing* through the imposition of *punitive sanctions*. Using this benchmark to assess a given mechanism, we might identify a potential deficit if, for example, the sanctions provided were not punitive in nature, or if they were limited to cases where deliberate wrongdoing had caused loss,[8] for example. Similarly, we might identify a potential overload where a mechanism goes further than anticipated by the benchmark – for example, by making punitive damages available

---

[8] For example, we might view the availability of punitive damages for the tort of misfeasance in public office as falling into this category as there is no liability without proof of harm: Ellen Rock, 'Misfeasance in Public Office: A Tort in Tension' (2019) 43(1) *Melbourne University Law Review* 337.

outside cases of deliberate wrongdoing, or by imposing liability on one party for the actions of another. We would craft different standards (and identify different gaps and overlaps) if we choose transparency, control, redress or deterrence as our guiding rationales.

The difficulty is that, if we accept the possibility that accountability may be underpinned by more than one rationale, we must in turn accept that our accountability benchmark may at times pull in different directions. So, for instance, the redress rationale might demand that liability be imposed on the government as an entity given its deep pockets, whereas the desert rationale might demand that liability be sheeted home to a wrongdoing official. Because these two demands are in opposition, we cannot expect that our accountability benchmark would demand that a single mechanism perform both simultaneously. Accordingly, it would be necessary either to define our accountability benchmark very narrowly so as to avoid this potential conflict (in which case we could not complain about accountability deficits arising outside the confines of that narrowly defined benchmark), or we must allow that accountability will be supported via multiple mechanisms. In other words, even if individual mechanisms might fall short of the benchmark when taken alone, they may produce accountability when taken together. Of course, the more mechanisms made available to support accountability, the greater the chances that they will overlap with one another.

This leads to the second key point made in this book, which is that accountability mechanisms must not be measured against a benchmark in isolation, but located within the wider accountability system. The identification of a potential gap or overlap can only ever be taken as a preliminary observation, pending consideration of whether that gap or overlap is ameliorated by the operation of the accountability system as a whole. So, for instance, some might say that the unavailability of judicial review in cases of outsourced public powers represents an accountability deficit. However, until we have considered the alternative sources of control over that outsourced power, we cannot say that the failure of judicial review to attach to those agents is really an accountability deficit. Similarly, we might reach the view that the simultaneous availability of punitive damages for the tort of misfeasance in public office and criminal punishment pursuant to the offence of misconduct in public office represents a potential accountability overload. However, until we have considered the interaction between these two causes of action and whether both in fact impose accountability in the same case, our observation will only ever be a preliminary one.

This book makes the argument that accountability systems encompass a range of accountability dynamics that must be understood in order to assess the potential presence of accountability deficits and overloads. First, it is necessary to consider the varying features between accountability mechanisms. So, while some are very accessible, others are more difficult to access; while some are expensive and time-consuming, others are more affordable and efficient; while some are flexible, others are more rigid; while some are coercive, others are more discretionary; while some operate autonomously, others rely on intervention; while some are independent, others are subject to supervision and control; and while some enjoy a degree of permanence, others exist at the whim of another party. When viewing mechanisms in isolation, there is a temptation to treat these various features as a collection of strengths and weaknesses (e.g. the ideal would be a mechanism that is accessible, cheap, flexible, coercive, autonomous, independent and permanent). However, when approaching accountability as a system, it is possible that a balance of features between mechanisms may better serve accountability overall. So, for instance, the courts can afford to adopt a more rigid approach in light of the flexibility offered by the ombudsman, and the office of the ombudsman can afford to be of a less permanent character in light of the permanence of the courts.

A second feature evident in viewing accountability mechanisms as a system is that they reflect a range of different types of relationship dynamics. Viewing mechanisms in isolation can give the mistaken impression that they operate independently and without regard to one another, giving rise to the over-diagnosis of accountability overloads. Returning to the earlier example, we might view the imposition of punitive sanctions pursuant to both the tort of misfeasance in public office and the criminal offence of misconduct in public office as producing a potential accountability overload. However, on closer inspection it becomes apparent that there are much more nuanced relationship dynamics in place between mechanisms in the system. In addition to *independent* relationships, where mechanisms may operate in parallel, mechanisms may operate in a *staged* manner (where one is a precondition of another), *mutually exclusively* (where one precludes another), *interdependently* (where mechanisms are interlocked with one another) or *co-operatively* (where mechanisms complement and assist one another). We cannot possibly reach a conclusion that an accountability shortfall or excess identified through use of our benchmark is in fact an accountability deficit or overload without locating the mechanism within this wider system, and appreciating the role played by these various dynamics.

This book serves both to highlight the limitations of the treatment of accountability deficits and overloads in the existing literature, and to offer a framework for future exploration of these ideas. If the concept of accountability is as important to supporting the legitimacy of government as we are given to believe, the task of identifying an appropriate balance between 'too much' and 'not enough' accountability is equally deserving of our attention.

PART I

Accountability Deficits and Overloads

The concept of accountability has been put to many uses in academic literature and public discourse. Not unlike the rule of law, it is touted as an essential feature of modern democratic regimes, evoking notions of justice, equity and good governance. What such descriptions lack in detail, they more than make up for in rhetorical appeal. But on winding back the rhetoric, what do we discover about the meaning of accountability, and how do we determine whether or not we have 'achieved' it? In particular, how do we know whether or not we are falling short of achieving accountability (accountability deficit) or going too far in pursuit of accountability (accountability overload)?

Part I of this book lays the groundwork to tackle this larger question. Chapter 1 introduces readers to the generally accepted definitions of accountability, drawing together areas of agreement from across a range of disciplines, and noting areas that remain in dispute. An appreciation of the state of the art on the concept of accountability is necessary to begin to explore the concepts of accountability deficit and overload. Chapter 2 introduces readers to these two concepts, noting the use to which they have been put in academic and political commentary, and begins to unpack the two 'hidden assumptions' that rest behind these concepts.

1

Defining Accountability

Though accountability remains a contested concept, there is general agreement that it refers to a relational mechanism that can be analysed within the framework of the questions: *who* is accountable, *to whom*, *for what* and *how*? One of the largest unresolved questions about accountability, as explored in this chapter, is whether it is simply a mechanical concept (i.e. a description of a mechanism with certain attributes) or more broadly reflects a value or ideal (i.e. the notion of being an accountable person). The conclusion drawn here is that it is particularly difficult to divorce the concept of accountability from a normative background in discussing concepts of accountability deficits and over-loads. Each of these concepts rests on the normative assumption that it is possible to identity an 'ideal amount' of accountability. Accordingly, at least in this context, accountability imports a normative dimension.

1.1 What Is Accountability?

It is commonplace to start an accountability analysis by stating that it is a concept that everyone agrees is a desirable attribute of democratic regimes. It is a 'golden concept that no one can be against',[1] a 'hurrah-word'[2] with which '[n]obody argues'.[3] Up until the end of the twentieth century, it did not feature prominently in discussions of public govern-ance.[4] Despite its subsequent meteoric rise in popularity and its

---

[1] Mark Bovens, 'Analysing and Assessing Accountability: A Conceptual Framework' (2007) 13 *European Law Journal* 447, 448.

[2] Mark Bovens, 'Public Accountability' in Ewan Ferlie, Laurence Lynn Jr and Christopher Pollitt (eds.), *The Oxford Handbook of Public Management* (Oxford University Press, 2005) 182, 182.

[3] Amanda Sinclair, 'The Chameleon of Accountability: Forms and Discourses' (1995) 20 *Accounting, Organizations and Society* 219, 219.

[4] Richard Mulgan, '"Accountability": An Ever-Expanding Concept?' (2000) 78 *Public Administration* 555, 555.

apparently inherent value,[5] the term is not often given a precise definition. A review of the literature indicates that 'accountability' is a term that means different things to different people in different contexts. There are nearly as many descriptions of accountability as there are legal, political and philosophical authors who have written on the topic. Sinclair describes the study of accountability as the exploration of 'a "bottomless swamp", where the more definitive we attempt to render the concept, the more murky it becomes'.[6] The two decades that have passed since she made this observation have done little to settle the waters, and much more to muddy them. Accountability is ascribed a number of different roles and functions, many of which differ according to context; however, there are a number of elements that are agreed upon.

One of the more widely accepted definitions of accountability is that put forward by Bovens, who defines it as

> a relationship between an actor and a forum, in which the actor has an obligation to explain and to justify his or her conduct, the forum can pose questions and pass judgement, and the actor may face consequences.[7]

This definition has resonated with a number of other authors who have adopted it either in whole or with minor qualifications.[8] Oliver offers a similar definition, of 'being liable to be required to give an account or explanation' and 'where appropriate, to suffer the consequences, take the blame or undertake to put matters right if it should appear that errors

---

[5] Melvin J Dubnick, 'Accountability as a Cultural Keyword' in Mark Bovens, Robert Goodin and Thomas Schillemans (eds.), *The Oxford Handbook of Public Accountability* (Oxford University Press, 2014) 23, 24.

[6] Sinclair (n 3) 221, borrowing phrasing from Robert Dahl, 'The Concept of Power' (1957) 2 *Behavioral Science* 201, 201.

[7] Bovens, 'Analysing and Assessing Accountability' (n 1) 450; Mark Bovens, 'Two Concepts of Accountability: Accountability as a Virtue and as a Mechanism' (2010) 33 *West European Politics* 946, 951; Mark Bovens, Thomas Schillemans and Paul 't Hart, 'Does Public Accountability Work? An Assessment Tool' (2008) 86 *Public Administration* 225, 225.

[8] See, e.g., Carol Harlow, 'Accountability and Constitutional Law' in Mark Bovens, Robert Goodin and Thomas Schillemans (eds.), *The Oxford Handbook of Public Accountability* (Oxford University Press, 2014) 195, 196; Jeff King, 'The Instrumental Value of Legal Accountability' in Nicholas Bamforth and Peter Leyland (eds.), *Accountability in the Contemporary Constitution* (Oxford University Press, 2013) 124, 127; Arnost Vesely, 'Accountability in Central and Eastern Europe: Concept and Reality' (2013) 79 *International Review of Administrative Sciences* 310, 313.

have been made'.[9] In Oliver's view, accountability 'is explanatory and amendatory'.[10] Sinclair's definition implies similar reasoning, as she defines accountability as 'a relationship in which people are required to explain and take responsibility for their actions',[11] while Strom sees it as 'a mechanism ... by which agency loss may be contained'.[12] In his view, there is an accountability relationship where (1) the agent 'is obliged to act on ... behalf' of the principal and (2) the principal can 'reward or punish' the agent in respect of that performance.[13] Mulgan's definition is more complex, as he looks at the 'core sense' of accountability, which he says has the features of being external, involving 'social interaction and exchange' and implying 'rights of authority', wherein the superior body has the 'rights to demand answers and impose sanctions'.[14] The definition employed by Grant and Keohane also speaks of rights of authority, as they define accountability as a 'right to hold [an actor] to a set of standards, to judge whether they have fulfilled their responsibilities in light of these standards, and to impose sanctions if they determine that these responsibilities have not been met'.[15] This definition is predicated on there being 'a relationship between power-wielders and those holding them accountable where there is a general recognition of the legitimacy of (1) the operative standards for accountability and (2) the authority of the parties to the relationship (one to exercise particular powers and the other to hold them to account)'.[16] Some authors have adopted narrower definitions than these. For Scott, '[a]ccountability is the duty to give account for one's actions to some other person or body'.[17] Further, Philp defines an accountability relationship in the sense that 'A is accountable with

---

[9] Dawn Oliver, *Government in the United Kingdom: The Search for Accountability, Effectiveness, and Citizenship* (Open University Press, 1991) 22. This definition is adapted from Colin Turpin, *British Government and the Constitution: Text, Cases and Materials* (Weidenfeld and Nicolson, 1990) 421–22.

[10] Oliver, *Government in the United Kingdom* (n 9) 22.

[11] Sinclair (n 3) 220–21.

[12] Kaare Strom, 'Parliamentary Democracy and Delegation' in Kaare Strom, Wolfgang Muller and Torbjorn Bergman (eds.), *Delegation and Accountability in Parliamentary Democracies* (Oxford University Press, 2003) 55, 62.

[13] Ibid.

[14] Mulgan, '"Accountability": An Ever-Expanding Concept?' (n 4) 555–56.

[15] Ruth Grant and Robert Keohane, 'Accountability and Abuses of Power in World Politics' (2005) 99(1) *American Political Science Review* 29, 29.

[16] Ibid.

[17] Colin Scott, 'Accountability in the Regulatory State' (2000) 27 *Journal of Law and Society* 38, 40.

respect to M when some individual, body or institution, Y, can require A to inform and explain/justify his or her conduct with respect to M.'[18]

Other authors offer less prescriptive definitions of accountability, seeing it as a sort of umbrella term that incorporates various other concepts. Harlow takes this approach in describing accountability as a 'portmanteau' into which may be packed a 'bundle of notions pertinent to modern systems of government' including 'democratic legitimacy, political responsibility, financial probity and audit'.[19] Koppell also conceives of accountability as an umbrella term that consists of five dimensions, being transparency, liability, controllability, responsibility and responsiveness.[20] An actor's accountability is assessed by reference to how it fulfils each of these dimensions, with transparency and liability acting as a basis for enquiries into the remainder.[21] Another commentator who takes this line is Dubnick, who defines accountability as a 'genus', for which the relevant 'species' are liability, obligation, answerability, obedience, responsibility, fidelity, responsiveness and amenability.[22]

These various definitions reveal a number of common streams of thought. One matter on which authors agree is that accountability is an *elusive and illusive concept* that is capable of performing various theoretical tasks; it is a 'chameleon',[23] a 'will-o-the-wisp',[24] an 'ever-expanding concept',[25] a 'portmanteau' containing 'a bundle of notions'[26] and an 'unspecified umbrella term'.[27] A second area of consensus is that accountability is a *relational concept*. It describes the dynamics of a relationship between two parties in which one is entitled to hold the other accountable for their actions. However, there are differences of

---

[18] Mark Philp, 'Delimiting Democratic Accountability' (2009) 57 *Political Studies* 28, 32.

[19] Carol Harlow, 'Accountability as a Value in Global Governance and for Global Administrative Law' in Gordon Anthony and others (eds.), *Values in Global Administrative Law* (Hart Publishing, 2011) 173, 178.

[20] Jonathan Koppell, 'Pathologies of Accountability: ICANN and the Challenge of "Multiple Accountabilities Disorder"' (2005) 65 *Public Administration Review* 94, 96.

[21] Ibid.

[22] Dubnick, 'Accountability as a Cultural Keyword' (n 5) 33.

[23] Sinclair (n 3) 219.

[24] Frederick C Mosher, 'The Changing Responsibilities and Tactics of the Federal Government' (1980) 40 *Public Administration Review* 541, 546, cited in Robert D Behn, *Rethinking Democratic Accountability* (Brookings Institution Press, 2001) 5.

[25] Mulgan, '"Accountability": An Ever-Expanding Concept?' (n 4).

[26] Harlow, 'Accountability as a Value in Global Governance' (n 19) 178.

[27] Vesely (n 8) 313.

opinion as to the source of this dynamic. Some appear to see it as an incident of the delegation of power from one party to another,[28] while others see it as a legal or moral duty stemming from the fact that one party is affected by the exercise of power by another.[29] Thirdly, there is general agreement that accountability is *coercive*, in the sense that it does not arise in situations of voluntary provision of information.[30] Fourthly, a minimum defining feature of an accountability relationship is that it requires the *provision of an account or justification* for a chosen course of conduct.[31] A fifth common thread in the literature is that accountability relationships can arise in a *wide variety of contexts*, not only within the area of public governance, but also in the private sector and social arena.[32] When examined more closely, the public governance context can be further broken down to refer to political accountability (accountability of the government to the public through political channels),[33] intra-political accountability (the accountability arrangements that take place within government institutions through hierarchy and supervision),[34] inter-political accountability (being the relationships that take place between government institutions)[35] and external accountability (being accountability arrangements that sit outside the political arena).[36] A further common theme is that accountability is a *value-laden term*. It is treated as closely related to, though perhaps not synonymous with, a number of other public governance concepts such as control,[37]

---

[28] This is the delegation model: Strom (n 12) 55; Richard Mulgan, *Holding Power to Account: Accountability in Modern Democracies* (Palgrave Macmillan, 2003) 12; Grant and Keohane (n 15) 31.

[29] This is the participatory model: Grant and Keohane (n 15) 31; Mulgan, *Holding Power to Account* (n 28) 13.

[30] Mulgan, *Holding Power to Account* (n 28) 11; Philp (n 18) 33.

[31] See, e.g., Mulgan, '"Accountability": An Ever-Expanding Concept?' (n 4) 555; Melvin J Dubnick, *Seeking Salvation for Accountability* (Annual Meeting of the American Political Science Association, Boston, 29 August–1 September 2002) 7.

[32] See, e.g., Jerry Mashaw, 'Accountability and Institutional Design: Some Thoughts on the Grammar of Governance' in Michael Dowdle (ed), *Public Accountability: Designs, Dilemmas and Experiences* (Cambridge University Press, 2006) 115.

[33] Oliver, *Government in the United Kingdom* (n 9) 25–26 ('public accountability'); Mashaw (n 32) 120 ('public governance').

[34] Mashaw (n 32) 120–21 ('a public administrative regime').

[35] Ibid 121; Oliver, *Government in the United Kingdom* (n 9) 23 ('political accountability').

[36] Oliver, *Government in the United Kingdom* (n 9) 27–28 ('administrative accountability').

[37] Mulgan, '"Accountability": An Ever-Expanding Concept?' (n 4) 563–66; Mulgan, *Holding Power to Account* (n 28) 18–20; Koppell (n 20) 97–98; Bovens, 'Analysing and Assessing

democracy,[38] dialogue,[39] equity,[40] justice,[41] liability,[42] responsibility,[43] responsiveness,[44] the rule of law,[45] the separation of powers[46] and transparency.[47]

Many authors see accountability as a *mechanism* that can be mapped out by reference to a series of questions which ask who is to be accountable to whom, about what and how?[48] The question of *who is to be held to account* seeks to identify the most appropriate party to place in the role of account-giver in a particular situation. This might be a straightforward proposition where there is one party that is solely and directly charged with exercising a particular power and producing a particular result. However, the task becomes more complicated in cases where there are

Accountability' (n 1) 453–54; Carol Harlow, *Accountability in the European Union* (Oxford University Press, 2002) 10.

[38] Strom (n 12) 55; Melvin J Dubnick, 'Accountability and the Promise of Performance: In Search of the Mechanisms' (2005) 28 *Public Performance and Management Review* 376, 380.

[39] Mulgan, '"Accountability": An Ever-Expanding Concept?' (n 4) 569–70.

[40] Bovens, Schillemans and 't Hart (n 7) 227.

[41] Dubnick, 'Accountability and the Promise of Performance' (n 38) 380.

[42] Koppell (n 20) 96; Bovens, 'Public Accountability' (n 2) 189.

[43] Koppell (n 20) 98; Dubnick, 'Accountability and the Promise of Performance' (n 38) 380; Mark Bovens, *The Quest for Responsibility: Accountability and Citizenship in Complex Organisations* (Cambridge University Press, 1998) 22–23; Bovens, Schillemans and 't Hart (n 7) 227; Mulgan, '"Accountability": An Ever-Expanding Concept?' (n 4) 557–58; Mulgan, *Holding Power to Account* (n 28) 15–18; Harlow, 'Accountability and Constitutional Law' (n 8) 197–98; Harlow, 'Accountability as a Value in Global Governance' (n 19) 174–75; Harlow, *Accountability in the European Union* (n 37) 6; John Braithwaite, 'Accountability and Responsibility through Restorative Justice' in Michael Dowdle (ed.), *Public Accountability: Designs, Dilemmas and Experiences* (Cambridge University Press, 2006) 33, 44.

[44] Mulgan, '"Accountability": An Ever-Expanding Concept?' (n 4) 566–69; Mulgan, *Holding Power to Account* (n 28) 20–22; Koppell (n 20) 98–99; Bovens, 'Analysing and Assessing Accountability' (n 1) 453; Bovens, Schillemans and 't Hart (n 7) 227; Dubnick, 'Accountability and the Promise of Performance' (n 38) 380.

[45] Harlow, 'Accountability and Constitutional Law' (n 8) 199–200; Carol Harlow and Richard Rawlings, 'Promoting Accountability in Multilevel Governance: A Network Approach' (2007) 13 *European Law Journal* 542, 546–47.

[46] Harlow, 'Accountability and Constitutional Law' (n 8) 200–01; Mulgan, *Holding Power to Account* (n 28) 20.

[47] Bovens, 'Analysing and Assessing Accountability' (n 1) 453; Bovens, Schillemans and 't Hart (n 7) 227; Koppell (n 20) 96–97; Harlow, *Accountability in the European Union* (n 37) 12.

[48] See, e.g., Bovens, 'Analysing and Assessing Accountability' (n 1) 454–55; Mulgan, *Holding Power to Account* (n 28) 22–23; Mashaw (n 32) 118; Philp (n 18) 42; Scott (n 17) 41; Grant and Keohane (n 15).

multiple parties that combine to produce an impugned outcome (particularly where there is no direct relationship between those parties),[49] or where one party exercises power on behalf of another. In the context of government powers, this difficulty is particularly relevant in the context of privatisation and outsourcing, where it becomes necessary to ask whether private contractors should be treated as part of the government apparatus for the purposes of holding them accountable for the exercise of public power.[50] In more complex scenarios such as these, it might be necessary to move beyond the individual accountability model and to place an organisation in the role of account-giver (corporate accountability), or to hold a superior accountable for the conduct of inferiors (hierarchical accountability), or to hold the various actors jointly accountable for the result (collective accountability).[51]

The question of *to whom an account is rendered* may refer to a number of different matters. For some authors, this question focuses on the accountability forum (for example, the courts, a commission of inquiry or the electoral process).[52] For others, this question is instead concerned with identifying the prosecuting party that is entitled to use that forum so as to hold an actor accountable. In this context, the entitlement to prosecute may derive from the fact that a person conferred the power and should therefore be able to supervise its performance (delegation model),[53] or from the fact that a person is affected by the exercise of power in a manner that confers a formal right to demand an account.[54]

The question of *about what an account is rendered* is context-dependent, focusing on the standards of conduct against which an actor's performance is to be measured. This question might look at the sources of such standards (for example, legal instruments, economic imperatives and social or democratic obligations),[55] or the standards themselves (for example, contravention of rules relating to procedure, performance, fairness, continuity and security).[56] The question of *how accountability is enforced* is a procedural question, which might focus on the procedures

---

[49] Mulgan, *Holding Power to Account* (n 28) 23.
[50] See, e.g., Scott (n 17) 41; Mashaw (n 32) 152.
[51] Bovens, 'Analysing and Assessing Accountability' (n 1) 458–59.
[52] Ibid 455–57.
[53] Grant and Keohane (n 15) 31.
[54] Mulgan, *Holding Power to Account* (n 28) 24–25.
[55] Ibid 28.
[56] See, e.g., Bovens, 'Analysing and Assessing Accountability' (n 1) 459–60; Scott (n 17) 42; Behn (n 24) 6–10.

employed by a particular accountability forum, or more generally on the process, procedure and outcome of the enquiry.[57] For example, Mulgan sees the accountability process as involving the three stages of 'information' (being 'initial reporting and investigating'), 'discussion' (being 'justification and critical debate') and 'rectification' (being 'the imposition of remedies and sanctions').[58]

Surprisingly missing from much of the accountability literature is the more fundamental question of why accountability is relevant at all? What is its function or purpose? It is to this question that we now turn.

1.2   Mechanism or Ideal?

The question of whether accountability is a normative concept remains the subject of ongoing debate in academic literature. The debate is framed in various ways, including whether accountability is a tool or a value, or whether it is targeted at internal or external motivations, or whether it applies retrospectively or prospectively. When boiled down, all of these debates are essentially disputes as to the function and purpose of accountability. A useful starting point in this analysis (and one which a number of authors adopt)[59] is the so-called Friedrich–Finer debate, which took place in the first half of the twentieth century. These two theorists represented opposing views in relation to the proper way of conceptualising the responsibility of public servants. For Finer, the proper role of a public servant was to act under the dictates of their superiors.[60] Public servants were required to account to ministers, who were in turn charged with taking action to ensure compliance.[61] For Friedrich, the proper role of a public servant was to exercise their functions rationally and responsibly.[62] Friedrich was in part influenced by the fact that ministers were incapable of actively monitoring the activities of public servants (either because of the technical nature of

---

[57] See, e.g., Mashaw (n 32) 118.

[58] Mulgan, *Holding Power to Account* (n 28) 30.

[59] See, e.g., Mulgan, '"Accountability": An Ever-Expanding Concept?' (n 4) 557; Bovens, 'Two Concepts of Accountability' (n 7) 949–50; Harlow, 'Accountability as a Value in Global Governance' (n 19) 179.

[60] Herman Finer, 'Better Government Personnel' (1936) 51 *Political Science Quarterly* 569, 580, cited in Michael Jackson, 'Responsibility versus Accountability in the Friedrich-Finer Debate' (2009) 15 *Journal of Management History* 66, 69.

[61] See Jackson (n 60) 71.

[62] Carl Friedrich, *Problems of the American Public Service* (McGraw-Hill, 1935) 30.

their activities, or because of the sheer volume of activities they would be required to supervise).[63] On this basis, Friedrich's argument was that the better course was to encourage improved administration through training and incentivising responsible behaviour.[64] The debate has been characterised in various ways by later authors. Finer himself described the distinction as one between 'a sense of duty' (Friedrich) and 'the fact of responsibility' (Finer).[65] Harlow describes it as a distinction between subjective accountability (Friedrich) and objective accountability (Finer).[66] Bovens describes it as a distinction between 'virtue' (Friedrich) and 'obedience' (Finer).[67] Jackson describes it as a distinction between 'eliciting responsible conduct' (Friedrich) and 'enforcing responsible conduct' (Finer).[68] For Mulgan, the difference can be seen as one between responsibilities that are internal (Friedrich) and external (Finer).[69] The debate may also be cast as a balance between expertise (Friedrich) and democratic authority (Finer).[70] Relevantly for present purposes, a further characterisation of the distinction is that between responsibility (Friedrich) and accountability (Finer).[71]

A number of accountability theorists frame accountability in terms of its normative value. For example, writing in the context of restorative justice, Braithwaite argues that there is no real justice in the absence of an offender taking active responsibility for their conduct, rather than simply being held passively responsible.[72] Further, Considine defines accountability as 'the proper use of authority ... in search of the most advantageous path to success',[73] while O'Connell describes accountability in terms of whether or not an actor has produced 'high quality of service ... at a lower cost ... while serving more citizens in a courteous

---

[63] See, e.g., Jackson (n 60) 71.

[64] Ibid.

[65] Finer (n 60) 581.

[66] Harlow, 'Accountability as a Value in Global Governance' (n 19) 179.

[67] Bovens, 'Two Concepts of Accountability' (n 7) 949–50.

[68] Jackson (n 60) 72.

[69] Mulgan, *Holding Power to Account* (n 28) 16.

[70] Jeremy Plant, 'Carl J Friedrich on Responsibility and Authority' (2011) 71 *Public Administration Review* 471, 476.

[71] Mulgan, '"Accountability": An Ever-Expanding Concept?' (n 4) 557; Jackson (n 60) 72.

[72] Braithwaite, 'Accountability and Responsibility through Restorative Justice' (n 43) 35.

[73] Mark Considine, 'The End of the Line? Accountable Governance in the Age of Networks, Partnerships, and Joined-up Services' (2002) 15(1) *Governance* 21, 22, cited in Bovens, 'Two Concepts of Accountability' (n 7) 950.

manner'.[74] Bovens concludes that such studies are essentially about the pursuit of good governance, evaluating the 'conduct of actors ... [and] the factors that induce accountable behaviour'.[75] Where such enquiries identify accountability deficits, they involve a value judgement regarding the propriety of an actor's conduct.[76] Bovens sees such research as a 'formidable task',[77] and has expressed a preference for limiting his study of accountability to its mechanical operation.[78] His preference is in part guided by his conclusion that 'there is no general consensus about the standards for accountable behaviour', and any such standards are in any event context specific.[79] While he acknowledges the importance of academic research into the normative aspects of accountability, he advocates maintaining a clear distinction in research into the two ideas. Philp is another commentator who advocates studying accountability divorced from its normative context.[80] He goes to considerable lengths to exclude normative concepts from his definition of accountability, arguing that questions of whether or not an actor is '"really" accountable' are bound up in normative judgements about whether or not an accountability relationship is achieving objectives that have been assigned to it.[81] He would prefer not to 'infuse' the relationship with such value judgements, but instead to identify a core description of the accountability relationship devoid of normative trimmings.[82]

While a purely mechanical understanding of accountability might be useful for some purposes, trespass into normative territory is inevitable when we come to discussions about accountability deficits and overloads. When we ask whether or not a particular arrangement or relationship produces an accountability deficit or overload, we are implicitly asking whether or not particular norms are being adequately upheld. If so, an

---

[74] Lenahan O'Connell, 'Program Accountability as an Emergent Property: The Role of Stakeholders in a Program's Field' (2005) 65 *Public Administration Review* 85, 86, cited in Bovens, 'Two Concepts of Accountability' (n 7) 950.

[75] Bovens, 'Two Concepts of Accountability' (n 7) 957.

[76] Ibid.

[77] Ibid 950.

[78] Bovens, 'Analysing and Assessing Accountability' (n 1) 450; Mark Bovens, Deirdre Curtin and Paul 't Hart, 'Studying the Real World of EU Accountability: Framework and Design' in Mark Bovens, Deirdre Curtin and Paul 't Hart (eds.), *The Real World of EU Accountability: What Deficit?* (Oxford University Press, 2010) 31, 35.

[79] Bovens, 'Analysing and Assessing Accountability' (n 1) 450.

[80] Philp (n 18).

[81] Ibid 36.

[82] Ibid.

actor is 'sufficiently' accountable. If not, we may identify an 'accountability deficit', and proceed to look at whether it is appropriate to enhance that particular accountability mechanism so as to achieve more robust enforcement of those standards. If the enforcement of norms has been over-catered for, we may identify an 'accountability overload' and query whether the mechanism should be adjusted so as to reduce the impact of that overload. By the time we come to ask whether a particular arrangement is an accountability mechanism, and whether it is functioning appropriately, we have already made the implicit judgement that there are underlying values that warrant reinforcement. Our analysis of the mechanism must necessarily take place within that context.

This approach is consistent with that adopted by Harlow. She concludes that accountability is not simply a mechanism, but has emerged 'as a constitutional principle approximating in value to the foundational liberal principle of the rule of law'.[83] She approves of Oliver's argument that 'accountability cannot be effectively imposed if the criteria against which conduct is to be measured in the process of calling to account are not made clear'.[84] On the basis of this observation, Harlow concludes that if standards are not in fact encompassed within the concept of accountability, then at a minimum they are 'an essential aspect of its context'.[85] Fisher agrees;[86] in her view, 'standard setting' is the most significant component of accountability,[87] in the sense that arguments in favour of increasing accountability are essentially 'about wanting to align governance regimes to a particular normative vision. The process of holding a decision-maker to account is a process of debating what the standards should be.'[88]

A slightly different perspective on this argument is taken up by Brennan et al in their treatise *Explaining Norms*.[89] Whereas Harlow, Oliver and Fisher focus on the normative foundations of accountability, Brennan et al argue that accountability is the conceptual foundation of norms themselves. For Brennan et al, the 'core function' of norms 'is to

---

[83] Harlow, 'Accountability as a Value in Global Governance' (n 19) 173.

[84] Dawn Oliver, 'Standards of Conduct in Public Life – What Standards?' [1995] *Public Law* 497, 497, cited in Harlow, *Accountability in the European Union* (n 37) 10.

[85] Harlow, *Accountability in the European Union* (n 37) 10.

[86] Elizabeth Fisher, 'The European Union in the Age of Accountability' (2004) 24 *Oxford Journal of Legal Studies* 495.

[87] Ibid 510.

[88] Ibid 513.

[89] H Geoffrey Brennan et al, *Explaining Norms* (Oxford University Press, 2013).

make us accountable to one another'.[90] In their words: 'Norms, then, construed as clusters of normative attitudes, are perfectly suited to the business of creating accountability. Other social facts, such as social practices and clusters of desires, are obviously not. Accountability is an out-and-out normative notion.'[91] Translating this idea into the present context, we would view public law norms as tools for reinforcing the accountability of government. Ultimately, reducing accountability to a description of a mechanism directs attention away from the raison d'être of that mechanism. The reason why we impose an accountability relationship on an actor is to achieve an end goal of 'accountability'; the mechanism exists because it provides for the enforcement of prescribed norms. In so doing, accountability takes on a normative quality in its own right. In Dubnick's words, it has 'been transfigured from an instrument of governing to ... a "virtuous practice"'.[92]

For those who deny accountability a normative role, it is particularly difficult to engage in systematic analysis of the concepts of accountability deficits and overloads. As will be explored in Part II of this book, the notions of accountability deficits and overloads rest on an assumption that there is some middle ground of an 'ideal amount' of accountability that has not been satisfied. This notion of an 'ideal amount' of accountability is an inherently normative one. We cannot hope to specify the situations where an accountability mechanism or system has not gone 'far enough' or has gone 'too far' without engaging with the question of how far the mechanism or system *should* have gone. What is that if not a normative question? At least in this respect, then, we must attribute accountability a normative role.

---

[90] Ibid 36.

[91] Ibid 38.

[92] Dubnick, 'Accountability as a Cultural Keyword' (n 5), 34.

2

Too Little or Too Much of a Good Thing?

One of the most prevalent themes in the accountability literature is claims about the 'amount' of accountability that applies in a given situation. There are claims of accountability 'deficits' (i.e. too little accountability) on the one hand, and claims of accountability 'overload' (i.e. too much accountability) on the other. This chapter seeks to draw out these claims and argues that, while these claims presuppose that accountability is a measurable concept, the literature often glosses over the underlying question of what is being measured, or how the measurement is to be conducted. This missing dimension of the literature is the core problem tackled in this book, which unpacks two of the hidden assumptions that underlie these claims. The first of these assumptions is that it is possible to identify some form of accountability benchmark, being a normative judgement as to the 'ideal amount' of accountability. The second is that it is possible to assess the universe of applicable accountability mechanisms against that benchmark, and to form a judgement as to whether the system underperforms (deficit) or overperforms (overload).

2.1 Accountability as a Measurable Commodity

Bovens et al define an accountability deficit as 'a condition where those who govern us are not sufficiently hemmed in by requirements to explain their conduct publicly – to legal, professional, administrative, social or political forums who have some sort of power to sanction them'.[1] Historically speaking, accountability deficits have attracted significant academic interest. Questions have been raised as to whether our system

---

[1] Mark Bovens, Thomas Schillemans and Paul 't Hart, 'Does Public Accountability Work? An Assessment Tool' (2008) 86 *Public Administration* 225, 229.

of governance contains accountability 'gaps'[2] in a range of contexts. One of the greatest sources of concern has been the expansion and fragmentation of the administrative state, and its perceived impact on the effectiveness of 'traditional' political accountability mechanisms.[3] For instance, ministerial responsibility does not 'bite' in the traditional manner if ministers do not (and perhaps cannot) have direct oversight over all of the activities that take place within their portfolios.[4] Similarly, the chain of accountability from voters to those who ultimately wield and exercise public power has been so attenuated that the ballot box cannot be viewed as an accountability mechanism that has any direct impact on the day-to-day operations of government. Two areas of supposed accountability deficits receiving significant attention in more recent discourse relate to accountability in the context of outsourced public functions[5] and in the context of network or multilevel governance, as in the case of the European Union.[6]

The counterpart to the range of arguments focusing on accountability deficits or gaps is the argument that accountability, far from being lacking in our system of governance, has in fact gone in the other direction. It goes without saying that if a number of institutions are simultaneously tasked with accountability functions, there will come a point where they overlap with one another. Scott identifies this as the 'redundancy' model, in which 'overlapping (and ostensibly superfluous) accountability mechanisms reduce the centrality of any one of them. In common parlance, redundancy is represented by the "belt and braces" approach, within which two independent mechanisms are deployed to ensure the system does not fail, both of which are capable of working on their own.'[7]

---

[2] Richard Mulgan and John Uhr, 'Accountability and Governance' in Glyn Davis and Patrick Weller (eds.), *Are You Being Served? State, Citizens and Governance* (Allen and Unwin, 2001) 152, 153.

[3] See, e.g., Richard Mulgan, 'Accountability Deficits' in Mark Bovens, Robert Goodin and Thomas Schillemans (eds.), *The Oxford Handbook of Public Accountability* (Oxford University Press, 2014) 545, 548; Mulgan and Uhr (n 2) 157.

[4] Mulgan, 'Accountability Deficits' (n 3) 548–49.

[5] See, e.g., Jerry Mashaw, 'Accountability and Institutional Design: Some Thoughts on the Grammar of Governance' in Michael Dowdle (ed.), *Public Accountability: Designs, Dilemmas and Experiences* (Cambridge University Press, 2006) 134; Richard Mulgan, 'Government Accountability for Outsourced Services' (2006) 65(2) *Australian Journal of Public Administration* 48; Mulgan, 'Accountability Deficits' (n 3) 549.

[6] See, e.g., Mulgan, 'Accountability Deficits' (n 3) 546; Mulgan and Uhr (n 2).

[7] Colin Scott, 'Accountability in the Regulatory State' (2000) 27 *Journal of Law and Society* 38, 52–53.

While there are no doubt failsafe-style benefits that may be ensured by such an approach, commentators have raised concerns as to whether this degree of overlap presents a threat to accountability, claiming instances of accountability 'overload',[8] 'overkill',[9] 'paradox',[10] 'trap',[11] 'dilemma'[12] and 'multiple accountabilities disorder'.[13] These labels point to various concerns that authors raise in circumstances where there is 'too much' accountability. For instance, some raise concerns about the potentially negative performance implications arising in situations where an actor is subject to numerous accountability demands pulling in different directions. For example, an actor may 'oscillate . . . between behaviours that are consistent with conflicting notions of accountability'.[14] Is accountability about following directions, or adhering to applicable rules? Is it about being transparent and facing consequences for past conduct, or responding to external demands in a forward-looking sense?[15] It is easy to see that if expectations are not clearly defined, an actor may potentially find themselves serving many masters, some of whom disagree with one another.[16] Obfuscation is also cited as a potential danger arising in situations of 'too much' accountability. For example, Mulgan suggests that, where there are multiple forums in which an agent might be held accountable, an agent may be tempted to 'forum-shop' by seeking the regime in which they will be subject to the least scrutiny, or least severe sanction.[17] Other potential negative effects include the 'blame game', where accountability processes become focused only on fault-finding to

---

[8] Bovens, Schillemans and 't Hart (n 1) 229.

[9] Maurits Barendrecht, 'Rule of Law, Measuring and Accountability: Problems to Be Solved Bottom Up' (2011) 3 *Hague Journal on the Rule of Law* 281, 294.

[10] Melvin J Dubnick, 'Accountability and the Promise of Performance: In Search of the Mechanisms' (2005) 28 *Public Performance and Management Review* 376, 395.

[11] Janet Kelly, 'The Accountability Trap' (2007) 96(3) *National Civic Review* 46; Mulgan and Uhr (n 2) 152.

[12] Robert D Behn, *Rethinking Democratic Accountability* (Brookings Institution Press, 2001) 10.

[13] Jonathan Koppell, 'Pathologies of Accountability: ICANN and the Challenge of "Multiple Accountabilities Disorder"' (2005) 65 *Public Administration Review* 94, 95.

[14] Ibid.

[15] Ibid 96.

[16] Arie Halachmi, 'Accountability Overloads' in Mark Bovens, Robert Goodin and Thomas Schillemans (eds.), *The Oxford Handbook of Public Accountability* (Oxford University Press, 2014) 560, 561.

[17] Richard Mulgan, *Holding Power to Account: Accountability in Modern Democracies* (Palgrave Macmillan, 2003) 221.

the detriment of redress.[18] Actors may also be drawn into attempts to
'game the system' to maximise the appearance of performance according
to accountability criteria,[19] or become too focused on short-term goals
associated with accountability metrics at the expense of paying attention
to longer-term organisational success.[20] Too much accountability may
also be thought to discourage innovation by fixing rigid standards
according to current knowledge.[21] A further aspect of the accountability
'overload' debate is a more pragmatic one; the burden of simply participating in various accountability proceedings reduces the time available to
perform the day-to-day operations with which an institution is
charged.[22] Bovens et al sum this point up with the quip that adminis-
trators 'spend half their time explaining to all sorts of accountability
forums what they intend to be doing, and the other explaining to them
why they did not get around to doing all these things'.[23]

Accountability overload may not only have implications for the government officials who are subject to the impugned range of accountability mechanisms; it may also produce negative effects for the individual
seeking to utilise them. The availability of a multitude of mechanisms
may produce 'appeal fatigue', with individuals withdrawing from their
goal of holding the government accountable in the face of the range of
options available, or lacking expertise to know which mechanism is most
appropriate.[24] The complexity of the system may also produce negative
overload for individuals who are faced with difficult choices between
seemingly competing mechanisms, each offering different structures in
time, cost and ease of use, and each promising slightly different potential
outcomes.

Whether or not we agree with these various concerns is not critical for
present purposes. All we need note is that when we take these arguments
together, it is possible to see that the literature abounds with claims as to

[18] Behn (n 12), cited in Halachmi (n 16) 561.
[19] Christopher Pollitt, *The Essential Public Manager* (Open University Press, 2003), cited in
Halachmi (n 16) 561.
[20] Halachmi (n 16) 561.
[21] Hans de Bruijn, 'Performance Measurement in the Public Sector: Strategies to Cope with
the Risks of Performance Measurement' (2002) 15 *International Journal of Public Sector
Management* 578, cited in Halachmi (n 16) 561.
[22] Mulgan, *Holding Power to Account* (n 17) 222.
[23] Bovens, Schillemans and 't Hart (n 1) 227–28.
[24] See, e.g., Gabrielle Appleby, Alexander Reilly and Laura Grenfell, *Australian Public Law*
(3rd ed., Oxford University Press, 2019) 294.

the sufficiency of accountability in various areas. Looking beneath the labels of 'gaps', 'deficits', 'overloads', 'traps', etc., it appears that all of these claims presuppose that accountability is a measurable phenomenon. That is, we can look at a public polity, institution, official or power and determine whether it is being held accountable to an appropriate degree (or too little, or too much). Despite the ubiquity of claims about the sufficiency of accountability, the literature is somewhat scant in its explanation of how sufficiency is to be measured. Bovens et al note that 'few if any of the parties to the debate specify which standards they employ. The literature is remarkably light on assessment tools and methods.'[25] This view is echoed by Scott, who notes that, while 'public lawyers almost universally regard [accountability mechanisms] as inadequate ... [i]t is rarely possible to discern how adequacy is actually being assessed'.[26]

This book adopts the position that there are two core limitations evident in many claims of accountability deficit and overload. The first is that many of these claims skate over the question of what accountability demands. If authors do not unpack this question, their analysis lacks the rudder needed to make good their claims of deficits and overloads. It is essential that we identify the 'normative yardstick'[27] sitting behind these claims in order to get a clear picture of the criteria against which accountability mechanisms are being assessed. Secondly, much of the accountability literature dealing with deficits or gaps tends to focus in on particular means of securing accountability to the exclusion of other (presumably less important) means. Mulgan notes that this is particularly the case in relation to claims of 'gaps' in political accountability mechanisms.[28] Such an approach risks presenting a 'distorted view'[29] of the nature and degree of claimed accountability gaps, as it fails to attribute appropriate weight to the contribution that might be offered via other sources.

These limitations can be explained through an example, as follows. It is a well-accepted proposition that damages are not recoverable in public

---

[25] Bovens, Schillemans and 't Hart (n 1) 230.

[26] Scott (n 7) 42–43.

[27] Mark Bovens, Deirdre Curtin and Paul 't Hart, 'Studying the Real World of EU Accountability: Framework and Design' in Mark Bovens, Deirdre Curtin and Paul 't Hart (eds.), *The Real World of EU Accountability: What Deficit?* (Oxford University Press, 2010) 31, 49. See also Mulgan, 'Accountability Deficits' (n 3) 553.

[28] Mulgan, 'Accountability Deficits' (n 3) 552.

[29] Ibid.

law proceedings in Australia: 'mere invalidation of an administrative decision does not provide a cause of action or a basis for an award of damages'.[30] Some might argue that the unavailability of damages for public law wrongs presents a potential accountability deficit.[31] However, such a claim presupposes that the accountability of government officials who are subject to public law norms can be measured, and found wanting. It is not immediately apparent, however, how that might be assessed. First, if we want to be able to describe judicial review proceedings as a sufficient (or insufficient) accountability mechanism, we would need to know what accountability *demands*. This presupposes that accountability has certain goals or functions. Implicit in this example, perhaps, is a suggestion that accountability demands the redress of individuals who are harmed by breach of a particular public law norm. Of course, much of the literature fails to unpack this normative dimension of the argument that there is an 'accountability gap'. Secondly, in order to sensibly speak about this supposed shortfall as a 'gap' we surely need to understand the wider accountability *context* in which this mechanism operates. The above deficit claim focuses on a particular type of accountability mechanism (i.e. the means by which the courts hold the government to account through judicial review) to the exclusion of all other mechanisms. For instance, this claim says nothing about the role to be played by damages in private law proceedings, the availability of ex gratia compensation, the powers of the ombudsman or the many other types of mechanisms that might potentially play a role in restoring the judicial review applicant. There is something quite unsatisfactory about describing the unavailability of damages as a deficit if the supposed gap is filled by an alternative mechanism.

Taking all of these matters together, this book adopts the position that in order to make a meaningful claim about the existence or otherwise of an accountability deficit (or overload), we need to be able to do at least two things. First, explain what it is that accountability *demands*, and second, explain whether that demand is being met *by the system* of applicable mechanisms. Parts II and III of this book set out some of

---

[30] *Chan Yee Kin v Minister for Immigration and Ethnic Affairs* (1991) 31 FCR 29, 41. See Ellen Rock and Greg Weeks, 'Monetary Awards for Public Law Wrongs: Australia's Resistant Legal Landscape' (2018) 41(4) *University of New South Wales Law Journal* 1159.

[31] This is perhaps an extension of Panetta's suggestion that government accountability would be increased through the introduction of a remedy in damages for wrongful administrative decisions: Rossana Panetta, 'Damages for Wrongful Administrative Decisions' (1999) 6 *Australian Journal of Administrative Law* 163, 179.

the difficult choices and complex analysis that would be required in order to move towards that ultimate goal. The balance of this chapter first looks at two of the more coherent attempts in the literature at measuring accountability.

2.2 Efforts to Measure Accountability

Recent literature presents two notable attempts at proposing a method that might be used to measure accountability. The first is that of Bovens et al in their 2010 study of accountability in the European Union.[32] Adopting Bovens' definition of accountability as a starting point,[33] the authors describe a framework that they intend for use in the systematic assessment of accountability arrangements.[34] The core of the framework is the identification of what the authors describe as the three 'theoretical perspective[s] on the rationale behind accountability'.[35] The first perspective they identify is the 'democratic perspective', in which the goal of accountability is to secure means for citizens to control their democratically elected representatives.[36] The second is the 'constitutional perspective', in which the relevant goal is preventing tyranny and abuse of power.[37] The third is the 'learning perspective', which is concerned with facilitating improvements in the delivery of public services.[38] The authors then identify evaluation criteria said to be relevant in assessing accountability by reference to these three perspectives. For the democratic perspective, the relevant criterion is concerned with identifying the extent to which a regime 'enables democratically legitimized bodies to monitor and evaluate executive behaviour and to induce executive actors to modify that behaviour in accordance with their preferences'.[39] Within the constitutional perspective, the relevant criterion considers '[t]he extent to which an accountability arrangement curtails the abuse of

---

[32] Mark Bovens, Deirdre Curtin and Paul 't Hart (eds.), *The Real World of EU Accountabil ity: What Deficit?* (Oxford University Press, 2010).

[33] See definition in text accompanying Chapter 1 n 7.

[34] Bovens, Curtin and 't Hart, 'Framework and Design' (n 27) 32.

[35] Ibid 50. The framework is based on earlier work described in Bovens, Schillemans and 't Hart (n 1).

[36] Bovens, Curtin and 't Hart, 'Framework and Design' (n 27) 50.

[37] Ibid 51–52.

[38] Ibid 52.

[39] Ibid 54.

executive power and privilege'.[40] Finally, within the learning perspective, the relevant criterion focuses on the extent to which an arrangement 'stimulates public executives and bodies to focus consistently on achieving desirable societal outcomes in the smartest possible fashion'.[41] The framework of perspectives and evaluation criteria set out by Bovens et al is intended to provide a foundation for 'the assessment of accountability relations', with the authors suggesting that the evaluation within each perspective 'may produce different types of accountability deficits'.[42] This evaluative challenge is then taken up by other contributors to their study.

The approach proposed by Bovens et al is subject to two core limitations (each of which the authors acknowledge) that prevent it from delivering on the ultimate goal of identifying whether or not there are in fact accountability deficits in a given system (here, the European Union). The first limitation is in the nature of the criteria that the authors use for assessment: '[t]hese building blocks cannot in themselves provide us with definite answers to the question whether accountability deficits in European governance exist'.[43] In order to answer that broader question, the authors note that it would be necessary to define a yardstick against which the assessment is being made. In other words, in order for the criteria identified by Bovens et al to be capable of identifying accountability deficits within each perspective, it would be necessary for the authors to say how far the arrangements need to go in order to 'sufficiently' support democracy, avoid the abuse of power and improve the delivery of public services. Without identifying those yardsticks, any conclusion that there is a deficit in an accountability arrangement necessarily conceals an underlying normative judgement about what it means to be accountable. Referring back to the language adopted above, the framework therefore lacks the 'rudder' that might otherwise be employed to allow it to measure the sufficiency of accountability. While Bovens et al have identified a yardstick that we can use to evaluate accountability, they have failed to tell us how long it is! Any claim of 'measurement' made using this yardstick is therefore a reflection of the views of the individual using the yardstick, rather than the content of the tool itself.

The second limitation of this approach is one of scale. As Bovens et al note, each particular agent or body that is selected for the purposes of

---

[40] Ibid 55.
[41] Ibid.
[42] Ibid 57.
[43] Ibid.

assessment 'has its own, multifaceted accountability regimes'.[44] The task of seeking to map out the full size and shape of that regime is a large undertaking, which the authors suggest might need to be explored in a series of monographs rather than a single volume.[45] For that reason, choices must be made as to which accountability arrangements will be the focus of the assessment. The difficulty with that approach is that, without considering the regime as a whole, we can only ever reach preliminary views on possible areas of deficit.[46] For instance, employing the framework in 2008, Bovens et al sought to evaluate a single type of mechanism: boards of oversight in The Netherlands.[47] Their analysis revealed that this mechanism aligns most closely with the 'learning perspective' of accountability rather than the constitutional or democratic perspectives.[48] While the analysis tells us some interesting things about the accountability contribution made by boards of oversight in the Netherlands, what it does not do is tell us whether their operation produces anything in the way of accountability deficits or overloads. That broader task, of course, can only be performed by holistically assessing the place of boards of oversight within the system of accountability mechanisms relevant in that context. As Mulgan reminds us, focusing on one mechanism or category of mechanisms without considering others risks presenting a 'distorted view'[49] of perceived gaps.

A second notable contribution to recent literature on measuring accountability is that of Brandsma and Schillemans, who propose the use of an 'accountability cube' as a 'mapping tool' in analysis of accountability processes.[50] The cube offers a visual depiction of the 'intensity' of a given accountability process across the three common phases of

---

[44] Ibid 58.

[45] Ibid.

[46] Wille's contribution to the study by Bovens et al is a notable exception in this regard, seeking to canvass a wide range of mechanisms applicable to the European Commission: Anchrit Wille, 'The European Commission's Accountability Paradox' in Mark Bovens, Deirdre Curtin and Paul 't Hart (eds.), *The Real World of EU Accountability: What Deficit?* (Oxford University Press, 2010) 63. However, the lack of normative rudder in the framework (discussed above) necessarily limits the conclusions that may be drawn.

[47] Bovens, Schillemans and 't Hart (n 1).

[48] Ibid 236.

[49] Mulgan, 'Accountability Deficits' (n 3) 552.

[50] Gijs Jan Brandsma and Thomas Schillemans, 'The Accountability Cube: Measuring Accountability' (2013) 23 *Journal of Public Administration Research and Theory* 953, 960.

accountability: information, discussion and consequences.[51] The authors propose that the cube can be used to measure a given accountability mechanism, producing a range of potential results. For instance, 'a situation with much information, intensive discussions and many opportunities to impose consequences' would fall within the portion of the cube that represents the 'most accountability'.[52] Conversely, a situation 'with little information, nonintensive discussions and few consequences' would fall within the portion of the cube that represents the least accountability.[53] It is suggested that the tool can be used to 'locate potential accountability deficits in one or more of the three analytically distinct phases of accountability'.[54] The authors go on to employ the accountability cube to assess the accountability arrangements of the European 'comitology' committees.[55]

Again, a core limitation of the method proposed by Brandsma and Schillemans (which is acknowledged by the authors) is that it does not resolve the underlying normative difficulties inherent in the identification of accountability deficits and overloads. The authors indicate that whether a deficit identified using the tool is 'normatively problematic' is a question that 'depends on one's normative theory of good governance'.[56] In this sense, while offering a useful tool for evaluation, it is not a 'normative tool' or 'yardstick'[57] in its own right. The authors suggest that the tool be used to identify potential areas of accountability deficit, following which it would be necessary to employ 'an appropriate normative benchmark' to assess that claim.[58] As with the framework offered by Bovens et al, then, the accountability cube can take us only so far in our attempt to identify accountability deficits and overloads within our system of governance. In order to transform a potential deficit into an actual deficit, it is necessary to develop and articulate the normative yardstick lacking within the cube itself.

The foregoing criticism of the assessment tools proposed by these authors is certainly not intended to diminish the importance of these contributions to the literature. As noted in Section 2.1, much of the

---

[51] Ibid. A visual depiction of the cube is presented at page 961.
[52] Ibid 960.
[53] Ibid.
[54] Ibid 961.
[55] Ibid.
[56] Ibid.
[57] Ibid 961–62.
[58] Ibid 963.

literature on deficits and overloads tends to gloss over the question of what is being measured and how that measurement is being conducted. In this respect, each is a welcome step towards developing a robust assessment tool. It is also not to suggest that the lack of a normative 'rudder' in the proposed tools is a glaring omission on the part of the authors. Each explicitly states their intention to adhere to a mechanistic, rather than normative, understanding of accountability in defining their tools.[59] Rather, the argument put forward here is that, when making claims of accountability deficits and overloads, at a minimum we need to be able to specify what accountability *demands* (Part II), and whether those demands are met by the *system* of applicable mechanisms (Part III). Without tackling these two issues, our analysis is limited to measuring the quantity of accountability mechanisms (i.e. listing the number of mechanisms which satisfy the definition of 'accountability') rather than the quality of accountability mechanisms (i.e. whether there is 'sufficient' or 'too much' accountability in a given circumstance by reason of the interaction between those mechanisms).

---

[59] Bovens, Curtin and 't Hart, 'Framework and Design' (n 27) 35; Brandsma and Schillemans (n 50) 961.

PART II

Benchmark of Accountability

One of the most significant limitations of existing discussions about accountability deficits and overloads is the failure to identify the yardstick against which a given arrangement is being measured. There is an inherent logical flaw in claiming that there is 'not enough' or 'too much' of something without specifying what 'enough' might mean. So, how might we take on the task of identifying what 'enough' accountability looks like? One approach would be to add a normative dimension to each aspect of the framework set out in Chapter 1. In other words, instead of asking simply 'who is held accountable?', we need to be able to offer an answer to the question 'who *should* be held accountable?'. Instead of 'to whom are they accountable?', we must decide 'to whom *should* they be accountable?'. Instead of 'for what are they held accountable?', we must ask 'for what *should* they be held accountable?'. Instead of 'how are they held accountable?', we must ask 'how *should* they be held accountable?'. In tackling this task, we would be moving beyond a mechanical analysis of the accountability contribution made by a given mechanism, and into the realm of asking what we *expect* of that mechanism. Were we able to do this, we might then have a basis to argue that the mechanism either falls short of expectations (accountability deficit) or overperforms in respect of those expectations (accountability overload).

The difficulty is that importing a normative dimension to each of these questions asks us to make very complex decisions about the nature and purpose of accountability and the means by which we wish to hold the government to account. For instance, in looking at the first question, 'who *should* be held accountable?', we must make decisions about whether we view the government as a collection of individual officials (a Diceyan approach), or as a corporate entity. We must choose whether to sheet home responsibility to a low-level official who may have made an error, or to make their superiors accept responsibility for that failing. In approaching these kinds of questions, we ultimately need to make difficult decisions about who in government ought to be held accountable in order for us to say that we have struck an ideal accountability balance. This book does not propose to provide definitive answers to these large philosophical questions. Instead, the task taken on in Part II of this book is to set out some of the possible options we might choose between, as well as some of the potential implications of those choices. Ultimately, this marks out the scale of the challenge before us in defining a normative benchmark for the 'ideal amount' of accountability, against which we might then proceed to measure accountability deficits and overloads. The very size of this challenge is a potential explanation for this gap in the existing literature.

This Part commences with one of the most important normative questions about accountability that up to now has received insufficient attention. That question is: what is the purpose of accountability? Why is it important, and what do we hope to achieve through imposing it (Chapter 3)? While there are a number of possibilities, this book outlines five potential rationales for accountability: transparency, control, redress, desert and deterrence. These rationales then serve to inform the remaining chapters in this Part, which respectively look at who should be held accountable (Chapter 4), to whom (Chapter 5), for what (Chapter 6) and how (Chapter 7).

3

Five Rationales for Accountability

One of the most important questions that must be tackled in seeking to import a normative dimension to the concept of accountability is to identify its purpose. Why is accountability important in the context of public governance; what is its rationale? Despite the significance of this question, much of the literature on accountability tends to gloss over it.[1] We cannot afford to avoid this question, however, if we are hoping to establish a benchmark of accountability. As set out in the following chapters, we can only make decisions about *who* should be held accountable if we have first thought about what we are hoping to achieve through targeting those agents. We can only make decisions about *to whom* those agents should be held accountable if we have first thought about what our purpose is in facilitating that arrangement. We can only make decisions about *for what* those agents are held accountable if we have first thought about why we are targeting particular conduct. And we can only make decisions about *how* we hold agents accountable if we have thought about what the goal of doing so might be. As put by Brandsma and Schillemans, '[t]he issue of expectations is central to the entire accountability process'.[2] This chapter briefly outlines a number of the possible rationales that we might draw on in establishing a normative benchmark of accountability.

Perhaps one of the more compelling arguments about the purpose of accountability in the context of public governance is that it is linked with the concept of legitimacy. On this view, we hold officials accountable to maintain and increase public confidence in our system of government.[3]

---

[1] Mark Bovens, Thomas Schillemans and Paul 't Hart, 'Does Public Accountability Work? An Assessment Tool' (2008) 86 *Public Administration* 225, 230.

[2] Gijs Jan Brandsma and Thomas Schillemans, 'The Accountability Cube: Measuring Accountability' (2013) 23 *Journal of Public Administration Research and Theory* 953, 956.

[3] Frederick Barnard, *Democratic Legitimacy: Plural Values and Political Power* (McGill-Queen's University Press, 2001) xi.

There is much to be said for the idea that, by government opening itself up to public scrutiny, the public is able to develop a degree of trust in government, which in turn contributes to its ongoing legitimacy. As Bovens et al argue, the existence of accountability mechanisms that facilitate transparency and dialogue between government and citizens 'can promote acceptance of government authority and the citizens' confidence in the government's administration'.[4] For Barnard, accountability functions as a 'gravitational centre in the legitimation of democratic governance',[5] essentially providing a foundation on which legitimacy might rest. On this view, effective accountability mechanisms are capable of fostering citizens' faith in a system of governance. Conversely, substandard accountability mechanisms may produce the inverse effect of eroding public confidence in the government.[6] For instance, if accountability mechanisms take on the character of empty processes we might have real concerns about whether those mechanisms are capable of going any way to support the legitimacy of government. This may be the case, for example, where an accountability forum simply engages in a box-ticking exercise with no real concern or motivation to test compliance with relevant standards. Perhaps more concerningly, empty accountability mechanisms and processes might even come to decrease confidence in government over time. We might perceive the empty mechanism as a shield being employed by government so as to avoid 'real' accountability via other means.

If we accept that legitimacy is an overarching goal in the pursuit of government accountability, the next step in defining a benchmark of accountability is to think in more concrete terms about the manner in which this goal is to be achieved. This book explores five possible perspectives that we might adopt in this respect.[7] The first possible rationale is that of transparency. It was noted in Chapter 1 that theorists

---

[4] Mark Bovens, Deirdre Curtin and Paul 't Hart, 'Studying the Real World of EU Accountability: Framework and Design' in Mark Bovens, Deirdre Curtin and Paul 't Hart (eds.), *The Real World of EU Accountability: What Deficit?* (Oxford University Press, 2010) 31, 53.

[5] Barnard (n 3) xi.

[6] Bovens, Schillemans and 't Hart, 'Does Public Accountability Work? ' (n 1) 239; Bovens, Curtin and 't Hart, 'Framework and Design' (n 4) 53.

[7] Koppell makes a similar argument, identifying transparency and liability as 'foundations, supporting notions that underpin accountability in all its manifestations': Jonathan Koppell, 'Pathologies of Accountability: ICANN and the Challenge of "Multiple Accountabilities Disorder"' (2005) 65 *Public Administration Review* 94, 96.

generally agree that a minimum defining feature of accountability is that it demands the provision of an account.[8] Koppell identifies transparency as 'the literal value of accountability', noting that '[b]elief in the openness of government to regular inspection is so firmly ingrained in our collective consciousness that transparency has an innate value'.[9] Furthering the objective of legitimacy, public scrutiny allows the public to develop trust in the government; justice is not only done, but seen to be done. On this view, our motivating force in pursuing government accountability would be to achieve transparency in government operations. We would prefer accountability processes that lay bare government operations for public scrutiny and we would bolster means of accessing information from government. This rationale would eschew governing behind closed doors, promote openness in decision-making (including through the provision of reasons) and favour efforts to make government communication meaningful[10] (the 'transparency rationale').

A second possible rationale for accountability might be that of control. Many theorists agree that a key function of accountability is to provide the account-holder with the ability to control the exercise of power by the account-giver. Mulgan and Uhr go so far as to describe this as the 'core purpose' of accountability.[11] Employing the principal–agent model, they see accountability as a tool to be employed by principals to ensure that their agents act in the interests of their principals rather than themselves.[12] Bovens describes this rationale for accountability as the 'democratic perspective', where 'public accountability is an essential condition for the democratic process'.[13] Accountability can on this approach be viewed as a 'chain of delegation', pursuant to which the ultimate account-holders (citizens) can pass judgement on government performance.[14] On this view, the motivating rationale for accountability is to facilitate control, allowing citizens to require the government to govern in

---

[8] Mark Bovens, 'Analysing and Assessing Accountability: A Conceptual Framework' (2007) 13 *European Law Journal* 447, 453; Carol Harlow, *Accountability in the European Union* (Oxford University Press, 2002) 12.

[9] Koppell (n 7) 96.

[10] Richard Mulgan, *Making Open Government Work* (Palgrave Macmillan, 2014) 4.

[11] Richard Mulgan and John Uhr, 'Accountability and Governance' in Glyn Davis and Patrick Weller (eds.), *Are You Being Served? State, Citizens and Governance* (Allen and Unwin, 2001) 152, 153.

[12] Ibid.

[13] Bovens, 'Analysing and Assessing Accountability' (n 8) 463.

[14] Ibid.

accordance with their interests. Our primary concern would be to facilitate accountability processes that enable citizens to exercise control over government, and to compel the government to act in accordance with the preferences of the public (the 'control rationale').

A third rationale that we might assign to accountability is that of redress. There are many authors who see redress as an essential feature of an accountability regime. Oliver sees accountability as an inherently 'amendatory' process, requiring matters to be 'put ... right if it should appear that errors have been made'.[15] Mulgan and Uhr agree, describing an accountability process as being of 'little value' in absence of 'redress'.[16] Mulgan notes that accountability entails 'appropriate rectification through the provision of compensation for victims', without which 'accountability seems frustrated'.[17] In similar terms Harlow and Rawlings describe 'reparation and effective redress' as 'key factors' in establishing legitimacy through accountability;[18] there is a risk that if wrongs are left unremedied, the value of accountability in reinforcing the legitimacy of government may be undermined. This idea is echoed in research which suggests that third parties who have witnessed injustice are in part restored when they observe the restoration of a primary victim.[19] If we accept this view, the redress of individuals who have been harmed by government wrongs is important not just for the individual, but also for wider society. We would therefore be concerned to ensure that victims of maladministration are not left without a remedy and have a means of accessing redress (the 'redress rationale').

Another possible rationale for accountability might be that of punishment. There are many theorists who incorporate notions of punishment into their definitions of accountability.[20] One of the more emphatic is Mulgan, who sees an accountability process as 'seriously incomplete'

---

[15] Dawn Oliver, *Government in the United Kingdom: The Search for Accountability, Effectiveness, and Citizenship* (Open University Press, 1991) 22.

[16] Mulgan and Uhr (n 11) 153.

[17] Richard Mulgan, 'One Cheer for Hierarchy – Accountability in Disjointed Governance' (2003) 55(2) *Political Science* 6, 10.

[18] Carol Harlow and Richard Rawlings, 'Promoting Accountability in Multilevel Governance: A Network Approach' (2007) 13 *European Law Journal* 542, 546.

[19] For an interesting study of this phenomenon in the context of workplace injustice, see Natàlia Cugueró-Escofet, Marion Fortin and Miguel-Angel Canela, 'Righting the Wrong for Third Parties: How Monetary Compensation, Procedure Changes and Apologies Can Restore Justice for Observers of Injustice' (2014) 122 *Journal of Business Ethics* 253.

[20] See, e.g., Richard Mulgan, *Holding Power to Account: Accountability in Modern Democracies* (Palgrave Macmillan, 2003) 9–10; Koppell (n 7) 96–97; Oliver, *Government in the*

without the possibility of the imposition of punishment,[21] this being one of the factors that distinguishes being 'called' to account from being 'held' to account:

> In many cases, particularly when mistakes have been made and things have gone wrong, we want to see something more than just transparency and communication, important though these functions are. We want appropriate rectification ... and penalties for those responsible. Without such responses, accountability seems frustrated. Particularly when an institution has caused a major disaster and loss of life, heads should roll. If heads stay stubbornly in place, as often happens, we think that accountability has been denied.[22]

To similar effect is Schedler's view that '[e]xercises of accountability that expose misdeeds but do not impose material consequences will usually appear as weak, toothless, "diminished" forms of accountability [which] will be regarded as acts of window dressing rather than real restraints on power'.[23]

If we turn to the literature on punishment we can identify two potential rationales, each of which might be relevant in discussions about accountability. These two rationales broadly reflect the 'retributivist' and 'consequentialist' justifications for punishment.[24] Retributivist justifications for punishment (which underpin Mulgan's argument)[25] are grounded in notions of desert.[26] On this view, we would hold agents accountable for particular conduct and using particular means because they *deserve* that treatment. This type of punishment is condemnatory in character. Punishment is the vehicle through which society is able to

---

United Kingdom (n 15) 22; Robert D Behn, *Rethinking Democratic Accountability* (Brookings Institution Press, 2001) 3; Ruth Grant and Robert Keohane, 'Accountability and Abuses of Power in World Politics' (2005) 99(1) *American Political Science Review* 29, 29–30; Kaare Strom, 'Parliamentary Democracy and Delegation' in Kaare Strom, Wolfgang Muller and Torbjorn Bergman (eds.), *Delegation and Accountability in Parliamentary Democracies* (Oxford University Press, 2003) 55, 62; Mark Bovens, *The Quest for Responsibility: Accountability and Citizenship in Complex Organisations* (Cambridge University Press, 1998) 39.

[21] Mulgan, *Holding Power to Account* (n 20) 10.

[22] Mulgan, 'One Cheer for Hierarchy' (n 17) 10.

[23] Andreas Schedler, 'Conceptualizing Accountability' in Andreas Schedler, Larry Diamond and Marc F Plattner (eds.), *The Self-Restraining State: Power and Accountability in New Democracies* (Lynne Rienner Publishers, 1999) 13, 15–16.

[24] Leo Zaibert, *Punishment and Retribution* (Ashgate Publishing, 2006) 4.

[25] '[A]ccountability implies an element of retributive justice': Mulgan, 'One Cheer for Hierarchy' (n 17) 10.

[26] Zaibert (n 24) 4, 7.

voice its disapproval of wrongdoing, and its judgement that the under-lying conduct is in some way reprehensible. In the accountability frame, punishment of this nature serves 'to underline the importance of the norms that were contravened'.[27] If we were to adopt a desert-based rationale of this nature, we might seek to define an accountability benchmark that centres on notions of responsibility and blameworthi-ness (the 'desert rationale').

The second camp of punishment justifications are those which can be classified as 'consequentialist', which draws on the idea that punishment is designed to achieve positive results going forward, such as reform or deterrence.[28] Such justifications potentially have an important role to play in the context of accountability: 'accountability ... can be seen as designed to influence the future as much as to judge the past'.[29] On this view, the norms that are reinforced through accountability mechanisms 'cast their shadows ahead'.[30] In Mulgan's view, the use of punishment in the accountability context has 'important deterrent effects on those held accountable'.[31] Bovens also sees deterrence as a function of accountability. He notes that the prospect of being held accountable 'often forces us to seek new ways of preventing such a situation from arising'.[32] For him, there is a clear link between accountability mechan-isms and better governance:

> The realisation that one will or might be held to account, the passive side of responsibility, stimulates people to behave responsibly, the active side. Giving account of oneself is therefore one of the most important means by which we can try to maintain the fragile public sphere and to make sure that the way in which society is arranged does not at crucial points slip through our collective fingers.[33]

In addition to deterring against undesirable behaviour, Bovens also emphasises the role that accountability plays in improving performance, which he discusses by adopting the language of 'learning'.[34] In his view, accountability should 'enhance ... the learning capacity and

---

[27] Bovens, *The Quest for Responsibility* (n 20) 39.
[28] Zaibert (n 24) 4.
[29] Mulgan, *Holding Power to Account* (n 20) 18.
[30] Bovens, *The Quest for Responsibility* (n 20) 39.
[31] Mulgan, *Holding Power to Account* (n 20) 18.
[32] Bovens, *The Quest for Responsibility* (n 20) 39.
[33] Ibid.
[34] Bovens, 'Analysing and Assessing Accountability' (n 8) 466.

effectiveness' of public officials.[35] He notes that, in this context, it is not only the individual who is the subject of an accountability enquiry who is targeted; others who see the outcome of a public enquiry also adjust their behaviour by reference to that outcome.[36] In this way, the imposition of sanctions and incentives does not only have the goal of deterring the particular individual against whom they are imposed. Seeing a colleague subjected to an accountability process and suffering sanctions can also influence the broader group of public officials subject to the same standards of conduct. This point is made clear by Behn. He notes that, through the act of holding a specific account-giver accountable, the account-holder 'seeks to influence the behaviour of all future public officials'.[37]

Not everyone agrees that accountability has a legitimate deterrent function. For example, Philp expresses concern that by making the threat of accountability a motivation for acting, there is a risk of eroding public officials' discretion and autonomy[38] – essentially another way of framing the concern that the imposition of punishment and sanctions may lead to defensive practices.[39] Doubts have also been expressed as to whether we can prove a link between accountability and improved performance[40] or 'ethical or morally responsible behaviour'.[41] If the experience of tort law researchers is anything to go by, the task of empirically proving deterrence (or over-deterrence) is likely to be fraught.[42] What we can say is that one of our *goals* in connection with accountability is to achieve both specific deterrence (influencing the individual official) and general deterrence (influencing onlookers) with a view to discouraging undesirable

---

[35] Ibid.

[36] Mark Bovens, 'Public Accountability' in Ewan Ferlie, Laurence Lynn Jr and Christopher Pollitt (eds.), *The Oxford Handbook of Public Management* (Oxford University Press, 2005) 182, 193.

[37] Behn (n 20) 14.

[38] Mark Philp, 'Delimiting Democratic Accountability' (2009) 57 *Political Studies* 28, 38.

[39] See also Mulgan and Uhr (n 11) 165; Bovens, 'Public Accountability' (n 36) 194.

[40] Melvin J Dubnick, 'Accountability and the Promise of Performance: In Search of the Mechanisms' (2005) 28 *Public Performance and Management Review* 376.

[41] Melvin J Dubnick, 'Accountability and Ethics: Reconsidering the Relationships' (2003) 6 *International Journal of Organization Theory and Behavior* 405, 406. Dubnick's observations are made on the basis of his review of the available literature, in which he failed to identify any factor which he believed provided the necessary link (or 'motivating force') between the act of account-giving and 'desirable' performance: Dubnick, 'Accountability and the Promise of Performance' (n 40) 395.

[42] See, e.g., Donald Dewees, David Duff and Michael Trebilcock, *Exploring the Domain of Accident Law: Taking the Facts Seriously* (Oxford University Press, 1996).

conduct and encouraging improved performance (the 'deterrence rationale'). The question of whether the means we select are capable of achieving those ends is one that must be left for another day.

To summarise, we might look to a number of potential rationales to
explain our purpose in holding the government to account, including
transparency, control, redress, desert and deterrence. This is not intended
to be a comprehensive statement of all possible rationales, as we might in
time identify others. The identification of these five rationales really
serves to make two points in Part II of this book. The first is that our
choice of rationale (or rationales) will necessarily influence the decisions
that we make in defining a benchmark against which we purport to
measure accountability deficits and overloads. For instance, in determining *who* should be held accountable we might adopt a very different
approach if our rationale is redress as opposed to desert. The former
would suggest that we select our account-giver on the basis of their ability
to perform restoration (e.g. how deep their pockets might be), whereas
the latter might suggest that we target the individual who has done
wrong. In this way, we might reach different answers to the questions
who, to whom, for what and *how* in defining an accountability benchmark depending on the rationale that we have identified. The second
point is that, unless we can narrow our choice to a single rationale, the
task of seeking to accommodate multiple rationales may bring our
choices into conflict with one another. Accordingly, we need to not only
identify relevant rationales for accountability, but also to make decisions
about how those rationales should be balanced against one another in
circumstances where they produce conflicting results. Bearing these two
points in mind, the following chapters demonstrate the size of the
challenge inherent in defining an accountability benchmark that we
might use to measure accountability deficits and overloads.

4

Who Should Be Held Accountable?

The first question accountability theorists often look to in describing accountability regimes is to ask: 'Who is being held accountable?'[1] In seeking to define a benchmark of accountability, we must rephrase this question as 'who *should* be held accountable?' In other words, which government agent or entity ought to be made to answer in an accountability forum? If we were able to provide an answer to this question, we might then have a basis to look for potential shortfalls or overlaps in our system of governance. This might be the case, for example, where the person who *should* be held accountable has avoided the relevant accountability mechanism, or where the wrong person has been subjected to the mechanism, or where the same party has unnecessarily been brought to account via multiple mechanisms. There are a number of difficulties that we must confront in seeking to decide who *should* be held accountable for the purposes of defining an accountability benchmark.

4.1 'Who' Is the Government?

The first difficulty to confront in deciding *who* ought to be held accountable for the purposes of our benchmark is the sheer complexity of modern government, with public power being divided between a host of interlocking institutions. On the traditional tripartite model, power is

---

[1] Mark Bovens, 'Analysing and Assessing Accountability: A Conceptual Framework' (2007) 13 *European Law Journal* 447, 454–55; Richard Mulgan, *Holding Power to Account: Accountability in Modern Democracies* (Palgrave Macmillan, 2003) 22–23; Jerry Mashaw, 'Accountability and Institutional Design: Some Thoughts on the Grammar of Governance' in Michael Dowdle (ed.), *Public Accountability: Designs, Dilemmas and Experiences* (Cambridge University Press, 2006) 118; Mark Philp, 'Delimiting Democratic Accountability' (2009) 57 *Political Studies* 28, 42; Colin Scott, 'Accountability in the Regulatory State' (2000) 27 *Journal of Law and Society* 38, 41; Ruth Grant and Robert Keohane, 'Accountability and Abuses of Power in World Politics' (2005) 99(1) *American Political Science Review* 29.

shared between the legislative, executive and judicial branches of government, with each of those branches being further devolved into complex
hierarchical structures. So, for instance, in the Westminster tradition, the
legislative branch is broken up into the Houses of Parliament, parliamentary committees and staff, and the courts operate as part of a complex
appellate hierarchy. The executive is more complex again, encompassing
at its core the cabinet and head of state, but more broadly including
various government departments and their employees, public and statutory authorities and agencies. To further complicate this description,
each of the institutions within the various branches of government is
then populated by individuals who may exercise power alone, or as
members of groups, or via internal hierarchies. The position becomes
more complex still in federal jurisdictions, with these power-sharing
arrangements being replicated across two levels of government.[2] To
speak generally of the accountability of 'government' conceals the size
and complexity of these structures; in defining a benchmark of accountability against which we might seek to identify accountability deficits and
overloads, we need to be able to unpack these nuances and be precise in
identifying *who* will be held accountable.

Further complexity arises because public powers are rarely conferred on
a discrete individual or institution who will then exercise that power from
start to finish. Frequently, there will be degrees of co-operation between
individuals and institutions in connection with the exercise of power. So,
for instance, the detention of an asylum seeker may follow a complex series
of interactions between officials sitting within various institutions of government. The initial detention may be effected by a border patrol officer;
officials within the relevant government department may collect information in relation to a claim for asylum; the responsible minister or a
senior official may make a decision to refuse a visa; a tribunal may refuse to
overturn that decision on merits review; a judge may decline to overturn
the decision on judicial review; and immigration officials may then give
effect to the detention. A flaw within one of these areas of activity
(e.g. crucial information missed during the initial investigation) may have
flow-on effects in relation to the course taken by later officials. This
'problem of many hands'[3] may make it very difficult to pinpoint an
individual or institution that might be held accountable for the end result.

---

[2] For example, the *Australian Constitution* divides power between the States and
Commonwealth.
[3] Bovens, 'Analysing and Assessing Accountability' (n 1) 457.

This problem will be exacerbated in circumstances where the relevant fault is not one that can comfortably be attributed to a particular individual or entity, but is more accurately described as a systemic fault. This may be the case, for instance, where a breakdown in the communication protocol between two entities means that the relevant procedure is not followed. *Who*, in that circumstance, ought to be held accountable for the result? Because government activity is frequently the result of a complex chain of interactions and co-operation between individuals and entities, it may be difficult to make choices about who ought to be held accountable in the design of our accountability benchmark.

This complexity is further compounded by the recent trend towards outsourcing of public functions to private contractors. Outsourcing to non-government entities and individuals is typical in modern government, with many hitherto public functions (such as the management of immigration detention facilities, prisons, health and disability services and so on) having been contractually handed over to private entities.[4] Concern that this outsourcing trend represents a potential area of accountability deficit[5] directs our attention to the question of *who* ought to be held accountable for the exercise of outsourced powers for the purposes of our accountability benchmark. Should these contractors be held directly accountable pursuant to the same regimes that apply to government entities? Should they be held accountable pursuant to alternative regimes? Ought the government be held accountable for the actions of private contractors? These questions require us to make normative judgements about whether we wish to require the government to answer for the conduct of those that perform functions on its behalf, or whether we are more concerned with requiring the party who has done wrong to answer for their misdeeds, or perhaps both? It is only once we have decided *who* ought to be held accountable for the purposes of our benchmark that we can then use that benchmark to assess whether outsourcing represents a potential area of accountability deficit.

Putting to one side the difficulties of mapping out the range of individuals and institutions that make up 'the government', there is in fact a much more important philosophical question we must confront in deciding *who* ought to be held accountable, which requires us to think about how we conceptualise 'the government'. The question of whether we should treat

---

[4] In the Australian context, see, e.g., Janina Boughey, Ellen Rock and Greg Weeks, *Government Liability: Principles and Remedies* (LexisNexis, 2019) ch 3.

[5] See, e.g., Mashaw (n 1) 134.

the government as a corporate entity or as a collection of individuals is one that has exercised the minds of political and legal theorists for centuries. As explored by McLean in her treatise on the elusive notion of the Crown, there are broadly two schools of thought.[6] The first, reflected in Blackstone's theory of the state, regards it as an abstract entity; a juridical person with its own moral personality that comes into being on the establishment of civil society.[7] On this view, the government might be understood as a corporate entity that exercises power through the acting mind and will of the sub-entities and individuals that constitute it. If we see the government in these terms, our accountability benchmark might answer the question of *who* ought to be held accountable by targeting mechanisms towards the over-arching entities of government, rather than towards the individuals who make up those entities. It would be necessary, then, to attribute the acts and will of government officials to the entities that they represent. The second school of thought, most prominently reflected in Dicey's theories, adopts a view of the state, not as an abstract entity, but as a collective of individuals.[8] If we were to adopt this model for the purposes of our accountability benchmark, the question of *who* ought to be held accountable would be more concerned with sheeting home responsibility to individuals who have contributed to an impugned outcome. All of this tells us that, in order to decide *who* ought to be held accountable in defining our benchmark, it would be necessary to come to a landing on a centuries-long debate regarding our conceptualisation of 'the government'.

4.2   A Rationale-Based Approach

Against this background, the sizeable task that we must confront in defining a benchmark of accountability is to decide who should be held accountable if we were to achieve some 'ideal amount' of government accountability. There are essentially three different models we might choose between.[9] The first is the *individual accountability* model, pursu-ant to which the task is to hold an individual accountable for their own

---

[6] Janet McLean, *Searching for the State in British Legal Thought: Competing Conceptions of the Public Sphere* (Cambridge University Press, 2012) ch 1.

[7] William Blackstone, *Commentaries on the Laws of England* (Clarendon Press, 1765–69).

[8] McLean (n 6) 3.

[9] Mark Bovens, 'Public Accountability' in Ewan Ferlie, Laurence Lynn Jr and Christopher Pollitt (eds.), *The Oxford Handbook of Public Management* (Oxford University Press, 2005) 182, 190–92. Bovens also identifies 'collective accountability' as a model pursuant to which any member (or members) of an organisation can be singled out to be held

acts and choices. Mulgan views this as the most 'central and straightforward' style of accountability, in which 'the person held accountable is the person who is responsible, in the sense of being the person who can choose to act or not to act in the performance of certain duties and who is therefore liable for praise or blame'.[10] Where multiple agents have been involved, the aim would be to share accountability according to the contribution of each. In the context of public governance, this model would (for example) demand that a public servant who was grossly negligent in the exercise of their duties, resulting in the deportation of the wrong person, be held personally accountable for that result. The second possible model is the *hierarchical accountability* model, pursuant to which one actor is held accountable for the actions of another. In many instances, it may be a superior being held accountable for the acts of an inferior, though there may be variations depending on context. In the above example, a government department might be held vicariously accountable for the negligence of the public servant. (As Bovens notes, it is possible that responsibility may nonetheless be shifted back to the individual wrongdoer after the fact.)[11] The third possible model is the *corporate accountability* model, pursuant to which an abstract entity is held accountable as a unitary actor for the acts and choices of those who represent it.[12] In the above example, the government department would be held directly (as opposed to vicariously) accountable for the negligence of the public servant on the basis that the negligent act was performed in the name of the department. So, which of these different models would represent the 'ideal amount' of government accountability for the purposes of defining the benchmark? Returning to the discussion set out in Chapter 3, our choice of *who* ought to be held accountable will be heavily influenced by the accountability rationale that we select (transparency, control, redress, desert or deterrence).

4.2.1 Who Should Provide the Answers?

The transparency rationale is concerned with exposing the machinations of government for public scrutiny. Adopting this rationale, the question

---

accountable for the actions of others. For present purposes, this can be subsumed within the notion of hierarchical accountability.

[10] Mulgan, *Holding Power to Account* (n 1) 23.

[11] Bovens, 'Analysing and Assessing Accountability' (n 1) 457.

[12] Ibid.

of *who* should be held accountable might direct our attention to identifying the best source of information. This might suggest a number of possible approaches. For instance, if we think that the best source of information is the person most directly involved in the relevant decision-making process or outcome, it might make sense to adopt the individual accountability model. Information would thereby be sourced 'straight from the horse's mouth', increasing the quality of the information provided and reducing the likelihood that explanations might be lost in translation. Within this model, the person who ought to provide the answers would be the judge who has decided a case, or the immigration official who has cancelled a visa, or the local government official who has granted a development application. We might, therefore, be wary of accountability arrangements in which only the head of the organisation operates as a source of information, with subordinates being 'muzzled'.[13] Such arrangements allow for the flow of information to be constrained and might result in 'public scrutiny [being] blunted'.[14]

While the individual accountability model might be considered useful in terms of sourcing the most accurate and rich information, there are a number of potential drawbacks to that approach. One such drawback is that (as outlined in Section 4.1) the nature of government operations and decision-making means that a matter is rarely dealt with from start to end by a single individual. Frequently, an outcome will be the result of a chain of interactions between various individuals and entities, making it difficult to isolate who might be best placed to act as the information-provider in a given instance. And, even if it were possible to receive explanations from all relevant parties, the complexity of the resulting picture will frequently fail to explain the situation as a whole. In such a situation, we might think that the corporate accountability model might offer a better contribution to the transparency of government, allowing information to be gathered from multiple sources and delivered through a single communication channel. The resulting information is then more likely to be compiled into a comprehensive and straightforward explanation than would be the case if the recipient were to receive multiple and potentially conflicting accounts from a range of parties.

A further reason we might wish to move away from the individual accountability model in certain circumstances is related to the notion of

---

[13] See, e.g., Richard Mulgan, 'One Cheer for Hierarchy – Accountability in Disjointed Governance' (2003) 55(2) *Political Science* 6, 11–12.
[14] Ibid 12.

legitimacy. While relying on an individual accountability model has the potential to target the individual who has engaged in the relevant conduct or made the relevant decision, we might wonder whether legitimacy is better supported by hearing from that individual's superiors or employers. We might have serious questions about the legitimacy of our system of government if the official government explanation for a mistake is left to a low-level public servant simply on the basis that they happen to be most closely involved. If the transparency rationale is concerned with reinforcing the legitimacy of government, a hierarchical model of disseminating information might reassure citizens that serious matters are being taken seriously and being dealt with at the highest levels. There is also something to be said for the idea that citizens may be more trusting of information provided by a senior official rather than a low-level public servant.

This discussion serves to demonstrate that, when adopting the transparency rationale, there are different choices we might make in deciding who ought to provide an explanation for government performance, with benefits and drawbacks to each. The individual accountability model potentially provides the most rich and accurate source of information; the corporate model is well suited to providing information about complex government processes; the hierarchical model has the potential to reinforce legitimacy by demonstrating that the government is taking a matter seriously. Because of the benefits and drawbacks to each model, it is difficult to select just one model to employ for the purposes of our benchmark of accountability; deciding who should provide the answers is quite simply a matter on which reasonable minds will differ and which might vary from situation to situation.

4.2.2 Whom Should We Control?

The second rationale explored in Chapter 3 is that of control. Under this rationale, the primary concern of accountability is to provide principals with the ability to control their agents, dictating the manner in which they exercise their power and bringing them back within boundaries when exceeded. The question of 'who' we should control for the purposes of establishing a benchmark of accountability is therefore concerned with identifying the party best placed to bring an exercise of power back within the boundaries that have been transgressed. In deciding which accountability model (individual, hierarchical or corporate) is best suited to this purpose, the most logical approach is to focus our attention on the conferral of power in each case, with the result that we would seek to control the repository of the power (i.e. the person or body responsible for its exercise). In some cases, this will reflect an individual accountability model. So, for instance, where a power to grant development consent has been conferred on the planning officer of a local council, an invalid exercise of power by that planning officer ought to attract a control order directed at that officer. Similarly, a misdirected exercise of a power conferred on a particular minister ought to attract a control remedy addressed directly to the minister. In circumstances where that planning officer or minister is the repository of the power, it makes little sense to direct a control order to other parties, such as their superiors or employers. This leads us to the conclusion that we ought to adopt an individual accountability model in such cases.

However, in other cases our focus on the conferral of power will lead us to adopt the hierarchical accountability model. So, for instance, in a case where one individual has exercised power on behalf of another (e.g. a low-level public servant has made a decision on behalf of their superior officers), we would adopt a hierarchical accountability model in issuing our order to the repository of power (the superior officer) in preference to the individual who exercised the power (the low-level public servant). Finally, in cases where the repository of power is an entity rather than an individual, we would adopt a corporate accountability model. So, for instance, where a power is conferred on a local council, or statutory body, or tribunal, we would be concerned with directing our control order to that relevant entity, rather than to the individual officer who happened to exercise power on behalf of the entity in the instant case. Therefore, if we adopt the control rationale for accountability, the question of *who* we should control might lead us to focus on identifying the repository of power. This would result in the employment of different accountability models in different situations.

4.2.3   Who Should Provide Redress?

The third accountability rationale explored in Chapter 3 is that of redress. This rationale is concerned with correcting the outcomes that arise by reason of a misdirected exercise of public power; it is about putting wrongs right.[15] If we adopt redress as our accountability

---

[15] Dawn Oliver, *Government in the United Kingdom: The Search for Accountability, Effectiveness, and Citizenship* (Open University Press, 1991) 22.

rationale, how would we answer the question 'who should provide redress?' On one view, we might say that the best means of achieving redress is to identify the party best placed to satisfy that demand – that is, the party with the most plentiful resources. This would likely lead us away from the individual accountability model, which would see the burden of redress claims rest on the individual official who can be said to have caused harm. Instead, we might reach the conclusion that the hierarchical or corporate accountability models are better suited to ensuring that the party being held accountable has the necessary resources to facilitate redress. If (as is likely to be the case in most circumstances) losses are to be remedied through the provision of a monetary award, the government coffers will in almost all cases be better resourced than those of individual government officials.[16] While many would be critical of the 'deep pockets' mentality as a driver of expanded government liability, the fact remains that the pool of funds available to resource redress is more substantial when adopting a corporate account- ability model than one premised on individual liability.

One of the core concerns regarding the adoption of a corporate or hierarchical accountability model for the purposes of redress centres not on the *ability* of governments to resource damages claims, but on the source and nature of those funds. Government coffers are, of course, filled through public taxation, exacted for the purposes of supporting public works and providing public services. As the argument goes, the redirection of these funds into redress of individuals who have been placed worse off as a result of government activity reduces the overall pool of funds available to perform these public functions. It follows that public services would be diminished or that higher taxes would need to be levied to support this expanded range of demands. And, as put by Stapleton in discussing government liability in tort, 'why should the accidents of tort litigation determine the allocation of public money to various activities?'.[17] In essence, if we adopt a corporate or hierarchical accountability model, it is not the government that is accountable to provide redress, but the public itself, either through the provision of taxes

---

[16] Peter H Schuck, *Suing Government: Citizen Remedies for Official Wrongs* (Yale University Press, 1983) 101.

[17] Jane Stapleton, 'Duty of Care: Peripheral Parties and Alternative Opportunities for Deterrence' (1995) 111 *Law Quarterly Review* 301, 313.

or compromising on the provision of public works and services.[18] However, these arguments take on less significance in light of the redress rationale for accountability. If our primary concern is to ensure that individuals harmed through government activity obtain redress, the fact that the government is in a better position to achieve this would likely outweigh our misgivings that the real underwriter of such liability is the tax-paying public.

In deciding between the hierarchical and corporate accountability models, the essential difference between the two is that, in the case of hierarchical accountability, the government would stand in for the primary wrongdoer, providing redress on their behalf. In comparison, the corporate accountability model would hold the government accountable directly, with the government providing redress for its own wrongdoing. One factor that might lead us to prefer the corporate accountability model is that it simplifies the process of identifying an appropriate defendant. This is particularly so in cases where losses are caused by systemic, rather than individual, fault. As was noted in Section 4.1, the nature of government is such that a victim's loss may have been produced through a complex series of interactions between officials and entities and as a result of various policies and procedures. It might be very difficult in such a case to pinpoint the particular individual who can be said to have caused the loss complained of. One benefit of the corporate accountability model is that this difficulty might be avoided through holding the government directly liable for systemic failings. If we are primarily concerned with redressing loss, we might welcome an approach to liability that reduces the burden on harmed individuals to pinpoint the particular government official or entity that can be said to have caused that loss.

4.2.4 Who Deserves to Be Punished?

The fourth accountability rationale explored in Chapter 3 is that of desert, being the goal of condemning past conduct. If we were to adopt this rationale, how would we answer the question of *who* should be punished? According to the desert rationale, an agent is punished on

---

[18] Harlow notes that this view does not reflect the reality that individual agencies operate within individual budgets rather than drawing on a general pool of funds, and that many government agencies are insured against liability: Carol Harlow, *State Liability: Tort Law and Beyond* (Oxford University Press, 2004) 25.

the basis that they deserve it; punishment stands as a public and symbolic expression of disapproval of blameworthy conduct. We might say that this rationale is most conformable with the individual accountability model, as this places the focus of accountability on identifying the individual who ought to be punished for their own wrongdoing. Punishment via the criminal law is the archetype of the individual accountability model in this respect, with the elements of criminal offences being primarily concerned with identifying the individual with the relevant mens rea and actus reus to establish the offence. For instance, a public official who has exercised their powers for personal gain may be found to have committed the offence of misconduct in public office, and be personally subject to penalties including imprisonment and fines. We would likely be satisfied that the individual accountability model has served the desert rationale of accountability well in such a scenario; the individual official who has engaged in egregious conduct has been publicly condemned for their behaviour on the basis that they deserve such recrimination.

While the individual accountability model might be thought to serve the desert rationale of accountability well in many cases, we might wonder whether there are circumstances that justify expanding beyond these boundaries. Are there circumstances in which we might wish to be able to condemn not only an individual official, but the government entity as a whole? This might be the case where, for example, the government has designed and implemented an egregious policy; to adapt Sir Leslie Stephen's famous example, the execution of all blue-eyed babies. If such a policy were to be implemented, we might wonder whether the condemnatory function of accountability captured by this rationale might be best achieved through targeting the government entity as a whole, rather than simply the individual officials who had the bad luck to be charged with its implementation. As put by Cane: 'The powerful functional case for government criminal liability is that it makes it harder for governments to offload on to individual public agents responsibility for what is done in the name of the government or the public.'[19] This might lead us to look to corporate accountability as a useful model for the purposes of the desert rationale. While the individual accountability model might represent the orthodox means of

---

[19] Peter Cane, *Responsibility in Law and Morality* (Hart Publishing, 2002) 267. For a similar point made in the context of tortious liability, see page 263 of that work.

achieving the desert goal of accountability, there might be some circumstances in which we may wish to look beyond it.

4.2.5   Whom Should We Deter?

Adopting the deterrence rationale, the primary function of accountability mechanisms would be to influence the future activity of government by disincentivising undesirable behaviour and/or incentivising desirable behaviour. The goal would be not only to target the individual official who has contravened a norm (specific deterrence), but also to influence others (general deterrence). The question of who ought to be held accountable would be concerned with targeting the parties that have the greatest capacity to influence future change, either for themselves or by setting an example for others.[20]

The individual accountability model would lead us to take the position that by subjecting an individual who has contravened a norm to an accountability process, we are likely to deter that individual from committing future infractions (specific deterrence) and deter others from engaging in similar conduct (general deterrence). To follow Dicey's line of thinking, for example, we might require an individual official to pay damages to their victim with a view to deterring that official from committing future infractions.[21] The question of whether the imposition of sanctions on individual officials in fact produces a deterrent effect is a fraught one, which, in the context of tort law, has exercised academic minds for decades.[22] If this experience is anything to go by, it may be very difficult to prove empirically that sanctions imposed via accountability mechanisms in fact deter individuals against future infractions.[23] Further, there are those who would suggest that, far from achieving the goal of improved performance, the imposition of sanctions on individuals in fact risks diminished performance. On this view, individuals who

---

[20] John Braithwaite, 'On Speaking Softly and Carrying Big Sticks: Neglected Dimensions of a Republican Separation of Powers' (1997) 47 *University of Toronto Law Journal* 305, 333.

[21] As Harlow notes, while Dicey does not explicitly embrace the deterrence model, he appears to assume that this will be a corollary of the imposition of tortious liability on individual officials: Harlow, *State Liability* (n 18) 23–24.

[22] See, e.g., Donald Dewees, David Duff and Michael Trebilcock, *Exploring the Domain of Accident Law: Taking the Facts Seriously* (Oxford University Press, 1996).

[23] In the context of accountability mechanisms more generally, see Melvin J Dubnick, 'Accountability and the Promise of Performance: In Search of the Mechanisms' (2005) 28 *Public Performance and Management Review* 376.

are at risk of exposure to sanctions as a consequence of their performance may be encouraged to adopt defensive practices.[24] So, for instance, an official may be disinclined to reject an application in circumstances where they are at risk of liability to the vexed applicant, and avoid making the 'tough decisions'.

A related risk, highlighted by Braithwaite, is that punitive sanctions targeted at individual wrongdoers may ultimately produce reactance, prompting the individual to adopt a defiant stance and resist the demand for improved behaviour;[25] an 'I'll show you!' response. To avoid this possibility, Braithwaite suggests that applying 'weak sanctions' to 'soft targets' is potentially more likely to produce the desired result of forward-looking change.[26] The aim is to deter, not through holding a few criminally responsible, but through more broadly targeting the range of 'actors with causative or preventative capability with respect to that abuse'.[27] A related aspect of the theory is that the best approach is not to target individual wrongdoers who stand to benefit from wrongdoing, but instead to seek out 'gatekeepers', being those who have the capacity to facilitate or prevent the agent's actions.[28] As the argument goes, there is more to gain by imposing the burden of compliance on a disinterested third party than on the agent who would otherwise benefit from their own wrongful conduct.[29] If we were to take these ideas on board, we would be concerned with holding accountable, not those who have done wrong, but those who have the capacity to influence prospective change. This might suggest a more hierarchical, rather than individual, model of accountability.

The individual accountability model is also open to criticism on the basis of its capacity to address systemic wrongdoing. As noted by Schuck, we would likely have doubts as to whether there is any utility in punishing a prison official for implementing a prison policy of solitary confinement.[30] This individual, having acted in accordance with the policy of their employer, is unlikely to regard punishment as a fair means of

---

[24] See, e.g., Richard Mulgan and John Uhr, 'Accountability and Governance' in Glyn Davis and Patrick Weller (eds.), *Are You Being Served? State, Citizens and Governance* (Allen and Unwin, 2001) 152, 165; Bovens, 'Public Accountability' (n 9) 194.
[25] Braithwaite, 'On Speaking Softly and Carrying Big Sticks' (n 20) 322–24.
[26] Ibid 318.
[27] Ibid 333.
[28] Ibid 334.
[29] Ibid 337.
[30] Schuck (n 16) 101.

deterrence, and others looking on are placed in the unenviable position of choosing between disobeying their employer and the risk of personal liability. An alternative option to facilitate the deterrence rationale in such cases would be to adopt the corporate accountability model. This would see government entities held accountable for the actions of their agents and employees, with a view to encouraging those entities to improve overall performance by better managing those agents and employees. This model aligns with Schuck's view that agencies are generally well equipped to facilitate deterrence.[31] In his view, there is more to be gained by targeting the agency than the 'street-level official' in light of the agency's knowledge, resources and powers, which position them to influence the future behaviour of their employees.[32] If we were to adopt sanctions that depend on the availability of significant resources (e.g. monetary payments), it might be argued that the 'deep pockets' of the government potentially cushion the impact of sanctions imposed on government agencies and departments. However, the reality is that these entities operate within the constraints of their budgets and must answer up the chain for overspends that might arise following the payment of substantial damages awards.[33] As for the individual accountability model, the question of whether applying particular sanctions to government entities in fact achieves deterrence as an empirically provable fact is likely to be a matter of debate. At best, we can say that particular sanctions might be applied with the goal of deterring undesirable conduct. We must say the same for the counter-argument that sanctioning entities might promote over-deterrence (i.e. where the threat of punishment fosters defensive practices). The lack of evidence of the effectiveness (or counter-productiveness) of sanctions against government entities is nonetheless a matter that we must bear in mind in defining our benchmark of accountability.

4.3 Summary

The foregoing discussion has demonstrated that there are many choices that we must make in deciding *who* should be held accountable, depending on which rationale for accountability we might adopt. So, for instance, while the desert rationale tends towards the individual

---

[31] Ibid 104.
[32] Ibid 104–05.
[33] On this point, see Harlow, *State Liability* (n 18) 25.

accountability model, the redress rationale tends towards the corporate accountability model. Even on adopting a particular rationale, there are then difficult choices to be made about which approach might best suit that rationale. So, for instance, if we adopt the transparency rationale, we might reach differing views on the best approach depending on whether we are concerned with identifying the richest source of information (the individual accountability model), or the most authoritative (the hierarchical or corporate accountability models). We might also find that different models are appropriate in different contexts. For example, in some situations we may think that sourcing detailed and accurate information from the person most closely connected is critical (e.g. when used as evidence in a court case), whereas in other situations we may be more motivated to ensure that information is made available efficiently. Therefore, the question of who should be held accountable is not always apparent, even with the assistance of the accountability rationales. What we can say, based on the discussion in this chapter, is that there is no one model that applies equally well to all accountability rationales and across all contexts; there are horses for courses.

This leads us to one of the most significant issues we must confront in seeking to identify a benchmark of accountability; how to balance competing rationales against one another. If we accept that accountability requires us to potentially support each of the five possible accountability rationales (transparency, control, redress, desert and deterrence), we must seek to adopt a benchmark of *who* should be held accountable that is capable of serving these various objectives. The difficulty is that there will be cases where these objectives are in tension with one another. So, for instance, one means of serving the redress rationale would be to adopt the corporate accountability model, requiring the government to make a monetary payment to a harmed individual. As outlined above, this approach might be preferred to the individual accountability model on the basis that the government is better resourced to finance such claims. In comparison, the desert rationale is far more conformable with the individual accountability model. In a case where an individual official has engaged in egregious conduct warranting condemnation, we might doubt whether that official is likely to suffer the requisite degree of condemnation if public funds are used to restore the individual they have harmed, leaving the official no worse off. Instead, we might wonder whether the goals of redress and desert may dually be served by requiring the individual official to directly foot the bill for the victim's loss in such a case (which in the legal context may be achieved through the provision of compensatory and punitive damages in tort). Of course, this might leave the victim at risk of losing out if the official happens to be impecunious. If we are to try and choose a single mechanism to provide accountability, the best choice for one rationale might produce an inversely negative effect for another. We must choose, in such a case, to prefer either punishment of the official or redress of the victim, or, perhaps, to hive off both rationales to be served through separate accountability processes. This complex balancing act would be further complicated if we were then to draw in the remaining accountability rationales of transparency, control and deterrence, each of which might lead us to look for different answers as to who should be held accountable.

To summarise, the foregoing discussion has demonstrated that, in seeking to establish a benchmark of accountability, the question of who ought to be held accountable is not a straightforward one, and will depend to a large degree on which rationale for accountability we adopt. If we need to accommodate more than one rationale, the decision is further complicated by attempting to balance these rationales against one another so as to achieve a result that best serves either the majority, or those we determine to be most important. Until we can reach a landing on these complicated questions, we will struggle to set a benchmark against which we can seek to identify accountability deficits or overloads. After all, we cannot hope to establish that an agent has escaped accountability if we cannot say that they ought to have been held accountable in the first place. If we wish to be able to take a firmer grasp on our claims of accountability deficits and overloads, the first step is to focus our attention on who should be held accountable by making clear what we are seeking to achieve (transparency, control, etc.), and arguing for the best means to achieve it (individual, hierarchical or corporate accountability models).

5

To Whom Should They Be Accountable?

As noted in Chapter 1, the question of *to whom* an agent is required to provide an account has been conceptualised in two ways in the literature.[1] The first conceptualisation focuses on the forum in which accountability is to be adjudicated.[2] So, for instance, the party *to whom* an agent is accountable would encompass bodies such as courts, ombudsmen, administrative tribunals, Parliament and so on. Accountability forums will vary, for example, in the manner in which they make accountability judgements. For the purposes of defining a benchmark of accountability, the nature of the accountability forum is better dealt with as a component of the question *how should an agent be held accountable* (see Chapter 7), rather than *to whom should an agent be accountable?* The focus of this chapter instead looks at the second conceptualisation of the *to whom* question, which focuses not on the accountability forum but on the party entitled to instigate the accountability process (referred to here as the '*prosecutor*'). So, for instance, only those who have a valid legal claim are entitled to secure government accountability via legal proceedings, and only those who are eligible to vote are entitled to participate in the electoral accountability forum. In some cases, a forum itself may also play the role of prosecutor. This will be the case, for example, where a forum is entitled to commence an own-motion enquiry.[3]

To redefine this conception of the *to whom* question as an accountability benchmark, it is necessary to decide who *should* be selected as a prosecutor for the purposes of deploying an accountability mechanism. In this respect, we can imagine a spectrum. At its broadest, we might have an entirely open regime that would allow any person to hold the

---

[1] See, e.g., Richard Mulgan, *Holding Power to Account: Accountability in Modern Democracies* (Palgrave Macmillan, 2003) 76.

[2] See, e.g., Mark Bovens, 'Analysing and Assessing Accountability: A Conceptual Framework' (2007) 13 *European Law Journal* 447, 455–57.

[3] See, e.g., *Ombudsman Act 1976* (Cth) s 5(1)(b).

government accountable. At the narrower end of the spectrum, we might limit access to only a particular group or individual to be charged with the accountability-enforcement role. In between, we might allow limited classes of individuals or groups with particular qualities or interests to access accountability mechanisms. As explored in the following discussion, there are two key difficulties that we will encounter in selecting the prosecutor(s) that best reflect an ideal benchmark of accountability. First, there are many factors that might influence a prosecutor's capacity and interest to undertake that role, and second, we will likely reach differing views on the best choice of prosecutor depending on which accountability rationale we are interested in promoting.

5.1   Capacity and Interest to Prosecute

If our overarching concern is to maximise the likelihood that the government will be held accountable, there are a number of different factors that might influence our selection of a prosecutor. One such factor is the *size* of the class. It goes without saying that if we increase the number of potential prosecutors, we also increase the likelihood one or more of them will be willing and able to hold the government to account. Conversely, limiting prosecutorial functions to a single point decreases that likelihood. In essence, increasing the size of the prosecutorial class allows us to 'hedge our bets' in the manner of the redundancy model of accountability.[4]

However, maximising the number of people who have the interest and resources to hold the government accountable (and thereby reducing the chances that no-one will do so) might not be our only concern. We might also wish to take into account the *skills* and *resources* of the prosecutor. For instance, there might be valid reasons to limit prosecution of criminal offences to a designated public prosecutor in preference to private prosecutors. If our concern is to maximise the likelihood of successfully holding the government accountable, we might think that an experienced prosecutor with the backing of relevant resources has greater prospects of satisfying that aim. We might similarly say that a further factor with the potential to increase the chances of a successful prosecution is *knowledge*. As distinct from prosecution skills and experience, a prosecutor may be better placed to perform their role if

---

[4] See Chapter 10, Section 10.1.

they have intimate knowledge of the facts and circumstances giving rise to the prosecution. So, for instance, a person who was on the receiving end of particular conduct will naturally be better placed to complain of it than a third party who has only received a second-hand version of those facts.

A further factor that might influence our choice of prosecutor is that of *motivation*. We might say, for example, that a person is particularly well motivated to undertake a prosecution if that role is part of their job description (e.g. a public prosecutor). We might also say that a person is more likely to engage in a prosecution if they stand to gain something as a result (e.g. the reversal of a decision that personally affects them). Others might wish to engage in a prosecution out of more altruistic motives, such as to help another or to protect a public interest (e.g. an environmental activist). Yet others might have a political agenda. If our sole concern was to maximise the likelihood of prosecution, we might wish to harness these various motivations so as to create a class of prosecutors that captures them. However, people may also have other, less altruistic, motives for bringing a prosecution (e.g. spite, vengeance or greed), and we would need to decide whether we are willing to capitalise on these in order to maximise the likelihood of prosecution. Similarly, a person might be more inclined to bring a prosecution when motivated by financial gain (e.g. receiving a windfall in the nature of a punitive damages award).[5] We could, therefore, increase the likelihood that accountability will be enforced by providing financial incentives for prosecution. However, in defining our benchmark of accountability we would need to consider whether allowing our accountability regime to foster profiteering might flood the system with unmeritorious prosecutions. If every 'real' accountability prosecution was matched with five purely speculative prosecutions, we might wonder whether the legitimacy of the system would be put at risk.

A further issue of motives that must be taken into account in defining the benchmark is those motives that might encourage a prosecutor *not* to exercise their entitlement. For example, we might be concerned that bias, corruption or self-interest might disincline an unscrupulous government employee from prosecuting 'their own'.[6] If we are concerned to avoid this possibility, or even the appearance of such a possibility, we might wish to

[5] Concerns about creating a 'windfall' underlie arguments against allowing punitive damages awards: Peter Cane, *An Anatomy of Tort Law* (Hart Publishing, 1997) 188.
[6] See, e.g., *Gouriet v Union of Post Office Workers* [1978] AC 435, 498.

ensure that the category of individuals entitled to prosecute a claim is wider than a defined government prosecutor. A related factor that might be relevant to our choice of prosecutor is *independence*. There might be reasons to prefer a prosecutor who is capable of making an independent assessment of the case, rather than being primarily influenced by questions of self-interestedness or retribution. This might decrease the likelihood of prosecutions being brought for ulterior purposes, and potentially increase public confidence in the accountability regime overall.

In summary, it is possible to see that one of the difficulties involved in defining the normative benchmark of *to whom* the government should be accountable is that there are a number of factors that might influence the likelihood of prosecution. On the one hand, we might think that allowing a very open regime will maximise the chance of a prosecution taking place, but on the other we might think that chances of successful prosecution are increased by limiting access to those with particular types of skills, resources, knowledge or motives. Striking an appropriate balance between these various factors will present a challenge in defining a benchmark of accountability.

5.2   A Rationale-Based Approach

The task of balancing the various factors that might define the class of prosecutors becomes even more complicated once we begin to think about the various rationales for accountability explored in this book. The question of 'to whom' the government ought to be accountable may admit different answers depending on which rationale for accountability we choose to adopt.

5.2.1   To Whom Should the Government Provide an Account?

The transparency rationale of accountability is closely aligned with notions of open government. In many respects, the question of to whom the government ought to provide an account might be answered 'everyone'. Ultimate transparency would be achieved if the government were to publicise all aspects of its internal operations and decisions and make all information publicly accessible. To a more limited extent, this accountability approach is evident in the duties of positive disclosure established under the Australian freedom of information regime, which requires agencies to publish certain information proactively. Such information includes, for example, details regarding the agency's structure, functions, appointments, annual reports, operational information and so on.[7] Provided that a person has the means of accessing the portal through which this information is made available (generally the agency website), any person is able to access this information at any time. This proactive accountability approach of widespread public access to government information is also evident in other aspects of government administration. For instance, in Australia proceedings in Parliament are publicised via free-to-air television and via publicly available transcripts, and court decisions are publicly available through open-access online sources and public libraries. Assuming that a person has the ability and means to access and interpret the information provided in this form, we can treat this information as essentially available to all. Of course, not all government information is made available in such a proactive sense. For other information, it is necessary to consider who should be entitled to *call* for the provision of an account; to whom should the government be obliged to provide information on demand?

If we are to adopt the transparency rationale for accountability, we would likely prefer a very widespread right to obtain access to government information. We would not wish, for example, for access to be limited to those sufficiently well connected or well resourced to exercise the privilege. In this respect, of the factors discussed above, our primary concern might be to maximise the size of the class of potential prosecutors, rather than limiting it to those with particular skills, knowledge and resources. In a practical sense, this would require that the mechanism we rely on to facilitate transparency does not contain barriers that might inhibit widespread access (e.g. high access fees). A perhaps more difficult question to consider is whether a person's motives for accessing information ought to play a role in our decision as to whether they ought to be excluded from the regime. For instance, should we be concerned that a person is seeking to access information for the purposes of personal financial gain, as opposed to some more altruistic, public interest-based motive? Again, if our primary concern is to facilitate transparency in government operations, we would likely be interested in adopting an accountability benchmark that prioritises transparency over any countervailing concerns about whether the person accessing information is 'deserving' of that access. In this

---

[7] *Freedom of Information Act 1982* (Cth) s 8.

respect, we might say that, for the purposes of the transparency rationale, the size of the class of prosecutors would potentially be the most
important factor influencing our choice of benchmark.

This approach is quite well-reflected in the Australian freedom of
information regime, which provides that 'every person has a legally
enforceable right to obtain access' to documents held by government
agencies.[8] While the agency is entitled to levy a charge for access to the
information,[9] before doing so the agency will take into account the extent
to which the charge might cause financial hardship to the applicant as
well as whether the provision of access to the information is in the public
interest.[10] Therefore, while the regime does not facilitate free access to
information to all, there is a mechanism built in for the purposes of
allowing free access in those cases where the applicant might not otherwise be able to afford it. The regime also provides that an applicant's
motives for accessing information are not a disqualifying factor.[11] In this
respect, the Australian freedom of information regime is relatively consistent with a benchmark that is concerned with enabling widespread
access to government information.

5.2.2   Who Should Be Entitled to Control the Government?

The control rationale for accountability is concerned with ensuring that,
when viewed through the lens of the principal–agent model, citizens have
the means to control their government and to ensure that it acts in
accordance with their interests. In thinking about *to whom* the government should be accountable for this purpose, one answer might be to say
that the relevant reference point ought to be the public as a whole. But
this overly simplistic response does not tell us very much about how the
'public as a whole' might hold the government accountable. In one sense,
elections represent a marking point for accountability of this nature;
the public goes to the ballot booth and casts a vote to either retain or
replace the incumbent government. The announcement of the outcome
of the vote can be seen to reflect a wholesale exercise of the public's
control over government. In countries that observe compulsory voting

---

[8] Ibid s 4(1) (definitions of 'agency', 'prescribed authority').
[9] Ibid s 29.
[10] Ibid s 29(5).
[11] Ibid s 11(2).

requirements, this system can be viewed as reinforcing this wholesale control by requiring all eligible voters to participate.

However, there are a number of matters that influence the extent to which the electoral vote reflects the judgement of 'the public' as a whole. As a starting point, it would be necessary to engage with the wealth of literature exploring drivers of voter choice.[12] There are also many institutional factors that must be considered. First, most electoral systems exclude certain classes of voters on the basis of age, citizenship and criminal status, for example. Can we say that the vote reflects the will of 'the public' in circumstances where categories of individuals are excluded from participation? Secondly, we must take into account the extent to which voting rights are equally weighted and distributed ('one vote one value'?),[13] as unequal distribution of voting rights might skew the conclusion that an election result represents public will. Thirdly, we would need to consider the relevance of the vote calculation method in our assessment. For example, a proportional representation method might be thought a better reflection of public control than a first-past-the-post system, as the former provides for representation in proportion to the amount of votes cast whereas the latter might see a party elected even though the majority of the public voted for other candidates.[14] Finally, perhaps one of the larger concerns about popular vote as a reflection of the will of the public is that it potentially leads to a risk of the 'tyranny of the majority'.[15] On this view, the election mechanism may not protect a minority that votes against a government elected by the majority. While this is not the place to explore this more wide-ranging debate, the key take-away point for present purposes is that there are limits on the extent to which an election result reflects the will of 'the public'; rather it may best be said to reflect the will of a *majority* of eligible and participating voters.

---

[12] See, e.g., Richard R Lau, Mona S Kleinberg and Tessa M Ditonto, 'Measuring Voter Decision Strategies in Political Behavior and Public Opinion Research' (2018) 82(1) *Public Opinion Quarterly* 911; Libby Jenke and Scott A Huettel, 'Issues or Identity? Cognitive Foundations of Voter Choice' (2016) 20(11) *Trends in Cognitive Sciences* 794.

[13] The Australian High Court rejected the argument that a permitted variation of 10 per cent between electorate sizes contravened any constitutional requirement of 'one vote one value' in *Attorney-General (Ex rel McKinlay) v Commonwealth* (1975) 135 CLR 1.

[14] Bryan Mercurio and George Williams, 'Australian Electoral Law: "Free and Fair"?' (2004) 32 *Federal Law Review* 365, 376–77.

[15] See, e.g., John Stuart Mill, *On Liberty* (Cambridge University Press, 1989).

Perhaps a more balanced response to the question of *to whom* the government ought to be accountable would be to say that the government should be held accountable, not just to the public as a whole, but at the same time to individual members of the public. If we were to adopt such a joint and several approach to the question of who ought to be entitled to control the government, we would potentially be able to balance our concern to ensure that the government adheres to an approach that best reflects the democratic interests of the majority, while also requiring them to be responsive to the needs of minorities. If we cannot shape a single mechanism so as to adhere to this benchmark, we might, for example, favour a balance of control via majority-based mechanisms (e.g. elections) with individual-based mechanisms (e.g. judicial review).

5.2.3   Who Should Be Entitled to Redress?

The redress rationale is concerned with ensuring that individuals who suffer harm as a consequence of government wrongdoing are not left to bear their own loss. The question of *to whom* the agent defined in Chapter 4 ought to be accountable would naturally centre on the harmed individual. For example, where a person is imprisoned as a result of an administrative error, there is little doubt that this individual is the person to whom the relevant government agent would owe an obligation of redress. However, as tort cases demonstrate for us, the matter will not always be so simple. One complicating factor is that there might be cases in which the ultimate victim (i.e. the person who in fact suffers loss or damage) is a number of steps removed from the initial government activity. So, for instance, in *Sutherland Shire Council v Heyman*[16] it was not the initial homeowners but the subsequent purchasers who were said to have suffered loss as a result of the local council's negligent inspections during construction. In such a case, latent loss may be transferred from one party to another, becoming apparent in the future. In other cases, the immediate class of victims may be of such a size as to make redress impractical or impossible. For example, the case of *Three Rivers District Council v Bank of England [No 3]* was a claim in which hundreds of depositors were said to have suffered loss as a result of the misfeasance of the Bank of England in its supervision of a failed banking institution.[17]

[16] (1985) 157 CLR 424.
[17] [2003] 2 AC 1.

Indeterminacy of loss is one of the chief concerns raised in the context of discussions about expanding the liability of government for regulatory-type functions, particularly in relation to pure economic loss as opposed, for example, to physical injury or property damage.[18] In order to define our accountability benchmark, it would be necessary for us to revisit a number of these well-rehearsed policy concerns and to reach a landing on whether government wrongdoing should render it liable to provide redress to all those who have suffered loss, or only a subset who are in some way more closely connected to that government activity (e.g. through time or physical proximity), or only those who have suffered certain types of loss.

Assuming that it is possible to define the victim(s) to whom the government would owe an obligation of redress, it is then necessary to consider who ought to be charged with seeking that redress. Should it be a right personal to the victim that only they can exercise? Or ought we establish an independent body whose role it would be to seek redress on a victim's behalf? At its broadest, we might even make the regime entirely open, allowing any interested person to take up the mantle and seek redress on behalf of a victim. In deciding *to whom* the government ought to have to answer in connection with repairing harm, we might conclude that the most coherent approach would be to focus on the interests of the victim. On one view, we might say that achieving redress is sufficiently important to the victim that we should allow broad rights of access to increase the chances that this outcome might be achieved. However, perhaps a more important factor to bear in mind is the victim's autonomy. We might, for example, be justifiably concerned if our benchmark of accountability provided a third party with the right to seek redress of an assault victim without their consent. There might be a multitude of reasons why that victim might wish to avoid subjection to an accountability process (e.g. not wishing to be brought into contact with their assailant) with the result that redress may not be their primary concern. The redress rationale is primarily victim-oriented and, as such, it might be fitting that the choice of whether to engage an accountability mechanism would in this context lie with the victim. This is not to say that the victim's choice not to seek redress should allow the wrongdoer to escape accountability; rather, that it may be a situation in which another rationale for accountability (e.g. the punitive rationale) might be engaged.

---

[18] Peter Hogg, Patrick Monahan and Wade Wright, *Liability of the Crown* (4th ed., Carswell, 2011) 249–50.

There may, of course, be cases where a victim is unable to exercise their choice to seek redress (e.g. due to age or disability), in which case we might think that the benchmark ought to allow a third party to bring proceedings on their behalf. However, we would likely consider these cases to be the exception rather than the rule if we take victim autonomy as our starting point.

To summarise, then, it seems that the approach most consistent with the redress rationale for accountability would be to say that the person *to whom* the agent defined in Chapter 4 should owe an obligation of redress is the victim who has suffered loss or damage as a consequence of government wrongdoing. We might also say that the most coherent approach would be to leave the choice of whether or not to seek redress with that victim, wherever possible. Of course, this conclusion leaves unresolved the much larger question of how we can define a 'victim' for the purposes of our accountability benchmark. This much more difficult problem is discussed in Chapter 6.

5.2.4   Who Should Be Entitled to Call for Punishment?

The final two rationales for accountability are tied to the notion of punishment: desert and deterrence. If we take these punishment rationales as our focus, how would we define our benchmark question of *to whom* the government must answer? There are a number of different options that we might explore in this respect. At its narrowest, we might limit the entitlement to seek punishment to a single defined point (e.g. a public prosecutor). A slightly broader approach would be to allow anyone immediately affected by the conduct complained of (e.g. a victim) to seek punishment. At its broadest, we would say that any interested party ought to be entitled to take steps to impose punishment on the government. In seeking to define a normative benchmark of accountability, we would need to decide which of these various options best supports the desert and deterrence rationales for accountability. Before thinking about the implications of each option, however, it is useful to return briefly to the underlying purpose of each of these rationales. The desert rationale is condemnatory in nature. It is concerned with ensuring that those who have committed wrongs of a particular nature (see Chapter 6) are punished on the basis that they deserve to be so. The deterrence rationale is more forward-looking in nature. It is concerned with improving public governance by discouraging both the wrongdoer and others from committing similar infractions going forward. In thinking about these two rationales, there are a number of factors that might influence our choice of prosecutor.

As a starting point, if our concern is to maximise the likelihood that prosecution will take place, we might think that the best approach is to open up the right of prosecution to allow anyone to seek punishment. By casting the net widely in the first instance, we might think to increase the likelihood that someone will take on the prosecution task. In so doing, we would likely also be interested in thinking about the potential *motivations* for commencing prosecution, as there is little utility in defining a large group of potential prosecutors, none of whom is interested in the role. There are a number of observations that we might make on this point. First, unless a person is charged with the duty of prosecution (discussed in the following paragraph), we would likely need to consider why individuals might be inclined to perform this task in defining our benchmark of accountability. There are a number of reasons why a person might potentially be motivated to prosecute. For instance, a person who is aggrieved might be interested in participating in a prosecution out of a desire for vengeance or retribution (well aligned with the desert rationale for accountability). Others might be motivated by the prospect of personal gain, which might be the case, for example, if punitive damages are available following a successful prosecution. Still others might have altruistic motives, seeking to prosecute in order to make a difference by discouraging that conduct going forward (aligned with the deterrence rationale for accountability). If we are concerned with maximising the likelihood of prosecution, we might try to harness these types of motivations by setting up procedures that encourage these individuals to take on the prosecution task.

However, we might be concerned less with the *likelihood* of prosecution, and more with the likelihood of *successful* prosecution. If that is the case, we might be better to think not simply about the quantity of potential prosecutors, but whether their qualities are likely to make them effective. So, for instance, we might consider that a person who has previous experience in prosecution and a good understanding of the relevant procedures may be better placed to achieve a successful result than someone for whom the task is new territory. We might also wish to ensure that our prosecutor is sufficiently well-resourced to enable them to effectively see the prosecution through. For example, if a successful prosecution requires production of certain categories of evidence, it is unlikely that we would want to define our benchmark of accountability so as to empower a prosecutor who lacked the resources to gather that evidence. In this respect, there is much to be said for carefully considering the use of a professional prosecutor, employed and funded for the dedicated role of engaging in public prosecution. A professional prosecutor would, of course, be well motivated to perform that function, quite simply because it would be their job to do so. Their professional role would also facilitate a degree of independence in the prosecution function. Rather than being swayed by notions of vengeance or greed, the professional prosecutor may be better placed to independently assess a situation and determine whether prosecution is warranted, thereby reinforcing the legitimacy of the function. A further factor in favour of using a professional, government prosecutor is one of optics: '[i]f punishment is the means by which society communicates its moral condemnation of bad acts, then the state is society's most appropriate proxy for communicating such condemnation'.[19] By assigning the task of condemnation to the government, we may reinforce the seriousness of the breach.

However, there is one potential limitation on the motivations of a professional prosecutor we would need to consider. Being a part of the machinery of government, we may be concerned that a professional prosecutor might not be inclined to prosecute government officials, either from self-interest (e.g. fear of retribution) or from the desire to 'protect their own'. This concern underpins the rationale for the continued availability of private prosecutions in the context of the criminal law. Writing in 1883, Sir James Fitzjames Stephen suggested that the rule was likely a result of English historical influences as opposed to a product of design.[20] However, in a passage cited with approval by Priestly JA in *Spautz v Gibbs*,[21] Stephen pointed to a potential justification for the availability of private prosecutions as follows:

> [N]o stronger or more effectual guarantee can be provided for the due observance of the law of the land, by all persons under all circumstances, than is given by the power, conceded to every one by the English system, of testing the legality of any conduct of which he disapproves, either on private or on public grounds, by a criminal prosecution. Many such prosecutions, both in our days and in earlier times, have given a legal vent to feelings in every way entitled to respect, and have decided peaceably, and in an authentic manner, many questions of great constitutional importance.[22]

---

[19] Miriam H Baer, 'Choosing Punishment' (2012) 92 *Boston University Law Review* 577, 603.

[20] James Fitzjames Stephen, *A History of the Criminal Law of England* (Macmillan, 1883) 496.

[21] (1990) 21 NSWLR 230, 247.

[22] Stephen (n 20) 496.

This sentiment is engaged in cases where matters of public interest or public policy are at issue. For instance, in *MacLaurin v Hall*, Pring J referred to *Stone's Justices' Manual* as authority for the proposition that

> when the offence is not an individual grievance, but is a matter of public policy and utility, and concerns the public morals, any person has a general power to inform and sue for the penalties, unless the Statute creating the offence contains some restriction or regulation limiting the right to some particular person or party.[23]

The notion of a constitutional mandate in favour of the availability of private prosecution can also be seen in concerns about relying solely on state officials to enforce the criminal law. What of circumstances where state prosecutors refuse to enforce the law? In such cases, the availability of private prosecutions can be seen to perform a critical role in reinforcing the rule of law. This notion is reflected in Lord Diplock's reference to the right of private prosecution in *Gouriet v Union of Post Office Workers* as a 'useful constitutional safeguard against capricious, corrupt or biased failure or refusal of those authorities to prosecute offenders against the criminal law'.[24]

Drawing these various arguments together, it is possible to see that, for the purposes of the desert and deterrence rationales, we would need to make choices about which approach is best adapted to achieving our aims. While we might think that the best chance of maximising the likelihood of a prosecution is to define a wide class of potential prosecutors, we may ultimately conclude that the chances of a successful prosecution are increased by limiting the task to a central professional prosecutor. However, to bolster the legitimacy of that role, we might also need to consider retaining a residual right for others to commence prosecutions in circumstances where the professional prosecutor declines to do so.

5.3   Summary

In summary, the question of *to whom* the parties discussed in Chapter 4 ought to be accountable is complicated by a number of matters. First, there are various factors that might contribute to our views about what makes a good prosecutor, including the size of the class, their resources,

---

[23] (1913) 13 SR (NSW) 114, 119 citing *Stone's Justices Manual* (40th ed, 1908) 866.
[24] [1978] AC 435, 498.

skills, knowledge and motivations. Secondly, the question of what makes a good prosecutor will differ depending on the accountability rationale that we adopt. So, while we might think that the task is best suited to a professional prosecutor in the case of the punitive rationales of desert and deterrence, we might favour a far more wide-ranging right of access in respect of the control and transparency rationales. Again, if we are seeking to define a benchmark of accountability, we need to be able to do so in a manner that accommodates these differing considerations.

6

For What Should They Be Accountable?

The third question that is frequently asked in the context of describing accountability mechanisms is *for what* the agent is held accountable. Using this descriptive framework we might say that an agent is accountable to explain their conduct with respect to 'finances', 'politics', 'law' and the like.[1] However, in order to transform this descriptive framework into a normative benchmark, we need instead to be able to answer the question 'for what *should* an agent be held accountable?' In other words, what conduct or outcomes do we think should attract the operation of an accountability mechanism if we are to achieve some 'ideal amount' of government accountability? The enormity of this undertaking is one of the most significant barriers that stands in the way of defining a benchmark that we might use to measure accountability deficits and overloads. There are quite simply as many answers to this question as there are people you might choose to ask. To catalogue the full range of options would likely fill the remaining space in this book, for which reason the following discussion is limited in scope. Thankfully, this lack of depth does not pose any serious limitation on this project, as the ultimate goal is to highlight the scale of the task of defining a benchmark of accountability. The point being made here is that, in order to adopt a normative benchmark of accountability, we would need to be able to come to a landing on what types of conduct would be targeted by the benchmark. The fact that there are so many options to choose between (including many not canvassed here) makes good that point.

One way of approaching the task would be to start by articulating the larger picture of 'for what' the government should be held accountable in terms of the different values we would expect the system to reflect.

---

[1] See, e.g., Richard Mulgan, *Holding Power to Account: Accountability in Modern Democracies* (Palgrave Macmillan, 2003) 28; Dawn Oliver, *Government in the United Kingdom: The Search for Accountability, Effectiveness, and Citizenship* (Open University Press, 1991) 23–28.

Even at this level of abstraction, however, the task is a difficult one. How would we choose which values are sufficiently important to be incorporated into the benchmark? Those who have attempted to cata-logue values underpinning public law, for example, point to such values as legality, fairness, consistency, rationality, integrity, honesty, good faith, openness, accessibility, participation, efficiency and effectiveness, amongst others.[2] While it is difficult to disagree with the merits of these various values, it is a large leap from identifying such a catalogue to crafting a benchmark pursuant to which government conduct might be measured. Values are slippery in nature and subject to evolution over time. If we allow the same to be the case in respect of our accountability benchmark, we would need to accept that the benchmark will be subject to ongoing development and may change and evolve in accordance with public expectations.

Even assuming that it is possible to identify a set of values we believe should underpin our accountability standards, a second difficult task is to define the standards that would give effect to these values. Adopting the above catalogue of values as a foundation, we would need to attempt to construct a benchmark pursuant to which the government would be held accountable for failing to exercise powers within legal boundaries (legality), for acting unfairly in the exercise of its powers (fairness), for exercising powers in an inconsistent or arbitrary manner (consistency) and so on. However, statements such as these are rather question-begging; a benchmark which provided simply that the government must not act 'unfairly' tells us very little about the types of conduct that would demand an accountability response. Instead, we would need to build up detailed sets of standards that reflect each of these values. For instance, we might adopt as part of our accountability benchmark a fair hearing rule, requiring that an affected individual have the oppor-tunity to be heard before an adverse decision is made against them. This standard would contribute to the accountability value of fairness, and a breach of that standard would be one for which the agent ought to be

---

[2] See, e.g., Chief Justice Robert French, 'Administrative Law in Australia: Themes and Values Revisited' in Matthew Groves (ed.), *Modern Administrative Law in Australia: Concepts and Context* (Cambridge University Press, 2014); Mark Aronson, 'Public Law Values in the Common Law' in Mark Elliott and David Feldman (eds.), *The Cambridge Companion to Public Law* (Cambridge University Press, 2015) 134, 144–45; Michael Taggart, 'The Province of Administrative Law Determined' in Michael Taggart (ed.), *The Province of Administrative Law* (Hart Publishing, 1997) 1, 3.

held accountable. But this would only be one small subset of the range of standards that would need to be constructed in order to give effect to the value of fairness. Until we are able to articulate the full set of standards that we say would represent government accountability, we cannot use our benchmark to point out potential accountability deficits (i.e. circumstances where a breach of a standard fails to enliven an accountability mechanism) or overloads (i.e. circumstances where a breach of a standard enlivens multiple accountability mechanisms, or the wrong ones).

A third difficulty in utilising a catalogue of values to define standards for the purposes of our accountability benchmark is that such values may at points come into conflict. To take an example from the above public law values, the most efficient means of dealing with a matter (e.g. accepting or rejecting all applications on the papers) may not be the most fair (e.g. by denying an individual a full opportunity to put their case). Unless we could be satisfied with an accountability benchmark that pulled in two opposite directions (i.e. simultaneously demanding both maximum efficiency and maximum fairness), we would need to be able to define our standards so as to strike an appropriate balance between these sets of values in circumstances where there is a tension between them. The task would be even further complicated if we permitted the standards to vary depending on context (e.g. if we were to say that fairness is more important than efficiency where individual rights are at stake). Again, then, defining our benchmark of accountability requires us to make difficult choices about what it means for the government to be 'accountable' in a given instance.

A final (and arguably the most difficult) aspect of the task before us is to articulate the manner in which our accountability benchmark would link the standards that we select to the various rationales of accountability. So, for instance, if we were to adopt the fair hearing rule as a relevant component of the benchmark, would we say that a breach of this standard (i.e. denying a fair hearing) is one that would enliven the desert rationale? We might have serious reservations about adopting a benchmark that imposed a condemnatory punitive sanction on an official who unknowingly excluded a party from being heard based on a mistake in the file paperwork. The real difficulty, then, is that we need to find a way to draw a link between each rationale, and the standard(s) that ought to enliven it. One way we might choose to explore this is to focus on two of the components that are relevant in defining standards of conduct: *fault* and *outcomes*.

6.1 Fault: Defining Standards by Reference to a Wrongdoer's State of Mind

The concept of fault might play a significant role in defining the standards of conduct that make up our accountability benchmark.[3] 'Fault' captures a range of factors relating to an agent's state of mind, including intention, motive, knowledge and belief. Looking first at intention, this refers to the degree of deliberateness attaching to an agent's state of mind, which might be intentional, reckless or negligent. Intention is essentially a deliberate choice of conduct which may or may not be designed to achieve certain ends.[4] Recklessness is one step behind intention, though it is also deliberate in nature.[5] Recklessness is 'awareness of a risk that certain consequences will result from conduct, and indifference to that risk';[6] where a risk taken is unreasonable, indifference or disregard to that risk will therefore amount to recklessness. In this context, it is important to distinguish between the idea of 'not caring' whether a risk may eventuate, and the legal notion of recklessness, which is more properly characterised as 'deliberately taking a known risk'.[7] Negligence is sometimes thought about in terms of 'inadvertence' or 'inattention';[8] however, it is more appropriately described as a failure to adhere to a prescribed standard.[9] In other words, an agent can be equally accountable for an oversight as for an intended consequence.

Motives are also often relevant when assessing fault. In simple terms, motivation refers to a person's reason for doing something. While related to the concept of intention, the two are not synonymous. For example, a person may drive a motor vehicle over the speed limit with a murderous desire to harm others, or out of a desire to experience the thrill of driving fast, or out of a desire to race an ill child to the hospital. In each case the conduct of driving over the speed limit is deliberate, but the motive for that intentional conduct differs. The consequences of that conduct (such as injury to a pedestrian) may therefore correlate with the motive (as in

---

[3] The following passages are based on earlier work which appears in Ellen Rock, 'Fault and Accountability in Public Law' in Mark Elliot, Jason NE Varuhas and Shona Wilson Stark (eds.), *The Unity of Public Law?: Doctrinal, Theoretical and Comparative Perspectives* (Hart Publishing, 2018) 171, 178–83.

[4] Peter Cane, 'Mens Rea in Tort Law' (2000) 20 *Oxford Journal of Legal Studies* 533, 535–36.

[5] Ibid 536.

[6] Ibid 535.

[7] Peter Cane, *Responsibility in Law and Morality* (Hart Publishing, 2002) 80.

[8] Ibid 79.

[9] Cane, 'Mens Rea in Tort Law' (n 4) 536.

the case of a murderous motive), or be an unintended side effect. This example also says something about the character of motives that may drive a person's behaviour. Good motives (such as racing an ill child to seek medical care) may in certain circumstances justify otherwise blameworthy conduct.[10] 'Bad' motives may be divided into the categories of intrinsically malicious or collaterally malicious.[11] Intrinsically malicious motives are those which are inherently reprehensible, such as wanting to use a motor vehicle to injure or kill others. Other such motives would include spite, or wanting to gain at the expense of another. Collaterally malicious motives are those which, while not intrinsically bad, are not authorised in the circumstances. The thrill-seeking desires of our dangerous driver would fall into this category, as would acting for personal gain or some other goal which the circumstances render inappropriate.

A person's knowledge may also contribute to their degree of fault. There are a number of observations that we can make about the relevance of a person's knowledge. First, the fact that a person turns out to have been wrong about what they thought they knew will not be determinative of fault. To take an example, a person may set fire to a house believing it was inhabited. If the house is in fact inhabited, we can say that the wrongdoer 'knew' of it. If it actually transpires that the inhabitants of the house had left by the back door before the fire was set, we cannot say that the wrongdoer 'knew' them to be inside, but we can say that the wrongdoer 'believed' them to be inside. In either case, we are concerned with attributing fault based on the wrongdoer's state of knowledge or belief, rather than the empirical correctness of their state of knowledge or belief. Secondly, there are varying degrees of knowledge that may be relevant in determining fault. For instance, we may define fault by reference to a wrongdoer's actual – subjective – knowledge or belief. Or we may extend fault to also capture knowledge that has been wilfully disregarded, in the sense that a wrongdoer has 'shut their eyes' to information, in the manner of recklessness as discussed above. We may further extend fault into an objective enquiry, so as to capture information that we say a wrongdoer 'ought to have known', or further, by imputing a wrongdoer with information (e.g. by finding that someone has constructive knowledge of information because of the manner or

---

[10] See, e.g., ibid 541.
[11] This is the terminology proposed by Cane: ibid 539.

location in which it was held).[12] Thirdly, we may think about knowledge as a temporal issue in defining fault. For example, we may impose fault on the basis of knowledge of past matters (e.g. a visa applicant's prior offences), or present matters (e.g. that there is presently a contract on foot containing certain terms, or the nature of a person's living accommodations),[13] or even future matters (e.g. if a fire starts in a faulty fireplace, it is foreseeable that it will cause damage to that property and to the neighbouring property).[14]

Sitting outside the concept of fault is the notion of strict liability. In circumstances where liability is strict, contravention of a prescribed norm will give rise to liability irrespective of whether or not the conduct coincides with fault, as defined by reference to intention, motives and knowledge. There are essentially four types of strict liability.[15] The most commonly thought-of variety is that of rights-based strict liability, which sees someone held liable for the infringement of a right irrespective of whether or not the infringement was intentional, reckless or negligent, as in the case of the tort of trespass. Activity-based strict liability arises where engagement in a particular activity (such as a relationship with another person) is seen as sufficient to impose liability, irrespective of fault. Outcome-based strict liability arises where a person is held responsible for causing a particular consequence irrespective of their fault. Finally, passive strict liability sees a person obliged to give up a benefit irrespective of whether or not there was some fault on their part in receiving it (as in the case of receipt of mistaken payments).

Taking these various ideas as a whole, we can see that fault is an amalgam of various enquiries into a wrongdoer's mind. We might pull together these ideas to describe three categories of fault, as follows. The first category, of *subjective fault*, would capture intentional conduct undertaken out of an inherently wrongful motive, such as spite, or desire to harm. Irrespective of motive, we might also include intentional or reckless conduct undertaken in the belief that harm would, or was likely to, arise. The second category, of *objective fault*, would not be concerned with the subjective intention, motives and knowledge. Instead, it would

---

[12] For example, a minister may be taken to have constructive knowledge of information contained in a relevant departmental file: *Minister for Aboriginal Affairs v Peko-Wallsend Ltd* (1986) 162 CLR 24, 31.

[13] *Moore v Secretary, Department of Social Services* [2015] AATA 669.

[14] *Pyrenees Shire Council v Day* (1998) 192 CLR 330.

[15] These four categories are identified by Cane: Cane, *Responsibility in Law and Morality* (n 7) 82–84.

be focused on what a person ought to have done, desired or known. Liability within this category of fault involves an implicit judgement that a person ought to have acted differently, or ought to have appreciated that their conduct was likely to have certain consequences for others. While it uses the label 'fault', what we are really dealing with in this category is a failure to comply with a standard of conduct.[16] The final category, of *strict liability*, is not a quality of fault, but instead reflects the proposition that liability attaches irrespective of fault. In this category, a wrongdoer's degree of intention, motives and knowledge are irrelevant, as is the question of whether the wrongdoer ought to have acted differently. Therefore, this category equally captures innocent and malicious contraventions of standards of conduct. It is important to note that these three categories of fault are not mutually exclusive. For example, a regulatory provision may make it an offence to cause water pollution in a certain area, irrespective of fault. If a person deliberately pollutes that river out of a desire to cause damage to a neighbour's property, we may not only conclude that they have contravened the strict liability provision, but also that their actions are intentionally malicious (subjective fault), and that they ought to have acted differently (objective fault).

Fault is a recurring theme in the literature on responsibility. Many explanations of responsibility employ as their starting point the idea that a person should only be held responsible in circumstances where they are culpable, and that a person can only be culpable in circumstances where they possessed a requisite level of mental engagement (usually that their conduct was intentional and the resulting consequences were intended, or at least foreseen).[17] For example, in *R v G*, Lord Bingham made the comment that:

> It is clearly blameworthy to take an obvious and significant risk of causing injury to another. But it is not clearly blameworthy to do something involving a risk of injury to another if one genuinely does not perceive the risk. Such a person may fairly be accused of stupidity or lack of imagination, but neither of those failings should expose him to conviction of serious crime or the risk of punishment.[18]

If we were to adapt this line of thinking for the purposes of our accountability benchmark, the idea of restricting responsibility (or accountability) to cases in which a person acted intentionally is bound up in the

---

[16] See, e.g., Cane, 'Mens Rea in Tort Law' (n 4) 536.
[17] HLA Hart, *The Concept of Law* (Clarendon Press, 1961) 173.
[18] [2004] 1 AC 1034, [32].

notion of choice: it is appropriate to hold people accountable for the consequences of the choices that they have made.[19] For this reason, we have little difficulty holding a person responsible (or accountable) if they have acted on the basis of subjective fault, out of a desire to cause harm, or foreseeing but not caring that they will cause harm. The rationale becomes more tenuous the further we move away from deliberate choice, or subjective fault, however.[20] On what basis can we impose liability where a person has not actually adverted to the possibility of harm in any subjective sense? Three possible justifications are the theories of unexercised capacity, outcome-responsibility and relational responsibility.

The idea of unexercised capacity informs Hart's justification for criminal punishment outside deliberate conduct. The crux of the theory is that a person might be held responsible not only for their deliberate conduct, but for failing to exercise 'the capacities and powers of normal persons to think about and control their conduct'.[21] In other words, if a person could have acted otherwise than they did, we can justifying holding that person responsible (or accountable) for the consequences of their unexercised choice not to take that alternative path. This enquiry becomes one part objective and one part subjective: we ask objectively whether a person has failed to act in accordance with reasonable standards, and then ask subjectively whether that person was in fact capable of meeting those standards. Such an approach excuses those who were unable to meet objectively established standards (e.g. by reason of physical or mental incapacity) and has been described as the 'individualisation of the negligence standard'.[22] It is in this respect that the unexercised capacity theory falls short of offering a complete explanation for the attribution of responsibility outside the context of deliberate wrongdoing. The enquiry into what an individual was capable of having done differently is essentially a subjective enquiry into the possible alternatives that were available to that individual. But the objective fault criteria considered here go further than this, being concerned with identifying what a reasonable person in the circumstances (not the individual in question)

---

[19] Cane, *Responsibility in Law and Morality* (n 7) 95.

[20] Ibid.

[21] HLA Hart, *Punishment and Responsibility: Essays in the Philosophy of Law* (2nd ed., Oxford University Press, 2008) 140.

[22] See, e.g., Michael Moore and Heidi Hurd, 'Punishing the Awkward, the Stupid, the Weak, and the Selfish: The Culpability of Negligence' (2011) 5 *Criminal Law and Philosophy* 147, 151.

might have done differently. In this sense, when we say that a person ought to have acted differently than they did, it is not a complete answer to say that there were factors outside the person's control that influenced their inability to meet minimum accepted standards of conduct. Therefore, the idea of unexercised capacity does not take us much further than liability based on subjective fault.

Outcome-responsibility, as posited by Honoré, provides a second possible justification for the imposition of responsibility outside the context of subjective choice. For Honoré, the notion of responsibility cannot be explained solely by reference to a person's behaviour, or fault, or choices.[23] Rather, it is also an obligation that can be voluntarily assumed (as in the case of a political leader who assumes responsibility in taking on that role), or may be imposed through societal norms (such as the responsibility owed to one's family).[24] Irrespective of its source, responsibility for Honoré 'involves a combination of actual or assumed control and risk', and within that frame it is appropriate that a person who is entitled to take the credit arising from their conduct is also subjected to the blame (or 'discredit').[25] In justifying non-fault-based liability, Honoré employs this notion of a credit–discredit balance book to argue that, when applied consistently and equitably over time, this broader framework of responsibility produces overall benefit for individual members of society.[26] However, he distinguishes between the idea of allocating outcome responsibility and liability: some 'extra element' is needed in order to superimpose a legal sanction on the allocation of responsibility more generally.[27] In addition to liability based on fault, Honoré argues that legal sanction may be appropriate where 'the conduct of the harm doer carries with it a special risk of harm of the sort that has in fact come about'.[28] Again, this theory does not take us much further in our accountability analysis. The attribution of responsibility for outcomes does not of itself extend to an obligation of repair; identifying Honoré's 'extra element' leads us into a circular hunt for the elusive justification for imposing punitive and reparative remedial responses outside cases of subjective fault.

[23] Tony Honoré, *Responsibility and Fault* (Hart Publishing, 1999) 126.
[24] Ibid.
[25] Ibid 130.
[26] Ibid 26–27.
[27] Ibid 27.
[28] Ibid.

The third theoretical justification holds more promise. This view, proposed by Cane, relies on the relational nature of responsibility to justify remedial responses outside cases of fault.[29] Unlike the unexercised capacity and outcome-responsibility theories, which are essentially focused on the wrongdoer, Cane's argument is that responsibility is a two-sided affair, that should take into account not only the acts and mindset of the wrongdoer, but the interests of the victim and society more generally. Through a distributional analysis, a balance is struck between the interests of the parties, in some cases therefore supporting the imposition of obligations to repair in absence of fault.[30] In other words, a person might be held responsible to repair outside cases of subjective fault by virtue of burdens inherent in the relationship between the parties. These observations take on particular significance in the context of accountability, which is by definition a relational concept. A relationship of accountability is one in which one party is entitled to hold another accountable for failure to meet defined standards of conduct. There is much to be said for viewing the operation of an accountability mechanism as the striking of a balance between the interests of the two parties to that relationship, which in some cases may justify the application of remedial responses from the courts outside cases of subjective fault.

Having explored what we mean by 'fault' and its potential relevance in the context of accountability, we can refer back to these ideas in thinking about the extent to which the various types of 'fault' should define the standards employed within an accountability benchmark.

6.2 Outcomes: Defining Standards by Reference to Whether Outcomes 'Matter'

A second concept that we might refer to in defining the standards that constitute our accountability benchmark is that of 'outcomes', used here to refer to the often intersecting legal notions of causation and remoteness. Causation is a somewhat amorphous concept, which in the legal context devolves into a range of technical tests. Rather than analysing the content of any of those legal tests, this section instead takes the lead from Hart and Honoré's search for the 'commonsense' or 'plain man's notion

---

[29] Cane, *Responsibility in Law and Morality* (n 7) 108.
[30] Ibid 108–09.

of causation'.[31] Hart and Honoré's goal resonates strongly with the present accountability analysis. When viewed through the lens of accountability, the ultimate objective of the mechanisms discussed here is to support the legitimacy of government. It is not for lawyers and judges to determine whether or not an accountability mechanism succeeds in this task. Rather, it is a matter for the people. It is understandable that the ordinary person would not be much impressed by an accountability mechanism which sought to assign responsibility for outcomes by reference to technical tests that sit uncomfortably with common understandings of fairness and justice. In this context, Hart and Honoré's goal of understanding causation by reference to 'the ordinary person's ideas of when it is fair to punish or seek compensation'[32] would appear to be a better starting point. Against this background, this section unpacks one of the core themes in the literature on personal responsibility: do outcomes 'matter'? Is an agent to be held accountable based on their actions, or on the basis of the results of those actions? This question raises broad philosophical issues around the concept of moral luck.

In asking whether outcomes 'matter' in a given scenario, a common way to frame the debate is by reference to a hypothetical example: two individuals (here called Attempter and Succeeder) independently make the decision to commit murder. Attempter decides to kill Lucky, and Succeeder decides to kill Unlucky. Both Attempter and Succeeder use the same type of gun, loaded with the same ammunition, position themselves the same distance from Lucky and Unlucky respectively, and fire their weapons with the same intention of causing their victims a fatal wound. As it transpires, Succeeder's bullet strikes and kills Unlucky, but Attempter's bullet misses and Lucky survives. While different explanations are offered for Lucky's survival (she happened to wear a bullet-proof vest that day, or to bend to pick something up from the ground at a fortuitous time, or Attempter was distracted at the final moment by an insect), the underlying idea remains the same: the fact of Lucky's survival is attributable to luck and not to some action or inaction on Attempter's part. The relevant question for present purposes is whether Attempter and Succeeder ought to be held accountable solely by reference to the quality

---

[31] HLA Hart and Tony Honoré, *Causation in the Law* (2nd ed., Oxford University Press, 1985) 1.

[32] Jane Stapleton, 'Law, Causation and Common Sense' (1988) 8 *Oxford Journal of Legal Studies* 111, 112.

of their fault (i.e. their conduct undertaken with the intention to harm Lucky and Unlucky), or by reference to the outcome of their conduct (i.e. Lucky's survival and Unlucky's death). In other words, is Attempter less blameworthy than Succeeder on the basis that luck intervened and preserved Lucky's life? And if so, ought Attempter to be subject to a lesser sanction than Succeeder?

This conundrum is one that has attracted many theorists over many years.[33] Those who advocate for equal sanction of Attempter and Succeeder believe that the outcomes of their respective actions are irrelevant to liability (equal sanction proponents). Those who advocate that Succeeder should be subject to a more severe penalty than Attempter believe that outcomes are relevant to the question of liability (differential sanction proponents). As a starting point in this debate, it is important to bear in mind that even amongst differential sanction proponents there is a general consensus that Attempter deserves to be sanctioned: '[t]here is no question that attempters and riskers deserve punishment even if they do not cause harm'.[34] The crux of the debate is, therefore, not directed at the question of whether Attempter ought to be sanctioned at all, but rather at whether Attempter deserves a more lenient sanction than Succeeder. The divergence in the literature between differential sanction and equal sanction proponents can often be traced to core disputes about identification of the underlying purpose of holding people responsible for their actions. In other words, the question of whether or not outcomes 'matter' is to a significant extent dependent on what objective we are seeking to achieve. These observations are particularly pertinent in thinking about defining standards of conduct for the purposes of the rationales of accountability as explored below.

---

[33] See, e.g., Sanford Kadish, 'Foreword: The Criminal Law and the Luck of the Draw' (1994) 84 *Journal of Criminal Law and Criminology* 679; Larry Alexander, Kimberly Kessler Ferzan and Stephen Morse, *Crime and Culpability: A Theory of Criminal Law* (Cambridge University Press, 2009); Michael Moore, *Causation and Responsibility: An Essay in Law, Morals, and Metaphysics* (Oxford University Press, 2009); David Lewis, 'The Punishment That Leaves Something to Chance' (1989) 18 *Philosophy and Public Affairs* 53, 53; George Fletcher, *A Crime of Self-Defense: Bernhard Goetz and the Law on Trial* (University of Chicago Press, 1988); Joel Feinberg, 'Equal Punishment for Failed Attempts: Some Bad but Instructive Arguments Against It' (1995) 37(1) *Arizona Law Review* 117, 117–18; Thomas Bittner, 'Punishment for Criminal Attempts: A Legal Perspective on the Problem of Moral Luck' (2008) 38 *Canadian Journal of Philosophy* 51; Jeffrey Brand-Ballard, 'Moral Emotions and Culpability for Resultant Harm' (2011) 42 *Rutgers Law Journal* 315, 317.

[34] Alexander, Ferzan and Morse (n 33) 172.

6.3 Defining Standards: A Rationale-Based Approach

Having discussed the notions of fault and outcomes at a high level, it is possible to start unpacking the possibilities of how we might frame our standards of conduct for the purposes of a benchmark of accountability.

6.3.1 Transparency: Accountability for 'Everything'

Transparency has been described in this book as a minimum defining feature of accountability. Its purpose is to make government activity accessible for public scrutiny, in order to facilitate public dialogue regarding both the ultimate outcomes of government activity and the processes that have been used to reach those outcomes. If our chief concern is to facilitate transparency, then we might reach the view that the government ought to be held accountable for 'everything'. We would not wish, for example, to limit access to information only to those circumstances where the government has already been shown to have acted in a faulty way. In fact, if we were to limit access to circumstances where the government has already been 'caught out', we would severely inhibit our capacity to uncover wrongdoing, which is antithetical to the notion of accountability. The transparency rationale would likely demand a very open-ended response to the question of *for what* the government ought to be held accountable in order to support this investigatory role.

It is also relevant to note that facilitating transparency does not only support the goal of uncovering potential wrongdoing. There will be cases in which transparency reveals commendable behaviours, attitudes and reasoning in our government officials. We can contribute to accountability by bringing examples of good and sound administration to light, thereby reinforcing public trust in our system of governance. In fact, if we only used the transparency function to uncover wrongdoing, we might even risk undermining public trust in government, presenting a skewed image of the degree of wrongdoing and corruption present within our system of governance. Instead, using transparency to expose all machinations of government might present a more balanced and accurate picture by locating incidences of wrongdoing within the broader picture of otherwise acceptable day-to-day government operations. In this sense, there is much to be said for the notion that, when viewed through the lens of the transparency rationale, the question of for what the government should be accountable would be answered: everything.

6.3.2   Control: Accountability for Excess of Power

The control rationale of accountability is reflected in the delegation model of government, its goal being to ensure that power is exercised by government agents in accordance with the interests of the citizens they represent. So, how would the concepts of fault and outcomes assist in determining whether the control objective of accountability is engaged? Looking first at the concept of fault, we might reach the view that the control rationale would embrace a strict liability approach for two key reasons. First, if we agree that the control rationale is concerned with ensuring that public power is exercised within defined boundaries, to limit control only to subjectively faulty (e.g. intentional or knowing) contraventions would be to redefine those boundaries in purely fault-based terms. Instead of setting a rule requiring agents to afford fair hearings (a strict approach), our accountability regime would only require agents to avoid *intentionally* failing to provide fair hearings. In so doing, we would shift the focus away from the value underpinning the original boundary (i.e. to ensure that power *is* exercised fairly) and instead construct a fault-based boundary (i.e. to ensure that agents *try* to exercise power fairly). This would have potential ramifications for our ability to define boundaries in which power can be exercised, as we would only be able to police boundaries drawn on fault-based lines.

A second reason we might adopt a strict liability approach to control is that it makes no real difference to our government agents, as it imposes no additional burden. As explored in Chapter 7, the means used to give effect to the control rationale are essentially concerned with reinforcing boundaries and requiring government agents to perform their roles within the confines of existing parameters. In circumstances where an agent is required to undertake some action, that action is, in essence, an existing, rather than new, obligation and redirects the official onto the path that they ought to have taken in the first place. For this reason, we might have no difficulty justifying control irrespective of an official's degree of fault; our benchmark of accountability might provide for control on a strict liability basis.

Looking, then, at outcomes, would we say that outcomes 'matter' for the purposes of attracting accountability's control objective? In answering this question, it is necessary to bear in mind the different ways of achieving control. As explored in Chapter 7, control may be achieved through reinforcing the boundaries of power, through unwinding expressions of incorrectly exercised power, or through requiring certain things be done, or not done, within permitted boundaries. For this reason, we can consider the suite of public law writs and remedies (certiorari, mandamus, prohibition, injunctive and declaratory relief) as various expressions of control over the exercise of public power. For the purposes of defining a benchmark of accountability, outcomes may play a role in deciding whether a control-based response is appropriate and, if so, of what type. So, for instance, we might say that, where an agent has already taken steps to bring the exercise of power back within permitted boundaries, control may be best achieved through a declaration of breach, thereby reinforcing those boundaries. Our benchmark would say, in such a situation, that there is no accountability deficit in not pursuing more intensive control-focused remedies, as there is no longer any transgression standing to be corrected. If there is no ongoing impact in a practical sense, there is nothing that needs to be 'controlled' in a forward-looking capacity. On the other hand, where an agent's decision has ramifications going forward (again determined by looking at the outcomes, or expected outcomes, of an agent's conduct), we might define our bench-mark so as to allow nullification of that decision. In yet other cases, where an agent's current course is likely to lead to particular outcomes (e.g. continued breaches), we might define our benchmark to allow more intense control-focused orders. So, for instance, where an agent has threatened to engage in conduct in excess of permitted boundaries, an order prohibiting that conduct may be the most appropriate expression of control.

Taking these ideas together, we might reach the conclusion that if we adopt the control rationale for accountability, a strict liability (rather than fault-based) approach is appropriate. The purpose of the control objective is to police the boundaries within which public power can be exercised and, viewed in that light, it is appropriate that any transgression, whether intentional, unreasonable or entirely innocent, is open to challenge: control is about accountability irrespective of fault. However, in exercising this control, the nature of the appropriate regulatory approach will be influenced by the second element of 'outcomes'; in some cases a mere declaration of breach will be sufficient to re-establish control, whereas in others a more coercive control-based approach will be appropriate. In determining which is the appropriate approach in a given case, it will be relevant to consider what impact the relevant remedy will have, an essentially outcome-focused enquiry.

6.3.3 Redress: Accountability for Causing Harm

One of the more difficult aspects of the benchmark to grapple with is the question of *for what* the government ought to be accountable for the purposes of the redress rationale. At first blush, the answer is quite a simple one: causing loss or damage. In this sense, it is possible that outcomes would play a critical role in defining the redress rationale. Returning to the hypothetical in Section 6.2, Succeeder (and not Attempter) would be the subject of an obligation of repair, though both might warrant punishment – see discussion in Section 6.3.4. But on closer inspection there are a number of difficult choices that we must make in determining the circumstances in which loss or damage ought to be remedied. The first key decision to be made is in defining the *types* of loss or damage that the benchmark would encompass. For instance, would it be limited to personal injury? Mental harm? Property damage? Pure economic loss? Interference with valued rights and interests (e.g. reputation, liberty)? Hurt feelings? The most expansive form of accountability benchmark would define loss or damage in very broad terms, so as to encompass any and all negative impacts on citizens, while a more narrowly defined benchmark would seek to classify only certain losses as 'worthy' of redress. As experienced in the law of tort, the task of deciding where a line might be drawn in defining the categories of loss and damage that the benchmark would protect is a complex one.

A second key difficulty in defining the benchmark is in determining the manner in which outcomes are to be attributed to an agent. '[C]ausation is a precondition' of obligations to repair harm,[35] but the much more difficult aspect of the enquiry is deciding what counts as 'causation' in a given instance. If the experience of tort lawyers is anything to go by, our benchmark will need to be quite sophisticated in delimiting the outcomes for which the government ought to be held accountable. As tort lawyers understand it, analysis of legal causation comprises two stages.[36] The first stage is a factual analysis, involving an objective enquiry into the factors that ultimately contributed to a particular outcome.[37] The second stage is one of attribution, requiring a value judgement as to whether an actor should be held responsible for the outcome.[38] Even the first, objective, stage of the enquiry is not an entirely straightforward matter. For the purposes of many torts, the Australian courts apply the 'but for' test of causation, pursuant to which a factor will

---

[35] Cane, *Responsibility in Law and Morality* (n 7) 139.

[36] Jane Stapleton, 'Perspectives on Causation' in Jeremy Horder (ed.), *Oxford Essays in Jurisprudence (Fourth Series)* (Open University Press, 2000) 61, 61–62.

[37] Ibid 62.

[38] Kit Barker et al, *The Law of Torts in Australia* (5th ed, Oxford University Press, 2012) 533.

qualify as a cause if the harm would not have been occasioned but for the conduct in question. In other words, the agent's conduct is a necessary condition of that harm.[39] Though it is widely used, the 'but for' test has been criticised as a somewhat blunt test of factual causation, on the basis that it can be over-inclusive (e.g. a person would not have been injured *but for* the fact that they were born), or under-inclusive (e.g. if a person is struck simultaneously by two lethal gunshots, their death cannot be said to have been occasioned *but for* either gunshot).[40] Instead, it has been suggested that the so-called 'NESS' test of causation might offer a more nuanced approach.[41] Pursuant to this test, something will be a factual cause if it can be called a 'necessary element for the sufficiency of a sufficient set'.[42] Unlike the 'but for' test, the NESS test is more sophisticated in accommodating cases of overdetermination, where two independent causes may alone have caused the harm. Rather than treating neither as a cause, the NESS test would treat both gunshots as sufficient to have caused the death.

Assuming that we can agree on the best way to identify factual causes of harm, we must then move into the second stage of the causation analysis, in deciding whether a particular cause ought to be singled out as a basis to hold an actor accountable. Problems of attributive causation are reflected in tort law through the use of such tests as *novus actus interveniens* (which considers whether a new event has 'broken' an existing chain of causation), remoteness of damage (which considers whether the nature or extent of damage is such that it should fall outside the scope of the defendant's liability) and apportionment of liability between concurrent tortfeasors. In defining a benchmark of accountability that requires redress of losses caused by the government, it would be necessary to grapple with these same types of issues.

A particularly curly question in connection with the outcomes of government activity (and one that has been raised against the

---

[39] Ibid.

[40] Ibid.

[41] See, e.g., Jane Stapleton, 'Choosing What We Mean by "Causation" in the Law' (2008) 73 *Missouri Law Review* 433. The 'NESS' algorithm was popularised by Wright, based on the original work of Hart and Honoré: Hart and Honoré (n 31); Richard Wright, 'Causation, Responsibility, Risk, Probability, Naked Statistics, and Proof: Pruning the Bramble Bush by Clarifying the Concepts' (1988) 73 *Iowa Law Review* 1001.

[42] Stapleton, 'Choosing What We Mean by "Causation" in the Law' (n 41) 472.

introduction of a public law remedy in damages)[43] is how to determine when unlawful government activity can be said to have 'caused' loss. In some cases, the matter may be straightforward. So, for example, if there is only one legal way in which power might have been exercised, we would likely be able to say that any departure from that approach is causally linked to a plaintiff's loss. But what of a situation where the same outcome might have been reached lawfully?[44] For instance, a decision reached following an unfair hearing might potentially have been made the same way had the hearing been fair. And a decision reached having taken into account an irrelevant consideration might potentially have been made the same way even disregarding that consideration. In circumstances where we seek to 'restore' an individual who has suffered loss as a result of these decisions, we risk being drawn into the task of deciding how the case would, or perhaps even should, have been decided in absence of the procedural irregularity. If we wish to define our accountability benchmark so as to embrace this approach, we would need to think carefully about our answers to the question dealt with in Chapter 5, namely *to whom* an obligation of accountability is owed. In particular, in cases where the courts are the forum charged with enforcement of accountability standards, there is a real question as to whether determining loss arising from government illegality moves the courts into the territory of deciding the *correct and preferable* decision. At least in Australia, this would present a potential separation of powers concern as the courts might have moved from a role of deciding the legality of a decision and into the realm of its merits.[45]

More complex still is the question of whether the benchmark would be limited to *unlawfully* caused loss, or whether a broader approach might be adopted that would also see the government liable for *lawfully* caused loss. Take, for instance, a circumstance in which a new law is introduced which has the effect of prohibiting a small number of individuals from carrying on their businesses. If we assume that the law is valid,[46] how would the accountability benchmark address that situation? If we wanted

---

[43] See, e.g., Paul Craig, 'Compensation in Public Law' (1980) 96 *Law Quarterly Review* 413, 438–39.

[44] These difficulties have arisen in the context of false imprisonment cases, where the quantum of damages may be influenced by whether the plaintiff would in any event have been detained legally: see the final paragraph in Section 8.3.2.5.

[45] *Attorney-General (NSW) v Quin* (1990) 170 CLR 1.

[46] For example, assume that the law does not fall foul of the constitutional guarantee of just terms for acquisition of property: *Australian Constitution* s 51(xxxi).

to define the benchmark so as to capture lawfully caused loss, we might look to the French system of administrative law as an example. The plenary jurisdiction of the French administrative courts not only provides remedies in circumstances where public power is exercised invalidly or in a faulty way, but also extends to allow indemnity on the basis of risk or equality before public burdens (*égalité devant les charges publiques*).[47] This extended jurisdiction recognises that even the lawful exercise of public power may result in a burden being imposed on an individual that more properly ought to be shared amongst the community,[48] providing compensation where a valid law prohibits a company from continuing to sell its products,[49] or where a valid decision not to remove a blockade prevents a ship owner from moving into port.[50] Would our accountability benchmark encompass redress in such circumstances? To say nothing of the legitimate concerns we may have about 'legal transplants',[51] to adopt this approach in constructing our benchmark would have significant ramifications for our benchmark of accountability. Our question of 'for what' the government ought to be held accountable would move away from one of defining particular standards of conduct (e.g. harm-causing conduct must only be undertaken in particular ways) and into one that more closely represents absolute liability.[52]

Even assuming that we narrow the scope of the benchmark to limit redress to cases of unlawfully caused loss, it is necessary to consider whether liability should be determined by reference to strict liability (i.e. liability for the outcomes of all unlawful conduct), objective fault (i.e. liability for the outcomes of breach of an expected standard of competence) or subjective fault (i.e. liability for the outcomes of only intentionally wrongful exercises of power). Again, our choice here will be guided by what we see as the core purpose of accountability. In adopting

---

[47] L Neville Brown and John Bell, *French Administrative Law* (5th ed., Oxford University Press, 1998) 193; Duncan Fairgrieve, *State Liability in Tort: A Comparative Study* (Oxford University Press, 2003) 137.

[48] Brown and Bell (n 47) 194.

[49] *La Fleurette* (CE 14 January 1938).

[50] *Sealink UK Ltd* (CE 22 June 1984).

[51] See, e.g., Carol Harlow, *State Liability: Tort Law and Beyond* (Oxford University Press, 2004) 43.

[52] It is worth noting here that the French system is not one of absolute liability. Even in that context, liability for lawfully caused loss is the exception rather than the rule: Fairgrieve (n 47) 148–49.

the redress rationale, we would be unlikely to prefer subjective fault as a qualifying feature of our benchmark. To require wronged citizens to prove that the government acted with particular qualities of fault (e.g. that it knew its actions to be wrongful, or was motivated by a wrongful motive, or acted unreasonably as well as unlawfully) would place significant hurdles in the way of an applicant, leaving many to bear their own loss. Instead, the approach that would be most conducive to serving the redress rationale would be to make the obligation of repair applicable irrespective of the degree of fault on the part of the government. Of course, in adopting an essentially strict liability approach to redress, we would be seen to be making choices that privilege redress over other concerns. So, for instance, we might be concerned about opening the government up to a 'flood' of demands for compensation, or diverting public resources into fixing past wrongs rather than providing public services going forward.[53] Ultimately, we are required to decide whether accountability through redress must at some point give way to concerns about the efficient use of government resources, which is separate to the task of defining an 'ideal' benchmark of government accountability.

6.3.4   Desert: Accountability for Deliberate Wrongdoing

In determining when the desert rationale for accountability might be engaged for the purposes of defining our benchmark of accountability, we might conclude that fault would play a leading role. This rationale is concerned with marking public condemnation of inherently wrongful conduct; abuse of public power in the traditional sense. We might think it appropriate that the sanctions that attach to this rationale be similarly characterised by notions of stigma and public disapproval. In the legal context, punitive sanctions are of their nature highly intrusive, not only imposing an immediate burden on an official (e.g. imprisonment or punitive damages), but also condemning them. It is this condemnatory character of punishment that might lead us to conclude that, for the purposes of our accountability benchmark, the desert rationale would be confined to cases of subjective fault, in line with the choice theory. Where a person has acted maliciously, or knowing they are likely to cause harm, it may be appropriate to impose a sanction that signifies the inherent

---

[53] In Cane's words, 'the more extensive governmental damages liability becomes, the more significant its implications for public spending': Peter Cane, 'Damages in Public Law' (1999) 9 *Otago Law Review* 489, 491.

wrongfulness of their conduct. However, to go further and extend the reach of punishment into objectively faulty and unfaulty conduct would risk undermining this primary condemnatory characteristic of the sanction.

But would fault be only a necessary condition of liability, or determinative? Would we decide that outcomes 'matter' for the purposes of accountability's desert rationale? In answering this question, it is useful to return to the Attempter and Succeeder hypothetical outlined in Section 6.2. Both Attempter and Succeeder have engaged in the same conduct with the same subjectively faulty mindset. Ought both receive the same punishment? Or should Succeeder be more roundly condemned on the basis that her desired outcome came about? Those who believe that punishment is based on desert take the view that we are entitled (or perhaps obliged) to punish someone because they 'deserve' to be punished. As noted in Chapter 3, the desert rationale for accountability would be similarly grounded in the idea of condemning reprehensible conduct. What would be the relevance of outcomes in this context?

For differential punishment proponents, a person is more blameworthy if they cause harm than if they try but fail to cause harm; Succeeder is thought to have done worse than Attempter when it is discovered that Unlucky has died, and is worthy of greater condemnation as a result. If we accept this proposition, we might be led to think that outcomes *do* matter for the purposes of desert and would agree with Moore that '"[c]ausation matters" seems a pretty good candidate for a first principle of morality'.[54] However, heeding Feinberg's admonishment, we must not be 'so fixated on actual harm that [we] keep ... searching for the question to which it is the right answer'.[55] Instead, it is necessary to unpack the 'moral magic' or 'moral power' that would lead us to include outcomes in our determination of moral responsibility.[56] Differential punishment proponents have sought to bolster their argument that outcomes affect moral responsibility in a number of ways. This is not the place for a detailed discussion of this range of arguments,[57] and

---

[54] Moore, *Causation and Responsibility* (n 33) 29.
[55] Feinberg, 'Equal Punishment for Failed Attempts' (n 33) 132.
[56] Alexander, Ferzan and Morse (n 33) 173.
[57] For other arguments, see Bittner, who quibbles with the design of the Attempter and Succeeder hypothetical, arguing that these actors are not representative of the population of people who attempt and complete crimes: Bittner (n 33) 57, and Fletcher, who argues that because of the popularity of the intuition that outcomes affect desert, there would be something anti-democratic in simply ignoring the view of the 'sensibilities of the

so only two of the more relevant are discussed here. The first centres around the idea that the unsuccessful attempter need not experience the same 'moral feelings' of shame, guilt and the like, that a successful actor does. Because the unsuccessful attempter has less to feel guilty about, the argument follows that they are therefore less blameworthy.[58] There are two reasons we might doubt this 'moral feelings' argument. The first is a question of proportionality. Kadish maintains that, in order for punishments to be considered proportionate, they must 'bear some relation to the degree of blameworthiness of the defendants' actions, not to what they think of themselves or to what they have become in some existential sense'.[59] If punishments were to be doled out by reference to a person's perceived degree of guilt associated with their conduct, there would be no consistent measure of blameworthiness, no yardstick against which we could determine which crimes warrant which punishments.

Another issue with the 'moral feelings' argument is that it does not entirely explain the relationship between these feelings and having caused harm. In some cases, there will be a disconnect between the two, which might call into question the soundness of the underlying principle. Brand-Ballard uses the example of a firing squad in which no member knows which rifle contains live ammunition.[60] When the firing squad executes a prisoner, it is not possible to determine which member of the squad is factually the cause of the prisoner's death. If the execution is subsequently discovered to have been wrongful, should only the actual killer feel guilt about their causal role in the death? Or should all members of the firing squad feel equally guilty? Brand-Ballard suggests the latter, arguing that whether or not a particular member's rifle contained live ammunition 'is not a fact with any moral significance'.[61] This might suggest that something other than causation is at play in the experience of moral feelings of guilt in such a case. This all casts doubt on whether the 'moral feelings' experienced by Attempter and Succeeder provide a sound basis on which to determine their respective desert.

The second argument frequently raised by differential punishment proponents is based on the concept of moral luck. Nagel's notion of

---

common people' in favour of abstract philosophical reasoning about concepts of desert and moral luck: Fletcher (n 33) 83, cited in Feinberg, 'Equal Punishment for Failed Attempts' (n 33) 126.

[58] Moore, *Causation and Responsibility* (n 33) 30.

[59] Kadish (n 33) 692.

[60] Brand-Ballard (n 33) 323–24.

[61] Ibid 324.

'moral luck' sees chance as a pervasive concept that arises in all aspects of our lives: '[w]hether we succeed or fail in what we try to do nearly always depends to some extent on factors beyond our control'.[62] He identifies four categories of luck,[63] being results-based (e.g. a bird happens to fly into the path of Attempter's bullet), constitutive (e.g. being a naturally jealous or greedy person), circumstantial (e.g. being thrust into a situation that provides the occasion for wrongdoing) and antecedent (i.e. that outcomes are the inevitable product of an agent's constitution and circumstances). Advocates of equal punishment are focused on results-based luck, arguing that Attempter should not escape punishment simply on the basis of luck attaching to the outcome of her conduct. However, differential punishment proponents would argue that to focus on results-based luck to the exclusion of other categories is inconsistent. Why should we be willing to ignore some matters that are attributable to luck (perhaps such as having a personality with a 'short fuse'), but not others (such as a mosquito distracting Attempter at the moment she squeezes the trigger)? Moore would say that we cannot have it both ways.[64] A whole host of matters sit behind the wrongful act that we might term to be 'luck' of one sort or another; if a person deserves to be punished in spite of those matters, we should equally be willing to punish them in spite of the role that luck plays in determining the ultimate outcome.

But is there a valid reason to distinguish between outcome-based luck and the other 'lucky' factors that might arise in a given case? For the equal punishment proponents, the issue comes down to a question of choice and control.[65] On this view, we can only really hold people responsible for matters over which they have control: choice is an active exercise of the control that we have over ourselves and our environment. If we choose to kick another person, we make a deliberate choice to move our leg in the attempt to make contact with that person. Whether or not the person sees the kick coming and manages to dodge out of the way is not within our control, but our choice to try to kick them is. Because choice is something that is inherently within our ability to control, Alexander et al argue that it is 'something law and morality can

---

[62] Thomas Nagel, *Mortal Questions* (Cambridge University Press, 1979) 25.

[63] Ibid 28.

[64] Michael Moore, *Placing Blame: A General Theory of the Criminal Law* (Clarendon Press, 1997) 233–46.

[65] For the perspective of differential punishment proponents on choice and control, see, e.g., Moore, *Causation and Responsibility* (n 33) 29.

influence'.[66] Similarly, Kadish takes the view that '[t]he settled moral understanding is that what you deserve is a function of what you choose'.[67] Equal punishment proponents believe that the quality of choice provides us with a basis on which to differentiate circumstantial luck from outcome luck. Kadish puts the position as follows:

> It may be that you would not have had occasion to make a choice that revealed your badness if you had better luck. Nonetheless, you did make a choice – nobody made you – and it is that choice for which you are blamed. It is a different matter, however, to say that chance occurrences that follow after you have made your choice determine what you deserve, for that is to rest desert upon factors other than what you chose to do.[68]

For Alexander et al, choice is also the critical distinguishing feature between outcome luck and other lucky influences in our lives; they suggest that 'the control we have over our choices – our willings – is immune to luck and is thus qualitatively and morally different from our control or lack thereof over our heredity and environment, the situations in which we find ourselves, and the causal consequences of our choices'.[69] For them, we have a kind of control over our choices that we do not have in respect of our make-up or circumstances, and this justifies treating results-based luck differently from other types. There is significant force in this argument. If we ascribe to the view that people are generally capable of making rational choice, the notion of choice provides a point at which to draw a line between the luck that precedes that choice, and the luck that follows. Irrespective of how a person came to be in the position that they are currently in, we believe that people have the ability to reason and choose whether to comply with prescribed norms.[70] In this sense, there would be no inconsistency in treating outcome-based luck as different from other types of luck.

Returning to the task of defining an accountability benchmark, we would need to make a decision to follow either the equal or differential punishment proponents. Would we define the benchmark so that the desert rationale would have a greater role to play in cases where wrongful conduct has resulted in loss? Inspired by the Attempter and Succeeder

---

[66] Alexander, Ferzan and Morse (n 33) 174.
[67] Kadish (n 33) 690.
[68] Ibid.
[69] Alexander, Ferzan and Morse (n 33) 190.
[70] Excluding questions of capacity (e.g. age or disability) that might otherwise influence our ability to make such choices.

hypothetical, we might think about how this scenario could translate into the public law context. Imagine that a statutory power allows Officer Attempter and Officer Succeeder to direct the provision of road improvement services, with priority to be ascertained by reference to greatest need. Though other roads are in much greater need of repair, each Officer decides to direct the improvement of their own residential streets in order to increase the values of their respective properties. The road crew directed by Officer Succeeder heads off immediately to repair the road as requested. Due to a GPS error, the road crew directed by Officer Attempter mistakenly repairs a neighbouring road, which turned out to in fact be in dire need of repair. As in the case of the attempted murder hypothetical, both officers have engaged in precisely the same actions and with the same motives; both have exercised their public powers in bad faith. The only relevant difference between the two cases is that Officer Succeeder obtains the benefit she intended, while Officer Attempter is foiled by an accident of luck. Should Officer Attempter be treated with greater leniency than Officer Succeeder?

Differential punishment proponents would regard Officer Succeeder as more blameworthy than Officer Attempter on the basis that she has managed to obtain the personal advantage she desired. But we might question whether this approach is the best means of punishing the abuse of public power. The public law norm that best encapsulates subjective fault – bad faith – is not framed by reference to the notion of causing harm, but is instead concerned with constraining the *manner* in which power is exercised. Certainly, there might be cases in which an exercise of power in bad faith produces an outcome of which we may disapprove; in the above hypothetical Officer Succeeder obtains the advantage of improving her own street at the expense of others, and in other more sinister cases, a malicious exercise of public power may cause damage to person or property. But the norm itself is concerned with preventing the exercise of power accompanied by a dishonest or malicious mindset, not the exercise of power so as to achieve an impugned result. If we were to say that Officer Succeeder deserves greater punishment than Officer Attempter, we might risk undermining the importance of the norm itself. Adopting this approach, we might decide to follow the equal punishment proponents in demanding that both Officer Attempter and Officer Succeeder be punished according to their conduct, rather than the lucky result that followed it.[71]

[71] Even if we reach the view that outcomes do not 'matter' for the purposes of the desert rationale, this does not mean that they do not 'matter' at all. As Alexander et al argue,

6.3.5   Deterrence: Accountability for Excess of Power

Turning finally to the deterrence rationale for accountability, we encounter different considerations in defining the benchmark of 'for what' we would hold agents accountable. Unlike the desert rationale, deterrence is not concerned with condemning those who deserve it. Instead, its aim is to foster improvements in public governance going forward, both by targeting the instant case (specific deterrence) and by using that as an example to reach others (general deterrence). If this is our goal, there would seem little to be gained in restricting this rationale to cases of subjective fault. If we were to limit the reach of accountability in this way, we would reduce our capacity to influence future negligent or unintentional breaches (the question of how we might hope to achieve deterrence is separately addressed in Chapter 7). Accordingly, we might decide on a strict liability approach for the purposes of the deterrence rationale.

A more difficult question is the role outcomes should play in delimiting the deterrence rationale. Returning to punishment theory, this question has posed some difficulty. Is deterrence better served by imposing equal punishment, or by more severely targeting those who cause harm? Thinking first about general deterrence, if we want to make examples out of Attempter and Succeeder to deter others from committing the same crime, some might say that it makes little difference whether we impose equal punishment: 'if the punishment for success does not deter [others], an equal punishment for failure certainly will not'.[72] If this reasoning is correct, general deterrence would not be an adequate justification for imposing equal punishment. However, even if this reasoning is sound in the context of intentional wrongdoing, the same cannot be said in relation to reckless or unintentional conduct.[73] Intentional wrongdoers (like Attempter and Succeeder) set out with the specific goal of bringing about a particular outcome, and so the prospect of equal punishment for trying but failing to achieve one's goal is unlikely to have any impact on others considering the same activity. However, by definition, reckless and negligent actors are not attempting to achieve a particular outcome, but instead are acting without sufficient regard to the legality of their actions,

---

though outcomes are irrelevant to assessing 'moral desert', it 'certainly matters whether actors succeed or fail': Alexander, Ferzan and Morse (n 33) 177. Rather, the point is that the relevance of outcomes would fall within one of the other grounds of liability (redress being a key example).

[72]   Kadish (n 33) 686.
[73]   Ibid.

or the outcomes that might follow. If a reckless or negligent actor does not have a harm-causing goal in mind, there is no deterrence gain in punishing an actor who causes harm more severely than an actor who (luckily) does not.

The same reasoning applies in respect of specific deterrence (i.e. deterring Attempter and Succeeder from reoffending in the future). If we wish to discourage an offender from engaging in the same conduct in the future, Kadish notes that it 'makes no sense' to impose different punishments for those who fail to cause harm and those who succeed.[74] This must be correct. If we assume that a bird flies into the path of Attempter's bullet, preventing Lucky's death, the differential sanction proponents would say that Attempter deserves a lesser punishment than Succeeder. How does this support the goal of specific deterrence? Attempter intended the same harm and engaged in the same conduct as Succeeder, but (through no credit of her own) failed to achieve her goal. Putting aside questions of reform or a sudden attack of conscience, why would Attempter be deterred by the prospect of a more severe punishment if she ultimately succeeds in her next attempt? On the basis of these observations, it appears that deterrence does not provide a basis on which to decide whether outcomes 'matter', as we lack the evidence needed to confirm that the imposition of differential punishments either bolsters or undermines the deterrence rationale.

6.4 Summary

As demonstrated in this chapter, deciding 'for what' an agent should be held accountable is likely the greatest hurdle that we must surmount in defining a benchmark of accountability. It requires us to return to general propositions about how we conceptualise the government (i.e. as a group of individuals or a corporate entity),[75] and what we expect of the government and the manner in which it exercises its powers. Further, the choices that we make for the purposes of one aspect of the bench mark (e.g. adopting an individualist conception of government) will have knock-on effects for dealing with later questions of *for what* those actors are to be held to account. Perhaps most difficult is the task of articulating the manner in which we would link the standards we select to the rationales of accountability we choose to adopt. So, for instance, how

[74] Ibid 684–86.
[75] This was discussed in Section 4.1 in Chapter 4.

would we decide whether a standard is one that warrants the extremity of the desert rationale, or the breadth of the control rationale? We would need to identify criteria that we might use to draw links between standards and rationales. Using the notions of fault and outcomes, this chapter has demonstrated that this is no small task, leading us into difficult territory of moral and legal philosophy.

7

How Should They Be Held Accountable?

The final question in the accountability framework set out in Chapter 1 was the question of 'how is the agent held accountable'. In its descriptive context, this question is concerned with identifying the procedures and outcomes of the accountability mechanism under review. It is possible to point to three different phases in this respect: investigation (i.e. initial provision of information), discussion (i.e. assessment and debate) and rectification (i.e. imposition of sanctions or remedies).[1] In defining a normative benchmark of accountability, we can group together these phases to ask *via what procedures should an agent be held accountable?* and *with what consequences?* Again, our answers to these questions will differ depending on which rationale for accountability we choose to adopt.

7.1 Via What Procedures?

The question of *via what procedures* an agent ought to be held accountable encompasses the two phases of 'information' and 'discussion' canvassed in the accountability literature. The information phase is an investigatory one, involving the initial provision of information by an agent to a forum, and initial investigation by the forum.[2] This may be by way of prepared reports, through the production of documents or through the provision of an oral account, for example. The second phase has been described as a 'discussion' phase.[3] In this phase, the information is examined, debated and tested, and the agent is given the opportunity to

---

[1] Authors use slightly different terminology: Richard Mulgan, *Holding Power to Account: Accountability in Modern Democracies* (Palgrave Macmillan, 2003) 30; Gijs Jan Brandsma and Thomas Schillemans, 'The Accountability Cube: Measuring Accountability' (2013) 23 *Journal of Public Administration Research and Theory* 953, 955.

[2] Mulgan, *Holding Power to Account* (n 1) 30; Brandsma and Schillemans (n 1) 955.

[3] Mulgan, *Holding Power to Account* (n 1) 30; Brandsma and Schillemans (n 1) 955.

justify their conduct. To these two process-oriented phases we might add a third, focusing on the process of adjudication pursuant to which the forum reaches its view as to whether the agent has complied with relevant standards. Though some include adjudication in the final recti-fication stage,[4] this conceals the many procedural components that might influence the manner in which the forum adjudicates the question of whether an agent has complied with accountability standards. To take an example, legal proceedings involve a range of processes across these three categories. The information stage is reflected in pre-trial investigatory procedures, including discovery and interrogatories and the filing of pleadings and evidence. The discussion phase is reflected in the adver-sarial nature of the trial itself, through the processes of admission of evidence and cross-examination. The adjudication phase is then reflected in the processes that influence the court's ultimate decision, including for example the burden of proof and the extent of the court's discretion to refuse or award relief.

In defining a benchmark of accountability, we would need to trans-form these descriptive ideas of process into normative ideas, asking by what procedures *should* an agent be held accountable. As with the other chapters in Part II, the answer we reach would largely depend on which rationale for accountability we choose to adopt. Looking first at the transparency rationale, procedures will play a very important role. This rationale is primarily concerned with facilitating public access to infor-mation for the purposes of maintaining the dialogue between govern-ment and citizen. While it may in some cases take on an investigatory function with a goal to uncovering evidence of wrongdoing, the trans-parency rationale can more generally be understood to play an important role in securing the legitimacy of government. In many ways, one of the most fundamental accountability mechanisms within our system of democracy – the electoral process – is underpinned by a requirement of transparency. As put by McHugh J in the *Australian Capital Television* case:

> If the institutions of representative and responsible government are to operate effectively and as the Constitution intended, the business of gov-ernment must be examinable and the subject of scrutiny, debate and ultimate accountability at the ballot box ... Before [the electors] can cast an effective vote at election time, they must have access to the information,

---

[4] Brandsma and Schillemans (n 1) 955.

ideas and arguments which are necessary to make an informed judgment as
to how they have been governed and as to what policies are in the interests
of themselves, their communities and the nation.[5]

The transparency function of accountability can be supported in a
number of ways. What is critical is that the means of accessing and
disseminating information are such that information is freely accessible.
For instance, the process of securing access to information would ideally
not involve a cost or administrative burden that operates to exclude some
members of the public from participation. Ideally, the channels through
which access is provided would also be inclusive – for example, by
making provision for people with disabilities. In order to support the
transparency function, it would likely be necessary that it be possible to
compel the production of information. While the voluntary provision of
information by government is no doubt capable of contributing to the
overarching objective of fostering legitimacy, it is the obligatory nature of
a process that transforms it into one of accountability.[6] Accordingly, any
limits on open access to information would only be relevant if there are
other concerns that outweigh those of accountability (e.g. we might
admit limits to freedom of information on the basis of national security).

Turning to the control rationale, its core concern is to ensure that
power is exercised within legal boundaries. As noted below,[7] the types of
remedies that are well adapted to this purpose are those capable of
confirming the legal boundaries within which power can be exercised,
prohibiting excess of those boundaries and compelling the exercise of
power within them. In order to achieve this purpose, the relevant procedures would likely need to be coercive in nature. We might, for
example, doubt whether the recommendatory powers of an ombudsman
rise to the level of 'control' envisaged by this rationale. Certainly, the
ombudsman mechanism plays a role in securing government accountability; however, we would likely look elsewhere within our accountability system if our primary concern is to control the government.

Supporting the redress rationale involves different considerations
again. This rationale is essentially victim-oriented, requiring that harm
be remedied. In thinking about the best means to achieve this goal, we
might be concerned, for instance, if the burden of making a claim for

---

[5] *Australian Capital Television Pty Ltd v Commonwealth [No 2]* (1992) 177 CLR 106, 231.
[6] Mulgan, *Holding Power to Account* (n 1) 11.
[7] See discussion of remedies and sanctions relevant to the control rationale in Section
7.2.1 below.

redress was of such a degree that it inhibited access to the mechanism. This might mean that we would favour minimised application fees and a simplified application process. We might also be disinclined to require a heavy burden of proof, or even go so far as to adopt a presumption in favour of redress of the victim that must be dislodged by the government. Of course, there must be a limit to the extent to which our accountability benchmark would be tipped in favour of the victim. As noted elsewhere in this book, accountability (here through redress) will not be our sole concern; we might also be interested in ensuring efficient use of public funds, amongst other matters. Again, the task of selecting the best means to facilitate this rationale of accountability and to give due weight to other legitimate concerns is a difficult one.

Unlike the redress rationale, the desert rationale is much more agent-focused, being concerned with condemning inherently wrongful conduct. The fact that the desert rationale is so tied up in notions of condemnation might lead us to be very careful in crafting the procedures used to impose punishment. We might, for instance, wish to ensure that the barriers to use of such an accountability mechanism are sufficiently high that only those with a particular interest are likely use it (e.g. a requirement of leave to proceed). We might also be concerned to ensure that the process through which punishment is delivered is a rigorous one, designed to ensure that the wrongdoer is in fact deserving of condemnation and that innocent parties are not mistakenly captured. This might lead us to impose a significant burden of proof,[8] for example, or to pass the case through multiple rounds of judgement, or to provide a right to appeal any sanction imposed. These types of limitations would serve to limit the chance of punishment being imposed in circumstances where it is not deserved, and to reinforce the seriousness of condemnation when it is warranted.

Finally, the deterrence rationale is concerned with facilitating improvements in public governance, by disincentivising undesirable conduct and incentivising desirable conduct. As discussed below, there remains much debate as to the best means to achieve these ends.[9] While deterrence remains in favour as a theoretical justification for the imposition of punitive sanctions, many question whether punitive sanctions are

[8] Alec Walen, 'Proof Beyond a Reasonable Doubt: A Balanced Retributive Account' (2015) 76 *Louisiana Law Review* 355, 362.
[9] See discussion of sanctions in the context of deterrence in Section 7.2.4.

in fact the best means to achieve those ends.[10] So, for instance, Braithwaite suggests that in place of highly punitive sanctions, deterrence might instead be better served through the imposition of 'broad, informal, weak sanctions'.[11] If we were to adopt such an approach, we might also move away from the procedures that suit the desert rationale. In place of agent-friendly procedures that give effect to highly condemnatory sanctions, we might instead favour procedures that are more apt to facilitate dialogue.[12] In that context, we would be less concerned with procedures that are directed at proving wrongdoing, and more concerned with flexible procedures that create an environment in which Braithwaite's 'soft target' will be more inclined to participate, listen and be open to taking steps to effect change in the future.[13]

To summarise, an accountability benchmark would likely anticipate different procedures for different accountability rationales. For transparency, the most fitting procedures would be those that facilitate ease of access to information, while the control rationale would be best supported by coercive procedures that balance the interests of the parties. The redress rationale might favour a prosecutor-friendly regime that limits the burden placed on the prosecutor to make good their claim for redress (e.g. limited application costs). The desert rationale, in contrast, might favour an agent-friendly regime in recognition of the condemnatory character of the sanctions sought (e.g. protections afforded by a significant burden of proof and rights of appeal). Finally, the deterrence rationale might be best supported through the adoption of flexible procedures that facilitate dialogue with a view to fostering improvements in performance.

7.2 With What Consequences?

The second aspect of the *how* component of the benchmark of accountability is concerned with identifying what consequences will follow the adjudication process. On adopting a rationale-based approach, the task becomes one of seeking to identify tools that are capable of securing the

---

[10] Braithwaite explores these ideas in John Braithwaite, 'On Speaking Softly and Carrying Big Sticks: Neglected Dimensions of a Republican Separation of Powers' (1997) 47 *University of Toronto Law Journal* 305.

[11] Ibid 333.

[12] Ibid.

[13] Ibid.

ends envisaged by each rationale. Because the transparency rationale is essentially process-driven, it is unnecessary to add anything to what has been said on this topic above.[14] The following discussion instead centres on the outcome-oriented rationales of control, redress, desert and deterrence.

7.2.1   Control: Regulatory Orders to Enforce Compliance with Legal Limits

The control rationale for accountability is concerned with providing a means to ensure that public power is exercised within legal limits, and in accordance with the public interest. In thinking about control as a rationale of accountability, it is necessary to bear in mind that, while control is central to accountability, we cannot say that all expressions of control are accountability mechanisms.[15] For example, the enactment of legislation may effect control or influence over conduct by demanding conformity to particular standards. However, the enactment of legislation is not itself an accountability mechanism; it is not premised on a relationship wherein one person is held accountable to another. Mulgan makes this point in terms that 'being accountable for alleged breaches of the law does not mean that compliance with the law is also an act of accountability or that the law itself is an accountability mechanism'.[16] Bearing this in mind, our benchmark of accountability for the purposes of the control rationale would be more concerned with identifying mechanisms that operate to reinforce (rather than create) limits on the exercise of power.

Strom sees control-based sanctions as essential in an accountability relationship. He defines accountability as an agency-based relationship in which the principal should have a 'veto power' (a power to quash or amend the account-giver's decisions) as well as a power to 'deauthorise' the account-giver by removing them from office or restricting their authority to act.[17] Sanctions of this nature potentially reinforce the

---

[14] See discussion of the transparency rationale in Section 7.1.

[15] Mark Bovens, 'Analysing and Assessing Accountability: A Conceptual Framework' (2007) 13 *European Law Journal* 447, 454.

[16] Richard Mulgan, '"Accountability": An Ever-Expanding Concept?' (2000) 78 *Public Administration* 555, 564.

[17] Kaare Strom, 'Parliamentary Democracy and Delegation' in Kaare Strom, Wolfgang Muller and Torbjorn Bergman (eds.), *Delegation and Accountability in Parliamentary Democracies* (Oxford University Press, 2003) 55, 62.

control-based character of accountability relationships, in which a key goal is to place limits on the exercise of power by defining and reinforcing the boundaries within which the agent can act. It is possible to think about each of these two functions (that is, defining boundaries and policing boundaries) as two distinct aspects of the control rationale; indeed, the character of the remedies that might be employed to serve each of these aspects can take different forms. So, for example, an order declaring that an official's conduct is illegal, or which has the effect of nullifying an official's decisions (which Strom would refer to as a 'veto power')[18] is aligned with the goal of defining the legal boundaries within which power can be exercised. More coercive powers, such as injunctive relief, go further, regulating conduct in a prospective capacity so as to police those boundaries going forward. These forward-looking powers might take a number of different forms, depending on the situation. For instance, the process may be either mandatory (in requiring something to be done) or prohibitive (in preventing something from being done). It may be highly prescriptive (e.g. requiring a particular decision to be made in a particular way) or permissive (e.g. requiring a particular outcome without specifying the means, or requiring a particular procedure without specifying the outcome). Whatever form the mechanism takes, it would seem that in order to achieve the goal of 'control' the mechanism would need to have a compulsory character.

7.2.2 Redress: Remedies to Restore

The redress rationale is primarily victim-oriented, its main concern being to ensure that harm is remedied. The means by which this outcome might be achieved will depend on the nature of the harm suffered, and what is possible to repair that harm. From the perspective of this accountability rationale, the ideal scenario would be to place the victim in the position they were in prior to the harm. In some cases, it will be possible to achieve this goal by, for example, requiring repair of property damage or the reinstatement of a cancelled licence. In other cases, the nature of the harm may be such that it cannot be corrected. In such a case, it may be possible to provide the victim with redress in a substitutionary form. So, for instance, a victim may receive a financial settlement in substitution for some impact on their health that cannot be remedied.

[18] Ibid.

Redress need not always be of such a formal type. It is well documented that proffering an appropriate apology may in many cases go some way towards resolving a grievance. While the link between apologies and reduction in litigation remains unproven, Vines has noted that 'people often sue wrongdoers because they are so enraged by the lack of an apology that a wrong which they would otherwise suffer without recourse to law becomes intolerable and litigation follows'.[19] The use of apologies may be particularly relevant where the victim's loss is of an intangible nature (e.g. pain, suffering or humiliation) rather than tangible (e.g. property damage or medical expenses).[20] In such cases, the victim seeks 'to publicly set the record straight by having the wrong acknowledged and to prevent further wrong doing'.[21] In the context of government maladministration, an apology may be particularly well adapted to serving the overarching objective of accountability. As recently noted in the Victorian Ombudsman's *Apologies* report, '[a]pologising is a mark of integrity for public authorities. It shows that the authority is transparent and accountable, and treats members of the public with courtesy and respect.'[22] Drawing these ideas together, it is possible to see that there is a range of different mechanisms that might be employed to facilitate redress in the context of government accountability. The question of which approach is best suited to the task will naturally depend on the nature of the loss or damage, and the circumstances of the case. What is critical to bear in mind is that redress is a victim-oriented rationale, and as such our focus is placed on the interests of the victim, rather than the impact on the wrongdoer.

7.2.3   Desert: Sanctions to Punish

The desert rationale is in distinct contrast to the redress rationale, being primarily focused on the wrongdoer. This accountability rationale is underpinned by a condemnatory approach, with a wrongdoer being punished on the basis that they deserve such treatment. Punishment is imposed as an expression of community outrage rather than with some

---

[19]   Prue Vines, 'Apologising to Avoid Liability: Cynical Civility or Practical Morality?' (2005) 27 *Sydney Law Review* 483, 483.

[20]   Alfred Allan, 'Functional Apologies in Law' (2008) 15 *Psychiatry, Psychology and Law* 369, 374–75.

[21]   Ibid 375.

[22]   Victorian Ombudsman, *Apologies* (April 2017) 5.

extrinsic goal of facilitating future change (which is the concern of the deterrence rationale discussed in Section 7.2.4 below). This expressive function of punishment is often used to justify punishment in the public sphere.[23] While many accountability theorists proclaim that punishment is an essential incident of accountability, most tend to gloss over the details of what that entails. Authors use 'punishment'[24] interchangeably with the language of 'retribution',[25] 'penalty',[26] 'sanction',[27] 'liability',[28] and 'suffering'[29] or 'facing'[30] consequences. Of those who engage in a more detailed analysis, a number refer to traditional remedies (such as termination of employment, fines, civil penalties and jail terms),[31] in addition to less formal types of sanctions (such as embarrassment and humiliation,[32] withholding of political support[33] and even the 'painful' nature of subjection to the accountability process itself).[34] But when we approach accountability from the perspective of the desert rationale, we might doubt whether some of these sanctions fit with that goal.

Writing in the criminal context, Hart defines the 'standard case' of punishment as (1) the infliction of pain or unpleasant consequences; (2) on the offender; (3) for an offence against rules; (4) intentionally administered by others; (5) within an authority set up in the legal

---

[23] See, e.g., Miriam H Baer, 'Choosing Punishment' (2012) 92 *Boston University Law Review* 577, 603.

[24] Mulgan, *Holding Power to Account* (n 1) 9; Robert D Behn, *Rethinking Democratic Accountability* (Brookings Institution Press, 2001) 3.

[25] Mulgan, *Holding Power to Account* (n 1) 9.

[26] Strom (n 17) 62; Mulgan, *Holding Power to Account* (n 1) 9.

[27] Mulgan, *Holding Power to Account* (n 1) 9; Ruth Grant and Robert Keohane, 'Accountability and Abuses of Power in World Politics' (2005) 99(1) *American Political Science Review* 29, 29; Strom (n 17) 62.

[28] Jonathan Koppell, 'Pathologies of Accountability: ICANN and the Challenge of "Multiple Accountabilities Disorder"' (2005) 65 *Public Administration Review* 94, 96–97.

[29] Dawn Oliver, *Government in the United Kingdom: The Search for Accountability, Effectiveness, and Citizenship* (Open University Press, 1991) 22.

[30] Mark Bovens, *The Quest for Responsibility: Accountability and Citizenship in Complex Organisations* (Cambridge University Press, 1998) 39.

[31] Behn (n 24) 3.

[32] Oliver, *Government in the United Kingdom* (n 29) 27; Behn (n 24) 3; Bovens, 'Analysing and Assessing Accountability' (n 15) 452; Andreas Schedler, 'Conceptualizing Accountability' in Andreas Schedler, Larry Diamond and Marc F Plattner (eds.), *The Self-Restraining State: Power and Accountability in New Democracies* (Lynne Rienner Publishers, 1999) 13, 16.

[33] Oliver, *Government in the United Kingdom* (n 29) 26.

[34] Bovens, *The Quest for Responsibility* (n 30) 39–40. See also Behn (n 24) 3.

system.[35] This definition encapsulates the *process* of punishment as Hart sees it, but what about its content? For Hart, the relevant content is the infliction of 'pain', or 'unpleasant consequences'. Other authors do not go this far, arguing that there must be something, if not painful, then intrinsically negative about a punishment in order for it to meet the definition. To this end, authors adopt the language of loss,[36] 'hard treatment',[37] and the like. But not every negative outcome is necessarily viewed as a punishment. Here, we may turn to Feinberg's distinction between punishments and 'mere penalties'.[38] In the latter category he places such outcomes as 'parking tickets, offside penalties, sackings, flunkings, and disqualifications'.[39] The heart of the distinction between penalties and punishments, for Feinberg, is the condemnatory character of the latter.[40] Adopting this rationale, there is substantial overlap between the rationales for the award of punitive sanctions and the desert rationale of accountability. As was noted in Section 6.3.4 in Chapter 6, condemnation is one of the defining features of the punitive function of accountability; the imposition of punishment in appropriate cases serves an expressive purpose in marking disapproval and reinforcing the norm that was contravened.

Adopting this approach, we would likely have no difficulty concluding that the imposition of a jail term or a fine would qualify as a desert-oriented sanction.[41] The recipient is branded as a wrongdoer and made to suffer loss of liberty or finances as a consequence. In contrast, we might be hesitant to characterise subjection to the accountability process as a fitting sanction for the purposes of the desert rationale. The fact that a wrongdoer has been called out for their infraction certainly goes some way towards contributing to government accountability more generally, but if they are left to then return to their lives with no repercussions we might doubt whether the desert rationale has been satisfied. Accordingly, in selecting sanctions for the purposes of the desert function, it would be

[35] HLA Hart, *Punishment and Responsibility: Essays in the Philosophy of Law* (2nd ed., Oxford University Press, 2008) 4–5. The five elements identified by Hart have been paraphrased and reordered.
[36] See, e.g., Thom Brooks, *Punishment* (Routledge, 2012) 5.
[37] Joel Feinberg, 'The Expressive Function of Punishment' (1965) 49 *The Monist* 397, 397.
[38] Ibid 398.
[39] Ibid.
[40] Ibid 400.
[41] Peter Cane, *Responsibility in Law and Morality* (Hart Publishing, 2002) 43.

necessary to consider whether the sanction in question provides the requisite degree of 'tar and feathering'.

7.2.4 Deterrence: Influencing Future Choices

The final accountability rationale considered here is that of deterrence. Unlike the desert rationale, which is primarily retrospective in nature, the deterrence rationale is concerned with influencing future choices, not only of the individual who may have done wrong in the instant case (specific deterrence), but also of others who witness the outcome (general deterrence). The question of how best to influence future behaviour is one that has troubled social scientists for many years. While deterrence is frequently offered as a justification for punishment,[42] there remain doubts as to whether punitive sanctions are necessarily the best means to achieve this goal. This may be particularly so in the public sphere. Research by Braithwaite suggests that abuse of public power is one context in which the threat of sanctions might not act as a useful deterrent.[43] Instead, this research suggests that in this context 'big sticks often rebound',[44] with individuals reacting in a defiant manner of 'getting mad rather than by ceasing to be bad'.[45] This phenomenon of 'reactance' (i.e. the motive of acting to regain a freedom that has been lost or threatened)[46] may therefore lead to a risk of backfire where sanctions are imposed in response to an abuse of public power.

The threat of sanction is, of course, not the only possible means available to influence future behaviour. Other possible approaches include the promise of rewards, reintegrative shaming strategies[47] and fostering dialogue. Braithwaite concludes that the dialogical approach is particularly promising,[48] wherein we 'replac[e] narrow, formal, and strongly punitive responsibility with broad, informal, weak sanctions – by making the many dialogically responsible instead of the few criminally responsible'.[49] By targeting a broad base of actors with weak sanctions, Braithwaite concludes that the risk of rebound is reduced. Brought into

---

[42] See, e.g., Hart, *Punishment and Responsibility* (n 35).
[43] Braithwaite, 'On Speaking Softly and Carrying Big Sticks' (n 10) 314–22.
[44] Ibid 360.
[45] Ibid 318.
[46] See Jack Williams Brehm, *A Theory of Psychological Reactance* (Academic Press, 1966).
[47] Braithwaite, 'On Speaking Softly and Carrying Big Sticks' (n 10) 319–20.
[48] Ibid 333.
[49] Ibid.

the present context of abuse of public power, this would involve targeting a broader range of actors (as discussed in Chapter 4) with weaker or non-punitive sanctions. On this approach, even the shame of being caught up in the accountability process itself might prove to be a sufficient incentive to engage in dialogue that could lead to improvements going forward.[50]

7.3   Summary

To summarise, we can see that there are a number of different means by which we might support the various rationales of accountability. As with the discussion of the other aspects of the accountability framework, it is also possible to identify tensions between these rationales. So, for instance, while highly punitive sanctions might be thought perfectly appropriate in the context of the desert rationale, such sanctions may potentially undermine the deterrence rationale if they produce a response of 'reactance'. There is an inherent tension between these two goals, as the greater the degree of condemnation (desert), the greater the risk of producing an indignant or defiant response in the wrongdoer (counter-deterrence). We can see a further example of such tension between the transparency and deterrence rationales. It was suggested that the best means of achieving transparency would be to adopt a very laissez-faire approach that would place all government decision-making under a public microscope. However, this approach might decrease an otherwise effective actor's internal motivation to perform; '[p]lants don't flourish when we pull them up too often to check how their roots are growing'.[51] If we cannot fashion a regime that is capable of meeting both demands, we must accept that one will fall by the wayside. And still, we must choose which of those rationales we will then prioritise. Here again we see that, in order to define a benchmark of accountability, we must not only carefully consider the best means to achieve our various goals but also make difficult choices about how to strike an appropriate balance between them when they come into conflict.

---

[50] Ibid 327.
[51] Onora O'Neill, *A Question of Trust* (Cambridge University Press, 2002) 19.

8

Defining and Deploying a Benchmark of Accountability

As described in the foregoing chapters of Part II of this book, one of the key steps in seeking to map out potential accountability deficits and overloads in our system of governance is to define a benchmark of accountability. Without articulating what 'enough' accountability looks like, it is very difficult to point to areas where there is either not enough or too much accountability. The foregoing chapters have explored one way of defining this benchmark, being to transform the descriptive accountability framework employed by many theorists (i.e. who is accountable, to whom, for what and how) into a normative framework (i.e. who *should be* accountable, to whom, for what and how). Those chapters have set out the size of the challenge before us in seeking to define this normative benchmark. Each question is attended by its own complications. So, for instance, in deciding *who* should be held account-able, we need to grapple with the complexity of our system of govern-ment, the implications of outsourcing and even the more theoretical question of how we conceptualise the government (i.e. as an entity or group of individuals). In deciding *to whom* the government should be accountable, we must think about the nature of the prosecution task and what motivates and allows individuals to take it on. In deciding *for what* the government should be held accountable, we need to return to difficult questions about the expectations we have of our government and the standards against which performance should be assessed. And in decid-ing *how* we should hold the government accountable, we need to return again to the question of what we are seeking to achieve.

What Part II of this book has demonstrated, in a more concrete sense, is that we would define our benchmark in different ways depending on the rationale we choose to assign to accountability. The rationales explored in this book are those of transparency, control, redress, desert and deterrence. So, for instance, in asking *who* should be held account-able, the desert rationale might prompt us to target an individual wrong-doer, whereas the redress rationale might prompt us to target the government itself (i.e. the entity with the greatest capacity to restore). And in asking *how* the government should be held accountable, the desert rationale might see us adopt punitive sanctions to facilitate condemnation, whereas the deterrence rationale might see us look for weaker sanctions that have the greatest capacity to encourage dialogue. However, adopting a rationale-based approach does not lead us to a simple solution to defining our benchmark. Even within a rationale we must sometimes make difficult choices between competing options. So, for example, in asking *who* should be held accountable for the purposes of the transparency rationale, we must choose between accessing the best source of information (i.e. the individual most closely connected with the decision or conduct), or the most authoritative source of information (i.e. the most senior official overseeing the matter), or the most coherent source of information (i.e. the government entity that can draw together all information and deliver it via a single channel).

A further challenge highlighted in Part II is that, assuming we can identify a 'best' way to support a given rationale, tensions might then arise between the various rationales. So, for instance, Chapters 4–7 suggest that the transparency rationale might be best promoted by adopting a very open approach to who should be accountable, to whom, for what and how. However, there is a risk that such an open regime might undermine the deterrence rationale, as some might say that constant interrogation might have negative impacts on performance (as opposed to encouraging improvements going forward). Similarly, while highly punitive sanctions might be thought to be the best means of supporting the desert rationale, there is a risk that the imposition of such sanctions on individuals may undermine the deterrence rationale if they lead to 'reactance', whereby the agent responds with defiance rather than improved performance.

If we allow that the concept of accountability might embrace more than one rationale, we must therefore make choices about how best to define the benchmark in light of these tensions. For instance, we might decide to prioritise one rationale over another, in which case we would need to accept that one dimension of our accountability framework might be weakened over time in order to strengthen another. Another option would be to try and find a 'middle ground', where rather than searching for the 'best' way of supporting each rationale, we look for an option that is capable of simultaneously accommodating both. In thinking about tension between accountability rationales, it is also important to consider whether it might be avoided if we allow our benchmark to consist of multiple strands. So, rather than trying to find a single answer to the question of *who* should be accountable *to whom*, etc., that will accommodate all rationales, we might instead provide a separate answer for each rationale, and offer different mechanisms to support those goals.

We must add to these considerations the further possibility that we might not wish to define a single, universal, benchmark of accountability. Instead, we might allow that the 'ideal amount' of accountability could differ across areas of government operation and across jurisdictions. We might accept, for example, that accountability would demand the strict enforcement of norms relating to corruption by high-level government officials, but that less exacting norms might be more appropriate in cases where a low-level public servant has acted in contravention of internal guidance regimes. The argument set out in this book is not that we must limit ourselves to a single, universal, standard to which all jurisdictions and areas of government must subscribe. Rather, the point being made is that when we are seeking to identify accountability deficits and overloads, we must be explicit in identifying whatever benchmark we have chosen for that purpose. In other words, we might legitimately use different yardsticks in our measurement of accountability deficits and overloads, provided that we give sufficient detail to allow others to compare their yardstick with our own.

To summarise, then, there are significant difficulties that we must confront in defining a benchmark of accountability. We must consider and articulate the underlying purposes of the concept of accountability, which requires us to revisit difficult philosophical questions about the structure and functions of government, and what we expect of the individuals and entities that constitute it. We must resolve tensions where the accountability goals we identify are in conflict with one another, and we must be able to define the benchmark we identify with sufficient precision that we can compare our chosen benchmark with those employed by others. The purpose of this book is to set out the scale of this challenge, rather than to provide neat answers to these difficult questions. In fact, the very complexity of the challenge is, I suspect, one of the reasons why we rarely see authors attempting to specify the accountability 'ideal' that they employ as a touchstone when making claims of deficit and overload. The failure is not one of oversight but rather one of scale and purpose; authors are more concerned with critiquing the area or mechanism under review than confronting the types of esoteric points raised here.

Thus far, the discussion in Part II of this book has been largely theoretical. In order to demonstrate the importance of facing the difficulties highlighted, this final chapter moves into uncharted territory by seeking to apply the ideas explored in Part II in a practical setting. What could we discover about accountability deficits and overloads if we were to deploy an accountability benchmark to measure the 'amount' of accountability delivered by given mechanisms in a particular situation? This chapter takes three real-world scenarios in which mechanisms have been called on to deliver accountability, and assesses them by reference to the framework set out in Part II. The selected examples are instances of government maladministration that have taken place in Australia in the past two decades, and paint a useful picture of accountability in practice.

8.1 A Hypothetical Benchmark

Before attempting to deploy a benchmark of accountability in practice, it is necessary to define one. As outlined in Part II of this book, this is no small task. In order to choose a benchmark of accountability, it is necessary to grapple with a number of very difficult questions. Most importantly, it is necessary to come to a landing on what we say the rationale or rationales of accountability might be. Does accountability entail transparency, or extend also to control? Does it entail redress of harm? Does it entail punishment of wrongdoing, and if so, is the underlying purpose of such punishment desert- or deterrence-oriented? Is accountability just about what has happened in the past, or also about facilitating improvements going forward? Perhaps accountability demands all of these outcomes, which brings us to the next key difficulty of defining a benchmark of accountability, namely, how to accommodate competing tensions between accountability goals. If we expect accountability mechanisms both to condemn poor behaviour (desert) and to foster improvements in administration (deterrence), we may find that a mechanism fails to meet either of our expectations to their fullest; a highly condemnatory mechanism might be inclined to produce unproductive defensive practices by officials who fear reprisal, whereas a dialogic-focused mechanism may lack the 'bite' necessary to satisfy community expectations of punishment.

In addition to these difficulties in accommodating accountability rationales, Chapters 4–7 also highlighted that there are further practical and philosophical dilemmas that must be confronted. We must be able to articulate what we mean when we speak of the 'government' and the exercise of public power. We must grapple with the realities of expanding government services and the encroachment of privatisation. We must enter moral terrain, asking on what basis we believe people ought to be held accountable for their decisions and conduct, including whether we are more concerned with motives or results. We must delve into psychological questions about what motivates human behaviour, driving people to utilise and respond to accountability mechanisms. Debates about these kinds of issues have attracted legal and moral philosophers for centuries precisely because there are no ready answers to these questions.

Putting this (not insubstantial) range of concerns to one side for the moment, we might ask what a 'benchmark' of accountability would look like if we attempted to define one? At a minimum, it would need to offer a normative response to the questions posed in Chapters 4–7: *who* should be accountable *to whom*, *for what*, via *what procedures* and with *what consequences*? As noted in those chapters, we would likely adopt different answers to these questions for each of the rationales for accountability explored in this book. Table 8.1 sets out one possible set of responses to these normative questions. Taken together, we can treat this as a 'hypothetical benchmark' of accountability.

Framing these elements into words, we could structure a five-part benchmark in the following terms:

(a) **Transparency rationale**: *All individuals/entities within government* would be accountable to *all members of the public* for *all government decisions and conduct* by *explaining and justifying* through *public dissemination of information*. If we take the view that transparency is a fundamental prerequisite to accountability, and that there needs to be means not only to respond to maladministration but also to discover it, we might demand mechanisms that offer the widest rights of access to the widest range of information. A benchmark that limits access to cases where there is evidence of potential wrongdoing, or limits access to a particular class of prosecutor, would not meet that objective. The hypothetical benchmark is therefore drafted broadly to provide widespread rights of access to information.

(b) **Control rationale**: The *individual/entity charged with exercising power* would be accountable to *all members of the public* for *unlawful exercise of power* through the imposition of *regulatory orders* imposed via *coercive procedures that are equally balanced between the parties*. The control rationale is concerned with defining and

Table 8.1 *Hypothetical accountability benchmark providing potential responses to the questions who should be accountable, to whom, for what, via what procedures and with what consequences?*

Rationale	Who	To Whom	For What	Consequences	Procedures
Transparency	All individuals/entities within government	All members of the public	All government decisions and conduct	Explain and justify	Procedures that facilitate public dissemination of information
Control	The individual/entity charged with exercising power	All members of the public	Unlawful exercise of power	Regulatory orders	Coercive procedures that are equally balanced between the parties
Redress	The government as an entity	Individuals who have suffered harm	Unlawful exercise of power causing harm	Reparative remedies	Prosecutor-friendly procedures
Desert	Individual public officials and government entities	A defined prosecutor (with residual rights for members of the public)	Deliberate wrongdoing (for an entity, where that conduct is engaged in in its name)	Punitive sanctions	Agent-friendly procedures
Deterrence	Officials or entities with the capacity to effect change	A defined prosecutor	Unsatisfactory rules, procedures or practices that should be discouraged or improved	Weak sanctions	Flexible procedures that facilitate dialogue

enforcing the limits applicable to public power. The hypothetical benchmark might meet that objective by providing widespread access to sanctions capable of containing public power, and by targeting the party charged with exercising that power. The selection of balanced procedures reflects the fact that the core concern of this rationale is the legality of government operations, rather than the protection of the rights of either the citizen or the official.

(c) **Redress rationale:** The *government as an entity* would be accountable to *individuals who have suffered harm* due to *unlawful government decisions and conduct* through the imposition of *reparative remedies* via *prosecutor-friendly procedures*. The redress rationale is concerned with providing a remedy to individuals who have suffered harm as a result of government decisions and conduct. The nature of redress entails that this rationale is engaged only where government activity results in loss of some kind, though it is by no means clear how we should define the limits of the reparable loss. The deliberately imprecise term 'harm' is selected here to prompt thinking about this question. In order to increase the prospects of redress, the government (rather than an individual official) is targeted as the account-giver, and the procedures adopted are prosecutor- rather than agent-friendly. The hypothetical benchmark limits the remedy to *unlawfully* rather than *lawfully* caused loss, though it is possible that some might advocate a wider recovery principle.[1]

(d) **Desert rationale:** *Individual public officials* would be accountable to a *defined prosecutor* (*with residual rights for members of the public*) for their *deliberate wrongdoing* through the imposition of *punitive sanctions* via *agent-friendly procedures*. This rationale is concerned with condemning abuse of power, and consistently with that objective it deploys highly punitive sanctions in order to reflect the significance of the wrongdoing. Given the condemnatory nature of the sanctions, we might think it appropriate that they are limited to cases of intentional wrongdoing, and that the procedures are agent-friendly in order to limit the chance that penalties will be imposed in cases where they are not deserved.

(e) **Deterrence rationale:** *Officials or entities with the capacity to effect change* would be accountable to a *defined prosecutor* in respect of

---

[1] E.g. the French legal system recognises a right to recover loss caused by lawful administration on the basis of the principle of equality before public burdens: see Section 6.3.3 in Chapter 6.

*unsatisfactory rules, procedures or practices that should be discour-
aged or improved* through the imposition of *weak sanctions* via
flexible procedures that facilitate dialogue. This rationale is concerned
with fostering improvements in public administration in a forward-
looking sense. To this end, the benchmark is defined to increase the
likelihood of facilitating positive change and therefore targets those
with the ability to achieve change with sanctions that are most likely
to encourage that response. Though many advocate the use of punitive sanctions as a deterrent, the hypothetical benchmark adopts this
less confrontational approach in line with Braithwaite's views of the
utility of 'weak sanctions' in fostering dialogue.[2]

There is still potential for tension between this series of benchmarks (e.g.
there might be tension between the desert and deterrence rationales if the
person who has the greatest capacity to effect change going forward is
also the individual wrongdoer). However, allowing the benchmark to
target different individuals, in different ways and for different conduct
reduces the likelihood of such tensions arising.

This hypothetical benchmark is offered subject to a number of caveats.
First, I wish to make it clear that I do not make any claim that this is an
ideal accountability benchmark, or even that it reflects my own finalised
views on the topic. While the choices made generally align with many of
the points drawn out in earlier chapters, those chapters also make clear
that there are a number of unresolved philosophical and practical questions that are beyond the scope of this book to settle. At best, then, this
hypothetical benchmark offers a set of tentative answers to a number of
difficult questions, and leaves for another day the broader task of
defending the choices made. A second caveat is that I leave open the
question of whether there might be more than one 'ideal' benchmark of
accountability. The ideal answers to the set of normative questions posed
in this book might legitimately differ as between contexts and jurisdictions. It might be perfectly acceptable to adopt different guiding rationales for accountability in different contexts, thereby altering our focus, for
example, from pursuit of desert to support of deterrence. Again, our
preferences in defining a benchmark involve complex choices about what
we expect of our government, which may differ by context and jurisdiction, and indeed, over time. Rather than seeking to prescribe a single,
universal, standard, the core concern of this book is to point out the

---

[2] See discussion in Section 7.2.4 in Chapter 7.

importance of making our choice of benchmark (whatever form it takes) explicit. It is only in doing so that we can have meaningful conversations about the nature of any deficit or overload identified by reference to that benchmark. A third caveat is that the focus of this book (and in turn, the content of the hypothetical benchmark) is accountability in the context of *public governance*. Accordingly, it would be necessary to consider appropriate adjustments that might be relevant in extending these ideas into other contexts, such as accountability in private sector markets.

Finally, this hypothetical benchmark is concerned only with furthering *accountability*, and is not intended to take into account other concerns or interests that may be inconsistent with, and even in some circumstances outweigh, those of accountability. For instance, while widespread access to information might be considered important when furthering the transparency objective of accountability, this objective in some situations might be outweighed by concerns to protect individual privacy, or national security, or commercial interests (amongst others).[3] A benchmark that demands extensive information access rights might therefore be criticised on the basis that it is not sensitive to legitimate concerns that are inconsistent with transparency in government decision-making. Likewise, a benchmark that demands redress of individuals who suffer harm as a consequence of maladministration might be criticised on the basis that it does not take into account the significant drain that this might place on public resources. In the real world, there are of course many countervailing concerns that would need to be taken into account alongside those of accountability. The hypothetical benchmark does not purport to take these competing interests into account, nor does it represent a value judgement that accountability is more important than such interests. But this does not limit the utility of the hypothetical. It may in fact be better to define our accountability benchmark independently of considerations that pull against it. We can use the hypothetical benchmark to identify a shortfall in a mechanism (e.g. that a freedom of information regime does not allow access to cabinet docu ments in opposition to the transparency benchmark),[4] but then justify

---

[3] This balancing act is reflected in Australia's freedom of information regime, which exempts the production of information in circumstances where its release could affect national security or public safety, or expose trade secrets, or reveal privileged advice, or affect personal privacy (*Freedom of Information Act 1982* (Cth) pt IV), or where complying with freedom of information obligations would unreasonably divert an agency from its operations (*Freedom of Information Act 1982* (Cth) ss 24, 24AA).

[4] *Freedom of Information Act 1982* (Cth) s 34.

departure from that benchmark by reference to countervailing concerns. The advantage of this approach is that it forces us to be explicit in our choices as to the circumstances in which we think departure from the accountability 'ideal' is justified.

Bearing these caveats in mind, deploying the hypothetical benchmark offers the opportunity to attempt to measure the 'amount' of accountability delivered in certain instances of government maladministration in the following sections.

8.2   The Eddie Obeid Corruption Scandal

Edward Obeid was a member of the upper house of Parliament in New South Wales between 1991 and 2011, also holding a position as a minister for a number of years during that period. Mr Obeid can be considered something of a controversial political figure, with a number of allegations of wrongdoing and corruption having been levelled against him during and after his term in office. For the purposes of applying our hypothetical accountability benchmark, this book focuses on one particular incident, relating to the grant of leases over government-owned property at Circular Quay, Sydney. The following facts are based on findings made in Mr Obeid's criminal prosecution for the common law offence of misconduct in public office.[5]

Mr Obeid's family held an interest in a company which operated a number of restaurants at Circular Quay. The restaurant premises were leased from a government body: the NSW Maritime Authority. Following a series of protracted lease renewal negotiations, the Maritime Authority proposed a policy pursuant to which all its lease agreements would be offered for competitive tender rather than giving existing tenants a preferential position. Before that policy was adopted, a new official (Mr Stephen Dunn) took up an appointment as a senior officer within the Maritime Authority. Mr Dunn had previously worked with Mr Obeid, and regarded Mr Obeid as something of a mentor. Soon after his appointment, Mr Obeid contacted Mr Dunn to express concern about the way in which existing tenants at Circular Quay had been treated by the Maritime Authority. Mr Obeid did not disclose his personal interest in those tenancies, and encouraged Mr Dunn to meet with a representative of the Circular Quay lessors. Following that meeting and a further

---

[5]   *R v Obeid [No 12]* [2016] NSWSC 1815.

series of phone calls with Mr Obeid, the Maritime Authority ultimately adopted a policy which required it to negotiate with existing tenants in the first instance. The company in which Mr Obeid's family held an interest was granted new leases at Circular Quay, which ran until terminated when the restaurants failed in 2012.

For present purposes, the substance of the concerns about Mr Obeid's conduct centre on his alleged use of his influence as a Member of Parliament to benefit his family's interests in relation to the Circular Quay leases. Looking at the hypothetical benchmark, Mr Obeid's conduct is most relevant in connection with the rationales of transparency, desert and deterrence:

(a) the **transparency** rationale might require a mechanism that could uncover the circumstances surrounding the leasing decisions, including Mr Obeid's involvement;
(b) the **desert** rationale might require the application of punitive sanctions to punish any intentional wrongdoing by Mr Obeid; and
(c) the **deterrence** rationale might require dialogue-driven sanctions designed to facilitate improvements in applicable procedures with a view to preventing future abuses of power of this nature.

A number of different mechanisms played roles in holding Mr Obeid accountable for his conduct in connection with the award of the Circular Quay leases, most notably investigation by the New South Wales Independent Commission Against Corruption (**ICAC**) and criminal prosecution for the offence of misconduct in public office. The following sections consider the extent to which the operations of these mechanisms align with the hypothetical accountability benchmark.

8.2.1   The New South Wales Independent Commission Against Corruption

Commissions of inquiry broadly sit within the executive branch of government on the traditional tripartite view of the separation of powers,[6] with at least some type of anti-corruption commission having been introduced across each of the Australian jurisdictions. While some

---

[6] With the exception of those institutions that are specifically identified as officers of Parliament: see, e.g., *Independent Broad-Based Anti-Corruption Commission Act 2011* (Vic) s 19.

are limited to investigating corruption in law enforcement[7] or the public service,[8] the most wide-reaching anti-corruption commissions have a generalist jurisdiction to investigate corruption in the public sector. Generalist anti-corruption commissions exist in all Australian states, and a similar body is under consideration at the Commonwealth level at the time of writing.[9] The NSW ICAC is one of the longest-running specialist anti-corruption commissions in Australia, and was introduced in 1988 in response to widespread concerns about corruption across all levels of NSW government.[10] The overarching objective of the ICAC is clearly aligned with accountability, with its empowering legislation having as its principal object 'to promote the integrity and accountability of public administration'.[11] It does so in two key ways: (1) by investigating and reporting on instances of corruption, and (2) by advising and assisting government officials and bodies with a view to reducing corruption going forward. The following sections consider the extent to which this agency satisfied the transparency, desert and deterrence aspects of the hypothetical accountability benchmark in Mr Obeid's case. To the extent that the ICAC's work underperformed against the hypothetical benchmark we might identify a potential accountability deficit, and to the extent that it overperforms against the benchmark we might identify a potential accountability overload.

8.2.1.1   Who Can the ICAC Hold Accountable?

The ICAC is able to investigate potential corruption by a relatively wide range of parties. Some types of corrupt conduct can be engaged in by 'any person',[12] and therefore extend to conduct engaged in by private individuals that affects the exercise of public power. However, most provisions focus on conduct engaged in by current or former 'public officials',[13] broadly defined to capture public servants, members of the police force, members of public authorities, judicial officers and a range of other

---

[7]   E.g. the Australian Commission for Law Enforcement Integrity.

[8]   E.g. the Australian Public Service Commission.

[9]   See Janina Boughey, Ellen Rock and Greg Weeks, *Government Liability: Principles and Remedies* (LexisNexis, 2019) ch 9.

[10]   New South Wales, *Parliamentary Debates*, Legislative Assembly, 26 May 1988, 673 (Nicholas Greiner, Premier, Treasurer and Minister for Ethnic Affairs).

[11]   *Independent Commission Against Corruption Act 1988* (NSW) s 2A.

[12]   Ibid s 8(1)(a), (2), (2A).

[13]   Ibid s 8(1)(b)–(d).

government officeholders.[14] Most importantly for present purposes, the provision captures Members of Parliament and ministers of the Crown. Accordingly, the ICAC was in a position to investigate Mr Obeid, who was a member of the NSW Legislative Assembly and a minister at various points during the time period in question. This aligns well with the desert rationale, which anticipates that a mechanism is able to target the individual official who engaged in wrongdoing.

In addition to its investigative function, the ICAC also has a more wide-ranging educatory role. These powers allow it to advise 'public authorities' and 'public officials' about changes the ICAC thinks necessary to reduce the likelihood of corruption and to 'promote the integrity and good repute of public administration'.[15] While the NSW Parliament is not included within the definition of 'public authority', it was nonetheless able to be the subject of recommendations for improvements in process pursuant to the ICAC's more general power to 'formulate recommendations for the taking of action that [it] considers should be taken in relation to its findings'.[16] As noted in Section 8.2.1.4 below, the ICAC was therefore able to make recommendations to the NSW Houses of Parliament regarding amendment of their Codes of Conduct.[17] Given that these are bodies with the capacity to effect change, there is a strong alignment with the deterrence rationale in the hypothetical benchmark.

8.2.1.2   Who Can Enliven the ICAC's Jurisdiction?

The ICAC's jurisdiction may be enlivened in a number of ways, including through complaints and referrals, but also on its own initiative.[18] Many bodies are empowered to refer matters to the ICAC; for some bodies (such as the Ombudsman, Commissioner of Police, principal officers of public authorities, and ministers), there is a mandatory duty to report suspected corrupt conduct to the ICAC.[19] Matters may also be referred to

---

[14] Ibid s 3 (definition of 'public official').

[15] Ibid s 13(1)(f).

[16] Ibid s 13(3)(b).

[17] The NSW ICAC had made recommendations to the NSW Parliament to reform its Codes of Conduct following a previous investigation involving Mr Obeid: NSW Independent Commission Against Corruption, *Reducing the Opportunities and Incentives for Corruption in the State's Management of Coal Resources* (October 2013) 8.

[18] *Independent Commission Against Corruption Act 1988* (NSW) s 20(1).

[19] Ibid s 11. See that provision for details of exceptions.

the ICAC by the NSW Parliament[20] and the NSW Electoral Commission.[21] However, it is not just government officials that may notify the ICAC about potential corruption issues; 'any person' is entitled to make a complaint to the ICAC about matters that 'may concern corrupt conduct'.[22] This broad complaints mechanism is tempered by the qualification that it is an offence to provide false information to the ICAC when making a complaint.[23]

In Mr Obeid's case, the ICAC acted on a complaint,[24] reportedly received via an anonymous phone tip-off.[25] Returning to the hypothetical accountability benchmark, the ability for 'any person' to complain to the ICAC is consistent with the transparency rationale, which demands widespread right of access to information about government decisions and activity. In relation to the desert and deterrence aspects of the benchmark, however, the fact that any person could instigate an ICAC investigation might be of some concern, as these aspects of the benchmark anticipate that prosecution be reserved to a defined prosecutor (though there may be a residual right of private prosecution). We might wonder, therefore, whether the ability for 'any person' to enliven the ICAC's jurisdiction raises the prospect of a potential accountability overload. However, it is necessary to bear in mind that the ICAC reserves discretion to decide whether or not a particular complaint warrants investigation.[26] In this sense, the question of 'to whom' Mr Obeid was accountable in this case represents a balance between the accountability rationales; a member of the general public was able to set the wheels of the ICAC in motion, but the ICAC acted as an independent prosecutor in determining that an investigation was in fact warranted.

---

[20] Ibid s 13(1)(b).

[21] Ibid s 13A.

[22] Ibid s 10.

[23] Ibid s 81.

[24] NSW Independent Commission Against Corruption, *Operation Cyrus: Investigation into the Conduct of The Hon Edward Obeid MLC and Others Concerning Circular Quay Retail Lease Policy* (June 2014) 9.

[25] Michaela Whitbourn, 'Ex-ICAC Boss Says Obeid Would Be a Free Man under Morrison's Plan', *Sydney Morning Herald* (14 December 2018) <https://www.smh.com.au/national/so-many-holes-former-icac-boss-slams-morrison-s-plan-20181214-p50m91.html> accessed 10 January 2019.

[26] *Independent Commission Against Corruption Act 1988* (NSW) s 10(2).

8.2.1.3   For What Did the ICAC Hold Mr Obeid Accountable?

The principal functions of the ICAC are to investigate potential corrupt conduct and to communicate the results of such investigation to appropriate authorities,[27] with a mandate to prioritise serious and systemic corruption.[28] The definition of corrupt conduct consists of two limbs: conduct must satisfy the requirements of s 8 of the Act (which sets out a range of types of conduct considered to be corrupt), but must not be excluded by s 9 of the Act (which sets out limits on the types of conduct that will be considered corrupt). Section 8 defines corrupt conduct to include conduct that either constitutes, or could affect, the 'honest or impartial exercise of official functions', involves a breach of public trust, involves misuse of information, could 'impair confidence in public administration', or otherwise affects the exercise of official functions including through bribery, blackmail, misconduct, fraud and so on. However, pursuant to s 9, such conduct can only be considered corrupt if it constitutes (a) a criminal offence; (b) a disciplinary offence; (c) reasonable grounds for termination of employment; or (d) for ministers and Members of Parliament – a substantial breach of a code of conduct. For ministers and Members of Parliament, the fact that conduct does not satisfy one of those four criteria does not preclude the ICAC from investigating if the conduct is such that it would cause a reasonable person to believe that it would bring the integrity of the relevant office into disrepute.[29] However, the ICAC cannot report findings of corruption unless the conduct is considered to be a breach of a law.[30]

Following its investigation, the ICAC determined that Mr Obeid had engaged in corrupt conduct. In particular, it made findings that Mr Obeid had misused his position as a Member of Parliament by making representations to government officials to change government policy so as to allow direct negotiation of leases at Circular Quay. The ICAC found that in doing so, Mr Obeid had (a) breached public trust in failing to disclose his family's interests in relation to the leases; and (b) exercised his functions as a Member of Parliament dishonestly and partially by pressuring officials to change government policy to benefit his family's

---

[27] Ibid s 13.
[28] Ibid s 12A.
[29] Ibid s 9(4).
[30] Ibid s 9(6).

financial interests.[31] Accordingly, Mr Obeid's conduct met the first limb of the 'corrupt conduct' definition set out in s 8. The ICAC further found that Mr Obeid's conduct satisfied the requirements of s 9, indicating that it was satisfied that an appropriate tribunal could find that Mr Obeid had committed the criminal offence of misconduct in public office, were the facts to be proved. The 'wilfulness and seriousness' of the misconduct was thought by the ICAC to be sufficient to warrant criminal punishment, and it was accordingly satisfied that it could make and report findings of corruption against Mr Obeid.

8.2.1.4   How Does the ICAC Deliver Accountability?

As noted in Chapter 7, the question of how an agent is held accountable consists of two ideas; first, the procedures employed by the forum in its accountability process, and secondly, the consequences or outcomes that can be imposed. The ICAC's processes consist of two stages: investigation and reporting. The investigatory powers of the ICAC are quite broad. During the course of conducting an investigation, the ICAC is able to enter and inspect premises, and require the production of information and documents,[32] including under warrant.[33] If determined to be in the public interest, the ICAC is able to conduct compulsory examination of witnesses, including under oath,[34] and has powers of arrest where a witness fails to answer a summons or is at risk of failing to attend.[35]

One of the ICAC's most significant powers of investigation is to conduct public inquiries.[36] In deciding whether to do so, the overriding question is one of public interest, which involves balancing of competing interests including the benefit of making the public aware of corrupt conduct, the seriousness of the alleged conduct, risk of undue prejudice to a person's reputation, and personal privacy.[37] The ICAC has published guidelines relating to the conduct of public inquiries, which make provision for procedural fairness.[38] The ICAC is not bound by the rules or

---

[31] NSW Independent Commission Against Corruption, *Operation Cyrus* (n 24) 60.
[32] *Independent Commission Against Corruption Act 1988* (NSW) ss 21–23.
[33] Ibid Pt 4 Div 4.
[34] Ibid ss 30, 35.
[35] Ibid s 36.
[36] Ibid s 31.
[37] Ibid s 31.
[38] NSW Independent Commission Against Corruption, *Public Inquiry Procedural Guidelines* (February 2018).

practice of evidence, and is intended to operate in an informal manner.[39] Witnesses are also not entitled to refuse to answer questions on grounds of privilege against self-incrimination.[40] However, the ICAC does adhere to a legal standard of proof in making findings, requiring that facts be proved on the balance of probabilities but with reference to the seriousness of the allegations.[41]

The ICAC's primary outcome-oriented processes are its reporting functions. It is able to prepare reports on any matters that have been the subject of an investigation, and must do so in cases where it has conducted a public inquiry or where a matter has been referred to the ICAC by Parliament.[42] The permitted content of reports is governed by legislation, as only findings of 'serious corrupt conduct' can be included,[43] and the ICAC is prohibited from expressing an opinion that a person has committed a criminal or disciplinary offence.[44] Accordingly, reports must tread a fine line between setting out sufficient grounds to justify a finding of corruption without expressing a conclusion that an offence has in fact been committed.

In Mr Obeid's case, the ICAC determined that, based on the complaint which had been made, it was in the public interest to conduct an investigation and launched 'Operation Cyrus'.[45] In conducting its investigation, the ICAC exercised powers to obtain access to documents and information, including through compulsory examination of a number of witnesses. Following this investigation, the ICAC determined that it was in the public interest to hold a public inquiry, which took place in late 2013. The ICAC published a report on its findings in June 2014, which was ultimately tabled in Parliament with a recommendation that the report be made public.[46] The report was subsequently made available

[39] *Independent Commission Against Corruption Act 1988* (NSW) s 17.
[40] Ibid s 37.
[41] See, e.g., NSW Independent Commission Against Corruption, *Operation Cyrus* (n 24) 56. The ICAC observes the '*Briginshaw*' standard of proof. The case of *Briginshaw v Briginshaw* (1938) 60 CLR 336 is taken as having established the principle that a judge will not find that serious allegations have been made out on the balance of probabilities unless they 'feel . . . an actual persuasion' (at 361) or reach 'comfortable satisfaction' as to that allegation (at 350).
[42] *Independent Commission Against Corruption Act 1988* (NSW) s 74(1)–(3).
[43] Ibid s 74BA.
[44] Ibid s 74B.
[45] NSW Independent Commission Against Corruption, *Operation Cyrus* (n 24) 10.
[46] Ibid 8, pursuant to *Independent Commission Against Corruption Act 1988* (NSW) s 78(2).

on the ICAC website,[47] and remains available on the website of the NSW Parliament.

Looking at the hypothetical accountability benchmark, these processes are well aligned with the transparency rationale, which requires the public dissemination of information. The general public was made aware of Mr Obeid's conduct both via the public inquiry process, and as a result of the final report published by the ICAC. In this respect, the accountability goal of transparency was well served as a result of the ICAC investigation. However, it is less clear how well the ICAC investigation process aligned with the desert aspect of the hypothetical accountability benchmark. The benchmark anticipates that desert-oriented mechanisms will impose punitive sanctions via agent-friendly procedures, and neither of these two expectations describes the ICAC process. First, the procedures employed by ICAC are far more prosecutor-friendly than agent-friendly. When compared with legal proceedings, the ICAC's powers to compel production of evidence are very robust; witnesses do not have the benefit of the privilege against self-incrimination or other legal controls on the admissibility of evidence, and the ICAC maintains flexible control over the manner in which inquiries are run. In this respect, the ICAC processes might be at risk of producing an accountability overload when measured against that aspect of the benchmark. Secondly, the ICAC does not deploy highly punitive sanctions as envisaged by the desert aspect of the benchmark, which anticipates the application of sanctions that condemn wrongdoing and reflect public outrage. Instead, the ICAC's powers allowed it to subject Mr Obeid to a public inquiry and to make a finding of corruption against him. While Mr Obeid would doubtless have considered this to be a very unpleasant experience, subjection to the ICAC process would not be sufficient to amount to punitive sanctions for the purpose of the hypothetical benchmark.

In addition to its corruption-investigation functions, the ICAC is also charged with functions directed towards the reduction of corrupt conduct in a forward-looking capacity. These include instructing, advising and assisting public bodies and officials on ways to eliminate corrupt conduct and promote integrity including through education strategies and changes to practices and procedures.[48] In Mr Obeid's case, the ICAC targeted the parliamentary Code of Conduct, describing it as a 'feeble

---

[47] Reports in relation to Mr Obeid are not available on the ICAC website at the time of writing.

[48] *Independent Commission Against Corruption Act 1988* (NSW) s 13(d)–(h).

document' that was 'virtually worthless' in addressing the corruption issues that had been identified. It reiterated a recommendation made in a previous report that the NSW Parliament ought to consider amending its Code of Conduct to address improper influence by Members of Parliament.[49] Each of the NSW houses of Parliament subsequently tasked committees with considering the implementation of this recommendation, and while both recommended revision of the Code of Conduct,[50] differences in approach meant that progress stalled.[51] A new code has since been drafted, but has not been adopted at the time of writing.[52] In looking at the deterrence rationale, the ICAC's recommendatory process is relatively consistent with the expectations of the hypothetical benchmark. By criticising the Code of Conduct and recommending reform to target improper influence, the ICAC employed weak sanctions to facilitate dialogue, setting in motion a movement towards change. However, it is worth pointing out the lengthy delay in progress towards adoption of the ICAC's recommendations, and lack of ongoing public dialogue about the issue.

8.2.2 Criminal Prosecution for Misconduct in Public Office

Following the findings of corruption made by the ICAC, Mr Obeid was prosecuted for the criminal offence of misconduct in public office.

---

[49] The ICAC had previously made this recommendation in a report prepared following another investigation into Mr Obeid's conduct, this time in connection with the grant of coal exploration licences: NSW Independent Commission Against Corruption, *Reducing the Opportunities and Incentives for Corruption in the State's Management of Coal Resources* (n 17) 42–43. The ICAC indicated that it did not consider it necessary to reiterate that recommendation in the present report: NSW Independent Commission Against Corruption, *Operation Cyrus* (n 24) 7–8.

[50] Parliamentary Privilege and Ethics Committee, Legislative Assembly (NSW), *Inquiry into matters arising from the ICAC report entitled "Reducing the opportunities and incentives for corruption in the State's management of coal resources"* (July 2014); Privileges Committee, Legislative Council (NSW), *Recommendations of the ICAC regarding aspects of the Code of Conduct for Members, the interest disclosure regime and a parliamentary investigator* (June 2014).

[51] Privileges Committee, Legislative Council (NSW), *Review of the Members' Code of Conduct 2018* (November 2018) 2.

[52] Parliamentary Privilege and Ethics Committee, Legislative Assembly (NSW), *Review of the Code of Conduct for Members* (June 2018); Privileges Committee, Legislative Council (NSW), *Review of the Members' Code of Conduct 2018* (n 51). The most recently adopted Code of Conduct for Members (May 2019) does not directly address improper influence of executive officials.

The criminal law can be viewed as an important mechanism in support of accountability's overarching objective of securing the legitimacy of government. The notion of accountability is implicit in many descriptions of the criminal offences that apply to the exercise of public powers by government officials. While public officials are subject to the same ordinary criminal law that governs the acts of private individuals,[53] there are also categories of offences that are specifically concerned with the exercise of public power, including abuse of office,[54] receipt of bribes[55] and breach of secrecy obligations.[56] It was the first of these three categories of offences that was relevant in Mr Obeid's case. The detailed elements of the abuse of office offence vary depending on jurisdiction, with New South Wales retaining the common law offence of misconduct in public office. That offence is made out where a public official, 'in the course of or connected to his public office ... wilfully misconduct[s] himself ... without reasonable excuse or justification' in light of the 'responsibilities of the office'.[57]

Alder advocates the adoption of accountability as the 'guiding principle' in connection with this offence,[58] noting that it hinges off the notion that 'the public has an interest in ensuring that anyone acting on behalf of the state, performs all their duties properly'.[59] Describing the offence as 'a constitutional fundamental',[60] and a 'hybrid, public-criminal law remedy',[61] Horder also points to an accountability rationale: '[The offence] provides an essential way in which, as a last resort, prosecutors and the courts can deter and punish (with an appropriate label) corrupt conduct on the part of legislators and other officials, and thereby make

---

[53] So, for instance, in absence of legal authority, the actions involved in undertaking an arrest might ordinarily constitute criminal assault. See Peter Cane, *Responsibility in Law and Morality* (Hart Publishing, 2002) 265.

[54] E.g. *Criminal Code* (Cth) s 142.2(1).

[55] E.g. ibid ss 141.1(3), 141.2(3).

[56] E.g. *Crimes Act 1914* (Cth) ss 70, 79.

[57] *R v Quach* (2010) 27 VR 310, 323 [46], cited with approval by the NSW Court of Criminal Appeal in *Obeid v The Queen* (2015) 91 NSWLR 226, 252–54 [133], [139].

[58] John Alder, 'Misconduct in Public Office: Modernising the Law' [2014] *Public Law* 369, 371.

[59] Ibid 370.

[60] Jeremy Horder, *Criminal Misconduct in Office: Law and Politics* (Oxford University Press, 2018) 2.

[61] Ibid 10–11.

the use of power accountable by reference to the standards of ordinary people.'[62]

Following the ICAC investigation, Mr Obeid was subsequently prosecuted for the common law offence of misconduct in public office before the NSW Supreme Court. After an initial trial was aborted when new evidence came to light during the hearing,[63] a second jury convicted Mr Obeid of the offence in June 2016, and he was sentenced to a term of imprisonment of five years with a non-parole period of three years.[64] Mr Obeid's appeal against that conviction was dismissed by the NSW Court of Appeal,[65] with special leave to appeal to the High Court of Australia refused.[66] The following sections consider the extent to which the criminal prosecution process aligned with the *transparency*, *desert* and *deterrence* aspects of the hypothetical accountability benchmark.

8.2.2.1 Who Can Be Prosecuted?

The common law offence of misconduct in public office is one that can only be committed by 'public officials'.[67] This is understood to include 'an officer who discharges any duty in the discharge of which the public are interested, more clearly so if he is paid out of a fund provided by the public'.[68] The offence has been applied to a broad range of officials including ministers, judges, police officers, prison officers, prosecutors, and employees of local government authorities, educational institutions and health care providers.[69] In marking out the reach of this offence, the courts have demonstrated a preference to maintain a degree of elasticity in the definition. In Mr Obeid's case, this degree of elasticity allowed the NSW Court of Criminal Appeal to extend the reach of the offence to Members of Parliament.[70] The Court cited with approval Zellick's description of a Member of Parliament as being 'a "public character"',

---

[62] Ibid 2.

[63] *R v Obeid [No 7]* [2016] NSWSC 132.

[64] *R v Obeid [No 12]* [2016] NSWSC 1815.

[65] *Obeid v The Queen* (2017) 96 NSWLR 155.

[66] *Obeid v The Queen* [2018] HCATrans 54.

[67] *R v Quach* (2010) 27 VR 310, 323 [46].

[68] *R v Whitaker* [1914] 3 KB 1283, 1296.

[69] See David Lusty, 'Revival of the Common Law Offence of Misconduct in Public Office' (2014) 38 *Criminal Law Journal* 337, 344–45.

[70] *Obeid v The Queen* (2015) 91 NSWLR 226, 250–51 [121]–[125].

'paid from public funds' and performing duties 'exclusively of a public nature'.[71] Also relevant for the Court was the 'level of trust' reposed in such officials and the fact that they are elected by the people.[72] Accordingly, the misconduct offence was capable of being utilised to hold Mr Obeid accountable in the present case.

Looking at the hypothetical benchmark, the misconduct offence is most clearly aligned with the desert rationale, in targeting the individual wrongdoer for their personal conduct. Mr Obeid was charged with the offence on the basis of his own acts and decisions in connection with the Circular Quay leases. The Court found that he had engaged in this conduct with a view to furthering his own and his family's financial interests, and as such the benchmark would deem it appropriate that Mr Obeid be made to answer for this conduct himself, rather than imputing his conduct to the government. The criminal law is also commonly thought of as a tool of deterrence, both with a view to deterring the individual wrongdoer from future infractions (specific deterrence) and others from following their example (general deterrence).[73] In sentencing Mr Obeid, the trial judge certainly took this view of the misconduct offence, noting that the goal of deterrence was 'especially strong' in such cases.[74] On this view of deterrence, the punishment of the individual wrongdoer is viewed as a disincentive to others who might be tempted to engage in similar conduct. Whatever we think of the deterrent capacity of criminal sanctions more generally, for present purposes this approach to deterrence is not well aligned with the hypothetical benchmark. Rather than seeking to engage in dialogue with those with the capacity to influence change going forward, in this situation Mr Obeid (at the time of his trial, an ex-parliamentarian) was used as an example to warn officials of the perils of abuse of office. This is not a good fit with the approach anticipated by the hypothetical benchmark. There are also limitations in relation to the transparency rationale, given the limited range of parties that can be prosecuted for the misconduct offence.

---

[71] G Zellick, 'Bribery of Members of Parliament and the Criminal Law' [1979] *Public Law* 31, 38, cited in *Obeid v The Queen* (2015) 91 NSWLR 226, 250 [123].

[72] *Obeid v The Queen* (2015) 91 NSWLR 226, 251 [124].

[73] See, e.g., David Dolinko, 'Punishment' in John Deigh and David Dolinko (eds.), *The Oxford Handbook of Philosophy of Criminal Law* (Oxford University Press, 2011) 403.

[74] *R v Obeid [No 12]* [2016] NSWSC 1815, [94].

8.2.2.2   Who Can Prosecute Government Misconduct?

As a general rule, modern criminal prosecutions are primarily the province of the state,[75] with the criminal trial standing as 'an accusatorial process in which the power of the State is deployed against an individual accused of crime'.[76] In the majority of cases, the relevant procedure is that a police officer will file an information with the relevant court. If the offence is an indictable one (as is the case for the offence of misconduct in public office), a committal hearing will be held, following which a public prosecutor will take carriage of the prosecution of the trial proceedings. While private citizens may play important roles in providing evidence, in the vast majority of cases the decision to prosecute will be driven by the state. Such prosecutorial decisions are insusceptible to judicial review,[77] thereby reducing the capacity of private individuals to compel prosecution of criminal offences.

However, the state's monopoly on prosecution is by no means absolute. Indeed, the historical position was that crimes were frequently prosecuted privately.[78] Following the emergence of the criminal jurisdiction up to the nineteenth century, private prosecution remained the primary means by which misdemeanours and felonies were punished.[79] Changes in social conditions and increasing incidences of petty crime in England in the eighteenth to nineteenth centuries revealed limitations in the private prosecution model, ultimately leading to the establishment of the office of public prosecution.[80] Though public prosecution is now the dominant means by which criminal offences are prosecuted in Australia,[81] it remains possible in most jurisdictions for an individual to mount a private prosecution unless Parliament has legislated to the contrary.[82] The potential ability for individuals to launch criminal prosecutions remains important from an accountability perspective, to accommodate

---

[75] Cane, *Responsibility in Law and Morality* (n 53) 268.

[76] *R v Carroll* (2002) 213 CLR 635, 643 [21] (Gleeson CJ and Hayne J).

[77] *Maxwell v The Queen* (1996) 184 CLR 501, 534.

[78] Tyrone Kirchengast, *The Victim in Criminal Law and Justice* (Palgrave Macmillan, 2006) 39.

[79] Ibid 60.

[80] Ibid.

[81] See, e.g., *Wilson v Official Trustee in Bankruptcy* [2000] FCA 1251, [14] (Emmett J).

[82] *R v Thompson* (1991) 58 A Crim R 81, 84. Parliament has abrogated this right in a number of Australian jurisdictions (see, e.g., *Criminal Procedure Act 2004* (WA) s 20(5)). In others statute reflects the common law position (see, e.g., *Crimes Act 1914* (Cth) s 30, *Criminal Procedure Act 1986* (NSW) s 14).

any shortfall in the state's capacity and interest to prosecute.[83] This is particularly so for public corruption offences, to counter any concern that government prosecutors will act to 'protect their own'.[84]

Turning to the hypothetical accountability benchmark, the transparency, desert and deterrence rationales represent a spectrum of prosecutorial options. The transparency rationale is most open, demanding that 'all members of the public' be entitled to utilise the mechanism. The deterrence rationale is most confined, limiting access to a 'defined prosecutor'. The desert rationale represents something of a midway point, anticipating that punitive sanctions will be sought by a 'defined prosecutor' with residual prosecutorial rights to be available to members of the public. In New South Wales (where Mr Obeid was prosecuted) the offence of misconduct in public office remains able to be prosecuted privately.[85] In Mr Obeid's case, however, the decision to prosecute was made by the Office of the Director of Public Prosecutions (**DPP**) following a recommendation by the ICAC.[86] The question of 'to whom' Mr Obeid was accountable is most clearly aligned with the desert aspect of the hypothetical benchmark; the primary position is that prosecution is left to a defined prosecutor, with residual public rights of prosecution. Had the DPP elected not to proceed with a prosecution, it is theoretically possible that a private citizen might have taken the initiative to commence proceedings, with the DPP having a right to then take over. This avoids the possibility or impression that the government prosecutor might act partially in pursuing sanctions against their fellow government official.

---

[83] In this respect, we might even consider the utility of the *qui tam* action, which allows a private prosecutor to take a percentage of the penalty payable by the convicted defendant. Braithwaite has argued that this device may have an important role to play in circumstances where state capacity to prosecute is at its weakest: John Braithwaite, 'Responsive Regulation and Developing Economies' (2006) 34 *World Development* 884, 895.

[84] This concern underpinned comments made by Gaudron, Gummow and Kirby JJ in the context of the utility of the Attorney-General's fiat in judicial review proceedings: *Bateman's Bay Local Aboriginal Land Council v Aboriginal Community Benefit Fund Pty Ltd* (1998) 194 CLR 247, 262–63 [38].

[85] *Criminal Procedure Act 1986* (NSW) s 14. The registrar must first consider whether there are grounds for the proceedings (*Criminal Procedure Act 1986* (NSW) s 49(2)) and, once commenced, the public prosecutor has a right to take over (*Director of Public Prosecutions Act 1986* (NSW) ss 9, 17).

[86] NSW Independent Commission Against Corruption, *Operation Cyrus* (n 24) 61.

8.2.2.3 For What Does the Misconduct Offence Hold an Agent Accountable?

The hypothetical benchmark anticipates that an accountability mechanism will be engaged in respect of (a) all government decisions and conduct (transparency), (b) deliberate wrongdoing (desert) and (c) the unlawful exercise of power that should be discouraged or improved (deterrence). Again, this represents something of a spectrum, with the transparency rationale being most open, the desert rationale being most limited and the deterrence rationale representing something of a midway point. The question of 'for what' Mr Obeid was able to be held accountable via his criminal prosecution is most clearly aligned with the desert rationale.

The common law offence of misconduct in public office is made out in circumstances where an official 'wilfully misconduct[s] himself'.[87] There are a number of types of conduct that are thought to fall within the ambit of the offence.[88] Only one of these specifically relates to excess of public power, which Finn describes as 'malfeasance'.[89] However, mere excess of power does not of itself amount to malfeasance, as it is necessary to show that the official had no honest belief that they had the power to act as they did, or alternately, that the conduct independently satisfies the elements of another crime, such as assault.[90] Further types of conduct that may give rise to liability include fraudulent conduct and malicious exercise of power,[91] being the 'doing of an otherwise lawful act in a fashion which is wrongful'.[92] It appears that the subjective element inherent in all of these descriptions of the misconduct offence aligns with the notion of deliberate wrongdoing as envisaged by the desert aspect of the hypothetical benchmark.

In Mr Obeid's case, it became clear that the elements of the offence were capable of capturing his conduct. Early on in proceedings, Mr Obeid's counsel argued that the offence could not be made out as Mr Obeid had acted recklessly rather than 'wilfully' in his dealings in relation to the Circular Quay leases; wilfulness, it was argued, was limited to

---

[87] *R v Quach* (2010) 27 VR 310, 323.

[88] For recent discussion of the scope of the offence in the United Kingdom and proposals for reform, see Horder (n 60).

[89] Paul Finn, 'Official Misconduct' (1978) 2 *Criminal Law Journal* 307, 310.

[90] Ibid 320–25.

[91] Ibid 310.

[92] Ibid 318.

'deliberate or voluntary' conduct.[93] However, in Chapter 6 it was noted that deliberate wrongdoing may extend beyond intentional wrongdoing and into the realm of reckless conduct (i.e. a subjective state of mind that involves an advertence to the possibility of an event, but deciding to proceed regardless). The trial judge took this broader view of the 'wilfulness' element, accepting that the offence may be made out 'where the accused is reckless as to whether their act or omission was in breach of the duties and obligations attaching to their office'.[94] On this point, Beech-Jones J borrowed from the words of Gillies in noting that:

> 'wilfully' imports mens rea in at least the technical sense of requiring that [the accused] intentionally *or recklessly* perform the forbidden act, while knowing *or suspecting* the existence of any such associated facts as are required to be proved by [the prosecution]. There is, as well, some authority to the effect that depending upon context, the word 'wilfully' imports knowledge *or suspicion* on the part of the [accused] that his act is forbidden by the law.[95]

In any event, it was unnecessary to resort to this extended definition of wilfulness in Mr Obeid's case. Following the jury's verdict, Beech-Jones J considered that it was 'inconceivable that [Mr Obeid] would not have known that he could not use his position as a parliamentarian to further his or his family's financial interests', accepting that Mr Obeid's conduct in this respect was intentional.[96]

Bearing these matters in mind, the misconduct offence is quite conformable with the expectations of the desert aspect of the hypothetical benchmark, which anticipates that punitive sanctions attach in cases of deliberate wrongdoing. The offence is also able to deliver on the remaining two rationales, as deliberately wrongful exercise of power falls within the scope of government decisions and conduct (transparency), and is an unlawful exercise of power that we would wish to discourage (deterrence). However, because these rationales are relevant beyond cases of deliberate wrongdoing, the misconduct offence makes only a limited contribution to these goals. To put the point more plainly, if the misconduct offence was the *only* means by which we were able to achieve transparency and deterrence in government decision-making, the limited

---

[93] *R v Obeid [No 11]* (2016) 260 A Crim R 94, 96 [8].
[94] Ibid 99 [23]. Approved in *R v Macdonald; R v Maitland* [2017] NSWSC 337, [17].
[95] *R v Obeid [No 11]* (2016) 260 A Crim R 94, 99 [20], quoting Peter Gillies, *Criminal Law* (4th ed., LBC, 1997) 766.
[96] *R v Obeid [No 12]* [2016] NSWSC 1815, [52].

range of conduct targeted by this mechanism would represent a potential accountability deficit.

8.2.2.4   Misconduct: By What Procedures Are Sanctions Imposed?

The next aspect of the misconduct offence to consider is the procedures pursuant to which sanctions are imposed. A detailed examination of court procedures is beyond the scale of this book. Instead, the following analysis focuses on three aspects of procedure: access to information, burden of proof and remedial discretion.

(i) **Access to Information**   The courts make a very useful contribution in providing public access to information. At the broadest level, the very fact that court proceedings are open to the public serves an important transparency function. There have been various formulations of the idea that the courts are, by their nature, open forums. One of the more well-known is that 'it is not merely of some importance but is of fundamental importance, that justice should not only be done, but should manifestly and undoubtedly be seen to be done'.[97] The fundamental requirement that cases are heard in an open court can be departed from only in exceptional circumstances, such as where public attendance or publication might prejudice the fairness of the trial.[98] A corollary of the requirement that the courts perform their work in public is that interested members of the public and the media have access not only to attend but also to publicise the content of proceedings. Perhaps one of the most important procedural contributions to transparency in the judicial process is the courts' publication of reasons. While the original justification for the provision of reasons stemmed from concerns about appellate rights,[99] more recently the judicial obligation to provide reasons has been linked with the administration of justice.[100] By laying bare the reasons that underlie judicial decisions, they can be scrutinised not only by the individuals who are immediately affected by the outcome of the case, but also by other members of the bench, academics,

---

[97] *R v Sussex Justices; Ex parte McCarthy* [1924] 1 KB 256, 259.

[98] Common law: see, e.g., *Scott v Scott* [1913] AC 417, 437; statute: see, e.g., *Court Suppression and Non-publication Orders Act 2010* (NSW).

[99] HP Lee and Enid Campbell, *The Australian Judiciary* (2nd ed., Cambridge University Press, 2012) 259.

[100] Justice Michael Kirby, 'Judicial Accountability in Australia' (2003) 6 *Legal Ethics* 41, 46.

the media, and the public more generally. This goal is furthered by the fact that, in most cases, judgments are published in accessible formats that can be widely accessed online. As has been argued in this book, this transparency process is a valuable means of securing the legitimacy of government.

A further means by which court processes support access to information is through mechanisms that allow access to government documents. Depending on the nature of the proceedings, pre-trial investigatory procedures may be used to compel officials to provide information, for example through discovery, subpoenas and interrogatories. These mechanisms are coercive in nature, allowing a prosecutor to bring the power of the court to bear in demanding the production of information that is relevant to the case (subject to claims of privilege and the like). Also depending on the type of proceedings, pleadings and evidence may further define the boundaries of the dispute between the parties and allow a prosecutor to draw the government respondent out on a particular issue. At the trial itself, the prosecuting party may have the opportunity to cross-examine and test the stories of officials involved in the dispute, clarifying outstanding questions about facts that may have previously been unclear. Again, because the courts adjudicate in public and the court's reasons are ultimately published, these procedural contributions can be viewed as playing a significant role in facilitating transparency not only within the confines of the courtroom, but more broadly.

In the context of Mr Obeid's prosecution, the utility of these various aspects of procedure was somewhat curtailed, both by the nature of criminal proceedings,[101] and by the use of non-publication orders during that case. The listing of Mr Obeid's trial, as well as a number of pre-trial applications and appeals from interlocutory decisions, were all made the subject of non-publication orders leading up to the first (aborted) trial.[102] The rationale for suppressing this information was to reduce material in the public domain that might otherwise have had a prejudicial impact on the fairness of the trial.[103] As a result, there could be no media publicity

---

[101] For example, an accused cannot be compelled to give evidence in criminal proceedings: *Evidence Act 1995* (NSW) s 17.

[102] *R v Obeid [No 4]* [2015] NSWSC 1442, [4]; *Obeid v The Queen [No 2]* (2016) 329 ALR 379.

[103] *R v Obeid* [2015] NSWSC 897. In the High Court, Gageler J's rationale was to avoid undermining the existing orders that had been made by judges in the NSW Supreme Court and Court of Appeal: *Obeid v The Queen [No 2]* (2016) 329 ALR 379, 383 [22].

about the fact that Mr Obeid was to be tried for the offence, of the outcomes of pre-trial applications or of the nature of the evidence presented at trial. The suppression orders ultimately lapsed – perhaps unintentionally – at the conclusion of the aborted first trial, but before the second trial commenced.[104] The second trial was then able to be publicised in the ordinary manner. The approach adopted in relation to publicity of the trial reflects a careful balance between the transparency rationale (which favours widespread access to information) and the desert rationale (which favours an agent-friendly approach in respect of the imposition of punitive sanctions).

(ii) **Burden of Proof**   In criminal law, the prosecuting party bears a significant onus both in terms of a legal and evidential burden. It is necessary to establish, 'beyond reasonable doubt', the legal elements making up the offence as well as evidentiary proof in support of those elements.[105] Returning to the hypothetical accountability benchmark, we would likely say that the criminal burden of proof (through which desert-oriented criminal sanctions are facilitated) is far more defendant-friendly than the civil burden of proof (through which control-oriented judicial review remedies and redress-oriented damages awards are facilitated). In this respect, the burden of proof in our hypothetical system aligns well with our benchmark. We can justify imposing a higher burden of proof for the criminal offence of misconduct in public office where the cause of action is desert-oriented: 'the justification for the [beyond reasonable doubt] standard ... is to be found in the retributive justification of punishment itself'.[106] If retribution is concerned with the ideas of punishing those who deserve it (and protecting those who do not) then adopting a higher burden of proof supports this goal.[107] By adopting this higher burden of proof, we reinforce the condemnatory features of the

---

[104] Following an unsuccessful application for a stay of the trial by the High Court, Gageler J made a non-publication order that was due to expire on a date after the first trial was due to conclude, with liberty to apply for variation: *Obeid v The Queen [No 2]* (2016) 329 ALR 379. After the first trial was aborted, no party applied for a variation and Gageler J's reasons were published online. The trial judge then lifted the non-publication orders made by the NSW Supreme Court on the basis that the publication of Gageler J's reasons negated their ongoing necessity: *R v Obeid [No 8]* [2016] NSWSC 388, [7].

[105] *May v O'Sullivan* (1955) 92 CLR 654, 657.

[106] Alec Walen, 'Proof Beyond a Reasonable Doubt: A Balanced Retributive Account' (2015) 76 *Louisiana Law Review* 355, 360.

[107] Ibid 426.

desert rationale of punishment, as we can assume that those who have met this high standard very likely deserve the punishment they receive. Were we to adopt a lower standard, such as that applicable in civil proceedings, we may risk capturing innocent parties and in turn undermine this condemnatory function.

(iii) **Remedial Discretion**   On conviction for the offence of misconduct in public office, the court has a relatively broad discretion to determine the appropriate sentence. As there is no specified maximum penalty for the common law offence of misconduct in public office, the sentencing judge in Mr Obeid's case utilised corresponding statutory offences as a reference point (i.e. seven years for bribery and corruption offences).[108] In sentencing Mr Obeid to a penalty of five years imprisonment, Beech-Jones J took into account a range of factors,[109] including the nature of the breach of duty, the damage occasioned to public confidence, principles of 'general deterrence and denunciation', the offender's prior good character (though to a lesser extent than in other cases) and other matters prescribed by statute.[110] The court also took into account mitigating factors, including that Mr Obeid had no record of previous convictions, that he was a person of good character, that he was unlikely to reoffend, that he had good prospects of rehabilitation and that he had co-operated in the conduct of the trial.[111]

This approach demonstrates the degree of discretion afforded to the court in determining the penalty applicable for the offence of misconduct in public office. While some offences prescribe more particular penalties or set maximum limits, the penalty for this common law offence is effectively at large. This highly discretionary process allows the court to take into account not only the nature of the offence, but also various mitigating factors that might weigh in the defendant's favour. Thus the court can adopt a flexible approach that tailors the sentence to the nature of the deliberate wrongdoing in which the offender has engaged, consistently with the desert aspect of the hypothetical accountability benchmark.

---

[108] *Crimes Act 1900* (NSW) Pt 4A; see *R v Obeid [No 12]* [2016] NSWSC 1815, [66]. His Honour considered the common law offence to be nonetheless more serious than these statutory analogues (at [70]).

[109] *R v Obeid [No 12]* [2016] NSWSC 1815, [82]–[94].

[110] Ibid [61]. See further *Crimes (Sentencing Procedure) Act 1999* (NSW) ss 3A, 21A(2)–(3).

[111] *R v Obeid [No 12]* [2016] NSWSC 1815, [129]–[132].

8.2.2.5   Misconduct: With What Consequences?

The final aspect of the hypothetical benchmark to consider is the *consequences* that flow from prosecution for the offence of misconduct in public office. As a common law offence, the penalties that may be handed down following a conviction for the offence are 'at large and in the discretion of the court',[112] with commonly imposed penalties including fines and terms of imprisonment. As was foreshadowed in Chapter 7, the literature on punishment broadly represents a battleground between retributivist and restorative justice theorists, arguing as to whether the function of punishment is one of condemning reprehensible conduct, imposing sanctions on those who deserve them, deterring future wrongdoing, reforming wrongdoers and a host of other possible explanations. In the context of this book, we can understand the retributivist approach to be aligned with the desert rationale of accountability. On this view, a primary function of punishment is to condemn intentional wrongdoing and mark public disapproval of conduct that would threaten the legitimacy of government if left unpunished. This accountability rationale is reflected in New South Wales sentencing legislation, which cites as two purposes of sentencing 'to make the offender accountable for his or her actions', and 'to denounce the conduct of the offender'.[113]

Imprisonment is the classic conception of criminal punishment: 'a clear case of punishment in the emphatic sense'.[114] It carries with it the 'symbolism of public reprobation'[115] that is key to the retributivist conception of legal punishment underlying the desert rationale of the hypothetical accountability benchmark. It is useful in this respect to consider the comments made by Beech-Jones J in sentencing Mr Obeid. Imposing a five-year term of imprisonment, Beech-Jones J placed weight on the public nature of the offence, describing it as a 'breach of trust in the form of a deliberate or reckless breach of a duty owed by a public official to the public'.[116] The 'real damage', for Beech-Jones J, was not reflected simply in the nature of the benefit obtained by Mr Obeid through his conduct, but instead was damage 'to the institutions of

---

[112] See *Blackstock v The Queen* [2013] NSWCCA 172, [8]. In Victoria, a ceiling of ten years' imprisonment applies: *Crimes Act 1958* (Vic) s 320.
[113] *Crimes (Sentencing Procedure) Act 1999* (NSW) s 3A.
[114] Joel Feinberg, 'The Expressive Function of Punishment' (1965) 49 *The Monist* 397, 398.
[115] Ibid 415.
[116] *R v Obeid [No 12]* [2016] NSWSC 1815, [79].

government and public confidence in them'.[117] It is useful to set out some of his Honour's concluding sentencing remarks in full:

> The overwhelming majority of parliamentarians are not motivated by an intention to enrich themselves or their families. Instead, they act in what they believe to be the best interests of the electorate, cognisant that the most likely reward for their service is persistent criticism and ultimately electoral rejection. The continuity and relative strength of our parliamentary democracy is a product of their efforts and the maintenance of public confidence in their honesty. All the work of parliamentarians can be destroyed by the wilful misconduct of only some of their members. Corruption by elected representatives consumes democracies. It destroys public confidence in democratic institutions. It opens up consideration of alternative modes of government, especially those that offer an illusion of security and order.[118]

We see here echoes of the overarching legitimacy objective of accountability, as his Honour links breach of trust with erosion of public confidence in the democratic system of government. It was on this basis that Beech-Jones J determined that the 'dominant considerations' in sentencing included 'denunciation and recognition of the harm done to the community',[119] and reached the view that no penalty other than imprisonment was appropriate.[120]

While a fine was not imposed in Mr Obeid's case, it is interesting to note its utility as an accountability sanction. By comparison to a term of imprisonment, a fine can be considered a less severe form of punishment, which is reflected in the New South Wales sentencing provision that imprisonment must not be imposed unless 'no penalty other than imprisonment is appropriate'.[121] As a form of penalty, a fine can be considered less intrusive than imprisonment from the perspective of an offender. While it may cause hardship in the immediate term, unlike a term of imprisonment it allows an offender to continue to engage in their social and professional life. Beyond this, there is a range of reasons why a fine might be considered a useful form of penalty: it can be tailored according to the severity of the offence and the means of the defendant; it can be reversed if a conviction is later discovered to be unsound; once

---

[117] Ibid [84].
[118] Ibid [137].
[119] Ibid [138].
[120] Ibid.
[121] *Crimes (Sentencing Procedure) Act 1999* (NSW) s 5(1).

exacted, there are no ongoing administration costs; and, perhaps most compellingly, the amount of the fine is reinvested into the public coffers.[122] This last point is particularly interesting in the context of the redress rationale for accountability. If we conceive of damage to public trust as a broadly conceived type of harm, we might think of the requirement to pay a fine into the central revenue as contributing to repair of that harm, increasing the funds available to improve public services going forward.

If imprisonment and fines are sufficiently condemnatory to satisfy the desert rationale of accountability, we might doubt whether they would fit with the deterrence rationale as it is framed in the present hypothetical.[123] The deterrence rationale looks to the imposition of *weak sanctions*, and if prison sentences and fines are of a condemnatory nature, it is difficult to see how they can also be characterised as 'weak sanctions'. This is reflected in Feinberg's distinction between punishments and 'mere penalties' described in Chapter 7 (see Section 7.2.3).[124] For Feinberg, to qualify as punishment a sanction must stand as a symbolic representation of society's condemnation of wrongdoing. If the weight of the sanction is not sufficiently severe to carry condemnation, then it will instead be of the character of a 'mere penalty'. Based on this analysis, we might reach the view that the penalties applicable for commission of the misconduct offence (and Mr Obeid's imprisonment) fall within the *desert*, rather than *deterrence*, category for the purposes of the hypothetical benchmark. This is certainly not to suggest that criminal penalties have no legitimate deterrent role in a more general sense. Rather, it demonstrates that if we construct a benchmark that seeks to achieve deterrence through the imposition of 'weak sanctions', we cannot then assign a serious penalty like imprisonment a deterrent function. To reiterate the observations made in Part II of this book, this is one of the inherent difficulties in defining a benchmark of accountability.

---

[122] Pat O'Malley, 'Theorizing Fines' (2009) 11 *Punishment and Society* 67, 67–68.

[123] As has been noted, this is not to say that there is no place for deterrence as a rationale for criminal law and criminal sanctions more generally. The point here is confined to the application of the *hypothetical* accountability benchmark.

[124] Feinberg, 'The Expressive Function of Punishment' (n 114) 398.

8.2.3   *What Does the Hypothetical Benchmark Tell Us in Eddie Obeid's Case?*

This section has deployed the transparency, desert and deterrence components of the hypothetical accountability benchmark to examine the operation of the NSW ICAC and the criminal offence of misconduct in public office in Mr Obeid's case. In doing so, neither mechanism was thought to meet all aspects of those various benchmark expectations:

(a) **Transparency**: In Mr Obeid's case, the ICAC's role was largely consistent with the hypothetical transparency benchmark. An anonymous member of the public was able to complain to the ICAC, thereby leading it to use its compulsory investigatory powers to uncover information about Mr Obeid's conduct. The ICAC was able to hold a public inquiry, which facilitated members of the public being made aware of these potential corruption issues, and was able to prepare a report on its findings that was both tabled in Parliament and publicly released. Criminal proceedings also made some contribution towards transparency through the principles of open justice which support public awareness of an accused's wrongdoing. However, criminal proceedings provide no direct right of access to information, and the content of the evidence presented is confined by the rules of admissibility and tactical choices by the parties. Further, in Mr Obeid's case, public awareness was hampered by the extensive use of non-publication orders in the lead-up to the trial. In this respect, we might conclude that the ICAC investigation was more closely aligned with the hypothetical transparency benchmark than the criminal proceedings.

(b) **Desert**: Criminal proceedings are well aligned with the expectations of the hypothetical desert rationale. Mr Obeid (a former Member of Parliament) was able to be prosecuted for his deliberate wrongdoing (using his position in an attempt to benefit his family's financial interests), by a defined prosecutor (in this case, the NSW DPP – though rights of private prosecution were also available). The procedures adopted were agent-friendly (e.g. the high burden of proof placed on prosecutors), and the sanctions imposed were highly punitive (i.e. a five-year term of imprisonment). On the whole, this mechanism can be viewed as conformable with the expectations of the desert rationale in the hypothetical benchmark.

    In contrast, the ICAC investigation is unlikely to be viewed as satisfying the desert rationale. The mechanism did meet the 'who', 'to whom' and 'for what' components of the benchmark in allowing a defined prosecutor to target Mr Obeid and to make findings that the misuse of his official position was 'wilful'. However, the ICAC investigation did not meet benchmark expectations of 'how' accountability was delivered; the hypothetical desert benchmark anticipates the imposition of highly punitive sanctions in order to reflect public outrage at the deliberate abuse of public power, and subjection to the ICAC investigation and reporting process is likely not sufficient to meet this expectation. Further, even if it was, the procedures employed by the ICAC would exceed the desert benchmark, which requires punitive sanctions to be delivered only via agent-friendly procedures. The extensive investigatory powers afforded to the ICAC, the informality of the process and lack of rigorous rules of evidence make it a decidedly prosecutor-friendly regime.

(c) **Deterrence**: The hypothetical benchmark is defined in terms that demand the application of 'weak sanctions' to 'soft targets' with a view to facilitating dialogue.[125] The ICAC's reporting function is well aligned with this expectation, allowing it to make recommendations to Parliament regarding the amendment of the parliamentary Code of Conduct to better address improper influence by Members of Parliament. While this process has not yet led to substantive change, it satisfied the benchmark's expectations of a flexible and dialogue-focused mechanism to discourage future wrongdoing. In contrast, the misconduct offence offers minimal contribution to this view of deterrence; there are likely better 'soft targets' than Mr Obeid who have the ability to facilitate forward-looking change. As a former parliamentarian, Mr Obeid is unlikely to have the ability to influence meaningful systemic change, such as a revision of ethical standards. Further, the sanctions imposed for the offence are highly punitive. Employing the hypothetical deterrence benchmark, we would likely say that the misconduct offence exceeds its expectations on this score.

If we were to accept the validity of the hypothetical accountability benchmark, it might lead us to draw a number of tentative conclusions about the accountability performance of the NSW ICAC and criminal

---

[125] See discussion in Section 8.5 below regarding the limitations of adopting this benchmark.

prosecution in Mr Obeid's case. For instance, the ICAC investigation was thought to be quite well aligned with the hypothetical deterrence benchmark. However, it was unable to deliver punitive sanctions of the nature anticipated by the hypothetical desert benchmark (though subjection to the public inquiry would doubtless have been an unpleasant experience for Mr Obeid). We might therefore reach the view that the consequences delivered in Mr Obeid's case fell short of the benchmark, representing a potential *accountability deficit*. At the other extreme, it was noted that the ICAC's highly prosecutor-friendly procedures went much further than the desert benchmark's expectation that sanctions be delivered via agent-friendly procedures. Again, if we adopt a desert-oriented accountability benchmark in the terms of the hypothetical, we might therefore reach the view that the procedures employed by the ICAC in Mr Obeid's case represent a potential *accountability overload*. The criminal prosecution for misconduct in public office also failed to meet all benchmark expectations. While broadly satisfying the hypothetical desert benchmark, the criminal prosecution fell short of the expectations of the deterrence rationale. While many maintain that criminal sanctions have a specific and general deterrent effect,[126] the hypothetical deterrence benchmark requires the application of 'weak sanctions' aimed at facilitating dialogue. When measured against that expectation, criminal prosecution represents a potential *accountability overload* as the sanctions imposed exceed those demands. Adopting Braithwaite's approach, the infliction of highly punitive sanctions might risk a counterproductive response of 'reactance' that would be contrary to the deterrence objective of fostering improvements in public service delivery.

Of course, these tentative conclusions must be read subject to a range of caveats which are explained in the conclusion to this chapter.[127] Further, as argued in Part III of this book the identification of a potential accountability deficit or overload in a particular mechanism can only ever stand as a preliminary observation until it is located within the wider context of mechanisms relevant in that situation. As explored in Chapter 11, the concerns raised here about the NSW ICAC investigation and criminal prosecution of Mr Obeid may be resolved when the two mechanisms are considered as part of an accountability system rather than as two mechanisms operating in isolation.

---

[126] See discussion of this point in Section 7.2.4 in Chapter 7.
[127] See Section 8.5 below.

8.3 *Ruddock v Taylor*: Damages for Administrative Error

The second accountability scenario used to demonstrate the application of the hypothetical benchmark is the imprisonment of Mr Graham Taylor pursuant to migration detention procedures in 2000. The authority for the detention was found to be legally unsound in judicial review proceedings, and Mr Taylor subsequently (and unsuccessfully) sought damages in civil proceedings pursuant to the tort of false imprisonment. This section considers the utility of judicial review and tort proceedings as accountability mechanisms in Mr Taylor's case.

Mr Taylor was born in the United Kingdom and moved to Australia as a young child in the 1960s. He did not apply for Australian citizenship, but held two forms of visa in recognition of the duration of his time spent in the country. He lived most of his life in a rural town in New South Wales, never leaving Australia. In 1996, Mr Taylor was sentenced to a term of three and a half years imprisonment after pleading guilty to a number of charges involving sexual offences against children. On his release from prison in 1999, Mr Taylor returned to his home town. Months later, Mr Taylor's visas were cancelled by the Minister for Immigration and Multicultural Affairs. The power to cancel was set out in s 501(2) of the *Migration Act 1958* (Cth), which allowed the Minister to cancel a visa if two conditions were satisfied: (a) 'the Minister reasonably suspects that the person does not pass the character test', and (b) 'the person does not satisfy the Minister that the person passes the character test'. The character test was statutorily defined to capture those with a substantial criminal record (i.e. having been sentenced to a term of twelve or more months' imprisonment).[128] Mr Taylor was arrested and taken into detention. Due to his history of offences against children, he was held in a state prison rather than an immigration detention centre. Mr Taylor brought judicial review proceedings before the High Court of Australia alleging denial of procedural fairness in the visa cancellation decision. Those proceedings were resolved in Mr Taylor's favour by consent, with Callinan J making orders of prohibition and certiorari. Mr Taylor was then released from detention and returned to his home after being held for a period of 161 days.

Months later, Mr Taylor's visas were again cancelled, this time by the Parliamentary Secretary to the Minister. A different provision was relied on this time, which allowed the Minister to cancel a visa without

---

[128] *Migration Act 1958* (Cth) s 501(6)–(7).

according natural justice if (a) 'the Minister reasonably suspects that the person does not pass the character test', and (b) 'the Minister is satisfied that the refusal or cancellation is in the national interest'.[129] Mr Taylor was again taken into custody and detained as a non-citizen in state prison facilities. Mr Taylor brought a second set of proceedings for judicial review. The High Court found in Mr Taylor's favour,[130] and he was released having been detained for a period of 155 days.

Mr Taylor subsequently commenced civil proceedings against the Minister, the Parliamentary Secretary and the immigration officers who detained him. The cause of action was the tort of false imprisonment. Mr Taylor obtained a judgment in his favour at first instance, and was awarded a relatively significant sum in damages.[131] Both parties appealed; the Commonwealth against the finding of liability, and Mr Taylor against the assessment of damages. The NSW Court of Appeal dismissed both appeals,[132] leaving the first judgment intact. On appeal to the High Court, the judgment was overturned in favour of the Commonwealth, finding that there was no liability in tort.

What, then, can the hypothetical accountability benchmark tell us about this scenario? The relevant accountability rationales would be as follows:

(a) the **transparency** rationale would require that there is a mechanism available to uncover the circumstances surrounding the cancellation decisions and Mr Taylor's detention;

(b) the **control** rationale would require a mechanism that delivers regulatory orders with a view to bringing the misdirected exercise of public power back within legal limits;

(c) the **redress** rationale would require the availability of reparative remedies to respond to Mr Taylor's two periods of unlawful detention; and

(d) the **deterrence** rationale would require dialogue-driven sanctions that foster improvements in immigration decision-making processes to prevent such circumstances arising in the future.

---

[129] Ibid s 501(3)(c)–(d).
[130] *Re Patterson; Ex parte Taylor* (2001) 207 CLR 391.
[131] *Taylor v Ruddock* (District Court of NSW, Murrell J, 18 December 2002). The amount awarded was AU$116,000.
[132] *Ruddock v Taylor* (2003) 58 NSWLR 269.

The desert rationale (which is concerned with punishing intentional wrongdoing) would not be relevant as the various officials in Mr Taylor's case acted in the belief that their conduct was lawful. The following sections consider the extent to which the mechanisms of judicial review and the tort of false imprisonment aligned with the relevant accountability objectives in Mr Taylor's case.

8.3.1 *Judicial Review*

Judicial review can be understood to be a keystone of the accountability system in Australia; for Mulgan, judicial review 'is in some respects the most powerful form of external review of executive action' and a 'fundamental prerequisite for effective executive accountability'.[133] While the courts do not tend to use the language of 'accountability' when describing their role in adjudicating these cases, the concept of accountability is manifest in two fundamental constitutional principles: the rule of law and the separation of powers.[134] We can view these three concepts as overlapping and interdependent on one another; the rule of law requires that government officials be bound by the law, accountability is the machinery for enforcement of that principle, and the separation of powers provides the framework within which that enforcement can take place.[135] In Australia, judicial review encompasses the body of law that provides for judicial review of executive, legislative and judicial power, with jurisdiction sourced in the common law, the *Constitution* and state and federal legislation.[136] In Mr Taylor's case, judicial review was sought pursuant to the High Court's jurisdiction under s 75(v) of the *Constitution*. The following sections explore the extent to which this

---

[133] Richard Mulgan, *Holding Power to Account: Accountability in Modern Democracies* (Palgrave Macmillan, 2003) 75–76. See also AJ Brown, 'Putting Administrative Law Back into Integrity and Putting Integrity Back into Administrative Law' (2006) 53 *AIAL Forum* 32, 32, describing administrative law as 'the law of public accountability'.

[134] This is an idea I have expanded on more fully elsewhere: Ellen Rock, 'Accountability: A Core Public Law Value?' (2017) 24 *Australian Journal of Administrative Law* 189, 190–92. See also Janina Boughey and Greg Weeks, 'Government Accountability as a "Constitutional Value"' in Rosalind Dixon (ed.), *Australian Constitutional Values* (Hart Publishing, 2017) 99.

[135] Rock, 'Accountability: A Core Public Law Value?' (n 134) 190. See further *Corporation of the City of Enfield v Development Assessment Commission* (2000) 199 CLR 135, 157 (Gaudron J).

[136] At the Commonwealth level, statutory jurisdiction to engage in judicial review is established under the *Administrative Decisions (Judicial Review) Act 1977* (Cth).

mechanism aligns with the expectations of the transparency, control, redress and deterrence aspects of the hypothetical accountability benchmark.

8.3.1.1   Who Is Held Accountable in Judicial Review Proceedings?

The hypothetical benchmark anticipates the availability of mechanisms that are variously able to target all individuals/entities within government (transparency), the individual/entity charged with exercising power (control), the government as an entity (redress) and officials or entities with the capacity to effect change (deterrence). In looking at the defendant in judicial review proceedings, this cause of action is most clearly aligned with the control rationale.

The reach of modern judicial review is very extensive, providing a means to challenge the exercise of power by individuals and entities within all three branches of government. While broad, this reach is not unlimited. One of the primary limits on the availability of constitutional review under s 75(v) of the *Constitution* is that it is only available in respect of decisions made by an 'officer of the Commonwealth'.[137] This phrase has been interpreted as limiting the constitutional review jurisdiction to individual office-holders, thereby excluding judicial review of decisions made by public corporations,[138] public entities operating at arm's length from the government[139] or state officers exercising federal power.[140] One of the most important limits on the reach of judicial review, for present purposes, is in respect of the ability to bring proceedings against private contractors who are charged with the exercise of public power. Unlike the approach adopted in the United Kingdom,[141] the Australian courts have not expanded the reach of judicial review (including under s 75(v)) to capture the exercise of outsourced public

---

[137] For a comprehensive overview, see Mark Aronson, Matthew Groves and Greg Weeks, *Judicial Review of Administrative Action and Government Liability* (6th ed., Thomson Reuters, 2017) [2.150]–[2.160].

[138] See, e.g., *Businessworld Computers Pty Ltd v Australian Telecommunications Commission* (1988) 82 ALR 499, 500.

[139] E.g. *Waterhouse v Australian Broadcasting Corp* (Unreported, Federal Court, Wilcox J, 21 October 1987); *Aboriginal Land Council (NSW) v Aboriginal and Torres Strait Island Commission* (Unreported, Federal Court, Hill J, 30 August 1995). See further Matthew Groves, 'Outsourcing and s 75(v) of the Constitution' (2011) 22 *Public Law Review* 3, 4.

[140] See, e.g., *R v Bevan; Ex parte Elias and Gordon* (1942) 66 CLR 452, 462.

[141] As represented in *R v Panel on Takeovers and Mergers; Ex parte Datafin Plc* [1987] QB 815.

power.[142] Though not relevant in Mr Taylor's case, this might raise the prospect of a potential area of accountability deficit.[143]

Putting to one side these particular difficulties of review under s 75(v), judicial review is generally well aligned with the task of targeting the repository of public power, as required by the control aspect of the hypothetical benchmark. So, rather than focusing only on an individual, or hierarchical, or corporate accountability model, we see that judicial review instead adopts whichever model is appropriate to target the person upon whom power has been conferred. We see that in cases where a power has been conferred on, and is exercised by, an individual, the appropriate respondent in judicial review claims will be that individual.[144] So, for instance, if a government minister makes a decision pursuant to a statutory power conferred on that minister, the appropriate respondent in proceedings for judicial review of that decision is that individual minister. In comparison, we see that in cases where power has been conferred on one party, but has been exercised by another, judicial review adopts the hierarchical model of accountability. For instance, in many cases an executive decision-maker will rely on reports or summaries prepared by their subordinates.[145] Deficiencies in that summary (e.g. failure to set out a material fact) are ultimately laid at the feet of the decision-maker rather than with the officers who prepared the summary.[146] The hierarchical accountability model is also reflected in the *Carltona*,[147] or 'alter ego', principle. While 'administrative necessity' allows a senior official to act through their subordinate officers in certain cases,[148] accountability ultimately rests with the senior official rather than with the individual officer who made the relevant error in line with

---

[142] See, e.g., Aronson, Groves and Weeks (n 137) [3.180]; Boughey, Rock and Weeks (n 9) [3.5.2].

[143] Janina Boughey and Greg Weeks, '"Officers of the Commonwealth" in the Private Sector: Can the High Court Review Outsourced Exercises of Power?' (2013) 36 *University of New South Wales Law Journal* 316, 323.

[144] This is reinforced by High Court procedural rules, which require that where an applicant seeks a writ of mandamus or prohibition is against an officer of the Commonwealth, 'the officer shall be described in the title of the proceeding by the office held' and that in all other cases, a defendant may either be named personally or by reference to their office: *High Court Rules 2004* (Cth) rr 25.02.2–25.02.3.

[145] For example, in *Minister for Aboriginal Affairs v Peko-Wallsend Ltd* (1986) 162 CLR 24, the minister relied on a summary of relevant facts prepared by departmental officers.

[146] Ibid 31.

[147] So named for the case of *Carltona Ltd v Commissioners of Works* [1943] 2 All ER 560.

[148] *Minister for Aboriginal Affairs v Peko-Wallsend Ltd* (1986) 162 CLR 24, 38.

an agency approach. Finally, we see that where power has been conferred on a government entity, and is exercised by individuals on behalf of that entity, judicial review adopts the corporate accountability model. The corporate approach is evident in the line of authority testing the reach of s 75(v) of the *Constitution*. For example, where a public body has made a decision, naming individual officers of that body as respondents to circumvent the 'officer of the Commonwealth' limitation has been described as 'colourable'.[149] This is because decisions made by such bodies represent 'collegiate acts' rather than 'the actions, conduct or decisions of the individual members'.[150] Likewise, in cases where a decision is made by a court or tribunal, that body, rather than the members or judges constituting it, is the appropriate respondent in judicial review proceedings.[151]

As a cause of action, judicial review is therefore well aligned with the *control* rationale for accountability, moving between individual, hierarchical and corporate accountability models with the goal of attaching liability to the party on whom public power has been conferred. In Mr Taylor's case, judicial review proceedings were brought respectively against Mr Ruddock[152] and Ms Patterson[153] in respect of the visa cancellation decisions made by each of them. These cancellation powers were conferred on 'the Minister',[154] and the court accepted that both Mr Ruddock and Ms Patterson were acting *as* the Minister for the purpose of exercising the relevant powers.[155] Mr Taylor's two judicial review proceedings were therefore conformable with the control aspect of the hypothetical benchmark, in targeting the repository of the power as the relevant respondent.

We might also say that judicial review proceedings are broadly consistent with the *deterrence* aspect of the benchmark, which anticipates the

---

[149] *Vietnam Veterans' Affairs Association of Australia New South Wales Branch Inc v Cohen* (1996) 70 FCR 419, 432–33 (Tamberlin J).

[150] Ibid 432; cf *Broadbent v Medical Board of Queensland* (2011) 195 FCR 438, 464 [103] and Aronson, Groves and Weeks (n 137) [2.160].

[151] E.g. *Re Refugee Review Tribunal; Ex parte Aala* (2000) 204 CLR 82, 90–91 [14]; *SAAP v Minister for Immigration and Multicultural and Indigenous Affairs* (2005) 228 CLR 294, 310 [43]; *Sinkovich v Attorney General (NSW)* (2013) 85 NSWLR 783, 787–88 [13].

[152] *Re Ruddock; Ex parte Taylor* [2000] HCATrans 101 (16 March 2000).

[153] *Re Patterson; Ex parte Taylor* (2001) 207 CLR 391.

[154] More precisely, the power in s 501(3) must be exercised by the Minister personally, while the power in s 501(2) can be exercised by the Minister or a delegate: *Migration Act 1958* (Cth) s 501(4).

[155] See, e.g., *Re Patterson; Ex parte Taylor* (2001) 207 CLR 391, 403 [17].

application of weak sanctions to officials or entities with the capacity to effect change. By targeting the party that is charged with exercising the power in question, judicial review proceedings narrowly concentrate their attention on the official that is in the most immediate position to alter the way in which that power is exercised going forward. We might take the view, therefore, that judicial review proceedings offer the repositories of government power specific guidance on the limits of their powers, thereby encouraging them to remain within those boundaries when the power is exercised in the future. We might also wonder whether other public officials might take heed of this guidance in exercising their own powers.[156] However, this flow-on general deterrent effect is not of the type envisaged by the deterrence rationale, which is more concerned with facilitating widespread systemic change. A more comprehensive approach, perhaps, would be one that targeted legislators and policy-makers with a view to better defining the scope of the powers in question, or offering guidance on the manner in which they should be exercised. That approach would have the benefit not only of influencing the exercise of the particular power in question, but could also more widely impact on related areas.

It is also less clear how well judicial review proceedings align with the remaining accountability rationales. The limited scope of parties amenable to judicial review proceedings offers minimal contribution to the transparency aspect of the benchmark, which anticipates a wider right of access to information about how a decision was made from *all individuals/entities within government*. We would also doubt the degree of contribution to the redress aspect of the benchmark, which is concerned with targeting the *government as an entity* rather than the individual repository of the power in question. In conclusion, when we look at the respondent in judicial review proceedings we would say that this cause of action most clearly aligns with the *control* aspect of the hypothetical benchmark.

8.3.1.2 To Whom Are They Accountable?

The hypothetical benchmark of accountability anticipates that, for the purposes of the control and transparency rationales, the government will

---

[156] For discussion of empirical research on the impact of judicial review on administrative decision-making, see, e.g., Simon Halliday and Colin Scott, 'Administrative Justice' in Peter Cane and Herbert Kritzer (eds.), *The Oxford Handbook of Empirical Legal Research* (Oxford University Press, 2010) 469.

be answerable to all members of the public. The remaining relevant rationales are, in contrast, more confined. The redress rationale limits access to those who have suffered harm, while the deterrence aspect of the benchmark anticipates that the government will be accountable only to a defined prosecutor. Judicial review proceedings employ the legal concept of standing to define the party entitled to commence a claim, and in looking at these rules it is possible to see a tension between these various expectations.

The approach to standing adopted by the Australian courts has been described as 'far from coherent',[157] with some cases suggesting a movement towards adopting a single test of standing, and others adopting different tests depending on the form of relief sought. This leaves a proliferation of similar, but distinct, tests that apply depending on the remedy and procedure adopted by an applicant. These tests range from a focus on the immediate parties to the decision, those with a 'legal specific right',[158] those who are 'aggrieved',[159] those with a 'special interest in the subject matter of the action'[160] and even 'strangers'.[161] While each of these tests purport to apply different standards, they all follow the same trajectory in focusing on the nature of the applicant's interest in the decision, asking whether they are a 'mere intermeddler or busybody',[162] as opposed to someone with a genuine grievance. In the Australian constitutional context, these standing limitations are also reflected in the High Court's jurisdiction to adjudicate 'matters', which limits the court's intervention to the determination of present judicial controversies (i.e. involving 'some immediate right, duty or liability') as opposed to hypothetical questions.[163]

Aside from the occasional expansion of standing tests to accommodate 'strangers', we can view all of these various tests as broadly aligned with the *redress* rationale for accountability. Certainly, the tests reveal a

---

[157] *Bateman's Bay Local Aboriginal Land Council v Aboriginal Community Benefit Fund Pty Ltd* (1998) 194 CLR 247, 279–80.

[158] *R v Commissioners of Customs and Excise; Ex parte Cook* [1970] 1 WLR 450.

[159] *R v Justices of Surrey* [1870] LR 5 QB 466.

[160] *Australian Conservation Foundation Inc v Commonwealth* (1980) 146 CLR 493, 527.

[161] Being persons 'without a relevant legal interest': *Re Refugee Review Tribunal; Ex parte Aala* (2000) 204 CLR 82, 104–05 [48]–[49].

[162] *United States Tobacco Co v Minister for Consumer Affairs* (1988) 20 FCR 520, 527.

[163] *Re Judiciary and Navigation Acts* (1921) 29 CLR 257, 265. The High Court has observed this degree of overlap: *Truth About Motorways Pty Ltd v Macquarie Infrastructure Management Ltd* (2000) 200 CLR 591, 637 [122].

preference for a person who, if not having suffered direct harm, has a personal bone to pick in relation to a government decision. This is a far cry from the expectation of the control rationale that a mechanism is accessible to 'all members of the public'. Calls for the abandonment of judicial review standing tests are certainly nothing new,[164] and allowing open standing would go some way towards bringing judicial review into alignment with the control and transparency rationales for accountability. 'Public interest' motivated claims may raise the spectre of very different types of issues as compared with claims motivated by private interests, and may be no less deserving of judicial scrutiny.[165] Indeed, there might be cases in which there is no party with the requisite degree of private interest (or inclination) to bring proceedings, leaving illegal government action to go unchallenged.[166] Against this, we must balance the reality that open standing would potentially shift the choice to litigate away from the parties most immediately affected by a decision,[167] with the effect, for example, that a person who has been granted a liquor licence might see it revoked following proceedings by a community group advocating greater regulation of alcohol. Such concerns might be of critical importance for the purposes of the redress rationale, which is concerned with leaving the choice of prosecution within the hands of the individual who has been harmed. However, the control rationale is driven by different considerations, namely to ensure that public power is exercised legally. If this is our core concern, open standing would appear to be an attractive option.

Some might argue that concerns about standing tests may be ameliorated by the mechanism of the Attorney-General's fiat, which allows a party to commence proceedings in the name of the Attorney-General.[168] For the purposes of the accountability benchmark, this mechanism performs two roles. First, this assigns a defined prosecutor the role of

---

[164] See, e.g., Louis Jaffe, 'Standing to Secure Judicial Review: Public Actions' (1961) 74 *Harvard Law Review* 1265; Mark Leeming, 'Standing to Seek Injunctions against Officers of the Commonwealth' (2006) 1 *Journal of Equity* 3.

[165] Peter Cane, 'Standing Up for the Public' [1995] *Public Law* 276, 277.

[166] There are of course other counter-arguments to consider: see, e.g., Carol Harlow, 'Public Law and Popular Justice' (2002) 65 *Modern Law Review* 1, 2.

[167] Elizabeth Fisher and Jeremy Kirk, 'Still Standing: An Argument for Open Standing in Australia and England' (1997) 71 *Australian Law Journal* 370, 373–74.

[168] Roger Douglas, 'Standing' in Matthew Groves and HP Lee (eds.), *Australian Administrative Law: Fundamentals, Principles and Doctrines* (Cambridge University Press, 2007) 158, 159.

managing public interest litigation, consistently with the demands of the deterrence rationale. Secondly, the ability of a public interest litigant to approach the Attorney-General may operate as a residual safety net in supporting the control rationale, ensuring that even if not 'all members of the public' can bring proceedings directly, there is at least a mechanism available to ask another to bring the proceedings in their stead. There are reasons, however, why we might have some concerns about relying on the fiat mechanism as residual 'safety net'. First, the decision as to whether or not to allow the fiat is a matter entirely within the discretion of the Attorney-General, with a decision to refuse being non-justiciable.[169] Secondly, there is a risk (however small) that, as a member of the government, the Attorney-General may conceivably be influenced by political motivations. This possibility was hinted at in *Bateman's Bay Local Aboriginal Land Council v Aboriginal Community Benefit Fund Pty Ltd*:

> it may be 'somewhat visionary' for citizens in this country to suppose that they may rely upon the grant of the Attorney-General's fiat for protection against ultra vires action of statutory bodies for the administration of which a ministerial colleague is responsible.[170]

From an accountability perspective, even this theoretical possibility is of importance, as perceived accountability shortfalls may pose as great a threat to public confidence in the legitimacy of government as those which are borne out.

In summary, we might conclude that the party *to whom* the government is accountable via judicial review proceedings reveals tensions within our hypothetical benchmark of accountability. In their orthodox form, standing rules tend to be more closely aligned with the redress rationale, notwithstanding that (as argued in Section 8.3.1.5 below) redress via judicial review remedies is largely a matter of co-incidence rather than design. The relaxation of these rules to facilitate public interest litigation – which would be a better reflection of the control and transparency rationales – has not been facilitated. While the availability of the Attorney-General's fiat might go some way towards ameliorating the limitations of standing rules, this has its limitations in cases where the fiat is denied, whether or not with the design of avoiding scrutiny of government activities.

---

[169] Ibid.
[170] (1998) 194 CLR 247, 262–63 [38] (Gaudron, Gummow and McHugh JJ).

In looking at the hypothetical accountability benchmark, the first observation that we might make is in respect of accountability overloads. The deterrence rationale anticipates that dialogue will be instituted by a *defined prosecutor*, and standing rules which provide a right of access to a class of individuals go beyond this expectation. At the other extreme, we might also be concerned about the potential for accountability deficits in connection with the transparency and control aspects of the hypothetical benchmark. This is because circumstances may arise (for example, government decisions about environmental matters) in which members of the public may be unable to establish standing. By limiting access to a defined class, the accountability mechanism of judicial review might in those cases give rise to an accountability deficit. These concerns, of course, did not play out in Mr Taylor's case. As an individual who was directly impacted by the visa cancellation decisions, it was uncontroversial that he would be able to establish standing to bring proceedings against the Minister and Secretary. We can conclude, therefore, that while the mechanism of judicial review might potentially fail to align with the hypothetical accountability benchmark in some circumstances, no such difficulties arose in Mr Taylor's case.

8.3.1.3 What Conduct Does Judicial Review Target?

Each of the aspects of the hypothetical benchmark target slightly different types of conduct. The transparency rationale is most broad, attaching to all government decisions and conduct. The control and redress rationales both target the unlawful exercise of power, with the additional qualification that the redress rationale is concerned only with circumstances where that exercise of power causes harm. Finally, the deterrence rationale is concerned with unsatisfactory rules, procedures or practices that should be discouraged or improved. In Australia, judicial review is most conformable with the control aspect of the benchmark, as it is concerned with controlling power in excess of jurisdiction.

The concept of jurisdictional error has come to play an extremely important role in the context of judicial review in Australia. For present purposes, jurisdictional error is relevant for two reasons. First, it plays a defining role with respect to the powers of each of the branches of government, as it provides a hard limit on the legislature's ability to remove the court's powers of judicial review.[171] Secondly, it determines

---

[171] See Section 11.2.1 in Chapter 11.

the types of relief that may be available, as establishing jurisdictional error is a prerequisite for entitlement to access the constitutional writs.[172] The concept of jurisdictional error therefore defines what types of *unlawful conduct* can be reviewed under s 75(v). In essence, a jurisdictional error is one that a decision-maker was not authorised to make, taking a decision-maker outside the legal reaches of their power.[173] The label has been described as 'conclusory',[174] in the sense that it describes an end product rather than offering a means to reach it. That means, at least for statutory powers, is through statutory interpretation, querying whether it was Parliament's intent that the particular error would result in the invalidity of the decision.[175] More recently, the High Court has had regard to the practical impact of the error in determining whether or not it is jurisdictional (i.e. whether 'compliance with the condition could have resulted in the making of a different decision').[176]

Given that each case must be decided by reference to the terms on which the power is conferred as well as the practical consequences of the error, it is not possible to offer a list of errors that will be treated as jurisdictional. It suffices to say that errors comprising essentially the full gambit of common law judicial review grounds (e.g. failure to accord procedural fairness, acting for an improper purpose, taking into account irrelevant considerations, acting in bad faith and so on) have been thought jurisdictional in one case or another.[177] What is clear is that before we can determine when relief pursuant to s 75(v) is available, an error must meet this threshold.[178] Perhaps more importantly, if our benchmark of accountability requires that control be achieved through

---

[172] For prohibition and mandamus, see *Plaintiff S157/2002 v Commonwealth* (2003) 211 CLR 476, 508 [82]. Certiorari does not extend to errors of law on the face of the record for the purposes of s 75(v): *Re Minister for Immigration and Multicultural Affairs; Ex parte Durairajasingham* (2000) 58 ALD 609, 617 [29]. In contrast, injunctive and declaratory relief in the context of s 75(v) may extend beyond jurisdictional error: *Plaintiff S157/2002 v Commonwealth* (2003) 211 CLR 476, 508 [82]; *Federal Commissioner of Taxation v Futuris Corporation Ltd* (2008) 237 CLR 146, 162 [47].

[173] See Boughey, Rock and Weeks (n 9) [5.2].

[174] Mark Aronson, 'Jurisdictional Error without the Tears' in Matthew Groves and HP Lee (eds.), *Australian Administrative Law: Fundamentals, Principles and Doctrines* (Cambridge University Press, 2007) 330, 344.

[175] *Project Blue Sky Inc v Australian Broadcasting Authority* (1998) 194 CLR 355.

[176] *Hossain v Minister for Immigration and Border Protection* (2018) 264 CLR 123, 135 [31].

[177] See, e.g., Caron Beaton-Wells, 'Judicial Review of Migration Decisions: Life after S157' (2005) 33 *Federal Law Review* 141. For a detailed overview of the grounds of judicial review, see, e.g., Aronson, Groves and Weeks (n 137) chs 4–9.

[178] Though note the observations at n 172 above.

attaching regulatory orders to the *unlawful exercise of public power* more generally, we must move beyond identifying conduct to which the constitutional writs *do* attach (i.e. jurisdictional error), and instead focus on the conduct to which they do *not*. In this context, our goal would be to define the concept of 'non-jurisdictional' error, which can be understood as comprising the residue of errors that fall beyond classification as jurisdictional. Examples of errors falling into this wider class as identified in recent cases include breach of a statutory requirement to provide reasons,[179] contravention of a state-based human rights charter[180] and assessing facts by reference to the wrong date.[181] Again, however, it is not possible to extrapolate a general rule from these findings, as the question of whether an error is jurisdictional (or non-jurisdictional) can only be determined through analysis of the relevant statutory scheme and the materiality of the error.

Returning to the hypothetical accountability benchmark, the control rationale has been defined such that it will be engaged in response to the *unlawful exercise of public power*. If we adopt a broad view of 'unlawfulness', we might not only be concerned to control conduct that goes beyond strict jurisdictional limits; we might also be inclined to define our benchmark to capture other errors which, though not jurisdictional, nonetheless involve a breach of defined legal boundaries. If we adopt this broad view of unlawfulness, we might doubt whether judicial review pursuant to s 75(v) would satisfy the benchmark. Most, if not all, of the available remedies under s 75(v) are confined by reference to the concept of jurisdictional error. While a wide variety of errors has been found to meet this criterion, there are many errors that may not. And if judicial review pursuant to s 75(v) is the means by which we seek to control the unlawful exercise of public power, then we would reach the view that it under-performs against that benchmark.

In Mr Taylor's case, his visa cancellations were effected pursuant to two separate decisions. In respect of the first decision, made by the

---

[179] *Re Minister for Immigration and Multicultural and Indigenous Affairs; Ex parte Palme* (2003) 216 CLR 212.

[180] *Bare v Independent Broad-Based Anti-Corruption Commission* (2015) 48 VR 129, 176 [139] (Warren CJ); 327 [617] (Santamaria JA), cited in Janina Boughey and Lisa Burton Crawford, 'Reconsidering *R (on the application of Cart) v Upper Tribunal* and the Rationale for Jurisdictional Error' [2017] *Public Law* 592, 600.

[181] *Hossain v Minister for Immigration and Border Protection* (2018) 264 CLR 123. This error was treated as non-jurisdictional on the basis that it did not affect the outcome of the decision (i.e. was non-material).

Minister, Mr Taylor alleged that he had been denied procedural fairness in light of a misleading representation made by departmental staff to the effect that he would have an opportunity to be heard, uncorrected in later dealings.[182] Ultimately, the Minister conceded the position and orders were made by consent quashing the cancellation decision.[183] Accordingly – though resolved by consent – judicial review proceedings in this first case enabled Mr Taylor to hold the Minister accountable for breach of an obligation of procedural fairness, which was a compulsory requirement in the exercise of the visa cancellation power.

In relation to the second decision, made by the Secretary, there were two separate bases on which the Secretary was alleged to have erred in the exercise of the power. The first, and which received the most attention, was a constitutional argument to the effect that the cancellation decision was beyond power because the relevant provision of the *Migration Act 1958* (Cth)[184] did not apply to Mr Taylor. By a majority of 4:3, it was held that the provision could not support the cancellation of Mr Taylor's visas as he was not an 'alien' for constitutional purposes.[185] In this respect, the case marked a turning point in 'alien' jurisprudence, overturning previous authority to the effect that a British subject who had lived in Australia since childhood could be deported pursuant to similar powers.[186] The new path, however, was quickly cut short, with the decision in Mr Taylor's case being overruled only two years later.[187] For present purposes, this evolving jurisprudence offers useful insights into the potential transience of the concept of 'unlawfulness' as a measure of 'for what' we hold an actor accountable. What was considered lawful in the year 2000 was considered unlawful in 2001, but was again lawful in 2003. The shift in legal boundaries was therefore to Mr Taylor's benefit in achieving the quashing of his visa cancellation decisions, but did not establish an impermeable legal boundary within which the government was required to act the following year.

---

[182] See *Re Ruddock; Ex parte Taylor* [2000] HCATrans 101 (16 March 2000).

[183] *Re Patterson; Ex parte Taylor* (2001) 207 CLR 391, 446 [165].

[184] *Migration Act 1958* (Cth) s 501(3).

[185] *Re Patterson; Ex parte Taylor* (2001) 207 CLR 391, 410 [44] (Gaudron J), 437 [136] (McHugh J), 497 [318] (Kirby J), 518 [377] (Callinan J).

[186] *Nolan v Minister of State for Immigration and Ethnic Affairs* (1988) 165 CLR 178.

[187] *Shaw v Minister for Immigration and Multicultural Affairs* (2003) 218 CLR 28. For further discussion, see Michelle Foster, 'An "Alien" by the Barest of Threads – The Legality of the Deportation of Long-Term Residents from Australia' (2009) 33(2) *Melbourne University Law Review* 483.

The second basis on which the Secretary's decision was argued to be unsound was in respect of more traditional administrative law grounds. The primary concern was that the Secretary had misapprehended the nature of the power conferred by s 501(3) of the *Migration Act 1958* (Cth).[188] Following guidance set out in a Departmental minute, the Secretary had proceeded on the mistaken understanding that Mr Taylor would have a later opportunity to make representations seeking revocation of the cancellation decision.[189] While the *Migration Act 1958* (Cth) did contain a revocation mechanism,[190] the basis for revocation was that the visa-holder had satisfied the Minister that they passed the character test; Mr Taylor's criminal conviction precluded him from ever satisfying that test, and accordingly there was no possibility he could succeed in seeking revocation under that provision.

Applying the hypothetical accountability benchmark to Mr Taylor's situation, we would likely say that the grounds for judicial review aligned most clearly with the control aspect of the benchmark. Both the grounds of breach of procedural fairness and misapprehension of jurisdiction operate to define the limits of government power and to police those boundaries. These concerns are well suited to the control benchmark's focus on the *unlawful exercise of power*, defining the legal limits of jurisdiction.

8.3.1.4 What Procedures Are Employed in Judicial Review Proceedings?

The next matter to consider is the extent to which the procedures adopted in judicial review proceedings align with the expectations of the hypothetical benchmark; the transparency rationale demands procedures that facilitate public dissemination of information, the control rationale anticipates coercive procedures that are equally balanced between the parties, the redress rationale anticipates prosecutor-friendly procedures and the deterrence rationale anticipates flexible

---

[188] Gaudron J further found error in the Secretary's failure to recognise that the provision required attention to the seriousness of the offence (*Re Patterson; Ex parte Taylor* (2001) 207 CLR 391, 419 [82]), and Kirby J further held that the material before the Secretary was insufficient to sustain a reasonable or rational conclusion that the visa ought to be cancelled (at 503 [332]).

[189] *Re Patterson; Ex parte Taylor* (2001) 207 CLR 391, 398 [1] (Gleeson CJ), 420 [83] (Gaudron J), 420 [87] (McHugh J), 437 [139] (Gummow and Hayne JJ).

[190] *Migration Act 1958* (Cth) s 501C(3)–(4).

procedures that facilitate dialogue. As with Mr Obeid's case, this section considers access to information, burden of proof and remedial discretion.

(i) Access to Information   As already discussed in the context of the Eddie Obeid corruption scandal,[191] the courts play an important role in contributing to transparency in government decision-making. In Mr Taylor's case, the legal forum enabled Mr Taylor to air his grievances in an open setting, unencumbered by the non-publication orders that featured so heavily in the *Obeid* litigation. The open nature of the forum as well as the courts' publication of reasons in respect of each decision in Mr Taylor's case each facilitated public access to information about the factual scenario underlying the dispute. In this respect, the judicial review proceedings in Mr Taylor's case were well aligned with the expectations of the transparency rationale.

Judicial review proceedings also offer coercive procedures that can be utilised to facilitate access to government information. However, in comparison to civil proceedings, investigatory and evidentiary procedures in public law cases are significantly more limited.[192] In Mr Taylor's case, this limitation was compounded by his selection of venue; the Full Court of the High Court of Australia does not engage in determination of factual disputes, preferring to proceed either on the basis of facts agreed between the parties, or to remit factual disputes for determination by another tribunal.[193] These limited opportunities for fact-finding were foreshadowed in the first judicial review proceedings before Callinan J, who indicated that it was 'highly unlikely' that the Full Court would entertain a trial of fact (including cross-examination) in relation to the content of statements made by immigration officials.[194] We would likely say, therefore, that in this respect, judicial review offers a potentially smaller contribution to the transparency rationale than criminal and tort proceedings.

A further limitation of judicial review proceedings is in respect of the power to compel the provision of reasons by a public official. The provision of reasons has been linked with the concept of accountability;

---

[191] See above Section 8.2.2.4(i).
[192] See, e.g., *Uniform Civil Procedure Rules 2005* (NSW) r 59.7.
[193] The power to remit is contained in *Judiciary Act 1903* (Cth) s 44.
[194] *Re Ruddock; Ex parte Taylor* [2000] HCATrans 101 (16 March 2000) [1180].

reasons are 'a necessary condition for securing the accountability and legitimacy of government action'.[195] The common law position in Australia is that there is no entitlement to reasons in respect of the decisions of executive officials.[196] However, we might speculate about whether the commencement of proceedings might influence the likelihood that a decision-maker will volunteer reasons for their decision. On the one hand, the prospect of being challenged through judicial review might negatively impact a government official's willingness to 'go into writing', or to explain themselves, for fear of those reasons being later used against them. On the other hand, the prospect of legal proceedings might potentially encourage officials to be transparent in the first instance. If an official believes that their decision or conduct is legally sound and that they have good reasons for so acting, might the official be prompted by the threat of legal proceedings to make those reasons clear?

In Australia, this incentive is bolstered by the fact that a discretionary decision might be regarded as legally unreasonable if it 'lacks an evident and intelligible justification'.[197] This threat might possibly be thought to *discourage* an official from providing reasons, in the belief that the reviewing court will closely scrutinise those reasons for the purposes of determining whether they are sufficiently 'intelligible' to justify the decision ultimately reached. However, it might also operate as an *incentive* to provide reasons, as a court's ability to apply 'unreasonableness [as] a conclusion'[198] is based on the proposition that 'where no good reason has been given by a decision-maker, a judicial review court may conclude that one did not exist'.[199] In turn, this might be thought to 'reduce the circumstances in which administrative

---

[195] Peter Cane, Leighton McDonald and Kristen Rundle, *Principles of Administrative Law* (3rd ed., Oxford University Press, 2018) 157. See also David Dyzenhaus and Michael Taggart, 'Reasoned Decisions and Legal Theory' in Douglas Edlin (ed.), *Common Law Theory* (Cambridge University Press, 2007) 134, 144.

[196] *Public Service Board (NSW) v Osmond* (1986) 159 CLR 656, 676 (Deane J). The position is not absolute, with reasons available in certain circumstances pursuant to the common law (see, e.g., *Campbelltown City Council v Vegan* (2006) 67 NSWLR 372, 394–96) and statute (see, e.g., *Administrative Decisions (Judicial Review) Act 1977* (Cth) s 13).

[197] *Minister for Immigration and Citizenship v Li* (2013) 249 CLR 332, 367 [76].

[198] Ibid.

[199] Matthew Groves and Greg Weeks, 'Substantive (Procedural) Review in Australia' in Hanna Wilberg and Mark Elliott (eds.), *The Scope and Intensity of Substantive Review: Traversing Taggart's Rainbow* (Hart Publishing, 2015) 133, 147.

decision-makers can safely exercise discretion without supporting their decision by an extensive statement of reasons'.[200]

Applying the hypothetical benchmark, we would likely say that when considering access to information, judicial review proceedings offer a number of useful procedural contributions to the transparency rationale. In Mr Taylor's case, his two judicial review proceedings facilitated public scrutiny of the visa cancellation decisions. He was able to present evidence as to the content of the decisions and communications received from relevant government officials, and to make submissions as to the errors made by decision-makers. All of this was published both in the public forum of the courtroom, as well as in a transcript of proceedings. The first proceedings were resolved by consent in Mr Taylor's favour, but the second proceedings (which were contested) were the subject of a judgment, with reasons published by the High Court. All of this aligned with the expectations of the transparency rationale.

(ii) **Burden of Proof**   Burden of proof does not feature as heavily in judicial review proceedings as it does in civil and criminal proceedings. In fact, factual inquiries have a much smaller role to play in the context of judicial review, which is concerned with testing the legality, rather than the merits, of government action.[201] As a general proposition, the party seeking to argue lack of jurisdiction bears the onus of establishing that issue,[202] though this burden may take a more onerous shape with grounds of review that are concerned with an official's subjective mindset (such as bad faith[203] and improper purpose).[204] We can view these varying approaches as attempting to accommodate different aspects of the accountability benchmark. For grounds of a technical or procedural nature, the ordinary onus of proof applies. Where the grounds are of a nature that aligns with concepts of subjective fault,[205] however, we see

---

[200] Ibid 148.

[201] *Attorney-General (NSW) v Quin* (1990) 170 CLR 1.

[202] *Municipal Council of Sydney v Campbell* [1925] AC 338, 343.

[203] 'Allegations that statutory powers have been exercised corruptly or with deliberate disregard to the scope of those powers are not lightly to be made or upheld': *Federal Commissioner of Taxation v Futuris Corporation Ltd* (2008) 237 CLR 146, 165.

[204] 'An improper purpose will not be lightly inferred': *Industrial Equity Ltd v Deputy Commissioner of Taxation* (1990) 170 CLR 649, 672.

[205] Ellen Rock, 'Fault and Accountability in Public Law' in Mark Elliot, Jason NE Varuhas and Shona Wilson Stark (eds.), *The Unity of Public Law?* (Hart Publishing, 2018) 171, 185–91.

that the onus shifts into a more agent-friendly form. In Mr Taylor's case, the grounds of review related to procedural and jurisdictional matters in which the government official was alleged to have misunderstood the statutory provision they were relying on, or had offered an insufficient opportunity to be heard. These grounds do not raise questions of the honesty or intentions of the decision-maker, and accordingly the ordinary onus of proof was relevant. We would likely be satisfied that this procedural aspect of judicial review proceedings was fairly balanced between the parties, as anticipated by the control aspect of the hypothetical benchmark.

(iii) **Discretion to Refuse Relief** Relief in judicial review cases is not available as of right, with the court retaining a discretion to refuse the remedies set out in s 75(v) of the *Constitution*.[206] Accordingly, the courts may decline to intervene in circumstances where the plaintiff has acted in bad faith or delayed in bringing their claim, or in circumstances where the order would be impractical or unnecessary, or where other remedies are available.[207] This operates as an important limitation on the operation of judicial review as an accountability mechanism, as even if an applicant can otherwise establish that the government has acted unlawfully, no remedy may issue if the applicant has acted in a disentitling manner, or if relief is otherwise futile or inappropriate. Having said this, the discretion is 'not to be exercised lightly against the grant of a final remedy' in circumstances where there is no further avenue of appeal.[208] Instead, the exercise of discretion should be guided by the sentiment that 'the courts should provide whatever remedies are available and appropriate to ensure that those possessed of executive and administrative powers exercise them only in accordance with the laws which govern their exercise'.[209] As a procedural mechanism, we can view the court's discretion to refuse relief in judicial review proceedings as being consistent with the benchmark requirement that procedures be balanced between the parties. By allowing the courts the discretion to refuse relief in

---

[206] *Federal Commissioner of Taxation v Futuris Corporation Ltd* (2008) 237 CLR 146, 172–73 [88].

[207] Aronson, Groves and Weeks (n 137) ch 17.

[208] *Re Refugee Review Tribunal; Ex parte Aala* (2000) 204 CLR 82, 107 [55] (Gaudron and Gummow JJ).

[209] *Corporation of the City of Enfield v Development Assessment Commission* (2000) 199 CLR 135, 157 [56].

appropriate cases (without undermining the rule of law), the courts have leeway to tip the balance back in favour of the government where that approach is warranted. In Mr Taylor's case, there was no question raised as to whether relief ought to be withheld, and accordingly these considerations did not arise.

8.3.1.5 What Consequences Are Delivered in Judicial Review Proceedings?

The final aspect of the hypothetical benchmark addresses the *consequences* delivered pursuant to an accountability mechanism. The transparency rationale anticipates that the government will be required to explain and justify its decisions and conduct. The extent to which judicial review meets this objective was outlined in the foregoing section. The remaining results-oriented rationales anticipate the availability of regulatory orders (control), reparative remedies (redress) and weak sanctions to facilitate dialogue (deterrence). Given the diversity of these expectations, it is unsurprising that judicial review proceedings do not satisfy all of them.

Depending on the nature of the claim, the available remedies in judicial review proceedings include declaratory and injunctive relief, and the writs of certiorari, prohibition and mandamus. Taken together, the functions of these remedies are to prohibit illegal conduct, to mandate required conduct, to nullify an illegal decision and to pronounce on the validity or invalidity of a particular course.[210] These functions are essentially regulatory in nature. They target the future behaviour of an official, restricting or mandating a course of conduct so as to confine it within legal bounds. A writ of prohibition and a prohibitory injunction each play a role of preventing an official from acting in reliance on an impugned decision or instrument, or (less frequently) from making the decision or instrument in the first place. The writ of mandamus and mandatory injunction also perform a forward-looking role. While the courts – particularly in the public law context – will be very reluctant to mandate a particular course of conduct, they will make an order that has the effect of coercing an official to do something that they are already obliged to do. In this way, both the mandatory and prohibitory orders are directed at the future conduct of an official so as to confine it within legal

---

[210] See further Ellen Rock, 'Accountability: A Core Public Law Value?' (n 134) 198–99.

bounds. These are orders of a regulatory nature, aligning with the control rationale.

Though not in the same way, the writ of certiorari and remedy of declaration can also be seen as falling within the regulatory category of remedial responses. Each of these remedies operates so as to define the legal limits within which power can be exercised, and thereby provides a measure of control over the conduct of officials. The writ of certiorari is used to 'quash' or 'annihilate'[211] the 'legal effect or the legal consequences' of an impugned decision,[212] thereby nullifying decisions and instruments that step outside the legal boundaries and depriving them of future effect. Similarly, though a declaration is non-coercive (i.e. it 'change[s] nothing'),[213] it is issued by the courts in the anticipation that government officials will act in conformity with its content.[214] If we view the function of these remedies as a means to police the boundaries within which power can legally be exercised, this takes on the character of a control-oriented remedial response.

However, we can also view these policing remedies as performing a deterrent function, particularly in the case of declaratory relief. Rather than taking legal effect to compel a particular outcome, a declaration of invalidity leaves the respondent to take such steps as they might choose to see the matter dealt with. While a declaration is made by the court in the expectation that it will be complied with,[215] its non-coercive nature affords the respondent greater opportunity to elect how to respond to it, thereby facilitating improvements going forward. As put by Varuhas, the public law declaration 'serves to mark and perhaps disapprove of unlawful conduct, as well as serving an 'educative' function, providing guidance to the administration as to how public powers ought to be exercised into the future and thus facilitating compliance and proper pursuit of public goals'.[216] When viewed in this light, it is possible to think about the

---

[211] *Ainsworth v Criminal Justice Commission* (1992) 175 CLR 564, 595 (Brennan J).

[212] Ibid 580 (Mason CJ, Dawson, Toohey and Gaudron JJ).

[213] Cane, McDonald and Rundle (n 195) 110.

[214] For example, the High Court would have issued declaratory relief regarding the validity of advice given by private contractors on the basis that the Minister would need to observe the declaration of invalidity if exercising discretion to consider that advice: *Plaintiff M61/2010E v Commonwealth* (2010) 243 CLR 319.

[215] Aronson, Groves and Weeks (n 137) [15.240].

[216] Jason NE Varuhas, 'The Development of the Damages Remedy under the *New Zealand Bill of Rights Act 1990*: From Torts to Administrative Law' [2016] *New Zealand Law Review* 213, 236.

declaration as performing a prospective regulatory function, albeit non-coercive in nature. Though there might be better ways to perform this educative role (e.g. we might more readily look to the ombudsman), we can see shades of the deterrence rationale in these policing remedies. However, we cannot take this point too far. Rather, the best characterisation of the orders available in judicial review proceedings is as a collection of regulatory remedies, well aligned with the control rationale for accountability.

Public law remedies have little role to play in connection with the remaining rationales of redress and desert. Looking first at redress, it is important to note that, while judicial review remedies may occasionally produce a reparative result in particular cases, these remedies have very limited capacity to restore the interests of those affected by the breach of public law norms. Four observations make this clear. First, the remedies are not focused in any meaningful way on the interests of the affected individual. As outlined above, each of the remedies is focused on the legality of the respondent's exercise of powers. With the exception of the tests for standing, the manner in and extent to which the applicant is affected by the conduct of the official is largely irrelevant to the determination of legality[217] and the applicability of the various remedies.

Secondly, the utility of these remedies from the perspective of an applicant is in many respects a matter of coincidence, rather than a reflection of the merits of their case. For instance, compare the position of an applicant affected by an invalid government decision to refuse an entitlement with that of an applicant affected by an invalid government decision to revoke an entitlement. In both cases the decision may be quashed, but with what result? Unless the decision is remade to different effect, the former applicant will still be left without the entitlement, while the latter will have theirs reinstated. In this way, the extent to which an applicant is restored via remedies in judicial review proceedings is a product of coincidence rather than the character of the remedy.[218]

Thirdly, while the available remedies provide the courts with a measure of control over government conduct going forward, this control does not rise to the level of allowing the court to restore an individual's interests. For instance, where an illegal decision is quashed and the court

---

[217] The High Court's recent indications that it will consider the 'materiality' of an error in determining whether or not it goes to jurisdiction may alter this position in some respects: *Hossain v Minister for Immigration and Border Protection* (2018) 264 CLR 123.

[218] *Attorney-General (NSW) v Quin* (1990) 170 CLR 1, 35–36 (Brennan J).

awards a writ of mandamus requiring the official to exercise their power according to law, it is not the role of the court to consider whether this will ultimately prove beneficial to the applicant. In some cases, there may only be one conceivable way in which the power may be exercised, with the effect that the writ will produce the result the applicant desires. However, this is the exception rather than the rule, and is not the object of the remedy.

Finally, even if a judicial review remedy achieves a result that restores the applicant for the future, none of the remedies enables the courts to repair harm that has been suffered in the interim.[219] To take a fairly benign example, the holder of a liquor licence may have their licence revoked pursuant to an invalid decision made by the issuing authority. Unless able to obtain urgent interlocutory relief, an applicant may wait months for the determination of their claim, and it is reasonable to assume that the loss and damage sustained during this period could be significant. Quashing the invalid decision may restore the licence going forward, but cannot repair the damage suffered while awaiting that result. Taken together, these observations demonstrate that while the available remedies in judicial review proceedings will occasionally produce a reparative effect for a plaintiff, this is not the object of those remedies. They are inherently regulatory in nature, and therefore align with the accountability objective of control, rather than redress.

Judicial review remedies also make no meaningful contribution to the desert rationale. For instance, some might say that there is a punitive element to publicly pointing out an official's mistakes; by declaring their decisions or conduct to be illegal in a public forum, the courts are exposing an official to condemnation. However, even on a broad view it is difficult to see how this would amount to punishment, as described in Chapter 7. There is no symbolic condemnation in the judicial pronouncement itself; it is merely an identification of the legal limits of public power. Further, it is difficult to see how a prohibitory or mandatory order requiring an official to exercise their powers legally is a form of punishment. Even if the official does not wish to exercise their powers, the courts are not imposing some new form of 'hard treatment', but are instead requiring the official to perform a pre-existing legal obligation.

---

[219] There is also no direct entitlement to damages in private law following successful judicial review proceedings: Ellen Rock and Greg Weeks, 'Monetary Awards for Public Law Wrongs: Australia's Resistant Legal Landscape' (2018) 41(4) *University of New South Wales Law Journal* 1159.

Importantly, the courts cannot tell an official *how* to exercise a discretionary power, but can only require an official to exercise a power within legal limits. It is very difficult to see how redirecting an official back onto the legal path aligns with the rationale of desert.

Taking these observations together, it appears that the purpose and function of the remedies available in judicial review proceedings would be aligned with the control rationale for accountability, though in many cases they may also support the deterrence rationale. In Mr Taylor's case, the applicable remedies awarded by the High Court were (1) a writ of certiorari to quash the visa-cancellation decision, and (2) a writ of prohibition to prevent it from being proceeded on. Consistent with the foregoing discussion, these remedies clearly align with the control rationale by policing the legal boundaries within which the visa cancellation powers were able to be exercised. These orders had the effect of confirming that the decision had been made illegally and could not be acted on. It is also relevant to note that, even though one of the grounds of illegality was subsequently overturned in an unrelated High Court decision (namely, the inapplicability of the visa cancellation power to Mr Taylor by reason of his non-'alien' status),[220] the later overruling had no retrospective impact on the security of the orders Mr Taylor had obtained.[221]

The practical effect of the orders saw Mr Taylor released from prison, as there was no longer any legal foundation to detain him. However – and importantly for the purpose of the redress rationale – the High Court had no power to correct the harm that Mr Taylor had occasioned as a consequence of his detention. Given the nature of the legal errors made were essentially procedural, Mr Taylor also was unable to rely on the Court's decision for assurance that a similar decision might not be made again pursuant to an alternate procedure. Indeed, during the course of the lengthy litigation history Mr Taylor's visas were cancelled twice; Ms Patterson was able to exercise her visa cancellation powers despite the fact that Mr Ruddock had earlier conceded that his own decision was attended by procedural error. All of this is consistent with the view that Mr Taylor's judicial review proceedings were concerned not with redress in respect of the damage he sustained as a consequence of his detentions, but with control of government power.

---

[220] *Shaw v Minister for Immigration and Multicultural Affairs* (2003) 218 CLR 28.
[221] *Ruddock v Taylor* (2005) 222 CLR 612, 658–59 [169]–[171] (Kirby J).

8.3.2 The Tort of False Imprisonment

Tort claims are a further category of legal causes of action that can be understood as contributing to government accountability. Though traditionally framed as a tool of corrective justice or economic deterrence,[222] we can also view tort law as a means by which individuals can hold the government accountable for its wrongdoing.[223] In Diceyan terms, government officials are bound by the 'ordinary law of the realm',[224] and 'are accountable for their conduct to a Court of Law'.[225] In fact, the use of tort law as a vehicle to challenge government conduct and decisions can be viewed as the earliest foundations of modern judicial review.[226] A variety of torts may potentially be commenced against government defendants. Because the government engages in many activities that are akin to private parties (including owning land, running businesses, acting as an employer, using roads) we can broadly conceive of just about all torts as potentially applying to government defendants in some circumstance or another. The more interesting question, for present purposes, is the extent to which private law tort actions will be relevant in cases where the government performs peculiarly governmental functions, including crafting and implementing policy, regulatory and coercive regimes. Various categories of tort actions may be relevant in that context, including misfeasance in public office and malicious prosecution to target the exercise of state power for unauthorised purposes;[227] negligence and breach of statutory duty to target the performance of governmental duties falling below a prescribed standard;[228] and the intentional torts of battery, assault and false imprisonment in connection with the

---

[222] Kit Barker et al, *The Law of Torts in Australia* (5th ed., Oxford University Press, 2012) 21–22.

[223] Peter Cane, 'Tort Law and Public Functions' in John Oberdiek (ed.), *Philosophical Foundations of the Law of Torts* (Oxford University Press, 2014) 148, 164; Carol Harlow, *Understanding Tort Law* (3rd ed., Sweet and Maxwell, 2005), 139–40.

[224] JWF Allison (ed.), *The Oxford Edition of Dicey* (Volume 1, Oxford University Press, 2013) 100.

[225] Ibid 112.

[226] Rock and Weeks (n 219).

[227] Ellen Rock, 'Misfeasance in Public Office: A Tort in Tension' (2019) 43(1) *Melbourne University Law Review* 337.

[228] The courts will accommodate statutory concerns within the common law duty of care and breach analysis for the purposes of negligence claims: see, e.g., *Crimmins v Stevedoring Industry Finance Committee* (1999) 200 CLR 1; *Pyrenees Shire Council v Day* (1998) 192 CLR 330; *Graham Barclay Oysters Pty Ltd v Ryan* (2002) 211 CLR 540; *Stuart v Kirkland-Veenstra* (2009) 237 CLR 215.

unauthorised use of state power to threaten, make contact with, or detain, citizens.[229]

Mr Taylor deployed the tort of false imprisonment in an attempt to recover damages for his detention consequent upon the invalid visa cancellation decisions outlined above. This tort has a venerable history in the context of government accountability, having been described by the courts as one of the most 'important constitutional safeguards of the liberty of the subject against the executive'.[230] While Mr Taylor was successful at first instance[231] and on appeal to the NSW Court of Appeal,[232] a majority in the Australian High Court ultimately found in favour of the government defendants.[233] The following sections consider the extent to which this cause of action aligned with the relevant accountability rationales in Mr Taylor's case.

8.3.2.1   Who Is Held Accountable Pursuant to the Tort of False Imprisonment?

Before considering how the transparency, control, redress and deterrence rationales were served in Mr Taylor's case, it is first useful to consider which of the accountability models this tort reflects, set out in Chapter 4. The *individual* accountability model, as noted in Chapter 4, is concerned with attaching consequences to the party responsible for the impugned act or decision. The tort of false imprisonment aligns well with this model, by looking first to attach consequences to the party responsible for restraining the plaintiff's liberty. In most cases, this will be a relatively straightforward analysis, as it will impose liability on the individual who physically restrains the plaintiff. However, assigning liability becomes more complex in cases, such as Mr Taylor's, where a number of actors have contributed to the ultimate imprisonment. In Mr Taylor's case, two levels of actors combined to achieve Mr Taylor's detention. First, there were the authors of the legal instruments that set in motion the procedures that led to Mr Taylor's detention – the Minister for Immigration (Mr Ruddock) and Parliamentary Secretary to the Minister (Ms Patterson). As outlined in the foregoing section, each was found in judicial review proceedings to have acted in excess of their powers in cancelling

---

[229] See, e.g., Boughey, Rock and Weeks (n 9) [15.5].
[230] *R v Governor of Brockhill Prison; Ex parte Evans [No 2]* [2001] 2 AC 19, 43.
[231] *Taylor v Ruddock* (District Court of NSW, Murrell J, 18 December 2002).
[232] *Ruddock v Taylor* (2003) 58 NSWLR 269.
[233] *Ruddock v Taylor* (2005) 222 CLR 612.

Mr Taylor's visas.[234] However, these officials did not personally detain Mr Taylor; detention was effected by the immigration officials who arrested Mr Taylor following his successive visa cancellations. Therefore the detention was the result of the decisions of high-level government officials that rendered Mr Taylor an apparently unlawful non-citizen, as well as the front-line government officials who put his arrest and imprisonment into effect.

The tort of false imprisonment contemplates liability in two situations. First, if an actor takes steps to imprison the plaintiff, or secondly if the actor is 'active in promoting and causing the imprisonment', such as to render their actions the 'proximate cause of the imprisonment'.[235] In this respect, Mr Taylor's case provides a useful factual scenario to appreciate the reach of the tort. For the front-line immigration officials who physically detained Mr Taylor, the first scenario was most relevant. For them, liability turned on the question of whether or not there was legal authority to detain. The officers were purporting to act pursuant to s 189 of the *Migration Act 1958* (Cth), which provides that: 'If an officer knows or reasonably suspects that a person ... is an unlawful non-citizen, the officer must detain the person.' In Mr Taylor's case, each of the respective immigration officials formed the view that Mr Taylor was an 'unlawful non-citizen' after being referred Mr Taylor's file and noting the visa cancellation decisions made first by Mr Ruddock and then by Ms Patterson.[236] As discussed in Section 8.3.2.3 below, the liability of immigration officials ultimately turned on statutory interpretation of s 189, which was held by a majority of the High Court to render the officials' actions lawful.

As to the second layer of actors – the authors of the visa cancellation decisions – liability fell into the second false imprisonment scenario outlined above, namely whether the conduct of these decision-makers could be viewed as the 'proximate cause of the imprisonment'.[237] The various judgments in the *Taylor* litigation reflect differing approaches to the liability of Mr Ruddock and Ms Patterson. Both at trial and on appeal to the NSW Court of Appeal, focus was directed to the roles these two

---

[234] The first cancellation was set aside pursuant to consent orders following a hearing before Callinan J: *Re Ruddock; Ex parte Taylor* [2000] HCATrans 101 (16 March 2000). The second was set aside following a High Court hearing: *Re Patterson; Ex parte Taylor* (2001) 207 CLR 391.

[235] *Myer Stores Ltd v Soo* [1991] 2 VR 597, 629 (McDonald J).

[236] *Taylor v Ruddock* (District Court of NSW, Murrell J, 18 December 2002) [25], [48].

[237] *Myer Stores Ltd v Soo* [1991] 2 VR 597, 629 (McDonald J).

decision-makers had played in Mr Taylor's detention, proceeding on the basis that the invalidity of the visa cancellation decisions necessarily rendered the imprisonment unlawful. Accordingly, provided that the requisite elements of directness and intention were established,[238] these judges would have held Mr Ruddock and Ms Patterson liable in tort. In contrast, a majority of the High Court considered that the determinative issue was the scope of s 189; if it authorised front-line immigration officials to detain Mr Taylor there could be no false imprisonment, either on the part of the front-line officials, or on the part of the authors of the visa cancellation decisions. Having found that s 189 did indeed grant such a power to detain Mr Taylor,[239] there could be no liability for either class of actors.

Applying the accountability benchmark, both of the foregoing categories of actors fall into the *individual* accountability model, by attaching liability to an actor on the basis of their own decisions and conduct. However, Mr Taylor's case also offers some insight into the extent to which the false imprisonment tort accommodates the *hierarchical* accountability model, which allows one party to be held accountable for the actions of another. In the legal context, this relationship is understood as one of vicarious liability. Vicarious liability derives from the nature of the relationship between the parties, and relevantly for present purposes, one of the most common relationships giving rise to such liability is that between master and servant. An employer will generally be held vicariously liable for the tortious acts of employees engaged in during the course of their employment,[240] a principle which operates equally in the government employment relationship. Some cases of government employment may raise difficult questions about the reach of the doctrine, such as where public functions are being performed under an independent contract or where the nature of the power exercised is one in respect of which the employee holds an 'independent discretion'.[241] None of these rules was tested in Mr Taylor's case; the Commonwealth government accepted that it was vicariously liable for the acts of the Minister and Parliamentary Secretary,[242] as well as those of

---

[238] See Section 8.3.2.3 below.
[239] See Section 8.3.2.3 below.
[240] See Barker et al (n 222) 752.
[241] *Cubillo v Commonwealth (No 2)* (2000) 103 FCR 1, 343 [1117] (O'Loughlin J). In NSW, see *Law Reform (Vicarious Liability) Act 1983* (NSW) s 8.
[242] *Taylor v Ruddock* (District Court of NSW, Murrell J, 18 December 2002) [112].

the immigration officials who had detained Mr Taylor.[243] To summarise, then, Mr Taylor's case demonstrates that the tort of false imprisonment can be deployed to target the individual tortfeasor (individual account- ability), and also to shift liability to their employer via the doctrine of vicarious liability (hierarchical accountability).

8.3.2.2   To Whom Are They Accountable?

In tort law, issues of standing are wrapped up in the elements of the cause of action, rather than being determined through stand-alone tests of eligibility to make a claim.[244] In order to determine *to whom* a government defendant is accountable in tort, we must look at the content of the relevant cause of action. For the purposes of the false imprisonment tort, it is the detention of the plaintiff that gives a right to commence proceedings. While there is no requirement to establish loss or damage (i.e. the tort is actionable per se),[245] the tort cannot be made out unless the plaintiff is actually detained. Accordingly, it is the act of detention that marks out the categories of individuals entitled to commence proceedings. In Mr Taylor's case, there was little doubt that he was an appropriate party to commence proceedings for false imprisonment.

8.3.2.3   For What Are They Accountable?

The tort of false imprisonment is actionable where the acts taken by the defendant are *direct*, *intentional* and lacking in *legal authority*. Each of these elements received attention in Mr Taylor's case. The element of directness is concerned with 'the sufficiency of the nexus between the defendant's act and the imprisonment'.[246] Returning to the discussion in Chapter 6, this element is essentially an outcome-focused enquiry, seek- ing to identify a requisite degree of attachment between a person's actions and their consequences. In the context of the false imprisonment tort, there are two ways in which this degree of attachment may arise. As discussed in Section 8.3.2.1 above, the first is in cases where a defendant is directly responsible for the imprisonment (i.e. liability of front-line officials who effect detention), and the second is in cases where the

---

[243] *Ruddock v Taylor* (2005) 222 CLR 612, 646 [127] (Kirby J).
[244] *Bateman's Bay Local Aboriginal Land Council v Aboriginal Community Benefit Fund Pty Ltd* (1998) 194 CLR 247, 264 [43].
[245] *Watson v Marshall & Cade* (1971) 124 CLR 621.
[246] *Ruddock v Taylor* (2003) 58 NSWLR 269, 277 [34].

defendant is active in 'promoting and causing the imprisonment' (e.g. liability of the authors of an instrument authorising the detention).[247] In the former situation, the element of directness will be a straightforward enquiry, looking at the immediate act of detention. The latter situation involves a more complex causation enquiry, seeking to identify whether the actor is the 'direct cause' of the imprisonment,[248] or whether 'the person who ultimately confines the plaintiff would not have acted at all but for the urging on the part of another'.[249] In Mr Taylor's case, not all judges considered this latter liability issue, with a majority of the High Court basing its decision on s 189 of the *Migration Act 1958* (Cth). It is nonetheless useful to consider how the element of directness was established to the satisfaction of other judges. For those who considered the matter, the ultimate act of detention was regarded as inseparable from the decisions to cancel Mr Taylor's visas. Directness was thought to be established because the detention was an 'inevitable consequence',[250] and 'virtually automatic' within the 'self-executing' scheme.[251]

The second element is that of intentionality. In the language employed in Chapter 6, this is a fault-based element, seeking to attach liability based on a person's state of mind in connection with their actions. For the purpose of the tort of false imprisonment, the courts have made clear that the element of intentionality is not tied to a defendant's motives. The courts rejected such an argument in Mr Taylor's case, confirming that wrongful imprisonment does not depend on 'how innocent, ignorant or even idealistic' the defendant may be.[252] Instead, the element of intention for the purpose of the tort centres on the concept of 'intention to detain'.[253] In most cases, the party that sets in motion the chain of events leading to an imprisonment will have 'actively sought that result'.[254] However, there will be cases – such as Mr Taylor's – in which a finding that a party was the direct cause of an imprisonment will not necessarily equate to a finding that this result was intended. For Mr Ruddock and Ms Patterson, Spigelman CJ concluded that they 'must have been aware' that

[247] *Myer Stores Ltd v Soo* [1991] 2 VR 597, 629 (McDonald J).
[248] *Ruddock v Taylor* (2003) 58 NSWLR 269, 276 [30] (Spigelman CJ).
[249] Ibid 277 [33] (Spigelman CJ).
[250] *Taylor v Ruddock* (District Court of NSW, Murrell J, 18 December 2002) [109]; *Ruddock v Taylor* (2005) 222 CLR 612, 645 [121] (McHugh J), 651–52 [143] (Kirby J).
[251] *Ruddock v Taylor* (2003) 58 NSWLR 269, 274 [12].
[252] Ibid 284 [73] (Meagher JA).
[253] Ibid 277 [36] (Spigelman CJ).
[254] Ibid 277 [35] (Spigelman CJ).

detention was an 'inevitable step' in the 'self-executing operation of the statute'.[255] Equating the situation with one in which a defendant throws a lighted squib into a marketplace,[256] his Honour concluded that the reflex actions of stallholders in tossing the threat amongst one another reflected a similar automatic function to the migration detention legislation.[257] Mr Ruddock and Ms Patterson could therefore be taken to have intended Mr Taylor's detention.

Perhaps the most complex element of the false imprisonment tort in Mr Taylor's case was that requiring a lack of *legal authority*. This is because there were two possible bases on which to find that Mr Taylor's detention was unlawful. The first, and that which absorbed the majority of attention, built on the finding in his previous judicial review proceedings that the visa cancellation power in the *Migration Act 1958* (Cth) did not apply to a British citizen who had been absorbed into the Australian community.[258] In his tort claim, Mr Taylor sought to extend this reasoning by arguing that it also precluded application of the detention power (i.e. s 189 of that Act). If correct, s 189 would offer no legal authority to support Mr Taylor's detention, thereby substantiating his false imprisonment claim. The High Court rejected this argument, finding that the earlier judicial review proceedings in respect of the visa cancellation powers had nothing to say about the applicability of the detention provision.[259]

The second basis on which Mr Taylor argued that his detention was unlawful was by reference to traditional administrative law grounds, namely that the visa cancellation decisions had been set aside for want of procedural fairness.[260] The High Court's orders in the earlier judicial review proceedings had the effect of quashing the visa cancellation decisions, and because an order for certiorari operates retrospectively,[261] the law recognised Mr Taylor as a valid visa-holder at the time he was

---

[255] Ibid 278 [37] (Spigelman CJ). See also Meagher JA at 284 [72].

[256] This was the factual scenario in the famed case of *Scott v Shepherd* (1773) 96 ER 525.

[257] *Ruddock v Taylor* (2003) 58 NSWLR 269, 278 [39]–[40] (Spigelman CJ).

[258] Such a person was thought not to be an 'alien' for constitutional purposes: *Re Patterson; Ex parte Taylor* (2001) 207 CLR 391, 410 [44] (Gaudron J), 437 [136] (McHugh J), 497 [318] (Kirby J), 518 [377] (Callinan J). Note that this finding was subsequently overturned by the High Court: *Shaw v Minister for Immigration and Multicultural Affairs* (2003) 218 CLR 28.

[259] *Ruddock v Taylor* (2005) 222 CLR 612, 624 [34].

[260] See Section 8.3.1.3.

[261] See *Ruddock v Taylor* (2003) 58 NSWLR 269, 275 [19]–[21] (Spigelman CJ).

taken into immigration detention. Mr Taylor argued that his circumstances therefore did not meet the legal conditions that would otherwise
have authorised the detention. Mr Taylor succeeded in his argument at
trial and on appeal to the NSW Court of Appeal. However, a majority of
the High Court found that it was a mistake to 'conflate' what they
considered to be two separate enquiries: 'one about the lawfulness of
the decision to cancel; the other about the lawfulness of the detention'.[262]
To treat the former as determinative of the latter was to misapprehend
the independent function served by s 189 of the *Migration Act 1958*
(Cth). Accordingly, this statutory provision took on a role of great
significance in Mr Taylor's false imprisonment claim.

Section 189 authorised an immigration official to detain a person if
they 'reasonably suspected' them to be 'an unlawful non-citizen'.
Mr Taylor accepted that s 189 would protect an official whose 'reasonable
suspicion' was based on a mistake of fact, but argued that the protection
could not extend to circumstances where the suspicion was based on an
error of law. If correct, the provision would have no application to
Mr Taylor, as the legal foundation on which immigration officials formed
their suspicion (i.e. the cancellation decisions) had been found to be
legally infirm. While this argument was accepted by a number of judges
during the course of this litigation,[263] a majority of the High Court found
that s 189 could be read as protecting reasonable suspicions that later
turned out to be incorrect: 'what constitutes reasonable grounds for
suspecting a person to be an unlawful non-citizen must be judged against
what was known or reasonably capable of being known at the relevant
time'.[264] Critically, 'what were reasonable grounds for effecting the
respondent's detention did not retrospectively cease to be reasonable'
when Mr Taylor's judicial review claim was determined.[265] Each of the
immigration officials who had acted to detain Mr Taylor had founded
their suspicion on the basis of 'what, on its face, appeared to be a regular
and effective decision', and in absence of any evidence of bad faith,
the majority found that there was therefore no doubt as to whether
the suspicion was reasonably held.[266] Before the High Court, then, the

---

[262] *Ruddock v Taylor* (2005) 222 CLR 612, 621 [24].
[263] *Taylor v Ruddock* (District Court of NSW, Murrell J, 18 December 2002) [128]; *Ruddock v Taylor* (2005) 222 CLR 612, 639 [100] (McHugh J).
[264] *Ruddock v Taylor* (2005) 222 CLR 612, 626 [40] (Gleeson CJ, Gummow, Hayne and Heydon JJ).
[265] Ibid.
[266] Ibid 628 [49]–[50] (Gleeson CJ, Gummow, Hayne and Heydon JJ).

scope of liability for false imprisonment became a matter of statutory interpretation as to the meaning of the phrase 'reasonable suspicion', with the majority concluding that the statute authorised the detention irrespective of the illegality of the instrument that had given rise to the suspicion.

If we return to the question of 'for what' an official is held accountable, we can make a number of observations about the false imprisonment tort in respect of the two key norm ingredients of *fault* and *outcomes*. In relation to outcomes, the tort is primarily concerned with the act of detention itself, rather than with the impact of that detention on the plaintiff. We can say this for a number of reasons. First, the tort is actionable per se, without any proof of loss or damage arising from the detention. Secondly, a plaintiff may recover damages for false imprisonment even in circumstances where they are unaware of the imprisonment.[267] And finally, the tort provides a remedy even in cases where the unlawfulness of the detention is of a technical character (i.e. the same decision could have been made legally).[268] However, this is not to say that the extent of any impact on the plaintiff is irrelevant, as these matters will be taken into account in determining the quantum of loss (discussed in Section 8.3.2.5 below). Thus, proof of harm may increase the size of the award, whereas ignorance and inevitability of the imprisonment may decrease the size of the award to one of only nominal damages.

Looking at the concept of fault, the elements of the false imprisonment tort demonstrate that it is an essentially strict liability tort.[269] It does require a degree of mental engagement in connection with outcomes; the defendant must have intended the outcome of detention, creating a mental link between that outcome and the defendant's knowledge and awareness that this would be the likely result. Otherwise, however, the defendant's knowledge and motives for acting are irrelevant for the purpose of the false imprisonment tort. A defendant cannot defeat a claim by arguing that they did not appreciate that their actions were unlawful, or that they were acting in good faith. As noted in Mr Taylor's case, the only circumstance in which the concept of bad faith might have played a determinative role was in the context of the detention power; the two immigration officials would not have fallen within the ambit of the 'reasonable suspicion' protection had they been acting in bad

---

[267] *Myer Stores Ltd v Soo* [1991] 2 VR 597, 615.
[268] See the final paragraph in Section 8.3.2.5.
[269] *Ruddock v Taylor* (2005) 222 CLR 612, 650 [140] (Kirby J).

faith.[270] Accordingly, we would say that this tort is more concerned with the *outcome* of imprisonment than with a defendant's *motives*.

8.3.2.4   Via What Procedures?

The next question to be addressed is the procedures employed in connection with the tort of false imprisonment.

(i) Access to Information   As with all legal proceedings, a tort claim for false imprisonment offers the opportunities of an open forum to air grievances as well as compulsory legal processes to facilitate access to information. However, these opportunities are more relevant in tort claims than in judicial review proceedings, which tend to be characterised by far more curtailed investigatory and evidentiary procedures.[271] In contrast, civil proceedings allow a plaintiff a significant range of opportunities to gather information from the government by making full use of pre-trial procedures such as discovery, subpoenas and interrogatories, and in-court procedures such as cross-examination. Along with allowing a plaintiff to test the government's justification for imprisonment, these procedures provide a plaintiff such as Mr Taylor the opportunity to tell their story in a public forum.

(ii) Burden of Proof   The tort of false imprisonment is determined by reference to the civil burden; 'the balance of probabilities'. The degree of proof required to meet this standard is regarded as 'well settled', with the burden being discharged if it is 'more probable than not'.[272] The onus rests on the plaintiff to establish the elements of the tort to this standard. However, once the plaintiff has established the elements going to imprisonment, it is a matter for the defendant to establish that the imprisonment was lawfully justified.[273]

(iii) Remedial Discretion   In tort proceedings, remedial discretion takes shape in the assessment of general damages. The principles taken into account are set out in the following section. As this discussion

---

[270]   Ibid 628 [50].

[271]   See Section 8.3.1.4(i) above.

[272]   *Miller v Minister of Pensions* [1947] 2 All ER 372, 374 (Denning J).

[273]   *Carnegie v Victoria* (unreported, Supreme Court of Victoria, Full Court, 14 September 1989) 4, cited in *Myer Stores Ltd v Soo* [1991] 2 VR 597, 625; *Cubillo v Commonwealth (No 2)* (2000) 103 FCR 1, 355 [1150].

demonstrates, the trial judge is able to exercise discretion in forming a view as to the appropriate award, having regard to these principles and awards made in previous cases.

8.3.2.5 With What Consequences?

Tort law can be viewed as consistent with a range of accountability rationales. Looking first at transparency, tort law can be regarded as a mechanism to facilitate scrutiny of government activity. It may serve as a 'tin-opener' used by 'pressure groups and crusading lawyers hoping to open up dark and windowless areas of public administration',[274] or as an 'ombudsman' or 'watchdog' to target the government with the 'glare of publicity'.[275] However, it is perhaps more common to consider tort law's remedial contributions to accountability, most relevantly, via damages awards. Damages awards may be compensatory (to cover loss suffered as a result of the conduct of another), restorative (to reverse a shift of resources from one person to another), disgorging (to retract a gain made by one person at the expense of another), punitive (to punish a person for their conduct towards another) or nominal (to mark that a wrong has been committed).[276] Damages, then, are a versatile remedy that can be put to a variety of uses. As noted by O'Malley, '[m]oney is probably the most frequently used means of punishing, deterring, compensating and regulating throughout the legal system'.[277]

It is possible to identify a number of different accountability rationales for damages awards in the context of the tort of false imprisonment.[278] The first, and most clear, is in connection with the *redress* rationale, which requires the availability of remedies that restore a plaintiff in

---

[274] Carol Harlow, *State Liability: Tort Law and Beyond* (Oxford University Press, 2004) 51.

[275] Allen Linden, 'Tort Law as Ombudsman' (1973) 51 *Canadian Bar Review* 155, 156.

[276] Peter Cane, 'Damages in Public Law' (1999) 9 *Otago Law Review* 489, 491. Cane would distinguish nominal damages on the basis these have a declaratory function, as opposed to a goal of enriching the recipient of the award 'at the expense of' the party making the payment. Legislation in a number of Australian states limits the availability of exemplary damages in personal injury claims (see, e.g., *Civil Liability Act 2002* (NSW) s 21).

[277] Pat O'Malley, *The Currency of Justice: Fines and Damages in Consumer Societies* (Routledge-Cavendish, 2009) 1.

[278] Though not considered as such in this book, a further possible rationale for accountability is that of vindication. It is worth noting that damages awards can also be understood as serving this purpose, and have been awarded to that end in the context of the tort of false imprisonment: see *Hook v Cunard SS Co* [1953] 1 WLR 682 and discussion in Justice James Edelman, Jason NE Varuhas and Simon Colton, *McGregor on Damages* (20th ed., Thomson Reuters, 2017) ch 17.

respect of harm they have suffered. In legal terms, this function is performed by compensatory damages, which make up for both pecuniary and non-pecuniary losses, damage and injuries with a view to placing the plaintiff in the position that they would have been in absence of the defendant's wrong.[279] This rationale is aligned with the redress function of accountability, by providing a monetary payment designed to repair harm. The basic foundation for the award of damages in false imprisonment cases relates to intangible forms of harm, including 'indignity, mental suffering, disgrace and humiliation, with any attendant loss of social status and injury to reputation'.[280] In assessing damages for these forms of harm, the courts will take into account the claimant's particular experience of imprisonment. There is no applicable 'daily tariff' relevant in the assessment, and while the duration of the term of imprisonment will be relevant, the earlier period of detention will attract a higher award due to the 'initial shock' of the deprivation of liberty.[281] The award of damages may also take into account any tangible losses suffered by a claimant as a consequence of their imprisonment (e.g. physical harm or loss of earnings).

In Mr Taylor's case, compensatory damages were initially awarded in respect of Mr Taylor's two periods of detention, of 155 and 161 days. The trial judge took into account a range of matters in determining the quantum of damages.[282] One of the most relevant factors, for the trial judge, was that Mr Taylor was detained within high-security divisions of the state prison system rather than immigration detention for the majority of his imprisonment. Based on his status as a convicted sex offender, Mr Taylor experienced significant fear for his safety, and was exposed to a number of incidents of threats and violence. According to medical evidence, Mr Taylor's existing mental and physical health conditions were exacerbated as a result of his incarceration. Against these matters, the trial judge also took into account that Mr Taylor's previous criminal conviction meant that he was a person of 'low repute' who would not feel the same degree of indignity as a person of good character, and that imprisonment was not unknown to him. On this basis, the general damages awarded consisted primarily of general damages for each of the two periods of imprisonment plus interest, with a small allowance for

---

[279] *Livingstone v Rawyards Coal Co* (1880) 5 App Cas 25.
[280] Edelman, Varuhas and Colton (n 278) 1514.
[281] Ibid 1514–15.
[282] *Taylor v Ruddock* (District Court of NSW, Murrell J, 18 December 2002) [136]–[140].

past and future medical expenses.[283] The Court of Appeal found no error in the trial judge's assessment of damages,[284] though the plaintiff was ultimately unsuccessful before the High Court.

A second accountability function that can be supported via remedies available in false imprisonment proceedings is the *desert* function, through the award of punitive damages. The desert rationale demands the availability of punitive sanctions designed to signal condemnation of reprehensible conduct. Punitive damages awards (sometimes styled 'exemplary' awards) have the purpose of punishing the tortfeasor. Whereas compensatory awards are focused on the interests of the victim, punitive awards are reflective of the conduct of the wrongdoer. Such awards are not made routinely; a plaintiff must establish that punitive damages are warranted having regard to the reprehensible nature of the defendant's conduct. The courts have used adjectives such as 'contumelious',[285] 'outrageous'[286] and 'oppressive'[287] to describe the types of conduct with which these awards are concerned. Of particular relevance in this context is that punitive damages are thought to be particularly appropriate in cases of *government* wrongdoing. When the English courts took steps to confine the availability of punitive damages in the 1960s,[288] one of the preserved categories in which such awards remained available was in respect of 'arbitrary and outrageous use of executive power',[289] as in cases of 'oppressive, arbitrary or unconstitutional action by the servants of the government'.[290] The Australian courts did not follow the English courts in limiting the availability of punitive damages in this way, but nonetheless have expressed similar sentiments regarding their particular utility in claims against government.[291] Punitive damages are well aligned with the desert rationale for accountability.[292] Their purpose is to condemn and mark public disapproval of the wrongdoer's conduct; they

---

[283] Ibid [153]. The amount awarded was AU$116,000.
[284] *Ruddock v Taylor* (2003) 58 NSWLR 269, 285 [81] (Meagher JA).
[285] *Gray v Motor Accident Commission* (1998) 196 CLR 1, 7.
[286] *Rookes v Barnard* [1964] AC 1129, 1223.
[287] Ibid 1226.
[288] Ibid.
[289] Ibid 1223.
[290] Ibid 1226.
[291] *New South Wales v Ibbett* (2006) 229 CLR 638, 648–50 [38]–[40] (Gleeson CJ, Gummow, Kirby, Heydon and Crennan JJ).
[292] For further detail, see Rock, 'Misfeasance in Public Office' (n 227).

serve to 'uphold and vindicate the rule of law'[293], or, in Harlow's words, constitute 'a constitutional principle of symbolic importance'.[294] This punitive function therefore ties back to the overarching accountability rationale of supporting the legitimacy of government.

Mr Taylor argued in his case that he should be entitled to punitive damages on the basis that the defendants 'detained him in a punitive prison environment, when he was not detained for the purposes of punishment'.[295] The trial judge was willing to accept that the defendants had 'inappropriately disregarded the plaintiff's interests in favour of their own convenience';[296] however, found that punitive damages were not warranted as the defendants' conduct 'was not driven by the sort of contemptuous disregard for proper process which characterises those cases in which exemplary damages have been awarded'.[297] Again, the Court of Appeal found no error in the trial judge's assessment; 'the Commonwealth, whatever its faults, was neither through its Ministers nor its officers guilty of behaving contumeliously, arrogantly or outrageously'.[298] Accordingly, the punitive function was not considered necessary in the context of Mr Taylor's tort claim.

There are those who might also argue that the award of punitive damages serves a *deterrent* as well as desert-oriented function. There are various judicial statements to the effect that punitive damages may be awarded with a view to deterring others from emulating the defendant's behaviour. In *Ashby v White*, Holt CJ indicated that 'publick officers ... ought to pay greater damages than other men, to deter and hinder other officers from the like offences'.[299] This deterrence rationale was echoed in *Kuddus*, with Lord Hutton indicating that:

> [t]he power to award exemplary damages in such cases ... serves to deter such actions in future as such awards will bring home to officers in command of individual units that discipline must be maintained at all

[293] *Kuddus v Chief Constable of Leicestershire Constabulary* [2002] 2 AC 122, 149, cited with approval in *New South Wales v Ibbett* (2006) 229 CLR 638, 649–50.

[294] Carol Harlow, 'A Punitive Role for Tort Law?' in Linda Pearson, Carol Harlow and Michael Taggart (eds.), *Administrative Law in a Changing State: Essays in Honour of Mark Aronson* (Hart Publishing, 2008) 247, 251.

[295] *Taylor v Ruddock* (District Court of NSW, Murrell J, 18 December 2002) [147].

[296] Ibid [150].

[297] Ibid.

[298] *Ruddock v Taylor* (2003) 58 NSWLR 269, 285 [81] (Meagher JA).

[299] *Ashby v White* [1703] 2 Ld Raym 938, 956.

times. In my respectful opinion the view is not fanciful ... that such
awards have a deterrent effect.[300]

Not all accept that punitive damages awards have (or are likely to
produce) a deterrent effect of this nature. For instance, in *Kuddus*, Lord
Scott of Foscote wondered whether deterrence was possible or likely
where liability to pay punitive damages fell to be paid by an employer
rather than the individual wrongdoer.[301] Perhaps more importantly,
for present purposes, the award of punitive damages does *not* meet with
the expectations of the hypothetical accountability benchmark. The
deterrent component of the benchmark, as framed, demands the application of *weak sanctions* to *soft targets*, with a view to facilitating
dialogue. On no account could the imposition of a punitive damages
award be viewed as a weak sanction. Therefore, if our accountability
benchmark was to be defined in those terms, we would not accept that
the award of punitive damages in a false imprisonment case would
meet that expectation.

Though not relevant in Mr Taylor's case, the final accountability
rationale that can be served by a damages award in false imprisonment
cases is the *control* rationale, which looks for the availability of regulatory
orders that serve the function of defining the legal boundaries within
which power can be exercised. It is possible to view nominal damages as
serving this purpose. In the context of the false imprisonment tort, this
category of damages plays a role in cases where the unlawfulness of the
detention is of a technical character. So, for example, where a plaintiff is
held pursuant to an order that is found invalid for want of procedural
fairness, the court may find the defendant liable even where the detention
was inevitable (i.e. it is inevitable that the plaintiff would have been
detained even if a fair process had been followed). In *R (Lumba)* this
principle was deployed by the UK Supreme Court to deny compensatory
damages to foreign nationals who were detained pursuant to an unlawful
government policy on the basis that they would in any event have been
detained pursuant to the applicable lawful policy.[302] In the Australian
context, the principle was relied on in the *Fernando* litigation to deny
compensatory damages to a plaintiff who stood in a similar position to

---

[300] *Kuddus v Chief Constable of Leicestershire Constabulary* [2002] 2 AC 122, 149 [79].
[301] Ibid 157 [108]; 161 [129]. See also Bruce Feldthusen, 'Punitive Damages: Hard Choices
and High Stakes' [1998] *New Zealand Law Review* 741, 761.
[302] *R (Lumba) v Secretary of State for the Home Department* [2012] 1 AC 245.

Mr Taylor.[303] Mr Fernando was detained pursuant to ss 189 and 196 of the *Migration Act 1958* (Cth) following the cancellation of his visa, and sought damages for false imprisonment on the basis that the cancellation decision was unlawful. The Federal Court extended the reasoning in the *Taylor* case to find that because the Act required officials to detain a person reasonably suspected to be an unlawful non-citizen, Mr Fernando's detention was inevitable irrespective of the invalidity of the cancellation decision.[304] As a result, only nominal damages could be awarded. In this respect, the false imprisonment tort may be viewed as playing a control-oriented role by confirming the illegality of an official's conduct where redress of loss is not relevant.[305]

8.3.3   What Does the Hypothetical Benchmark Tell Us in Mr Taylor's Case?

In Mr Taylor's case, we might make the following observations in relation to the application of the hypothetical accountability benchmark:

(a) **Transparency:** Both judicial review and tort proceedings make similar contributions to transparency through the open nature of the court forum and the publication of judicial reasons, allowing Mr Taylor to air his grievances and open the government to public scrutiny. However, the contribution of judicial review proceedings to transparency are somewhat limited by the restrained fact-finding opportunities in (at least) High Court cases, and by the lack of a common law right to obtain reasons from government decision-makers. In contrast, tort proceedings offer greater access to procedures prior to and during proceedings which can facilitate access to information from government.

(b) **Control:** Judicial review proceedings are generally well aligned with the control-oriented hypothetical benchmark. Most notably the core concern of the applicable remedies is to police the boundaries of public power in cases where it has been exercised unlawfully. However, in some cases there might be concerns about shortfalls against the benchmark. For example, where public power has been

---

[303] *Fernando v Commonwealth* (2014) 231 FCR 251.

[304] Ibid 268 [82] (Besanko and Robertson JJ).

[305] It may also be argued that awarding damages in such cases would serve a vindicatory function: see Jason NE Varuhas, *Damages and Human Rights* (Hart Publishing, 2016) 61–66.

outsourced to private contractors, we might be concerned that judicial review proceedings are unable to target the repository of public power. Likewise, standing rules might potentially prevent the public from testing the legality of government decisions in cases that do not affect individuals in the requisite manner. Neither of these issues arose for consideration in Mr Taylor's case, who had sufficient standing to challenge decisions made by Mr Ruddock and Ms Patterson.

The tort of false imprisonment will also be well aligned with this aspect of the hypothetical benchmark in some cases. Most notably, if a claimant's detention arises out of a procedural irregularity, nominal damages may be awarded to mark the unlawful infringement, thereby serving a regulatory function. However, the tort will go beyond the confines of the control rationale in cases where more than nominal damages are awarded, as was the case for Mr Taylor.

(c) **Redress**: The false imprisonment tort is most closely aligned with the hypothetical redress rationale; the lack of fault element and focus on the unlawfulness of detention each reflect the expectations of the benchmark, as does the provision of compensatory damages to remedy both tangible and intangible harm arising from loss of liberty. However, one clear shortfall against the benchmark is in respect of *who* the tort targets; the benchmark anticipates a corporate-style approach to liability to ensure that systemic wrongs can be addressed, and that a party with sufficient resources is available to facilitate redress. Instead, the tort tends to focus on the individual contributions to the ultimate detention, backed by vicarious liability. While this addresses the latter issue, it does not assist in respect of the former.

We would be unlikely to conclude that judicial review proceedings satisfy the expectations of the redress rationale, either in Mr Taylor's case or more generally. As set out above, remedies in judicial review proceedings are not concerned with curing loss, with any utility on this front being a matter of coincidence rather than design. While Mr Taylor was released from prison as a consequence of his successful judicial review proceedings, he was unable to have his losses rectified, or to achieve any certainty that his visas would not be cancelled again in the future. All of this is consistent with the conclusion that judicial review proceedings are not well aligned with accountability's redress rationale.

(d) **Deterrence**: Neither judicial review nor the false imprisonment tort aligns well with the expectations of the deterrence rationale. In judicial review proceedings the issue of declaratory relief goes some way towards satisfying the hypothetical deterrence benchmark, in allowing the courts to issue non-coercive directions as to the boundaries within which power can be exercised. However, it would be a stretch to describe judicial review proceedings as a dialogue-enhancing mechanism designed to facilitate systemic change. The false imprisonment tort falls short of the hypothetical benchmark in various respects, not only in terms of who the tort targets but also in terms of the strength of the applicable remedies. The closest reflection of this rationale would be in respect of the award of nominal damages, which might be regarded as a weak sanction. On the whole, we would be unsatisfied that this mechanism is likely to generate constructive dialogue with a view to improving government processes.

As this summary demonstrates, neither judicial review nor false imprisonment proceedings are capable of satisfying all of the transparency, control, redress and deterrence expectations to their fullest. Both mechanisms offered meaningful contributions to the transparency rationale, drawing upon court processes and procedures to facilitate access to information and public scrutiny of government decisions and conduct. We might flag this as a potential issue of *accountability overload*, to the extent that both proceedings facilitate public scrutiny of the same set of circumstances and require government officials to answer publicly for the same conduct on multiple occasions. The extent of this overlap is addressed in Chapter 11. It was further concluded that neither cause of action was likely to make any meaningful contribution to the deterrence rationale, as court proceedings are by their nature concerned with resolving an individual dispute rather than facilitating dialogue about systemic change going forward. If Mr Taylor's case is one that demands deterrence, we might highlight this as a potential area of *accountability deficit*.

Turning to the particulars of Mr Taylor's case, it is clear that judicial review played the most meaningful role as an accountability mechanism both in terms of control and redress. It offered Mr Taylor a chance to verify that the visa cancellation decisions which led to his imprisonment were in fact made unlawfully, both because the power could not be understood as extending to Mr Taylor in a constitutional sense, and also on procedural fairness grounds. The remedies awarded (one set by consent and the others following a contested hearing) operated to expunge those decisions from the administrative record and resulted in Mr Taylor being released from prison. In this sense, judicial review remedies succeeded in policing the boundaries of public power, and restoring Mr Taylor's liberty in a prospective sense.

Mr Taylor's chief concern, then, was to seek redress in a retrospective sense, for which he relied on the tort of false imprisonment. At trial and on appeal, the courts took a holistic view of the concept of 'unlawfulness', regarding the visa cancellation decisions as critically linked to the decision by immigration officials to detain Mr Taylor. The false imprisonment case was ultimately thwarted by the interpretation of s 189 of the *Migration Act 1958* (Cth) adopted by five members of the High Court, who read the phrase 'reasonably suspects' as applicable whether or not the foundation for that suspicion was legally infirm. This had the effect of severing the link between the legal validity of the cancellation decisions and the legal validity of the decision to detain; it was possible for s 189 to afford lawful justification for imprisonment even where informed by an unlawful administrative decision. Mr Taylor's failure to obtain compensation for his period of detention therefore says more about the fluid notion of 'unlawfulness' than it does about the capacity of this tort to provide effective redress for unlawful detention. If we perceive there to be an accountability shortfall in Mr Taylor's case, we might say that it stems not from the structure of the tort, but from the breadth of the detention power conferred on immigration officials pursuant to s 189.

8.4   Australian Apprenticeships Incentives Program: Maladministration by Private Contractors

The third accountability scenario measured against the hypothetical benchmark relates to the administration of a government scheme, the Australian Apprenticeships Incentives Program. The particular circumstances which engage the accountability benchmark relate to losses suffered by applicants which arose out of misleading and incorrect advice provided by private contractors administering the Program. This section considers the two accountability mechanisms that were brought to bear: the Commonwealth Ombudsman, and compensation pursuant to the Scheme for Compensation for Detriment caused by Defective Administration (CDDA Scheme).

The Incentives Program was an administrative scheme managed by an Australian Commonwealth government department.[306] The overarching purpose of the Program was to contribute to skills and workforce development through the provision of incentive payments to employers who offered apprenticeship positions. While the Program was overseen by a government department, individual decisions about eligibility and entitlements for incentives were made, in the first instance, by so-called Australian Apprenticeships Centres, which were private organisations contracted to perform that role on behalf of the government.[307] Two small business owners applied for entitlements under the Program, with each relying on eligibility advice provided by their relevant Apprenticeships Centre.[308] The first (Mr A) planned to take on a mature-aged apprentice, and was incorrectly advised by his Centre that this would make him eligible to receive a weekly subsidy payment. In fact, that aspect of the scheme had been discontinued and only a lump sum payment was available. The second small business owner (Ms M) supported a number of employees to commence tertiary qualifications, anticipating that she would receive an incentive on their completion of the course. Part way through the course, the Program policy was altered so that payments would only be available for completions up to a particular date. Seven months prior to that deadline, Ms M's Centre wrote to her, providing unclear information which led Ms M to believe the policy change did not affect her eligibility. Two months prior to the deadline, the Centre issued a further letter which confirmed that the deadline did in fact apply to Ms M. At this point, there was insufficient time left for Ms M's employees to complete their courses prior to the deadline, and Ms M was denied access to completion payments.

Complaints by Mr A and Ms M were investigated by the Commonwealth Ombudsman, who considered the means by which Mr A and Ms M could be compensated. The structure of the CDDA Scheme prevented compensation being awarded via that mechanism. This case study provides interesting fodder for discussion in the context of government accountability because it involves complainants who assert that they were

---

[306] The then Department of Industry, Innovation, Climate Change, Science, Research and Tertiary Education.

[307] Commonwealth Ombudsman, *Making Things Right: Department of Education and Training, Compensation for Errors Made by Contracted Service Providers* (Report No 1, March 2015) 5.

[308] Ibid 6–7.

left worse off as a result of the provision of unclear advice about the operation of a government scheme, with the alleged wrongdoing having been committed by private contractors working on behalf of the government. We would likely say that this scenario engages the following aspects of the hypothetical benchmark:

(a) the **transparency** rationale would require a mechanism to uncover the circumstances surrounding the provision of advice by Apprenticeship Centres;
(b) the **redress** rationale would require the availability of reparative remedies to correct the harm suffered by Mr A and Ms M in reliance on misleading and incorrect advice provided by Apprenticeship Centres; and
(c) the **deterrence** rationale would require dialogue-driven sanctions to foster improvements in the operation of government programmes managed by private contractors, and appropriate delineation of responsibilities between those entities.

The following sections measure the accountability performance of the Commonwealth Ombudsman and CDDA Scheme against the hypothetical benchmark.

8.4.1   Commonwealth Ombudsman

Mr A and Ms M each complained to the Commonwealth Ombudsman about the difficulties they had experienced in their dealings with their respective Apprenticeship Centres. Ombudsmen regimes have long been linked with the concept of accountability,[309] performing a role as an accountability mechanism of 'last resort' for aggrieved citizens.[310] McMillan has described the office as one of 'accountability "watchdog"',[311] viewing it as one of the 'non-judicial accountability bodies' that supplement the role of the courts in 'controlling government and ensuring integrity'.[312]

---

[309] See Greg Weeks, *Soft Law and Public Authorities: Remedies and Reform* (Hart Publishing, 2016) ch 11.

[310] See, e.g., Anita Stuhmcke, 'Ombuds Can, Ombuds Can't, Ombuds Should, Ombuds Shan't: A Call to Improve Evaluation of the Ombudsman Institution' in Marc Hertogh and Richard Kirkham (eds.), *Research Handbook on the Ombudsman* (Edward Elgar Publishing, 2018) 415, 418.

[311] John McMillan, 'Re-thinking the Separation of Powers' (2010) 38 *Federal Law Review* 423, 437.

[312] Ibid 423–24.

We would likely conclude that this mechanism is most clearly aligned with the *deterrence rationale*, although it also contributes to a range of other objectives.

8.4.1.1   Who Can Be Investigated?

The Commonwealth Ombudsman has a relatively broad remit in terms of who it may investigate, with empowering legislation conferring a function to investigate government departments and 'prescribed authorities',[313] defined to include statutory bodies, statutory office-holders and Commonwealth-controlled companies, amongst others.[314] The Ombudsman is prohibited from investigating the actions of ministers, Members of Parliament and judges,[315] with the result that the core focus of the Ombudsman's work is directed at the administrative machinery of government. From an accountability perspective, one of the most important extended applications of the Ombudsman's jurisdiction is in respect of the actions of private contractors, or 'Commonwealth service providers', which captures contractors and subcontractors who provide 'goods or services, for or on behalf of the Department or prescribed authority, to another person who is not a Department or prescribed authority or the Commonwealth'.[316] The effect of the relevant empowering provision is to deem the actions of a contractor to have been taken by the department or prescribed authority with whom the contract is held,[317] with the result that the Ombudsman can investigate actions taken by private contractors on behalf of the government. For the purpose of the Incentives Program, the Ombudsman had jurisdiction to investigate the actions of Apprenticeship Centres taken on behalf of the relevant government department.

8.4.1.2   Who Can Instigate an Investigation?

The jurisdiction of the Commonwealth Ombudsman can be engaged in a number of ways. Most relevantly, for present purposes, the Ombudsman is empowered to investigate a matter 'in respect of which a complaint has been made'.[318] The complaints process is not onerous, allowing a complainant to lodge their complaint either orally or in writing, with no

---

[313] *Ombudsman Act 1976* (Cth) s 5(1).
[314] Ibid s 3(1) (definition of 'prescribed authority').
[315] Ibid s 5(2).
[316] Ibid s 3BA. For further discussion see Boughey, Rock and Weeks (n 9) [3.6].
[317] *Ombudsman Act 1976* (Cth) s 3(4B).
[318] Ibid s 5(1)(a).

rigorous forms or fees.[319] There are no standing limitations that restrict rights of access to the complaints mechanism,[320] though the Ombudsman retains discretion to refuse to investigate a matter if the complainant lacks interest in the subject matter of the complaint.[321] The Ombudsman can also decline to investigate on a range of other grounds, including where the complaint is frivolous, vexatious or not made in good faith, where other mechanisms are more appropriate to resolve the complaint, or more broadly, where investigation 'is not warranted having regard to all the circumstances'.[322] The Ombudsman also has an own-motion jurisdiction,[323] allowing for the investigation of matters that might come to light through alternative sources such as media reports. We would say, therefore, that the Ombudsman mechanism facilitates very broad rights to instigate a complaint, with the Ombudsman retaining discretion to proceed.

8.4.1.3   What Can Be Investigated?

The Ombudsman has jurisdiction to investigate actions that relate to a 'matter of administration',[324] a phrase that has proved difficult to define and has been the subject of ongoing litigation. The key point to be drawn from this litigation history is that matters of administration are institutionally defined, requiring a distinction between matters that arise or are reasonably incidental to the 'executive function of government', and those which are concerned with the judicial or legislative functions of government.[325] As with the definition of 'who' may be investigated, the core rationale for this distinction appears to be to confine the Ombudsman's role to the investigation of day-to-day administration of the executive branch government. The types of wrongdoing that the Ombudsman is concerned with identifying are reflected in the types of findings that can be made,[326] which are generally concerned with processes rather than outcomes.[327] Available findings include opinions as to

---

[319] Ibid s 7. The Ombudsman may require a complainant to reduce their complaint to writing (sub-s (2)).
[320] Ibid s 7(1).
[321] Ibid s 6(1)(b)(ii).
[322] Ibid s 6.
[323] Ibid s 5(2).
[324] Ibid s 5(1)–(2).
[325] *Glenister v Dillon* [1976] VR 550, 558; *Booth v Dillon (No 3)* [1977] VR 143, 144.
[326] These are set out in *Ombudsman Act 1976* (Cth) s 15.
[327] See, e.g., Stuhmcke (n 310) 415, 418.

the legality of the action,[328] or to more broadly conceived notions of fairness (i.e. that the action, or the rule or practice it was based on, was 'unreasonable, unjust, oppressive or improperly discriminatory').[329] The Ombudsman may also form opinions that the action was based on mistake of fact or law, or, most broadly, that it was 'in all the circumstances, wrong'.[330] The reach of the jurisdiction of the Ombudsman was sufficiently broad to enable it to investigate the administration of the Incentives Program. The key findings recorded in the final report included that the Apprenticeship Centres had provided unclear and incorrect advice, and that both Mr A and Ms M had suffered loss by reason of that advice.[331]

8.4.1.4   By What Procedures?

The Ombudsman is able to exercise a range of investigative powers during the course of investigating a matter of administration. These powers allow the Ombudsman to require the production of documents and statements of information,[332] to require a person to attend and answer questions (including on oath),[333] and to enter premises.[334] These powers extend to the investigation of private contractors.[335] There are very limited circumstances in which an individual is entitled to refuse to comply with the Ombudsman's request, with usual grounds such as the privilege against self-incrimination and legal professional privilege being inapplicable.[336] Failure to comply without reasonable excuse is further punishable as an offence.[337] Accordingly, we would say that the Ombudsman's investigative powers are quite wide-ranging. On the other hand, there are significant protections for agencies and witnesses built into the Ombudsman's investigative jurisdiction. A range of procedural fairness requirements apply, with the Ombudsman being required to notify the relevant department or prescribed authority of the proposed

---

[328] For example, the Ombudsman may make findings that discretionary power was exercised for an improper purpose, or by reference to irrelevant considerations: *Ombudsman Act 1976* (Cth) s 15(1)(c).

[329] Ibid s 15(1)(a)(iii).

[330] Ibid s 15(1)(a)(v).

[331] Commonwealth Ombudsman, *Making Things Right* (n 307) 7.

[332] *Ombudsman Act 1976* (Cth) s 9(1).

[333] Ibid ss 9(2), 13.

[334] Ibid s 14.

[335] Ibid ss 14(a)(ii).

[336] Ibid s 9(4). The information and documents produced are inadmissible in evidence.

[337] Ibid s 36.

investigation.[338] The Ombudsman must also allow a person or agency an opportunity to make submissions before making a report that is critical of that person or agency.[339] Perhaps the most notable procedural aspect of Ombudsman investigations is that they take place in private,[340] with the result that the production of documents and examination of witnesses is not a matter of public record. Some investigations culminate in the publication of a report,[341] but many more are resolved without publicity. For example, in the same year that the Ombudsman published its report on the Incentives Program, approximately 2,300 matters were investigated but only four were the subject of an in-depth investigation and published report.[342]

8.4.1.5   With What Outcomes?

Following an investigation, the Ombudsman has a limited range of powers to follow through on the outcome of the investigation, including to report on their findings[343] and to make recommendations about action that should be taken in response to those findings. These recommendations might include that the agency reconsider the matter, vary or cancel the impugned decision, alter an applicable rule or procedure, take steps to 'rectify, mitigate, or alter the effects' of the impugned decision or conduct, or 'that any other thing should be done'.[344] Importantly, the Ombudsman's recommendations are non-coercive; no penalty arises from an agency's failure to comply. The Ombudsman has the power to publicise a report if in the public interest to do so,[345] but the only real consequence that the Ombudsman can deliver in cases of non-compliance is to report 'up the chain' to the Prime Minister and Parliament.[346] Having said this, the office of the Ombudsman is generally regarded as an effective accountability mechanism.[347] This is supported by the Ombudsman's own observations in its 2017–18 Annual Report,

---

[338] Ibid s 8(1).

[339] Ibid s 8(5).

[340] Ibid s 8(2).

[341] Ibid s 35A.

[342] Commonwealth Ombudsman, *Annual Report 2014–15* (October 2015) 12. The report indicates that the office received 21,044 in-jurisdiction complaints, 11 per cent of which proceeded to an investigation.

[343] See, e.g., *Ombudsman Act 1976* (Cth) s 15(1), (6).

[344] Ibid s 15(2).

[345] Ibid s 35A.

[346] Ibid ss 16–17.

[347] See, e.g., sources cited in Chapter 9 n 7, and Weeks (n 309) ch 11.

which recorded that in that year, agencies had accepted 75 per cent of recommendations made in published reports.[348]

Following the investigation into the conduct of Australian Apprenticeship Centres, the Ombudsman published a report in March 2015.[349] Having concluded that the Centres had provided incorrect advice to Mr A and Ms M, the Ombudsman considered the possible means by which their loss could be redressed. The first option considered was whether it was open to the Department to make payments to the complainants pursuant to the Program policy, for example, by waiving the problematic eligibility criteria.[350] The Ombudsman concluded that Ms M's situation could potentially have been dealt with as an 'exceptional circumstance' within the policy framework, on the basis that if the Centre had provided clear and accurate advice in its first letter, Ms M could have taken steps to ensure that she met the revised completion deadline. Accordingly, that aspect of the eligibility criteria could have been waived such that Ms M could receive completion payments pursuant to the policy. However, this approach could not assist Mr A, because the Centre had advised him of his eligibility to access a scheme that had been discontinued. There was no way to waive eligibility criteria to allow Mr A payments within the scope of the current policy scheme. The Ombudsman further considered the possibility of compensation pursuant to the CDDA Scheme. As noted in Section 8.4.2 below, this Scheme was determined to be inapplicable because the loss was caused by a private contractor rather than government agency.[351]

The Ombudsman made three recommendations in its report. Two of these related to the Department's approach to situations such as that of Mr A and Ms M in the future. One recommendation was that the Department adopt a more flexible approach to application of the policy, pursuant to which it might waive strict application of eligibility requirements where incorrect advice prevented an applicant from meeting those requirements (which would have avoided Ms M's loss).[352] Another was that the Department provide guidance to its decision-makers to ensure that they did not unreasonably penalise applicants who revised their plans to maintain eligibility following changes in Program policy (which

---

[348] Commonwealth Ombudsman, *Annual Report 2017–18* (October 2018) 18.
[349] Commonwealth Ombudsman, *Making Things Right* (n 307).
[350] Ibid 9–10.
[351] Ibid 11.
[352] Ibid 13.

again would have resulted in a favourable result in Ms M's case).[353] The Department accepted each of these recommendations, and committed to taking steps to implement the required changes. The final recommendation related to compensation. The Ombudsman recommended that the Department implement a scheme equivalent to the CDDA Scheme, which would allow it to provide compensation in circumstances where contracted service providers (rather than government officials) had engaged in defective administration.[354] The Department declined to adopt this recommendation on the basis that such a change should be addressed at a whole-of-government level.

8.4.2   CDDA Scheme

The second mechanism considered in this case was the CDDA Scheme, which is a form of discretionary compensation mechanism, operating alongside act of grace and waiver of debts mechanisms.[355] The scheme was originally established in 1995, and has undergone a series of revisions since that time.[356] In a report prepared in 1999, the Commonwealth Ombudsman acknowledged the link between ex gratia compensation and accountability in the context of recommending the adoption of a more flexible approach to such mechanisms.[357] The Ombudsman indicated that greater flexibility in the award of discretionary compensation was consistent with the existing trend towards viewing 'compensation for service delivery failures as a way of strengthening accountability for service delivery'.[358] When we look at the CDDA Scheme within the rubric of the hypothetical accountability benchmark, we see that it is most relevant to the redress rationale, though there were significant limits to its utility in the present case.

8.4.2.1   Who Is Held Accountable?

The CDDA Scheme is limited in its application to non-corporate Commonwealth entities.[359] This means that it does not apply to government

---

[353] Ibid 14.

[354] Ibid.

[355] Weeks (n 309) 252–56.

[356] See ibid 254.

[357] Commonwealth Ombudsman, *To Compensate or Not to Compensate* (September 1999) [9].

[358] Ibid.

[359] Department of Finance (Cth), *Scheme for Compensation for Detriment Caused by Defective Administration* (Resource Management Guide No 409, November 2018) [13]–[16] 'CDDA Scheme'.

departments or government corporate entities. Importantly for present purposes, the Scheme does not apply in circumstances where the conduct complained of was engaged in by a private contractor acting on behalf of the government. Accordingly, there was no possibility of applying the CDDA Scheme to the actions of Australian Apprenticeship Centres, even where their actions would have fallen within the Scheme had they been undertaken by a government agency. The Ombudsman was critical of this limitation, noting that a government agency should not be entitled to 'contract itself out of the moral responsibility to compensate members of the public for losses caused by [its] program's defective administration'.[360]

8.4.2.2 Who Can Obtain Relief?

There are no standing limitations for access to the CDDA Scheme, being applicable to 'individuals, businesses and other bodies' who suffer loss as a result of maladministration.[361] This broadly framed entitlement is consistent with the expectations of the redress rationale.

8.4.2.3 What Conduct Is Targeted?

The CDDA Scheme may be engaged in cases where a person suffers detriment as a result of defective administration. Looking first at the concept of 'detriment', the CDDA guidelines allow compensation for both economic and non-economic losses.[362] In respect of the latter, compensation is informed by legal principle and is available for personal injury, emotional distress and damage to reputation, but not for injured feelings. Economic loss is limited to reasonably foreseeable loss where it arises from a lost opportunity or is said to have been caused by incorrect advice. Expectation losses (e.g. a benefit a claimant hoped to receive from the government based on misleading advice) are specifically excluded.[363] In the present case, the Department denied that Mr A or Ms M had suffered any loss on the basis that, at best, they had been disappointed at not receiving incentive payments for which they had been advised they were eligible. The Ombudsman accepted that the lost expectation of incentive payments fell outside the CDDA Scheme, but expressed the view that consequential losses arising from reliance on incorrect advice could be compensated. As noted by the Ombudsman, the very nature of

---

[360] Commonwealth Ombudsman, *Making Things Right* (n 307) [5.3].
[361] Department of Finance (Cth), *CDDA Scheme* (n 359) [35].
[362] Ibid [60]–[67].
[363] Ibid [57].

an 'incentive' payment is to shape behaviour, and costs of action taken in pursuit of the incentive could therefore be treated as consequential losses.[364]

The next aspect defining 'for what' the CDDA Scheme provides accountability is the concept of defective administration, which captures two broad circumstances. The first relates to the application of appropriate administrative procedures, either where there is a 'specific and unreasonable lapse' in complying with an applicable procedure, or a failure to institute an applicable procedure.[365] This is measured against a 'standard of diligence' expected of 'reasonable officers acting in the same circumstances with the same powers and access to resources'.[366] The guidelines also make clear that unreasonableness can arise on a systemic view: 'Cases may arise where individual instances of administrative omissions or errors may not be regarded as unreasonable when considered in isolation from each other, but may constitute defective administration when considered in totality and in the context of the combined impact of the omissions or errors on the claimant.'[367] The second circumstance in which the Scheme operates is in connection with the provision of advice, encompassing both acts (i.e. the provision of 'incorrect or ambiguous' advice), as well as omissions (i.e. the failure to give 'proper advice').[368] It is unnecessary to establish unreasonableness or intent in such cases.[369]

The Ombudsman was of the view that the conduct of Australian Apprenticeship Centres fell within this latter category in failing to provide 'clear and correct' advice to Mr A and Ms M.[370] The advice given to Mr A was 'undoubtedly incorrect and outdated', while the advice to Ms M was 'initially ambiguous and then only corrected when it was already too late' for Ms M to act on it.[371] Looking at the redress rationale, it is engaged in cases of *unlawful exercise of public power*. Unless we take a very broad view of the concept of unlawfulness, we would likely say that the CDDA Scheme goes further than the strict requirements of the benchmark, as it is capable of applying to circumstances that traditional

---

[364] Commonwealth Ombudsman, *Making Things Right* (n 307) [4.32].
[365] Department of Finance (Cth), *CDDA Scheme* (n 359) [17].
[366] Ibid [46].
[367] Ibid [47].
[368] Ibid [17].
[369] Ibid [48].
[370] Commonwealth Ombudsman, *Making Things Right* (n 307) [4.1].
[371] Ibid.

legal remedies would not address. Indeed, this is the very point of the CDDA Scheme, as it is not intended to apply in circumstances where legal liability would arise.[372] As discussed in Chapter 11, this mechanism is intended to perform a gap-filling role rather than being available in parallel with other remedial mechanisms.[373]

8.4.2.4   By What Procedures?

The most notable feature of ex gratia compensation mechanisms is their inherently discretionary nature. Even where a case falls squarely within the examples of maladministration set out in the Scheme guidelines, the decision-maker retains ultimate discretion to determine whether a payment ought to be made, confined by the general requirement that the decision 'must be publicly defensible'.[374] The decision-maker is required to comply with procedural fairness requirements, including providing opportunities to make submissions and to respond to adverse material.[375] The Scheme is intended to operate quite separately from the legal system, both in terms of its coverage and in terms of the manner in which determinations are made. A claimant need not prove their case through the submission of 'incontrovertible' documentary evidence.[376] Instead, it is necessary only for there to be 'sufficient evidence' to allow the decision-maker to form an opinion that defective administration has taken place. All of this is consistent with the redress rationale, which looks for agent-friendly procedures.

8.4.2.5   With What Consequences?

The ultimate outcome of the CDDA Scheme is the provision of compensation, which is designed to place the claimant in the position they would have been but for the defective administration.[377] There is no ceiling on the amount that can be paid under the Scheme, meaning that it can be a very effective remedy in circumstances where it applies. Unfortunately for Mr A and Ms M, compensation was not available under the Scheme

---

[372] See Department of Finance (Cth), *CDDA Scheme* (n 359) [23]: 'The CDDA Scheme is not to be used in relation to ... claims in which it is reasonable to conclude that the Commonwealth would be found liable, if the matter were litigated.'

[373] See Section 11.3.2 in Chapter 11.

[374] Department of Finance (Cth), *CDDA Scheme* (n 359) [18].

[375] Ibid [40].

[376] Ibid [49].

[377] Ibid [69].

due to the involvement of private contractors in administering the Incentives Program.

8.4.3   What Does the Hypothetical Benchmark Tell Us in the Australian Apprenticeships Centres Case?

When comparing the performance of the Ombudsman and CDDA Scheme against the hypothetical accountability benchmark, we might make the following observations:

(a) **Transparency:** The office of the Commonwealth Ombudsman has useful investigatory and inquisitorial functions that allow it to access government information, including from private contractors. It may also be thought that the lack of immediate legal consequences flowing from an Ombudsman's report could improve the likelihood of co-operation during the course of investigations, and therefore the prospect of uncovering evidence of maladministration.[378] The fact that the Ombudsman's investigations are conducted in private is a significant limit on the contribution to transparency. While it is true that the Ombudsman prepares reports in some of its investigations (including its investigation into Mr A's and Ms M's cases), this represents only a small percentage of the work performed by the Ombudsman without attendant publicity. Again, this limits the extent to which we can regard the Ombudsman as a complete response to the demands of the transparency rationale. The CDDA Scheme offers no contribution to transparency. Applications are dealt with internally by the relevant decision-maker without publication of outcomes.

(b) **Redress:** The CDDA Scheme is clearly linked to the redress rationale for accountability, providing a monetary remedy designed to compensate financial and non-financial loss. In some respects, this mechanism's reach is wider than the requirements of the benchmark; the hypothetical benchmark requires redress only in cases of loss caused by the unlawful exercise of government power, whereas the CDDA Scheme is capable of applying to the misdirected application of procedure and provision of advice. In other respects, the Scheme is too narrow to satisfy the benchmark, as the exercise of public power by non-government agents is not captured. It was this limitation

---

[378] See Section 9.4 in Chapter 9.

which prevented its operation to remedy the losses occasioned by Mr A and Ms M.

The Ombudsman is well positioned to investigate cases of systemic (as opposed to individual) wrongdoing, and is able to recommend the redress of harm arising from government maladministration either within the context of taking steps to 'rectify' or 'mitigate' the effects of government conduct, or the broader power to recommend 'that any other thing should be done'.[379] While this may prompt the provision of a reparative remedy, the Ombudsman's lack of determinative power would likely prevent us from classifying this mechanism as meeting the expectations of the hypothetical redress benchmark. In the present case, none of the recommendations made by the Ombudsman was directed towards facilitating an immediate remedy for either Mr A or Ms M.

(c) **Deterrence:** The office of the Ombudsman is extremely well aligned with the expectations of the hypothetical deterrence benchmark. First, it is worth noting that the jurisdiction of the Ombudsman extends beyond traditional notions of 'unlawful' conduct as understood within the legal system, capturing more broadly conceived understandings of unacceptable practices. Notably, the Ombudsman's investigative powers allow it to target systemic issues, and to address its recommendations to the entity responsible for managing that area, rather than targeting individual wrongdoers. We would also be satisfied that the use of recommendations, rather than coercive determinations, would fit well with Braithwaite's notion of 'weak sanctions'.[380] Finally, the process of investigation and reporting is clearly well aligned with a dialogue-based approach. Entities participate in the investigation process, and are made aware of the Ombudsman's findings prior to the final report. This dialogue is reflected in the fact that an agency's responses to draft recommendations are included in the final report.

This summary tells us that the Ombudsman was very well positioned to facilitate deterrence in this case, by establishing dialogue with the relevant government department that was capable of facilitating

---

[379] *Ombudsman Act 1976* (Cth) s 15(2).

[380] John Braithwaite, 'On Speaking Softly and Carrying Big Sticks: Neglected Dimensions of a Republican Separation of Powers' (1997) 47 *University of Toronto Law Journal* 305, 318.

meaningful changes in the management of similar cases in the future. In particular, the Department committed to undertaking training to improve staff awareness of the manner in which the eligibility requirements should be interpreted, including in the context of requests for review of decisions made by Apprenticeship Centres.

The Ombudsman was also able to contribute to transparency in this case, by utilising broad investigative powers and publishing a report to facilitate public scrutiny. Importantly, however, this is not an inherent feature of this mechanism; many investigations are resolved without in-depth investigatory procedures or publicity, which limits the extent to which we would regard the Ombudsman as a complete response to the demands of the transparency rationale and revealing a potential area of *accountability deficit*. Indeed, we might view this as an example of the dangers of tension between accountability rationales. Were the Ombudsman to have a mandate of conducting investigations in public and publicising opinions and recommendations, we might have legitimate concerns about the extent to which this might undercut the effectiveness of the deterrence rationale. Many regard the non-coercive and conciliatory approach of the Ombudsman as an important factor which contributes to agencies' willingness to comply with investigations.[381] Accordingly, attempts to plug any potential accountability deficit in the transparency contributions of the Ombudsman might have knock-on effects in respect of the deterrence function.

We can also observe that neither mechanism met the expectations of the redress rationale in this case. The Ombudsman's report was directed towards systemic changes that could assist future complainants in the positions of Mr A and Ms M. These recommendations highlighted the inapplicability of the other mechanism considered in this case study; the CDDA Scheme.[382] The foregoing analysis demonstrates that this mechanism is capable of providing an effective reparative remedy that would likely have been engaged in the circumstances of the complainants' cases, had the government acted directly rather than through private contractors. We could regard this limitation of the CDDA Scheme as a potential area of *accountability deficit*.

---

[381] See Chapter 9 n 7.

[382] As noted below, it is possible that an alternative form of compensation was available to the complainants (see Section 11.3.2 in Chapter 11).

8.5   Conclusion

The position taken in Part II of this book is that claims of accountability deficit and overload conceal a hidden choice about what accountability demands in a normative sense. In order to make that assessment explicit by defining an accountability 'benchmark', it would be necessary to confront, and resolve, a range of difficult questions that do not admit of easy answers. This chapter has demonstrated the scale of this challenge by adopting a hypothetical accountability benchmark and deploying that benchmark in three real-world scenarios. This undertaking reveals a number of difficulties that stand in the way of giving body to the concepts of accountability deficit and overload.

First, it is clear that we are a long way from being able to define an accountability benchmark, or benchmarks. The hypothetical chosen here represents an overly simplified set of assumptions about how accountability is best achieved for particular purposes, and skips over the difficulties that have been highlighted in Chapters 4–7 of this book. The uncertainties that underpin these tentative choices are emphasised when we seek to apply the hypothetical benchmark to real-world scenarios. For example, the hypothetical benchmark employs the term 'unlawful' in a number of places to define the circumstances in which particular rationales would be engaged. This deceptively simple label could be interpreted in a variety of different ways; for example, does it mean excess of jurisdiction in the broad public law sense, or an act expressly forbidden by law? We might say the same of terms such as 'harm' and 'unsatisfactory'. Any claim of accountability deficit or overload identified through the application of such a general benchmark necessarily entails a value judgement about the types of conduct for which we believe an actor ought to be held accountable, which is precisely the problem that defining a benchmark seeks to address.

A further example of this difficulty can be seen in the framing of the hypothetical 'deterrence' rationale. For the purpose of the hypothetical, the deterrence rationale is said to demand the application of 'weak sanctions' to 'soft targets' with a view to facilitating dialogue, in line with Braithwaite's views.[383] However, as has been highlighted in a number of places throughout this chapter, there are many who would maintain that punitive sanctions have a legitimate role to play in facilitating specific and general deterrence (i.e. deterring the individual wrongdoer from

---

[383] Braithwaite, 'On Speaking Softly and Carrying Big Sticks' (n 380).

future infractions as well as discouraging onlookers from following suit). By defining the hypothetical benchmark so as to demand 'weak sanctions', we necessarily come to regard punitive sanctions as exceeding benchmark expectations and therefore as producing a potential accountability overload for the purposes of the deterrence rationale. So, for example, it was concluded that Mr Obeid's criminal prosecution might be regarded as an accountability overload in the sense that it applied a harsh punitive sanction as opposed to one designed to facilitate dialogue and encourage change. To the extent that we disagree with this conclusion, it is open to us to revisit (and redefine) the hypothetical benchmark so as to demand the use of punitive sanctions to facilitate deterrence. Of course, this would lead to criticism on the alternate basis that the application of punitive sanctions risks a response of 'reactance' that is counterproductive in the pursuit of dialogue and meaningful systemic change.[384] All of this confirms that we are a long way from being able to define a defensible accountability benchmark. As has already been stated, our present lack of an accountability benchmark is likely less a matter of oversight than a reflection of the sheer scale (and perhaps even impossibility) of the task of defining one. What this chapter demonstrates is that we cannot circumvent the challenges outlined in Part II of this book by adopting an overly simplified benchmark that is to be fleshed out in practice.

A second point to note is that there is something of a disjuncture between analysis of accountability mechanisms in the abstract, and application in the context of a particular case. For instance, when looking at judicial review it was noted that the available remedies are essentially control-oriented, being concerned with policing the boundaries of public power rather than with assisting a particular individual in respect of their circumstances. However, it was also noted that in Mr Taylor's case, judicial review remedies were capable of generating a reparative result, as he was released from prison as an immediate consequence of quashing the impugned visa cancellation decisions. Therefore, while judicial review remedies are not redress-oriented in the abstract, they achieved a redress-oriented result in Mr Taylor's case.[385] Similarly, it was noted that, when taken in the abstract, the tort of false imprisonment is capable of making meaningful contributions to the control rationale, by providing nominal

---

[384] Which is the argument made by Braithwaite: ibid.

[385] Of course, this does not take into account the losses (e.g. deprivation of liberty) which Mr Taylor occasioned prior to the order being made.

damages in cases where the unlawfulness of the detention is of a technical character. This potential was not realised in Mr Taylor's case as the facts did not engage that aspect of the tort. Because of this disjunct between the abstract analysis of a mechanism and its practical operation in a particular case, it is necessary to take care in diagnosing accountability deficits and overloads. A single case study, taken alone, cannot provide us with a complete picture of a mechanism's accountability contributions. Instead, this view must be formed by reference to a fulsome analysis of the mechanism in the abstract, as well as its operation across a range of different cases. Occasionally, a shortfall in a particular mechanism may only become apparent when realised in an unusual or difficult case.

Finally, this chapter made clear that while each scenario enlivened a number of the rationales for accountability, none of the given mechanisms was capable of meeting the demands of all relevant rationales. Most mechanisms were more clearly aligned with one, or perhaps two, rationales, and failed to meet the expectations of others. In some cases, this even rose to the level of evidence of tension between accountability rationales. For example, it was noted that the criminal sanctions imposed on Mr Obeid were well aligned with the desert rationale, but were very poorly aligned with the deterrence rationale. If we were to identify this deterrence shortfall as an accountability deficit, efforts to remedy that deficit by reducing the punitive effect of applicable sanctions would have an inverse impact on the desert rationale. Likewise, it was noted that investigation by the Ombudsman was very well aligned with the expectations of the deterrence rationale, but fell far short of the expectations of the transparency rationale. If we were to cite this lack of transparency as an accountability deficit, attempts to remedy that shortfall by increasing public awareness of investigations might impact negatively on agency compliance (and therefore deterrence). All of this tells us that, if we accept that accountability entails a range of different normative objectives, we must also accept that one mechanism cannot meet our expectations across all rationales. Instead, the various rationales are better targeted through the combined efforts of a range of mechanisms. This requires a systemic approach to accountability, which is considered in Part III of this book.

PART III

The Complexity of Accountability Systems

> Public accountability ... is not a simple quantum ... It consists of countless
> relationships, between different accountees and account-holders over differ-
> ent issues, not reducible to a single measure or variable. For any accountabil-
> ity deficit, as for any accountability relationship, we must always specify
> answers to the standard questions: who, to whom, for what, and in what
> way.[1]

The second main dilemma that must be confronted by those who wish to
assess accountability deficits and overloads is the task of understanding
accountability mechanisms not simply as a series of individual mechanisms in isolation, but as part of a system. This dilemma is evident in a
number of different ways in claims about accountability deficits and
overloads. For instance, a generalised claim that a government official
has not been held accountable in a given situation involves an implicit
reference to the universe of mechanisms pursuant to which that official
could have been held accountable; in other words, this is a claim that the
official has 'fallen through the net'. For obvious reasons, it is necessary to
have some understanding about the shape and structure of this 'net' to
make such a claim. It is also necessary to have some understanding of the
wider accountability system in making claims about the limitations of a
particular mechanism. If we focus on one style or group of accountability
mechanisms to the exclusion of others, the identification of any accountability deficit must necessarily be a preliminary observation; after all,
until we know whether other accountability mechanisms operate so as to
ameliorate shortcomings in one mechanism, how can we know whether
the perceived deficit is meaningful? To pick up the example mentioned in
Chapter 2, some might make the argument that the unavailability of

---

[1] Richard Mulgan, 'Accountability Deficits' in Mark Bovens, Robert Goodin and Thomas
Schillemans (eds.), *The Oxford Handbook of Public Accountability* (Oxford University
Press, 2014) 545, 553.

damages in judicial review proceedings represents an accountability deficit inasmuch as wronged individuals go unrestored. However, can we really describe this as a 'deficit' if we have not considered the role that other mechanisms (for example, tort law and ex gratia compensation amongst others) might play in filling that gap? In Mulgan's words, to look for accountability gaps within a single or discrete set of mechanisms is inclined to produce a 'distorted view' of the size or nature of any deficits that are identified.[2]

At the other extreme, failing to understand the nature and shape of the accountability system also affects our analysis of accountability overloads. Can we say that there is an accountability overload simply by pointing to the *quantity* of accountability mechanisms that potentially apply to a particular actor? It is one thing to note the potential for accountability overload by listing the number of mechanisms that potentially apply in the context of an exercise of statutory discretion by a government minister (e.g. judicial review, merits review, tort liability, ministerial responsibility, party discipline, a Royal Commission); it is quite another to explore the manner in which these various mechanisms coalesce to hold that minister accountable. Is one mechanism a precondition of another? Will one mechanism fall away in the face of a conclusion reached pursuant to another? Is one mechanism thought to be a failsafe that applies where all other mechanisms fail? The position adopted here is that claims of accountability overload cannot simply point to the number of mechanisms in play but must also assess the interrelationship between them. As Elliott suggests, 'accountability can, and should, take several forms ... [which] demands that accountability be supplied by a range of functionally-complementary institutions applying a diversity of criteria and approaches'.[3]

Part III of this book explores two key ideas that we need to grapple with in order to understand mechanisms as a *system* of accountability, rather than a collection of mechanisms working alone. Chapter 9 explores the delicate balance of features between these various mechanisms. So, for instance, while some mechanisms are flexible, others are rigid. And while some are coercive, others are recommendatory. If we were to look at each mechanism only in isolation, it might be tempting to

[2] Ibid 552.
[3] Mark Elliott, 'Ombudsmen, Tribunals, Inquiries: Re-fashioning Accountability Beyond the Courts' in Nicholas Bamforth and Peter Leyland (eds.), *Accountability in the Contemporary Constitution* (Oxford University Press, 2013) 233, 258.

classify some features of mechanisms as 'weaknesses' (e.g. when looked at alone, the ombudsman's lack of coercive powers might be thought to be a weakness of that mechanism: the 'toothless tiger'). However, when understood as part of a wider accountability system in which other mechanisms (e.g. the courts) have more coercive powers, we can instead view the ombudsman's recommendatory role as a potential strength, facilitating a more co-operative dynamic than might be achieved through the courts. For this reason, it is crucial to understand accountability mechanisms as a system that contains a delicate balance of features. Chapter 10 goes on to look at the manner in which the various accountability mechanisms interlock within the system, and notes that we can observe a wide variety of relationships in play when these mechanisms perform their accountability roles. For instance, mechanisms may operate independently, mutually exclusively, in stages, interdependently, co-operatively or as checks on one another. The nature of these relationship dynamics plays a key role in defining the shape of the accountability system. It is critical that we appreciate the nature of these relationships in order to have any hope of making good a claim of accountability deficit or overload.

9

Features in Balance

The various tools and mechanisms that make up accountability systems operate in quite different ways. One set of differences relates to the circumstances in which the mechanisms apply (for example, differences in the classes of government officials and entities that can be held accountable, and differences in the standards against which they are judged). However, putting these variations to one side, we can also observe a range of differences in the *features* of the various mechanisms, including their cost, duration, degree of flexibility and independence, amongst others. Sometimes these features are viewed in terms of 'strengths' and 'weaknesses' of the various mechanisms. So, for example, some might suggest that there is a potential accountability deficit arising out of the cost and duration of legal proceedings.[1] The argument made in this chapter is that, rather than thinking about these features in terms of 'strengths' and 'weaknesses' of individual mechanisms, it is more instructive to think about them as forming part of a patchwork of interacting and overlapping mechanisms. On this view, we may determine that traditionally conceived 'weaknesses' of individual mechanisms may be framed in less negative terms by viewing them as part of the larger systemic picture.

9.1 Accessibility

The first differentiating feature that we can observe between the mechanisms is their *accessibility*. Are these mechanisms designed for access by individuals, or must we rely on others to initiate the mechanism? In comparing the various mechanisms, we can see that there is a mixture of access entitlements. Some mechanisms are designed so as to be directly

---

[1] This is an example tested by Mulgan: Richard Mulgan, 'Accountability Deficits' in Mark Bovens, Robert Goodin and Thomas Schillemans (eds.), *The Oxford Handbook of Public Accountability* (Oxford University Press, 2014) 545, 554.

accessible by individuals (e.g. elections, courts, tribunals, freedom of information). Other mechanisms are designed to be operated by the government (most notably, the mechanisms of responsible government and parliamentary committees). This is not to say that one approach is more valuable than another. Certainly, there might be accountability concerns if all mechanisms were entirely within the hands of government, with citizens left to trust that they will be utilised. However, there might equally be concerns if all mechanisms required input from citizens in order to operate. Some issues may not attract the attention of particular individuals, or might only affect individuals who lack the means to air their concerns through available mechanisms. In such cases there is great utility in having mechanisms designed for use by government officials, such as the role of the Attorney-General in judicial review proceedings where others lack standing.[2]

9.2   Cost

A second differentiating feature is the *cost* of utilising particular mechanisms, both in terms of time and resources. While some mechanisms are free to access (for example, elections and complaints to ombudsmen), others require significant financial resources (for example, court proceedings). Similarly, while some have a fairly quick turnaround time (for example, election results are relatively immediate), others, such as legal proceedings, are far more time-consuming. On one view, we might think that all accountability mechanisms ought to be efficient in their operation and freely accessible to anyone. Certainly, there are valid criticisms of the enormous financial and time burden of bringing legal challenges before the courts and consequent limitations on access to justice.[3] However, when we view the collection of mechanisms as a system, some of these concerns may be alleviated. So, while an individual may not have the resources to bring a claim before the courts, they may potentially be able to air their concerns through comparatively less expensive and more efficient mechanisms, such as tribunals (which are assigned the objectives of operating in a manner that is 'economical' and 'quick').[4] Indeed, putting to one side concerns about limits on access to justice, there might

---

[2] See discussion in Section 8.3.1.2 in Chapter 8.
[3] See, e.g., Australian Law Reform Commission, *Managing Justice: A Review of the Federal Civil Justice System* (Report No 89, 2000) ch 4.
[4] *Administrative Appeals Tribunal Act 1975* (Cth) s 2A(b).

be views that the immense time and financial cost of legal proceedings is useful from the perspective of diverting individuals into less extreme mechanisms, leaving legal challenge as a tool of last resort. Irrespective of whether we believe that the substantial costs of access to some of the 'big ticket' accountability mechanisms are justified, some of our concerns about the costs of such mechanisms can be alleviated when we see that others are available free of charge.

9.3   Flexibility

The *flexibility* of the mechanisms is also a point of differentiation. Some mechanisms operate according to strictly defined rules of practice and procedure. So, for example, there are clearly defined protocols that confine the operation of elections and the management of legal proceedings through the courts. At the other end of the spectrum, some mechanisms are inherently flexible and discretionary in nature. Tribunals, for example, are intended to operate 'with as little formality and technicality, and with as much expedition' as possible.[5] Ex gratia compensation also falls squarely at this end of the spectrum, with decision-makers having very broad discretion to determine entitlements to compensation informed only by non-binding guidelines. Ombudsmen regimes are also inherently flexible in nature, having broad discretion both in terms of whether to investigate and the manner in which investigations are conducted.

9.4   Coerciveness

Similarly, there are differences between the *coerciveness* of the various mechanisms. Some mechanisms are able to use legal force to compel compliance with accountability objectives. Many, for example, are able to compel compliance with the accountability objective of transparency. Courts and tribunals can require the production of documents and the provision of reasons both prior to and during trial. Parliament can hold a minister in contempt for failure to produce documents,[6] and individuals can use freedom of information regimes to compel the production of documents held by government departments and agencies. Royal commissions and ombudsmen are conferred powers that give them legal

[5] Ibid s 33(1)(b).
[6] *Egan v Willis* (1998) 195 CLR 424.

force in the course of conducting their investigations. However, there are far fewer mechanisms that can act coercively in pursuit of the remaining objectives of accountability. The courts have coercive accountability powers, in being able to make orders mandating or prohibiting conduct (control), imposing fines and terms of imprisonment (punishment) and requiring payment of compensation or rectification (redress). To a certain degree, the doctrine of ministerial responsibility entails a degree of coercion. Convention requires the resignation of a government that lacks the confidence of the lower house and, should the government refuse to comply with the convention, the Governor-General has coercive reserve powers to dismiss the government on that basis. However, other mechanisms are far less coercive in their nature. So, for example, as noted in Chapter 8, the New South Wales Independent Commission Against Corruption (ICAC) has power only to make findings and recommendations in relation to issues of corruption, not to prosecute or impose penalties. Similarly, ombudsmen have powers only to recommend particular courses of action (including the provision of redress) to government. Failure to comply leads only to reporting 'up the chain', rather than to the imposition of any more coercive sanction.

Again, however, we should not view lack of coerciveness necessarily as a 'weakness' in terms of accountability functions. As many have noted, the fact that ombudsmen lack coercive powers can lead to greater likelihood of compliance with investigations.[7] Therefore, far from being a weakness, the lack of coercion may in fact be viewed as a strength of the model. Of course, if ombudsmen were the only available accountability mechanism within our system of government, we might be concerned that they lack the power to achieve the results-focused accountability objectives of control, redress and punishment. However, when we take a systemic approach, we are able to appreciate that a varying degree of coercion across the system is important to achieving accountability on a wholesale basis. This point is reflected in Schedler's description of accountability as a 'radial concept', pursuant to which the various stages

---

[7] Richard Mulgan, *Holding Power to Account: Accountability in Modern Democracies* (Palgrave Macmillan, 2003) 97; Carol Harlow, *State Liability: Tort Law and Beyond* (Oxford University Press, 2004) 122; Carol Harlow and Richard Rawlings, 'Promoting Accountability in Multilevel Governance: A Network Approach' (2007) 13 *European Law Journal* 542, 555; Mark Elliott, 'Ombudsmen, Tribunals, Inquiries: Re-fashioning Accountability Beyond the Courts' in Nicholas Bamforth and Peter Leyland (eds.), *Accountability in the Contemporary Constitution* (Oxford University Press, 2013) 233, 246.

of the accountability process – from information gathering through to the imposition of sanctions – 'are continuous variables that show up to different degrees, with varying mixes and emphases'.[8] We can therefore appreciate the important accountability role played by a non-coercive mechanism, provided that coercion exists somewhere else within the system.

9.5 Autonomy

A further feature that differs between mechanisms is their degree of *autonomy*; are the mechanisms proactive or reactive? Some mechanisms are engaged only through specific procedures. So, for example, the courts can adjudicate only on cases that are brought before them. Indeed, at the federal level in Australia, the separation of powers prevents the conferral of non-adjudicatory power (such as advisory roles) on courts.[9] This is a significant limit on the operation of the courts as an accountability mechanism, as they can operate in that capacity only when called on to adjudicate a dispute about existing rights (assuming the case otherwise falls within jurisdiction). Similarly, freedom of information and ex gratia compensation regimes are engaged only when an individual seeks to use them. In comparison, other mechanisms are able to play a far more proactive role. So, for example, ombudsmen have the power to investigate matters of their own volition, rather than waiting for a complaint to be made. Similarly, the NSW ICAC is able to investigate 'on its own initiative' as well as in response to complaints,[10] and also performs an ongoing educative role.[11]

9.6 Independence

There are also differences in terms of the *independence* of the various mechanisms. For instance, the courts are regarded as distinctly independent from the other branches of government. The concept of judicial

---

[8] Andreas Schedler, 'Conceptualizing Accountability' in Andreas Schedler, Larry Diamond and Marc F Plattner (eds.), *The Self-Restraining State: Power and Accountability in New Democracies* (Lynne Rienner Publishers, 1999) 13, 17.

[9] Such is the effect of the Australian High Court's jurisdiction with respect to 'matters': *Australian Constitution* s 75.

[10] *Independent Commission Against Corruption Act 1988* (NSW) s 20(1).

[11] Ibid s 13.

independence requires the courts to remain free of influence from the
political branches of government:

> At the heart of judicial independence, although not exhaustive of the
> concept, is decisional independence from influences external to proceed-
> ings in the court, including, but not limited to, the influence of the
> executive government and its authorities.[12]

Accordingly, the courts exercise their accountability function entirely
independently of the other branches of government. The importance of
judicial independence was recently highlighted in Australia in the context
of criticisms made by Commonwealth ministers regarding the sentencing
approach of the Supreme Court of Victoria in terrorism cases that were
sub judice.[13] In light of the threat of prosecution for contempt, the
ministers withdrew their comments and eventually made apologies to
the Court. The Court ultimately accepted these apologies and declined to
pursue contempt charges. However, in connection with handing down
sentences in the relevant cases, the Victorian Court of Appeal published a
statement in which it emphasised that the rules of contempt of court
'exist to protect the independence of the judiciary in making decisions
that bind governments and citizens alike ... [and] to protect public
confidence in the judiciary'.[14] Thus, judicial independence is not merely
an aspiration but a fundamental ideal enforceable through the law of
contempt.

   Although not to the same fundamental degree as the courts, there are
other institutions within the accountability system that enjoy a degree of
independence. Tribunals and ombudsmen are considered to be independent of the executive, notwithstanding that the orthodox view of
the separation of powers places them within the executive branch of
government. This independence is established by providing some security of tenure, as, like judges, these office-holders can be removed during
the term of their appointment only following resolution by both houses
of Parliament on defined grounds, including misbehaviour or incapacity.[15] However, there are limits to this independence, as demonstrated

---

[12] *South Australia v Totani* (2010) 242 CLR 1, 43 [62].

[13] Relevantly, *DPP (Cth) v MHK (a pseudonym)* [2017] VSCA 157 and *DPP (Cth) v Besim*
[2017] VSCA 158.

[14] *DPP (Cth) v Besim [No 2]; DPP (Cth) v MHK (a pseudonym) [No 2]* (2017) 52 VR 296,
298 [10].

[15] *Administrative Appeals Tribunal Act 1975* (Cth) s 13; *Ombudsman Act 1976*
(Cth) s 28.

through government influence on resourcing[16] and appointments. The independence of Australia's most prominent administrative tribunal (the Administrative Appeals Tribunal, or AAT)[17] was recently brought under threat in the context of media comments made by the Minister for Immigration and Border Protection, who intimated that decisions of the AAT that went against the government may have been influenced by political appointments.[18] Seemingly in response to these criticisms, the Acting President of the AAT noted in a judgment soon afterwards that:

> The very existence of the Tribunal and the independent, quasi-judicial model adopted for it means that, inevitably, there will be tension from time to time between Ministers and others whose decisions are under review ... They can be lessened if each element of our system of government understands and respects the role of the other.

> That does not mean that Tribunal decisions are immune from criticism. It does mean that ... any member who allowed himself or herself to be persuaded as to an outcome by partisan or political rhetoric by a Minister, any other administrator or the popular press would be unworthy of the trust and confidence placed in him or her by His Excellency the Governor-General and untrue to the oath or affirmation of office which must be taken before exercising the Tribunal's jurisdiction. For those members who do not enjoy the same security of tenure as judges, that may call at times for singular moral courage and depth of character.[19]

The subsequent round of appointments to the AAT has since been criticised as being substantially political in character.[20] Despite some of these concerns, the role of the AAT can be viewed as entailing a degree of independence and impartiality.

At the other end of the spectrum, there are mechanisms that cannot be viewed as independent. So, for example, the dominance of the party

---

[16] See, e.g., Brogan Elliot, 'The Hidden Influences That Limit Governmental Independence: Controlling the Ombudsman's Apparent Independence' (2013) 21 *Australian Journal of Administrative Law* 27, 33–34.

[17] For an overview, see, e.g., Peter Cane, *Administrative Tribunals and Adjudication* (Hart Publishing, 2009).

[18] Caitlyn Gribbin, 'Peter Dutton Blames "Politics" As Bid to Deport Six Refugees Fails', *ABC News Online*, 16 May 2017 <http://www.abc.net.au/news/2017-05-16/peter-dutton-blames-politics-over-blocked-bid-to-deport-refugees/8530060> accessed 10 January 2019, referring to comments made by Mr Dutton in an interview with radio station 2GB.

[19] *Singh (Migration)* [2017] AATA 850, [17]–[18].

[20] Michael Koziol, 'George Brandis Clears out "Infuriating" Administrative Appeals Tribunal', *Sydney Morning Herald*, 28 June 2017 <http://www.smh.com.au/federal-politics/political-news/george-brandis-clears-out-infuriating-tribunal-20170628-gx071l.html> accessed 10 January 2019.

system might be viewed as curtailing the independence of the legislative branch in utilising principles of responsible government to hold the executive to account. Further, some mechanisms are embedded within the institutions being held to account, with the effect that they take on the character of 'self-regulatory' mechanisms. Thus, parliamentary committees facilitate accountability from within Parliament, and the availability of ex gratia compensation from the executive branch is determined *by* the executive branch.

9.7　Permanence

A further differentiating feature between the various mechanisms is their *permanence*, in the sense that some mechanisms are enduring or open-ended while others are convened for a term or purpose, or are subject to abolition. At the permanent end of the spectrum we might place the mechanism of judicial review. The Australian High Court has held that it is beyond the power of Parliament to legislate so as to exclude the High Court's power to engage in review for jurisdictional error.[21] For this reason, judicial review for jurisdictional error can be regarded as a foundational accountability mechanism in Australian governance. This can be compared with accountability via criminal and tort law, as the government can legislatively confine or remove the availability of these mechanisms. Representative government supported via popular election is a further permanent mechanism; the *Australian Constitution* requires that Members of Parliament be 'directly chosen by the people',[22] and Parliament's power to limit the right to vote is therefore limited.[23] Accountability via responsible government is of a perhaps slightly less permanent character; as a matter of convention, this doctrine is subject to alteration over time, rather than operating as a permanent guarantee. At the other end of the spectrum sit those mechanisms that are essentially creatures of statute. Tribunals, commissions of inquiry, ombudsmen and freedom of information regimes are all inherently subject to substantial alteration, and even abolition, in accordance with the will of Parliament. This impermanence is exacerbated by the government's ability to withhold resources from these bodies.

---

[21] *Plaintiff S157/2002 v Commonwealth* (2003) 211 CLR 476.
[22] *Australian Constitution* ss 7 and 24.
[23] *Attorney-General (Ex rel McKinlay) v Commonwealth* (1975) 135 CLR 1.

9.8 Summary

This chapter has demonstrated that there is indeed a range of differences between the features of the various mechanisms constituting an accountability system. Some are more independent than others, some are more flexible, some have more coercive powers and so on. However, the argument drawn out here is that it is a mistake to describe these features as 'strengths' and to therefore criticise lack of these features in a particular mechanism as a 'weakness' (or sometimes, accountability deficit). Certainly, it is a good thing from an accountability perspective to have a permanent, independent, cheap, efficient, flexible and coercive means of securing accountability. However, these features need not all exist within a single mechanism. In fact, by spreading out these features amongst various mechanisms, we can introduce a degree of 'give and take' within the system that enhances accountability overall. Picking up the example set out above, an ombudsman's lack of coercive powers may limit the extent to which they can compel the government to provide redress to an individual who has suffered loss. However, that lack of coerciveness may lead to greater likelihood of compliance during ombudsmen investigations. Provided that there is coerciveness somewhere else within the system (for example, through the courts), the ombudsman's lack of coercive powers contributes to, rather than detracts from, accountability. This demonstrates the fundamental importance of viewing accountability across the whole of the system, rather than focusing on mechanisms in isolation. By focusing on mechanisms rather than systems, we risk misunderstanding the contribution made by various features of the mechanisms when taken as a whole.

10

Relationship Dynamics in the System

One of the most critical ideas to capture when treating accountability mechanisms as constituting a system is the dynamics of the relationships between those mechanisms. This idea was explored by Scott in his well-known article on accountability in the regulatory state, in which he put forward two models of extended accountability systems: interdependence and redundancy.[1] The interdependence model refers to the ways in which mechanisms operate to hold one another accountable. The redundancy model, in contrast, employs the idea of 'overlapping (and ostensibly superfluous) accountability mechanisms', which operate so as to 'reduce the centrality of any one of them'.[2] For Scott, this model represents a 'belt and braces' approach,[3] in which 'two independent mechanisms are deployed to ensure the system does not fail, both of which are capable of working on their own'.[4]

On closer analysis of accountability mechanisms, it is apparent that there are in fact many more nuances in the relationship dynamics between mechanisms within an accountability system.[5] As Scott's redundancy model envisages, some of the mechanisms are indeed designed to operate simultaneously and entirely independently. However, others are interdependent, in the sense that they interact and interlock in some way. Others have a staged relationship, where one operates as a precondition of another. Conversely, in others the operation of one precludes the operation of another. Another style of relationship is a co-operative type, where the mechanisms complement and assist one another. Importantly, it is necessary to accept that, while some mechanisms have been designed

---

[1] Colin Scott, 'Accountability in the Regulatory State' (2000) 27 *Journal of Law and Society* 38.
[2] Ibid 52.
[3] Ibid 53.
[4] Ibid.
[5] This possibility is explicitly acknowledged by Scott, indicating that there are 'at least two different models': ibid 50.

to operate in harmony with one another, others are in positions of competition or tension. The overall structure is strengthened through the interplay between opposing forces that weigh against one another to hold it in balance. This idea of tension is critical in Scott's analysis, as he views conflict or tension between mechanisms as an inevitable by-product of employing a system approach to accountability. Our goal, according to Scott, should not be to 'iron out' that conflict, but instead 'to exploit it to hold regimes in appropriate tension'.[6]

10.1 Independent

It is convenient to start with the most straightforward type of account-ability relationship, being that between *independent* mechanisms. Mech-anisms in this style of relationship can be viewed as operating in parallel to one another; two trains travelling under their own steam whose paths do not cross. This is not to say that there is *no* relationship between them. To remove one may disrupt the status quo in a manner that has a knock-on effect on the other. However, in terms of their day-to-day operation, mechanisms in an independent relationship may operate without regard to one other. As noted above, this dynamic aligns with Scott's redun-dancy, or 'belt and braces' model.[7] The availability of multiple mechan-isms provides a sense of safeguard, ensuring that where one mechanism falls short, others are available to take up the slack. Redundancy in mechanisms, as Scott reminds us, offers important benefits in terms of operating as a 'failsafe'; 'where one fails the other will still prevent disaster'.[8]

This independent type of accountability dynamic treads a fine line between patching up potential accountability deficits, on the one hand, and creating accountability overloads on the other. This is because while there is a safeguard benefit where numerous mechanisms operate in parallel, there is also a greater risk of them overlapping at some stage. As highlighted in Chapter 2, where an agent is subject to numerous competing accountability demands, this may lead to an overall reduction in their performance.[9] It is, therefore, necessary to closely examine independent mechanisms to determine whether they strike the correct

---

[6] Ibid 57.
[7] Ibid 53.
[8] Ibid.
[9] See discussion in Section 2.1 in Chapter 2.

balance between failsafe and overload. Looking at the Australian accountability system, it is possible to identify a number of ways in which the system establishes independent mechanisms. For example, the fact that a person has been acquitted in the context of disciplinary or criminal proceedings via legal mechanisms does not preclude an investigation by an ombudsman.[10] This failsafe dynamic is also visible where a senior official within a government department bungles an important decision; there is nothing to prevent Members of Parliament employing mechanisms of ministerial responsibility to hold the relevant minister accountable, at the same time that the official is the subject of review via disciplinary proceedings, while the affair is simultaneously scrutinised via the media. These three accountability mechanisms are able to operate largely in parallel, with each serving its own independent accountability function. If one falls short in its operation, the remaining mechanisms operate as 'failsafes'.

The legal system provides further examples of the failsafe dynamic. For example, if a plaintiff has succeeded in obtaining damages in a tort claim, there is nothing to prevent that same conduct being the subject of a criminal prosecution. Further, if the state fails to prosecute a criminal offence, an interested party may be able to bring a claim in tort.[11] In such a case, the punitive objective of accountability may be achieved via a civil suit, notwithstanding that the most relevant mechanism for that purpose (i.e. prosecution of a criminal offence) may have fallen short. However, the arguments here do not all go one way, as allowing mechanisms to operate independently does not always simply thicken the shape of the accountability system pursuant to which wrongdoers can be held accountable. For instance, if tort proceedings are used to challenge criminal conduct, these will be determined by reference to a lower burden of proof (the balance of probabilities, rather than beyond reasonable doubt). While a finding of liability in tort is ostensibly less condemnatory than a criminal conviction for an equivalent offence, there is

---

[10] *K v NSW Ombudsman* [2000] NSWSC 771, [88] (Whealy J): 'The functions performed by the Ombudsman are quite different and distinct from the disciplinary function.'

[11] This is an idea explored by Stapleton in the context of the use of tortious proceedings following failed criminal prosecution of murder and rape offences: Jane Stapleton, 'Civil Prosecutions Part 1: Double Jeopardy and Abuse of Process' (1999) 7 *Torts Law Journal* 244; Jane Stapleton, 'Civil Prosecutions Part 2: Civil Claims for Killing or Rape' (2000) 8 *Torts Law Journal* 15. As to the vindicatory function of certain categories of torts, see also Jason NE Varuhas, *Damages and Human Rights* (Hart Publishing, 2016).

potentially a risk of miscarriage of justice arising where tort proceedings are used to achieve a condemnatory 'branding' of the defendant.[12] We might also wonder whether frequent use of less exacting causes of action (that is, tort proceedings rather than a criminal prosecution) has the potential to undermine the overall accountability regime. In this book, the punitive function of accountability is regarded as important to condemn abuse of public power. There is a potential risk that this condemnatory purpose may eventually be undermined if alternative mechanisms that lack this essential characteristic are used in place of traditional criminal prosecution.[13]

10.2 Mutually Exclusive

A second type of relationship dynamic is the *mutually exclusive* variety. This dynamic is the opposite of the independent style of relationship. Rather than both mechanisms being able to operate independently in parallel, in a mutually exclusive dynamic the operation of one mechanism precludes the operation of another. This may occur in a number of different ways. First, an individual may 'succeed' via one accountability mechanism, causing another to be redundant. So, for example, if an investigation by the ombudsman leads to a settlement involving compensation for loss suffered as a result of maladministration, other mechanisms (such as legal liability and ex gratia compensation) would thereby become irrelevant. Alternatively, this type of relationship might arise where an individual 'fails' in the context of one mechanism, leading to the unavailability of another. So, for example, if an individual cannot establish that an official has exceeded the scope of their powers in a public law sense, they will not thereafter be able to claim that the official has committed trespass without legal authority. Failure at the first hurdle precludes success at the second.

A mutually exclusive dynamic might also arise where mechanisms are precluded from operating simultaneously. A prime example of this type of mutually exclusive relationship is in the context of contempt of court.

---

[12] See Stapleton, 'Civil Prosecutions Part 1' (n 11) 248.

[13] Stapleton makes a similar point in questioning whether it is satisfactory that rape prosecutions take the character of 'mere' civil wrongs given the enormity of the feminist struggle to have had rape treated seriously by the criminal law: ibid.

Where a matter is before the courts, this may preclude the operation of other mechanisms such as media scrutiny and consideration by Royal Commissions,[14] for example. Similarly, if criminal proceedings are on foot, the New South Wales Independent Commission Against Corruption (ICAC) is entitled to continue its investigation but must do so in private and defer reporting on its findings until after the conclusion of those legal proceedings, thereby limiting its contribution as an accountability mechanism during that period.[15] A further example of a potentially mutually exclusive dynamic exists where a matter is within the 'exclusive cognisance' of Parliament, such as where parliamentary privilege would prevent the determination of issues in legal proceedings. As discussed below, this relationship dynamic was raised unsuccessfully by Mr Obeid in the context of arguing that Parliament, rather than the courts, should have exclusive jurisdiction in respect of the misconduct of Members of Parliament.[16]

The legal system contains a number of rules and doctrines that have the effect of creating mutual exclusivity between causes of action. We can see a subtle reflection of this approach in the court's preferences for certain causes of action or remedies over others. For example, the court may not be willing to afford relief via judicial review proceedings in circumstances where a right of appeal could have been exercised, or where an appeal remains to be determined.[17] This approach is also evident in the description of the writ of mandamus as a 'remedy of last resort'.[18] While not applied in a literal sense by the courts,[19] this may see preference afforded to a civil action for damages over an application for mandamus to compel a duty for the expenditure of public funds.[20] Where the courts utilise their discretion to refuse relief in this way, this has the effect of privileging certain causes of action or remedies over

---

[14] Fiona Roughley, 'Royal Commissions and Contempt of Court: The Effect of Curial Proceedings' (2015) 38 *University of New South Wales Law Journal* 1123.

[15] *Independent Commission Against Corruption Act 1988* (NSW) s 18.

[16] See text accompanying Chapter 11 n 52.

[17] *Federal Commissioner of Taxation v Futuris Corporation Ltd* (2008) 237 CLR 146, 153 [10]. See further Mark Aronson, Matthew Groves and Greg Weeks, *Judicial Review of Administrative Action and Government Liability* (6th ed., Thomson Reuters, 2017) [17.90].

[18] Aronson, Groves and Weeks (n 17) [17.100].

[19] Ibid.

[20] Ibid; Enid Campbell, 'Private Claims on Public Funds' (1969) 3 *University of Tasmania Law Review* 138, 148; Enid Campbell, 'Enforcement of Public Duties Which Are Impossible to Perform' (2003) 10 *Australian Journal of Administrative Law* 201, 205–06.

others, supporting a mutually exclusive approach that prevents remedies from overlapping with one another.

The mutually exclusive relationship dynamic is more explicitly reflected in the broad doctrine of estoppel by record and the court's inherent power to stay proceedings for abuse of process.[21] So, for example, *res judicata* prevents re-litigation of causes of action,[22] issue estoppel prevents a party from raising an issue in subsequent proceedings that has already been determined in earlier proceedings[23] and *Anshun* estoppel[24] allows the court to stay later proceedings that seek to agitate a matter that ought to have been raised and dealt with in earlier proceedings.[25] To similar effect, the rule against collateral attack operates to prevent subsequent proceedings that invite the court to make an order that is inconsistent with, or might 'tarnish'[26] an earlier judgment.[27] Various public policy concerns justify these types of rules;[28] however, in the context of discussions about accountability, we might also point to a further potential rationale for making causes of action mutually exclusive: reducing the potential for accountability overloads. If a government official or department is required to respond to multiple forms of legal attack either simultaneously or consecutively, this may give rise to some of the risks of accountability overload that were cited in Chapter 2 (e.g. decision paralysis, difficulty in prioritising which standards to comply with, reduction in time and resources and so on). Consistently with these concerns, legal principles such as these operate to create relationships of

---

[21] See further Ellen Rock, 'Resolving Conflicts at the Interface of Public and Private Law' (2020) 94 *Australian Law Journal* 381.

[22] *Blair v Curran* (1939) 62 CLR 464, 532 (Dixon J), cited in JD Heydon, *Cross on Evidence* (11th ed., LexisNexis, 2017) 258–59.

[23] *Blair v Curran* (1939) 62 CLR 464, 531 (Dixon J).

[24] Named for the High Court's decision of *Port of Melbourne Authority v Anshun Pty Ltd* (1981) 147 CLR 589. The *Anshun* doctrine is often treated as a subset of estoppel by record, but may more accurately be classed as a feature of the court's inherent power to stay proceedings for abuse of process: Justice KR Handley, 'Anshun Today' (1997) 71 *Australian Law Journal* 934, 940.

[25] Another aspect of this discretion is to allow the courts to stay civil proceedings pending resolution of criminal proceedings (discussed in relation to 'staged' mechanisms in Section 10.3 below).

[26] *Giannarelli v Wraith* (1988) 165 CLR 543, 573–74.

[27] For discussion of circumstances in which collateral challenge is available, see the discussion of 'interdependent' causes of action in Section 10.4 below.

[28] These include pragmatic concerns (e.g. duplication of costs), concerns of fairness to the parties and concerns relating to the legitimacy of the court system: see Rock, 'Resolving Conflicts at the Interface of Public and Private Law' (n 21) 391–93.

mutual exclusivity between causes of action, as the choice to bring the first proceeding (depending on its outcome) may operate to preclude the possibility of bringing later proceedings.

Another set of legal rules create mutual exclusivity between judicial remedies in certain circumstances, preventing the remedies arising out of the causes of action from overlapping with one another. As was noted in the examples explored in Chapter 8, judicial remedies align with the objectives of accountability in differing ways. Adopting the hypothetical benchmark, it was noted that while judicial review remedies are essentially regulatory in nature and criminal sanctions are essentially punitive in nature, damages in tort are capable of performing a wider range of functions, including redress (i.e. compensatory damages) and punishment (i.e. punitive or exemplary damages).[29] Given the degree of overlap between the various categories of remedies, there is the potential that if all causes of action were to operate *independently*, at some point the same set of circumstances may lead to the award of overlapping categories of remedies. For example, if a public official received a fine for the offence of misconduct in public office, and was subsequently required to pay punitive damages to a plaintiff in the context of a tort claim, the official would be doubly punished in respect of the same conduct. In order to prevent a situation such as this, the law contains a number of rules that operate to make certain remedies *mutually exclusive* of one another. One notable example is in respect of the award of exemplary damages alongside criminal sanctions. If a wrongdoer has already been convicted of a criminal offence, the position is that exemplary damages cannot be awarded provided that the criminal punishment was 'substantial'.[30] According to the Australian High Court, 'it would be a most unusual case in which it was open to a civil court to conclude that the outcome of those criminal proceedings did not take sufficient account of the need to punish the offender and deter others from like conduct'.[31] Because the objective of criminal punishment overlaps with that of punitive damages awards, awarding punitive damages following a criminal conviction amounts either to a second-guess of the criminal court's assessment or

---

[29] Tort damages may also be ascribed a deterrent function; however, as noted above, this style of remedy does not align with the notion of 'weak sanctions' adopted for the purpose of the hypothetical benchmark: see discussion in Section 8.3.2.5 in Chapter 8.

[30] *Gray v Motor Accident Commission* (1998) 196 CLR 1, 14 [40].

[31] Ibid 15 [46].

to a duplication of the punishment imposed.[32] The position may be otherwise if later criminal proceedings are only a possibility, or have been commenced but not yet been finalised.[33] Further complications arise if a defendant has previously been *acquitted* of a criminal offence arising out of the same facts. The Australian courts do not view a criminal acquittal as an impediment to the award of exemplary damages in later tort proceedings.[34] This approach is justified as there is no fundamental disconnect between an acquittal in criminal proceedings and the award of exemplary damages in civil proceedings.[35]

These various legal rules offer useful insights into an accountability system that embraces the *mutually exclusive* relationship dynamic. The dynamic is underpinned not only by concerns of accountability overload (e.g. the prospect of 'double punishment'), but also concerns about maintaining the integrity of the system overall.

10.3 Staged

A third type of relationship is the *staged* dynamic. This type of relationship will be relevant where the engagement of one mechanism is viewed as a precondition of another. Structuring mechanisms in a staged way can assist in resolving some of the tension between them; as Mulgan argues, 'potential conflict between competing accountability demands can be mitigated by establishing clear priority between them'.[36] So, for example, an applicant might be required to have their grievance considered by a particular body before alternative avenues of appeal become available.[37] Within the legal system, this type of dynamic was evident in

---

[32] Ibid 14 [42]–[43]. See also *W v W* [1999] 2 NZLR 1, 7.

[33] *Gray v Motor Accident Commission* (1998) 196 CLR 1, 15 [48]. See also *W v W* [1999] 2 NZLR 1, 8.

[34] *Gray v Motor Accident Commission* (1998) 196 CLR 1, 15 [47]; *Niven v SS* [2006] NSWCA 338; *Whitbread v Rail Corporation New South Wales* [2011] NSWCA 130. The New Zealand courts have adopted a different approach: *Daniels v Thompson* [1998] 3 NZLR 22, 51.

[35] *Niven v SS* [2006] NSWCA 338, [63].

[36] Richard Mulgan, *Holding Power to Account: Accountability in Modern Democracies* (Palgrave Macmillan, 2003) 222.

[37] This style of staged review procedure applies in the context of review of freedom of information decisions at the Commonwealth level, where an applicant must generally seek review by the Information Commissioner before taking the matter to a tribunal: *Freedom of Information Act 1982* (Cth) s 57A.

the (now-defunct)[38] felonious tort rule, which prevented a plaintiff from commencing proceedings in tort for conduct amounting to a criminal offence unless a criminal prosecution had been finalised or its failure otherwise explained.[39] In modern parlance, this form of staged dynamic is reflected in the court's power to stay proceedings for abuse of process. For instance, where both criminal and civil proceedings have been commenced (or where criminal proceedings are 'on the cards'),[40] the defendant may apply for a stay of the civil proceedings pending resolution of the criminal proceedings. If awarded, this has the effect of making the completion of the criminal proceedings a precondition of the subsequent civil proceedings, thereby staging the causes of action. The staged dynamic may also be relevant in a more theoretical (rather than procedural) way, where a finding of one type operates as a precondition to a finding of another. For example, there have been times where the courts have restricted government liability in negligence by imposing a precondition which required a plaintiff to demonstrate that the government had acted ultra vires in a public law sense before opening up the negligence enquiry.[41] These types of constraints require a plaintiff to meet one accountability hurdle before being eligible to confront another. It is important to note that, in the context of these staged dynamics, success at one hurdle is a threshold issue and does not necessarily imply success at the next.

The staged dynamic may also be evident where certain types of mechanisms are classified as being of a 'gap-filling', or 'last resort' variety, to be employed only after other options are exhausted. Thus, ex gratia compensation is intended to operate in a gap-filling capacity, with non-binding guidelines prepared for decision-makers under the relevant schemes indicating that in circumstances where the government would otherwise be legally liable, these payments are not appropriate.[42]

---

[38] *Ceasar v Sommer* [1980] 2 NSWLR 929, 931 (Needham J): 'it would be wrong to regard the rule ... as a rule of law applying in New South Wales today'. See also *McMahon v Gould* (1982) 7 ACLR 202, 205 (Wootten J).

[39] *Smith v Selwyn* [1914] 3 KB 98. See Clifford Pannam, 'Felonious Tort Rule' (1965) 39 *Australian Law Journal* 164, 166.

[40] *Citation Resources Ltd v Landau* (2016) 116 ACSR 410, 423 [49].

[41] For further detail, see Ellen Rock and Greg Weeks, 'Monetary Awards for Public Law Wrongs: Australia's Resistant Legal Landscape' (2018) 41(4) *University of New South Wales Law Journal* 1159.

[42] Department of Finance (Cth), *Scheme for Compensation for Detriment Caused by Defective Administration* (Resource Management Guide No 409, November 2018) [23]; Department of Finance (Cth), *Requests for Discretionary Financial Assistance under the Public*

Accordingly, the guidelines relating to the grant of act of grace payments provide that '[i]f a person is claiming that a decision is incorrect at law, existing legal review mechanisms must be used'.[43] The Commonwealth Ombudsman performs a similar 'last resort' role,[44] which is reflected in its power to decline to investigate a matter in circumstances where an individual has not availed themselves of an applicable legal challenge.[45]

10.4   Interdependent

A fourth type of relationship dynamic is that where mechanisms are *interdependent* upon one another. Mechanisms in this type of relationship can be viewed as symbiotic, as they interact at various points without one overtaking the other. So, for example, a merits review tribunal may overturn a government decision, and then remit that decision back to the original decision-maker to be retaken. There is a degree of interrelationship between the two mechanisms in such a context, as the end outcome for the applicant is driven by the collective interaction between these two mechanisms. Similarly, the mechanism of public protest is interdependent upon the media in performing its accountability function. Protesters may rely on traditional or social media to communicate their intention to demonstrate, and the impact of the demonstration is then amplified via media publicity after the fact. Interdependency may also arise in an institutional sense, where functions and roles are intertwined in some way. An example of this can be seen in relation to judicial accountability mechanisms. Judicial review, criminal law and tort law are all separate causes of action. However, in an institutional sense they are all managed by the courts. In some cases, there is a divisional separation between the causes of action, with defined procedures allocating certain types of matters to certain courts, or divisions within courts. However, there may also be degrees of interrelationship in some cases. We can also observe a degree of institutional interdependence where officers from one mechanism are employed to perform roles

Governance, Performance and Accountability Act 2013 (Resource Management Guide No 401, April 2018) [3]–[6].

[43] Department of Finance (Cth), *Requests for Discretionary Financial Assistance* (n 42) [6].

[44] See, e.g., Anita Stuhmcke, 'Ombuds Can, Ombuds Can't, Ombuds Should, Ombuds Shan't: A Call to Improve Evaluation of the Ombudsman Institution' in Marc Hertogh and Richard Kirkham (eds.), *Research Handbook on the Ombudsman* (Edward Elgar Publishing, 2018) 415, 418.

[45] *Ombudsman Act 1976* (Cth) s 6(2).

within another. A good example of this is the operation of parliamentary committees, which are by their nature staffed by members of the legislative branch. Within the limits of the *persona designata* doctrine, judges may also be 'borrowed' from the courts to act as tribunal members, or to head commissions of inquiry, for example.

It is possible to see this style of dynamic within legal doctrine, in cases that permit collateral challenge. This doctrine enables a plaintiff to use one cause of action for the purposes of pursuing what might have been achieved in another. For instance, a successful defence to a criminal prosecution might depend on a challenge to the validity of the instrument that creates the offence, or a successful tort claim might depend on establishing the invalidity of the statutory instrument that might otherwise have authorised the tortious conduct. The validity point might have been raised directly by way of judicial review proceedings, but might also be attacked collaterally in the relevant criminal or tort proceedings. The reason we can consider this an example of an *interdependent* relationship is that one cause of action is being used to achieve indirectly a result that could have been achieved directly through use of another.[46] There are, therefore, symbiotic features to the relationship between the two causes of action, with a finding in one by its nature resolving a question that might have been raised in the other. It is also possible to see this dynamic in certain categories of remedies that are available only in tandem with others. One of the best examples of this is the relationship between punitive and compensatory damages, as the former are regarded as 'parasitic' on the latter;[47] exemplary damages are not available if the claim for compensatory damages was unsuccessful, as '[i]f there is no host, there can not be a parasite'.[48]

10.5   Co-operative

A fifth type of relationship is that between *co-operative* mechanisms. This type of relationship may exist where various mechanisms exchange information and resources in working towards a common goal. This dynamic is seen, for example, in the legislative requirement that the NSW ICAC is to work in co-operation with that State's Ombudsman

---

[46] See further Rock, 'Resolving Conflicts at the Interface of Public and Private Law' (n 21) 384–86.

[47] *XL Petroleum (NSW) Pty Ltd v Caltex Oil (Australia) Pty Ltd* (1985) 155 CLR 448, 468–69.

[48] *Fatimi Pty Ltd v Bryant* (2004) 59 NSWLR 678, 690 [73].

and other government agencies.[49] Similarly, while the NSW ICAC is not entitled to commence criminal proceedings of its own volition,[50] it is able to do so after seeking the advice of the Director of Public Prosecution and, in doing so, will provide evidence gathered during the course of its investigation.[51] The co-operative dynamic is also reflected in the various rules that govern the admissibility of findings in one set of legal proceedings in another. So, for instance, the rules of estoppel by record will operate to bind parties to findings made in earlier proceedings, and evidence of criminal conviction may be adduced as evidence in later civil proceedings.[52]

Co-operation may also be more subtle than these examples. It may be that there are instances in which the mere operation of one mechanism facilitates the operation of another, even without deliberate co-operation between them. Scott has noted this style of relationship in discussing the system of accountability applicable in the context of prisons regulation: 'With prisons, the development of litigation strategies has been both supportive of and supported by the work of the prisons humanity regulators, and notably the inspectorate and the ombudsman, the regulators providing better information which may be used in litigation, litigation providing more robust definitions of appropriate norms relating to the treatment of individual prisoners.'[53] We can view this as an almost cyclical relationship, where results of one mechanism feed into the practices of another, gradually enhancing the performance of the agent being held to account.

10.6 Reciprocal

The final type of relationship dynamic explored here is that of *reciprocity*,[54] pursuant to which mechanisms can be understood as holding

---

[49] *Independent Commission Against Corruption Act 1988* (NSW) s 16(1)(b).

[50] *Criminal Procedure Act 1986* (NSW) s 14A.

[51] *Independent Commission Against Corruption Act 1988* (NSW) s 14(1)(a).

[52] See, e.g., *Evidence Act 1995* (NSW) s 92(2) and other state equivalents, which alter the common law position reflected in *Hollington v F Hewthorn & Co Ltd* [1943] KB 587. No such allowance is made in respect of the admission of civil judgments in criminal proceedings (see, e.g., *Evidence Act 1995* (NSW) s 91).

[53] Scott (n 1) 56.

[54] This label is adopted by Andreas Schedler, 'Conceptualizing Accountability' in Andreas Schedler, Larry Diamond and Marc F Plattner (eds.), *The Self-Restraining State: Power and Accountability in New Democracies* (Lynne Rienner Publishers, 1999) 13, 26.

one another accountable. In the literature, this dynamic is referred to in a variety of ways, as relationships of 'compounded accountability',[55] 'mutual accountability',[56] 'circles of guardianship',[57] 'interdependency'[58] or a 'lattice of leadership'.[59] The common thread in these various theories is that accountability may be enhanced by arranging institutions into relationships of reciprocal or mutual scrutiny. Unlike a linear approach, which would simply layer a new guardian to guard existing guardians, the reciprocity approach evident within the accountability system involves creating and reinforcing relationships between existing mechanisms in the system. Adopting Scott's language, this type of model views the regime as being held 'in a broadly acceptable place through the opposing tensions and forces generated'.[60]

At its core, the tripartite separation of powers model is an accountability structure of this type, with powers being divided between institutions that are then charged with responsibility for scrutinising one another's exercise of those powers. The accountability system approach discussed in this chapter involves layering further accountability mechanisms on top of this base-level separation of powers, resulting in more comprehensive and nuanced layers of checks and balances. For example, an individual can bring judicial review proceedings before the courts to confirm that other mechanisms (such as ombudsmen) have acted validly within the scope of their powers,[61] and a parliamentary committee may be charged with overseeing the performance of an anti-corruption commission.[62]   There are two key benefits arising out of these types of relationships of reciprocity. The first is that the presence of external checks may improve the performance of an accountability mechanism.

---

[55] Mulgan, *Holding Power to Account* (n 36) 230.

[56] Bruce Stone, 'Administrative Accountability in the "Westminster" Democracies: Towards a New Conceptual Framework' (1995) 8 *Governance* 505, 518; AJ Brown, 'The Integrity Branch: A "System", an "Industry", or a Sensible Emerging Fourth Arm of Government?' in Matthew Groves (ed.), *Modern Administrative Law in Australia: Concepts and Context* (Cambridge University Press, 2014) 301, 315–16.

[57] John Braithwaite, 'On Speaking Softly and Carrying Big Sticks: Neglected Dimensions of a Republican Separation of Powers' (1997) 47 *University of Toronto Law Journal* 305, 349.

[58] Scott (n 1) 50–52.

[59] John Uhr, *Terms of Trust: Arguments over Ethics in Australian Government* (UNSW Press, 2005) 78–81.

[60] Scott (n 1) 52.

[61] E.g. *K v NSW Ombudsman* [2000] NSWSC 771.

[62] For example, the Committee on the Independent Commission Against Corruption oversees the NSW ICAC.

In Mulgan's words, '[h]ow well they perform their function as agents of public accountability depends very heavily on how accountable they are themselves for their own performance'.[63] In essence, it can be anticipated that an accountability mechanism will function more effectively in its role when the performance of that role is also subject to external scrutiny. A second key benefit arising out of this relationship dynamic is the establishment of legitimacy. As noted in Chapter 4, the government is more likely to be regarded as legitimate if it is accountable. The same goes for accountability mechanisms themselves; these mechanisms are more likely to be regarded as legitimate if they are held accountable for the way in which they perform their accountability functions.[64] Because of the role relationships of reciprocity play in improving performance and fostering legitimacy, this dynamic is an important feature of the accountability system.

10.7 Summary

This chapter has explored the range of different relationship dynamics that may exist between accountability mechanisms. Not only do mechanisms differ as between their features, but they also interlock and overlap in highly complex ways. In some cases they operate independently, but in others there are elements of mutual exclusivity, staging, interdependency, co-operativeness and reciprocity. Only by coming to grips with each of these areas of complexity can we build up a picture of accountability mechanisms as a 'system' rather than an ad hoc collection of paths towards government accountability. Understanding accountability mechanisms as a system is critical to the broader project of identifying potential accountability deficits and overloads. It makes no sense to point to a 'gap' by reference to a single mechanism unless we consider whether that gap is plugged by an alternative mechanism, and it is also no answer to point to an alternative mechanism without first understanding whether the dynamic between those mechanisms allows it to perform a relevant 'gap-filling' role. Similarly, it makes no sense to point to 'overlaps' simply by noting

---

[63] Mulgan, *Holding Power to Account* (n 36) 230.
[64] This is an idea explored by Black in the context of polycentric regulatory regimes: Julia Black, 'Constructing and Contesting Legitimacy and Accountability in Polycentric Regulatory Regimes' (2008) 2 *Regulation and Governance* 137, 149.

the existence of numerous mechanisms that target similar actors or conduct. Rather, we need to think about the dynamics between those mechanisms to determine if they do indeed operate simultaneously. In other words, potential gaps and overlaps may be ameliorated when we adopt a systemic approach to understanding accountability.

11

Mapping Out a System in Practice

Chapters 9 and 10 have described some of the complexities that arise when we approach accountability mechanisms on a systemic basis. This final chapter places these ideas in a practical setting, picking up the examples that were examined in Chapter 8: the Eddie Obeid corruption scandal, the detention of Graham Taylor following invalidly made visa cancellation decisions, and harm caused by reliance on inaccurate advice given by private contractors in the context of the Australian Apprenticeships Incentives Program. As canvassed in that chapter, the key mechanisms employed in each scenario were, respectively, a New South Wales Independent Commission Against Corruption (ICAC) investigation and criminal prosecution, judicial review and false imprisonment proceedings, and an Ombudsman investigation and discretionary compensation scheme. That chapter highlighted some of the ways in which these various mechanisms might measure up against a hypothetical accountability benchmark. This chapter takes that analysis a step further, by exploring the ways in which these mechanisms operate as an accountability system in each scenario.

11.1 NSW ICAC and Criminal Prosecution

When taken in isolation, each of the NSW ICAC and criminal prosecution for the offence of misconduct in public office fell short of meeting the full expectations of the transparency, desert and deterrence rationales of the hypothetical accountability benchmark. The ICAC was unable to deliver punitive sanctions and lacked the agent-friendly procedures appropriate to a punitive mechanism, and criminal prosecution was too punitive to provide the dialogue-focused approach favoured by the deterrence rationale. We might position these inconsistencies in the benchmark as potential accountability deficits and overloads (i.e. the ICAC delivered insufficient accountability on the desert rationale, and the criminal prosecution delivered too much accountability on the deterrence rationale). It might go without saying, given the approach that has been presented in this book, that this claim misses the point that we do not need to locate all of our accountability objectives within a single accountability mechanism. We might validly allow mechanisms to focus their attention on one objective rather than multiple, and the shortfalls in one mechanism may be ameliorated by the strengths in another. This section adopts a systemic view of the accountability mechanisms that were brought to bear in Mr Obeid's case.

11.1.1   Features of the System

As set out in Chapter 9, an accountability system represents a widespread patchwork of features that vary as between accountability mechanisms. To reiterate the points made there, a lack of independence in one mechanism may not represent an accountability concern if another available mechanism enjoys significant independence. In looking at the ICAC and the criminal offence of misconduct in public office, there are a number of areas in which the two mechanisms share similar features.

In relation to *accessibility*, both mechanisms are accessible to individuals in the sense that a member of the public can provide information that kick-starts an enquiry. In Mr Obeid's case, the ICAC investigation was commenced after an anonymous phone tip-off. The ease of reporting potential corruption to ICAC is supported by the ability to remain anonymous, and by specific protections against liability for defamation.[1] Initiating a criminal investigation is likewise accessible to members of the public, who are able to provide a tip-off to police. However, in neither case can members of the public ensure that an investigation actually takes place. There is no provision for individuals to launch an ICAC investigation, as the discretion to investigate remains with the ICAC. In contrast, the criminal law does make provision for members of the public to ensure that proceedings are commenced, via the mechanism of private prosecution. As noted in Section 8.2.2.2 in Chapter 8, while the orthodox position is that criminal prosecutions are maintained by the state, there remains a residual right for private individuals to commence criminal proceedings (though the financial burden is likely to reduce the relevance of this mechanism, as discussed in the paragraph below). It is also worth noting that public access to the accountability forum is stronger in

---

[1] Matters published to the ICAC are treated as absolutely privileged: *Defamation Act 2005* (NSW) s 27(2)(d), Sch 1(19).

respect of criminal proceedings than an ICAC inquiry. The ICAC has a discretion to decide whether or not to conduct a public inquiry in connection with an investigation, with the overarching consideration being whether a public inquiry is in the public interest.[2] This is to be determined by weighing the benefits of exposing corruption against concerns about the reputation and privacy of those being investigated.[3] Even if an inquiry is to be held in public, the ICAC retains a discretion to hold part of the inquiry in private if in the public interest to do so.[4] In contrast, court proceedings are much more geared towards public access; the principles of open justice require court proceedings to be open to the public and that judicial reasons be published, unless there are compelling reasons not to (as was thought to be the case in Mr Obeid's initial aborted trial). In comparing the two mechanisms, then, we would say that criminal proceedings are on the whole more accessible to private individuals than an ICAC corruption inquiry.

The *cost* of both mechanisms is again comparable when looking at the ability for an individual to report potential wrongdoing for investigation. There is no fee applicable when making a report about potential corruption issues either to the ICAC or to police. Individuals do not need to commit any significant time or resources (including time away from employment or travelling) in order to make a report which might trigger an investigation. However, the costs associated with each mechanism differ in looking at the conduct of proceedings. There is no provision for private individuals to compel the ICAC to investigate potential corruption. And while the available budget for the ICAC might limit the extent of its capacity to engage in investigative operations,[5] accountability does not depend on the resources of individual prosecutors as is the case for some mechanisms. In similar terms, the capacity for the state to commence criminal prosecutions can be considered limited by the time and resources of the public prosecutor. In contrast, private prosecutors face significant cost barriers to commencing a criminal prosecution. Legal proceedings are excessively costly and time consuming, significantly

---

[2] *Independent Commission Against Corruption Act 1988* (NSW) s 31.
[3] Ibid s 31(2).
[4] Ibid s 31(9).
[5] For instance, when the NSW Government made cuts to the ICAC's funding in 2015–16, the Commissioner warned this may reduce the number of investigations that could be commenced and maintained compared with previous years: NSW Independent Commission Against Corruption, *Annual Report: 2015–16* (October 2016) 3.

limiting the utility of the criminal law as an accountability mechanism where the state declines to prosecute.

Both the ICAC and criminal law are also comparable in terms of their *coerciveness*. In the context of both ICAC investigations and criminal prosecutions, there are strong mechanisms available to facilitate the production of evidence. Police have extensive powers to draw on in the context of a criminal investigation, and the courts likewise have wide-ranging powers to control the conduct of criminal proceedings. The ICAC can also use compulsory powers in the course of its investigations, including in entering premises and demanding the production of information and documents,[6] with authorised officers being entitled to use reasonable force in executing search warrants.[7] The ICAC is also empowered to compel witnesses to appear before the Commission to give evidence or produce documents,[8] and may issue a warrant for the arrest of a witness if it is believed that they will not appear in response to the summons.[9] Witnesses who are summoned to provide evidence are not entitled to refuse to appear, to answer a question or to produce a document, even where that evidence might incriminate them.[10] These coercive investigative powers are further backed by threats of sanctions for non-compliance, as failure to comply may be punished as contempt,[11] or as a criminal offence.[12]

While the ICAC and prosecution for the criminal offence of misconduct in public office might be broadly comparable in respect of their accessibility, cost and coerciveness, there are a number of features that differ as between the mechanisms. The first difference is in respect of their *flexibility*. The ICAC is specifically designed to adopt a flexible approach in its procedures. Pursuant to its governing legislation, the ICAC 'is not bound by the rules or practice of evidence and can inform itself on any matter in such manner as it considers appropriate',[13] and is required to 'exercise its functions with as little formality and technicality as is possible'.[14] In contrast, criminal proceedings employ highly technical rules in relation to the admissibility of evidence and the manner in

---

[6] *Independent Commission Against Corruption Act 1988* (NSW) ss 21–23.

[7] Ibid s 43.

[8] Ibid s 35.

[9] Ibid s 36.

[10] Ibid s 37. The evidence is not, however, admissible in later legal proceedings: s 37(3).

[11] Ibid ss 98–100.

[12] Ibid ss 82, 83, 86.

[13] Ibid s 17(1).

[14] Ibid s 17(2).

which proceedings are conducted. These differences in flexibility reflect the overarching purposes of each of the two mechanisms; the ICAC is primarily concerned with investigating and uncovering potential corruption, whereas criminal prosecutions are intended to punish corruption once proved. In these circumstances, it is appropriate that the ICAC is able to deploy more flexibility in its approach while a criminal prosecution is more rigid.

There are also significant differences in relation to the *autonomy* of each of these two mechanisms. The ICAC enjoys a significant degree of discretion in determining whether, and how, to investigate potential corruption. It need not wait until it receives a complaint or referral, but can instead determine for itself whether there are circumstances that warrant investigation on its own initiative.[15] While the legislative regime identifies matters that the ICAC may have regard to in exercising its discretion (e.g. whether the alleged corruption is of a trivial nature or occurred a long time ago), these are non-prescriptive and non-exhaustive, leaving the ICAC with a significant degree of autonomy in deciding whether to investigate.[16] The ICAC also has discretion in determining whether to conduct a public inquiry (as opposed to a private investigation) in a particular case, though this is guided by the overarching requirement that it be in the public interest to do so.[17] In contrast, the courts have no autonomy in commencing a criminal prosecution; it is the prosecutor and not the forum that determines whether a criminal prosecution will take place. The courts operate on an inherently adversarial approach, and while the courts may strike out a case that has no prospects of success, the courts play no role in determining whether proceedings ought to be commenced in the first place. In this respect, the ICAC has significantly more autonomy than the courts as an accountability forum.

In contrast, we would say that the courts enjoy a greater degree of *independence* than the ICAC in exercising their functions in criminal prosecution cases. On the traditional tripartite model of the separation of powers the ICAC forms part of the executive branch of government,[18]

---

[15] Ibid ss 13(1), 20.

[16] Ibid s 20(3): the ICAC may have regard to 'such matters as it thinks fit'.

[17] Ibid s 31.

[18] Note that some would advocate conceiving of such mechanisms as a 'fourth branch' of government rather than as part of the executive: see, e.g., Bruce Ackerman, 'The New Separation of Powers' (2000) 113 *Harvard Law Review* 633; Justice JJ Spigelman, 'The Integrity Branch of Government' (2004) 78 *Australian Law Journal* 724; Robin Creyke,

though it is intended to operate as an independent body. Indeed, its very name includes the word 'Independent', and the stated objects of its governing legislation include to 'promote the integrity and accountability of public administration by constituting [the ICAC] as an independent and accountable body'.[19] There is some degree of independence in the process of appointing Commissioners to the ICAC. Commissioners cannot be a current Member of Parliament or the judiciary, and must be either a former judge or be qualified for appointment as a judge.[20] Appointments are made by the Governor,[21] with a veto power afforded to a relevant parliamentary committee.[22] While there is some room for a political approach to appointments, the requirement of eligibility for judicial office means that Commissioners will have experience of the independent methodology of the court system. Perhaps a stronger limitation on the independent functioning of the ICAC is executive control over resourcing. The ICAC's ability to investigate corruption is dependent on budgetary constraints, as evidenced by the impact of significant funding cuts delivered in 2016–17. In its annual report, the ICAC indicated that following these cuts it had been required to deploy 'a rigorous selection process in determining which investigations are undertaken by the Commission in the face of decreased resources'.[23] In other words, this reduction in resources had forced the ICAC to narrow its investigative focus to a discrete set of inquiries.

In contrast, the courts enjoy a very significant degree of independence, perhaps the most significant within the accountability system. As discussed in Section 9.6 in Chapter 9, judicial independence is jealously guarded by the Australian courts, and is supported via the separation of powers. By dividing the *Australian Constitution* into three chapters that

---

'An "Integrity" Branch' (2012) 70 *AIAL Forum* 33; John McMillan, 'Re-thinking the Separation of Powers' (2010) 38 *Federal Law Review* 423; AJ Brown, 'The Integrity Branch: A "System", an "Industry", or a Sensible Emerging Fourth Arm of Government?' in Matthew Groves (ed.), *Modern Administrative Law in Australia: Concepts and Context* (Cambridge University Press, 2014) 301.

[19] *Independent Commission Against Corruption Act 1988* (NSW) s 2A(a).

[20] Ibid sch 1 cl 1.

[21] Ibid s 5(1).

[22] Ibid s 64A. The Committee on the Independent Commission Against Corruption is a joint committee of the NSW Parliament (s 63). In respect of Assistant Commissioners, the Commissioner is to be consulted on the persons to be appointed, but does not have a veto power (s 5(2)).

[23] NSW Independent Commission Against Corruption, *Annual Report: 2016–17* (October 2017) 25.

specify the powers of each of the Parliament, executive and judicature, its framers were taken to have established a functional separation of powers.[24] The strongest feature of this separation is in respect of judicial power,[25] as the *Boilermaker's* principle prevents the conferral of non-judicial power on courts at the federal level in Australia, and the conferral of judicial power on any individual or body other than a court.[26] While the Australian States do not recognise a strict separation of powers, the *Kable* principle extends some of the implications of the federal separation of judicial power to state level.[27] In the context of discussing government accountability, the separation of judicial power has an important role to play. By insulating the courts from legislative and executive interference and supporting their ongoing impartiality from politics (including through the power to punish contempt where proceedings are *sub judice*),[28] we can view the courts as an independent promoter of government accountability, and we are more likely to trust the courts to perform their accountability role because they are institutionally and functionally 'separate' from the policy-driven mechanics of government.

Finally, in looking at the *permanence* of these two mechanisms we would again say that the courts enjoy a greater degree of permanence than the ICAC. As a creature of statute, the ongoing powers and even existence of the ICAC is subject to the will of Parliament. This susceptibility to change was demonstrated in 2016, when the NSW government introduced legislation to alter the structure of the ICAC with the effect that the single Commissioner was to be replaced by a three-member panel (a Chief Commissioner and two part-time Assistant Commissioners).[29] The effect of the changes was to oust the then-current Commissioner from her position – though she was entitled to reapply – and to decrease the autonomy of the new Chief Commissioner by providing that certain powers, such as the power to conduct a public inquiry, were subject to the approval of at least one of the Assistant Commissioners.[30]

---

[24] *Attorney-General (Cth) v The Queen* (1957) 95 CLR 529, 537.

[25] The division between the legislative and executive branches is far less strict, as s 64 of the *Australian Constitution* requires ministers to be Members of Parliament.

[26] *R v Kirby; Ex parte Boilermakers' Society of Australia* (1956) 94 CLR 254.

[27] The principle derived from *Kable v DPP (NSW)* (1996) 189 CLR 51, as refined in subsequent cases: see, e.g., *South Australia v Totani* (2010) 242 CLR 1; *Kirk v Industrial Court (NSW)* (2010) 239 CLR 531.

[28] See Section 9.6 in Chapter 9.

[29] *Independent Commission Against Corruption Amendment Act 2016* (NSW).

[30] *Independent Commission Against Corruption Act 1988* (NSW) s 6(2).

The then-Commissioner described the changes as 'an unprecedented attack on the independence and effectiveness' of the ICAC.[31] These concerns were voiced more plainly in Parliament, with the opposition suggesting that the legislative changes were a means to achieve 'constructive dismissal' of the current Commissioner in 'revenge' for political embarrassment suffered by the government as a result of an ICAC investigation into wrongful receipt of election donations.[32] The changes proceeded notwithstanding this criticism, demonstrating that even a long-standing accountability mechanism such as the ICAC is subject to curtailment by legislative amendment.

In contrast, the courts are of a much more permanent character. The *Australian Constitution* makes specific provision for the Australian court system, providing for the establishment of the High Court,[33] and by confirming its jurisdiction to hear appeals from 'the Supreme Court of any State'.[34] As discussed below,[35] there are some aspects of jurisdiction that cannot be removed from either Federal or State courts. In respect of the criminal law, the courts have something of a monopoly on criminal punishment, as non-judicial bodies cannot be empowered to exercise judicial powers of punishment.[36] However, it does remain open to Parliament to alter the scope and content of the *offences* that can be adjudicated before the courts. The offence of misconduct in public office is a common law offence in New South Wales. By virtue of the doctrine of parliamentary sovereignty, it is open to the State Parliament to replace the offence with a statutory form (with or without modifications), or even to abolish it altogether, though to do so might invite significant public scrutiny and protest. We might therefore say that the offence itself is not of a permanent character (though to abolish it might prove politically difficult), whereas the forum which adjudicates the offence is here to stay.

Taking these various observations together, we can see that there are differences between the features of the ICAC and criminal offence of

---

[31] The Hon Megan Latham, 'Statement Regarding the Independent Commission Against Corruption Amendment Bill 2016' (15 November 2016).

[32] New South Wales, *Parliamentary Debates*, Legislative Assembly, 15 November 2016, 62 (Paul Lynch, Member for Liverpool).

[33] *Australian Constitution* s 71.

[34] Ibid s 73.

[35] See discussion of judicial review jurisdiction below in Section 11.2.1.

[36] *Chu Kheng Lim v Minister for Immigration and Local Government and Ethnic Affairs* (1992) 176 CLR 1, 27.

misconduct in public office as accountability mechanisms. In some respects, the two mechanisms are relatively similar; both are able to deploy highly coercive measures to enforce compliance with their accountability-enforcing procedures. In the early stages of investigation, both mechanisms are relatively cost-effective and accessible, in the sense that each can be kick-started as a result of an informal complaint or report with no fees or forms, and can even be anonymous. However, once the formal procedures begin, each mechanism becomes less accessible and more costly. During an investigation and inquiry, the ICAC retains discretion to deny access to the general public. And while it is theoretically possible for a private individual to commence a criminal prosecution, the cost and burden of doing so would prove to be a major disincentive. At the other extreme there are a number of ways in which the two mechanisms differ. The ICAC has significant autonomy in pursuing its accountability functions, while the courts can only adjudicate on matters brought before them. However, the courts enjoy much more security in terms of their independence and permanence than the ICAC, which is subject to legislative amendment and threats of defunding. All of this tells us that there are indeed variations in this small accountability system, as between the ICAC and the criminal offence of misconduct in public office.

11.1.2   System Dynamics

It is also important to consider the relationship dynamics between the mechanisms applicable in Mr Obeid's case. As outlined in Chapter 8, Mr Obeid was initially investigated by the NSW ICAC between 2012 and 2013. It gathered a range of evidence during the course of compulsory witness examinations and document production requests, held a public inquiry and ultimately made findings that Mr Obeid had engaged in corrupt conduct. Subsequently, Mr Obeid was prosecuted for and convicted of the criminal offence of misconduct in public office and sentenced to a term of imprisonment of five years. If we fail to take into account the relationship dynamics between these two accountability dynamics, we would take the view that Mr Obeid has been subjected to two independent forms of accountability process. To the extent that these mechanisms serve similar accountability objectives, we might therefore reach the view that this represents a potential accountability overload, with Mr Obeid having been subjected to numerous mechanisms with respect to the same conduct. There are two responses to this, however.

The first is that the mechanisms do not in fact serve the same purposes. In subsequent civil proceedings in Mr Obeid's case, Hammerschlag J noted that the ICAC's investigative function 'bears no relation to a civil or criminal trial before a court with jurisdiction to resolve factual and legal issues in a dispute between contending parties'.[37] As was highlighted in applying the hypothetical accountability benchmark in Chapter 8, the ICAC investigation was most closely aligned with the transparency and deterrence rationales, whereas the criminal prosecution was most closely aligned with the desert function. By focusing on different rationales, the potential for overlap in functions is significantly reduced. Even setting this to one side, however, these two accountability mechanisms are not simply independent sources of accountability, but sit in a more complex relationship with one another.

In terms of the timing of the two accountability processes, we might wonder whether there is a *staged* dynamic in play between the ICAC investigation and subsequent criminal prosecution. The ICAC undertook the initial functions of uncovering information and documents that tended to incriminate Mr Obeid, and conducting a public inquiry that allowed for him to be cross-examined on that information. The criminal prosecution was commenced only after the conclusion of the ICAC process and findings of corruption, thereby staging the two accountability mechanisms to follow on from one another. However, these two mechanisms do not represent the staged dynamic in the fullest manner explained in Chapter 10 because there is no rigid hierarchy between the two. The fact that the ICAC had commenced an investigation would not have precluded police from doing so, with a criminal prosecution to follow in the ordinary course. In fact, the ICAC's empowering legislation specifically contemplates that the ICAC may 'commence, continue, discontinue or complete any investigation' notwithstanding that criminal proceedings may be on foot.[38] The only restriction is in respect of the transparency of such proceedings, as the ICAC must complete its investigation in private and defer reporting until after the conclusion of proceedings in order to avoid prejudicing the accused's right to a fair trial.[39] In this sense, there was no formal requirement for a criminal prosecution to be staged until the conclusion of the ICAC investigation.

---

[37] *Obeid Snr v Ipp* (2016) 338 ALR 234, 251 [87].
[38] *Independent Commission Against Corruption Act 1988* (NSW) s 18(1).
[39] Ibid s 18(2).

Instead of staged, the better characterisation of the relationship between the ICAC and criminal prosecution mechanisms in this case would be *co-operative*. As discussed in Chapter 10, mechanisms will be in a co-operative dynamic where they share information and resources in working towards a common goal. There are three key ways in which the ICAC and criminal prosecution mechanisms exhibit a co-operative approach. The first is in connection with the ICAC's investigative powers, as governing legislation requires that when conducting its investigations, the ICAC is to 'work in co-operation with law enforcement agencies' so far as is practicable.[40] The legislation also makes provision for a co-operative approach between the ICAC and the Director of Public Prosecutions (DPP) after the conclusion of ICAC's investigative role. The DPP is able to request that the ICAC exercise its powers to issue search warrants, enter premises and obtain documents and information for the purpose of gathering evidence to be used in a criminal prosecution.[41] Information about the extent to which these co-operative investigatory procedures were used in Mr Obeid's case is not public knowledge. As a general observation, however, it is clear that there is significant scope for the ICAC to work together with police and the DPP in connection with investigating potential corruption.

The second key example of co-operation between these mechanisms is in respect of the choice to commence a criminal prosecution. The ICAC does not have the power to make findings of criminal guilt[42] or to commence prosecutions of its own volition.[43] However, the ICAC does have the power to consider whether it should seek the advice of the DPP in relation to the commencement of criminal proceedings (which must be noted in its report),[44] and is able to commence such proceedings with the approval of the DPP.[45] In the course of considering a proposed prosecution, the DPP is able to 'liaise' with the ICAC but is required to

---

[40] Ibid s 16(1).

[41] Ibid s 52A.

[42] *Balog v Independent Commission Against Corruption* (1990) 169 CLR 625, 633.

[43] *Criminal Procedure Act 1986* (NSW) s 14A. Prior to 2015, the ICAC had proceeded on the assumption that it had the power to commence criminal prosecutions for common law offences in the local court. This was brought into doubt in *Director of Public Prosecutions (NSW) v McDonald* [2015] NSWLC 7 (Grogin LCM). The relevant legislation was subsequently amended to provide an express right to commence proceedings after seeking the advice of the NSW DPP: *Criminal Procedure Act 1986* (NSW) s 14A.

[44] *Independent Commission Against Corruption Act 1988* (NSW) ss 13(5)(b)(1), 74A(2)(a).

[45] *Criminal Procedure Act 1986* (NSW) s 14A(1).

exercise independent judgement in forming an opinion as to whether prosecution may proceed.[46] In Mr Obeid's case, the ICAC included the following statement in its report:

> The Commission is of the opinion that consideration should be given to obtaining the advice of the DPP with respect to the prosecution of Edward Obeid Sr for the criminal offence of misconduct in public office in relation to his representations to [senior government officials] to change government policy with respect to Circular Quay leases without disclosing to them that his family had interests in Circular Quay leases and would benefit financially from such a change in policy. [These senior officials] could provide evidence of the representations and the fact that Edward Obeid Sr did not disclose his interest. Documentary and other evidence of the Obeid family interests in Circular Quay leases at the relevant times would also be available.[47]

The DPP agreed that there was sufficient evidence to proceed with the prosecution.[48] The manner in which the matter was brought before the courts reflects co-operation between the ICAC and DPP, with the former pulling together the evidence necessary to consider prosecution and support the indictment, and the latter taking the formal steps necessary to commence proceedings.

The third way in which these two mechanisms co-operate with one another is in respect of the sharing of evidence. As noted in this chapter, the ICAC gathered a range of evidence in the course of investigating Mr Obeid's conduct, including obtaining documents and information, interviewing witnesses and in the context of the ultimate public inquiry. While information and documents produced by witnesses during examinations or inquiries are not generally admissible in criminal proceedings (unless the witness fails to object),[49] the ICAC is tasked with gathering evidence that may be admissible in criminal prosecutions and providing it to the DPP, either during or after the completion of an investigation.[50] The courts have confirmed that the effect of these provisions is to abrogate the common law principle that the prosecution must make its

---

[46] Ibid s 14A(3).

[47] NSW Independent Commission Against Corruption, *Operation Cyrus: Investigation into the Conduct of The Hon Edward Obeid MLC and Others Concerning Circular Quay Retail Lease Policy* (June 2014) 61.

[48] NSW Independent Commission Against Corruption, *Annual Report: 2014–15* (October 2015) 105.

[49] *Independent Commission Against Corruption Act 1988* (NSW) s 37(3).

[50] Ibid s 14(1).

case without assistance from the accused, thereby allowing transcripts of compulsory public examinations to be used in criminal proceedings.[51] As highlighted above, in Mr Obeid's case the ICAC foreshadowed in its report that the evidence of senior government officials as well as documentary and other evidence was available to support the criminal prosecution.

To summarise, then, the relationship between the ICAC and DPP in prosecuting the offence of misconduct in public office can best be understood as primarily a *co-operative* one, with the ICAC playing a role of information-gatherer in the event that a criminal prosecution is to follow a finding of corruption. As a matter of academic interest, it is also interesting to note the dynamics that can be observed in some of the other mechanisms that formed part of the system which held Mr Obeid accountable for his wrongdoing. First, as a Member of Parliament, the powers and privileges of Parliament might be thought to have had a role to play in Mr Obeid's case. In his criminal trial, Mr Obeid argued that the Supreme Court had no jurisdiction to hear the case because his matter was within the 'exclusive cognisance' of Parliament. If he was correct, we would describe the relationship between the powers of Parliament and the prosecution for the offence of misconduct in public office as *mutually exclusive*; the engagement of parliamentary jurisdiction would preclude the possibility of criminal proceedings. Mr Obeid's argument centred on the principles of parliamentary privilege, relying on McHugh J's statement in *Egan v Willis* to the effect that '[w]hat is said or done within the walls of a parliamentary chamber cannot be examined in a court of law'.[52] Because his conduct was connected with his parliamentary role, Mr Obeid argued that it was for Parliament, and not the courts, to exercise its available powers to address the matter.[53] The NSW Supreme Court[54] and Court of Appeal[55] disagreed. Mr Obeid was charged not with breaching a parliamentary rule, but with a common law offence,[56] and the exercise of the Court's jurisdiction did not impact the dignity of the Parliament or the maintenance of its powers and

---

[51] *Macdonald v The Queen; Maitland v The Queen* (2016) 93 NSWLR 736, 760 [107]. The position may be otherwise if criminal proceedings are already on foot when the examination takes place.

[52] *Egan v Willis* (1998) 195 CLR 424, 461 [67].

[53] *Obeid v The Queen* (2015) 91 NSWLR 226, 235 [34].

[54] *R v Obeid [No 2]* [2015] NSWSC 1380.

[55] *Obeid v The Queen* (2015) 91 NSWLR 226.

[56] Ibid 235 [36].

privileges in a manner that would necessitate exclusive jurisdiction.[57] Accordingly these two mechanisms ought to be treated not as mutually exclusive, but as independent from one another.

A further mechanism that played a role in Mr Obeid's case was media publicity. Both the ICAC inquiry and criminal prosecution attracted significant media interest, with Mr Obeid being labelled as 'corrupt' in news reports following findings made by the ICAC.[58] The extent of media criticism of Mr Obeid was relevant at two points in the context of Mr Obeid's criminal hearing. First, prior to the hearing there was a question as to whether Mr Obeid ought to be tried by a judge alone, rather than a jury, as it was argued a jury might be influenced by the content of these media reports. The trial judge was satisfied that these concerns could be overcome through the use of appropriate directions and orders prohibiting publication of the trial.[59] The second way in which media publicity played a role in Mr Obeid's criminal proceedings was in connection with sentencing. Mr Obeid argued that the judge ought to take into account that he suffered a form of 'extra curial punishment from extensive media coverage', causing him humiliation.[60] The circumstances of Mr Obeid's wrongdoing gave Beech-Jones J reason to pause in considering whether public humiliation ought to be taken into account as a mitigating factor in sentencing:

> In this case the offender is a public figure, the offending did involve the abuse of a public position and the media reports that have been tendered do not sensationalise facts that are either irrelevant or trivial to the offending conduct. Instead, they are concerned with an issue of public importance, namely, political corruption. In those circumstances it seems incongruous that the consequential public humiliation should mitigate the sentence.[61]

However, on the state of authorities, Beech-Jones J thought that it would still be appropriate to treat significant adverse media publicity as a mitigating factor if it could be said to have physically or psychologically affected the offender.[62] Because Mr Obeid had not provided evidence of

---

[57] Ibid 237 [50].

[58] A number of such news reports are detailed in *R v Obeid* [2015] NSWSC 897, [36].

[59] *R v Obeid [No 4]* [2015] NSWSC 1442, [75]. See also *R v Obeid* [2015] NSWSC 897, [74].

[60] *R v Obeid [No 12]* [2016] NSWSC 1815, [98].

[61] Ibid [101].

[62] Ibid [102]. The inconsistency in authority stemmed from *Ryan v The Queen* [2001] 206 CLR 267, 284–85 [53] (McHugh J), 303–04 [123] (Kirby J) and 319 [177] (Callinan J).

such an impact, this media publicity was considered relevant 'only in the relatively limited sense'.[63] These two examples demonstrate that the media and criminal prosecution do not operate entirely independently from one another within the accountability system. The courts are able to exercise powers to limit the adverse effect of media publicity on the fairness of a trial (for example, by hearing a case in absence of a jury, or through making non-publication orders), and in determining the ultimate sanction to be imposed (by taking into account public opprobrium as a factor in sentencing). We would likely class this as an *interdependent* relationship, as both mechanisms interact with one another throughout the accountability process.

A further relationship dynamic of interest in Mr Obeid's case is that of *reciprocity*, which is the dynamic concerned with ensuring that accountability mechanisms are themselves accountable for the manner in which they perform their role. The NSW ICAC is subject to a number of checks on its powers, including two that are specified in its governing legislation: an independent auditor[64] and a joint parliamentary committee.[65] The courts can also operate as a check on the ICAC, as proceedings for judicial review can be commenced in order to confirm the legal boundaries within which the ICAC can exercise its powers.[66] The law of tort can also be put to use as a check on the exercise of ICAC's powers. Following a separate ICAC corruption investigation,[67] Mr Obeid brought proceedings against the ICAC, the Commissioner, its legal counsel and two of its officers alleging that each had committed the tort of misfeasance in public office.[68] While Mr Obeid was unsuccessful in his claim, the proceedings demonstrate the ability for the courts to utilise private law causes of action to check the exercise of power by the ICAC and its staff. All of these mechanisms are *reciprocal*, in the sense that they provide an external check on the ICAC's performance of its accountability functions.

---

[63] *R v Obeid [No 12]* [2016] NSWSC 1815, [103].

[64] Inspector of the Independent Commission Against Corruption: *Independent Commission Against Corruption Act 1988* (NSW) s 57A.

[65] The 'Committee on the Independent Commission Against Corruption': ibid s 63.

[66] E.g. *Independent Commission Against Corruption v Cunneen* (2015) 256 CLR 1.

[67] The ICAC separately investigated Mr Obeid in respect of conduct relating to the grant of mining tenements: NSW Independent Commission Against Corruption, *Investigation into the Conduct of Ian Macdonald, Edward Obeid Senior, Moses Obeid and Others* (July 2013).

[68] *Obeid Snr v Ipp* (2016) 338 ALR 234 (trial), and *Obeid v Lockley* (2018) 98 NSWLR 258 (appeal).

11.1.3   Summary

The Eddie Obeid corruption scandal provides a useful demonstration of the accountability ideas discussed in Parts II and III of this book. The ICAC inquiry and criminal prosecution proceedings both played important, albeit distinct, roles in holding Mr Obeid accountable for his conduct. If we were to measure each mechanism against the hypothetical benchmark, we would of course find that they both fall short; the ICAC was unable to deliver a punitive outcome as warranted by the wrongdoing occasioned, and criminal proceedings were too punitive to fulfil the expectations of the deterrence rationale. What this scenario demonstrates, however, is that different mechanisms might validly focus on different aspects of our accountability benchmark. Rather than expecting a single mechanism to meet the full gambit of accountability objectives reflected in the hypothetical benchmark, we might instead hive off particular functions to be the focus of different mechanisms. Because the ICAC focuses more squarely on uncovering wrongdoing (transparency) and supporting agencies to prevent corruption going forward (deterrence), this allows it to utilise more flexible approaches appropriate to those functions, leaving the offence of misconduct in public office to fulfil the task of punishing Mr Obeid (desert) with the protection of the rigorous evidential procedures of the criminal law.

In addition to being directed at different accountability *objectives*, we can also see that the two mechanisms possess different *features*. While both are similar in terms of their accessibility and coerciveness, they differ in terms of their flexibility, autonomy, independence and permanence. To the extent that we might otherwise be concerned that there are two mechanisms directed at delivering accountability in respect of the same conduct, the fact that they embody such differences alleviates some of these concerns. The operation of both mechanisms also provides us with some insight into the *relationship dynamics* that are in play within accountability systems. This scenario has demonstrated that the ICAC and criminal law operate in a relatively co-operative manner, as opposed to employing an independent or staged approach. Again, to the extent that we might be concerned that accountability tasks are being duplicated, this co-operative dynamic might explain the utility of dividing roles between separate mechanisms. To summarise, the operation of the ICAC and criminal prosecution in Mr Obeid's case demonstrate that in order to discuss potential accountability deficits and overloads, we need to be able to do two things. First, we need to be clear about the benchmark against which we are measuring the performance of a given mechanism or mechanisms. Secondly, we need to be able to understand the mechanisms under scrutiny as a system, which requires a comparison of the features of individual mechanisms, and an understanding of the relationships between them. After completing this analysis in respect of Mr Obeid's case, it is possible to understand accountability as the product of the joint efforts of a number of mechanisms.

11.2 Judicial Review and Tort Law

The second scenario explored in Chapter 8 was the imprisonment of Graham Taylor pursuant to immigration detention procedures following the cancellation of his visas. Those cancellation decisions were quashed by the courts in judicial review proceedings, and Mr Taylor subsequently brought civil proceedings seeking damages based on the tort of false imprisonment. It was noted that when applied strictly, we might regard this scenario as giving rise to a potential accountability overload (i.e. the transparency rationale is targeted twice, with officials being called to answer in the same forum in respect of largely the same subject matter on two occasions). It was further noted that there was a potential accountability deficit in respect of the deterrence rationale, as both sets of proceedings were ill-equipped to facilitate the kind of dialogue anticipated by that aspect of the benchmark. Finally, it was noted that each mechanism was most closely aligned with one accountability rationale (i.e. judicial review with the control rationale, and false imprisonment with the redress rationale), though there was a degree of interplay and overlap between these functions. This section compares the features of these two mechanisms and the ways in which they interact in order to understand their operation as an accountability system.

11.2.1 Features of the System

At first glance, we might wonder whether there is any sense in seeking to compare and contrast the features of judicial review and false imprisonment proceedings, given that both sit within the legal system. Unsurprisingly, there is a close degree of alignment between these two accountability mechanisms, with both being managed by the courts pursuant to legal norms and procedures. We would likely say that there are equivalent degrees of *flexibility*, *coerciveness* and *autonomy* when we compare the operation of these two legal causes of action. However, even within this homogenous corner of the broader accountability system, it is possible to identify a number of points of difference as between the features of these two mechanisms.

In terms of *accessibility*, rules of standing govern access entitlements to commence each type of claim. As was highlighted in Chapter 8, questions of standing in tort proceedings are bound up in the elements of the cause of action. In false imprisonment proceedings, the class of eligible plaintiffs is defined by reference to the element of detention, with only those who are in fact deprived of their liberty being entitled to commence proceedings.[69] In contrast, judicial review proceedings are open to a wider class of applicants, with standing being defined by reference to a person's interest in the subject matter of the claim.[70] When we compare these two standing tests, we would say that while false imprisonment proceedings are narrowly confined to the party immediately impacted by the tortious conduct, judicial review proceedings offer access to a wider class that can demonstrate a recognised link with the impugned decision. Accessibility is therefore wider in respect of this latter cause of action.

In terms of *cost*, all forms of legal proceedings will sit at the more extreme end of the scale when compared with other mechanisms such as complaining to an ombudsman. Both judicial review and false imprisonment proceedings are an expensive and time-consuming exercise, requiring parties to input significant resources into court fees and (in most cases) legal representation. When we compare the two, however, we would likely say that civil proceedings in which it is necessary to engage in extensive fact-finding inquiries (including evidence as to loss and damage) are likely to be more costly in terms of time and resources than judicial review proceedings.

We can also identify points of difference in relation to *independence* and *permanence* in respect of these two causes of action. Australian courts enjoy a constitutional mandate in respect of their judicial review function in Australia. With the principle in *Marbury v Madison*[71]

---

[69] See Section 8.3.2.2 in Chapter 8.
[70] See Section 8.3.1.2 in Chapter 8.
[71] 5 US (1 Cranch) 137 (1803), 177 and 180 (Marshall CJ):

> It is emphatically the province and the duty of the judicial department to say what the law is ... [T]he particular phraseology of the constitution of the United States confirms and strengthens the principle, supposed to be essential to all written constitutions, that a law repugnant to the constitution is void; and that the courts, as well as other departments, are bound by that instrument.

regarded as 'axiomatic' in the Australian context,[72] the courts have the exclusive role of determining the legality of legislative and executive action. The exclusivity of this role is reflected in the Australian courts' reluctance to engage with the doctrine of deference, which allows courts in other common law jurisdictions to defer to executive agencies as to the interpretation of ambiguous statutory provisions.[73] Preserving this function for the exclusive domain of the courts reinforces their *independence* in determining the meaning of the law. The constitutional foundation for judicial review also buys it a significant degree of *permanence* in Australia. The Australian courts have come to recognise an 'entrenched minimum provision of judicial review',[74] representing a minimum content of review power that cannot be withdrawn from the courts or abrogated over time. While this finding is strictly only applicable at the Federal level, the courts have since held that a similar restriction applies at State level.[75] In contrast, no such constitutional protection exists for civil claims, including the tort of false imprisonment. Parliament may legislate to make a plaintiff's task of establishing elements going to liability more difficult,[76] or to confer immunity on particular classes of government defendant,[77] to restrict access to remedies,[78] or even to abolish the cause of action altogether. All of this reinforces the conclusion that as a cause of action, judicial review confers on the courts a more independent and permanent accountability role than a civil claim for false imprisonment.

We can conclude, then, by noting that it is possible to identify differences between the features of accountability mechanisms even where they operate in a similar context. When we wish to make observations about potential accountability gaps and overlaps between these mechanisms, it is necessary to bear these points of difference in mind.

---

[72] *Australian Communist Party v Commonwealth* (1951) 83 CLR 1, 262.

[73] For discussion, see Janina Boughey, 'Re-evaluating the Doctrine of Deference in Australian Administrative Law' (2017) 45(4) *Federal Law Review* 597.

[74] *Plaintiff S157/2002 v Commonwealth* (2003) 211 CLR 476, 513 [103].

[75] *Kirk v Industrial Court (NSW)* (2010) 239 CLR 531, 580–81 [98]–[100].

[76] This was the effect of the legislative provisions in *Ruddock v Taylor* (2005) 222 CLR 612, which authorised detention on the premise that an officer held a 'reasonable suspicion' that a person was an unlawful non-citizen: *Migration Act 1958* (Cth) s 189.

[77] In Australia, Crown immunity in tort has been abrogated by statute: see, e.g., *Judiciary Act 1903* (Cth) s 64.

[78] For example, aggravated damages are not available in NSW for causes of action based in negligence: *Civil Liability Act 2002* (NSW) s 21. This legislation also introduces caps and thresholds in respect of damages for economic and non-economic loss (Pt 2 Div 2–3).

11.2.2   System Dynamics

Having identified some of the similarities and differences in the features of the legal accountability 'system' that was brought to bear in Mr Taylor's case, it is further necessary to consider the relationship dynamics in play. As argued in Chapter 10, claims of accountability deficit and overload must take into account the ways in which accountability mechanisms overlap and interact. Looking first at the degree of *independence* between these two mechanisms, tort proceedings can be viewed as an important alternative to judicial review proceedings in challenging the exercise of public power, and may potentially play an ameliorating role in circumstances where judicial review is not available (for example, where power has been outsourced to private contractors).[79] The independence of these causes of action is further reflected in the fact that their remedies are not interchangeable: 'the mere invalidation of an administrative decision does not provide a cause of action or a basis for an award of damages'.[80] This is not to say that the fact that conduct is ultra vires may not otherwise be relevant to liability in tort (as noted in Chapter 8, this was an integral aspect of Mr Taylor's false imprisonment claim). However, the point is that ultra vires conduct per se will not translate into a claim for civil damages. The courts have declined a number of invitations to develop the common law along these lines,[81] and so we can treat the remedies flowing from tort claims as independent of proceedings for judicial review.

However, there are limits to this independence. Rather than representing a simple binary system, various legal rules and doctrines move these causes of action into other types of relationship dynamic. In many cases, the application of these rules will depend on matters that will naturally

---

[79] Matthew Groves, 'Outsourcing and Non-delegable Duties' (2005) 16 *Public Law Review* 265, 268.

[80] *Chan Yee Kin v Minister for Immigration and Ethnic Affairs* (1991) 31 FCR 29, 41.

[81] For example, note the failure of the *Beaudesert* tort (which might have afforded damages for harm that was the 'inevitable consequence' of 'unlawful' conduct): *Beaudesert Shire Council v Smith* (1966) 120 CLR 145 overruled in *Northern Territory v Mengel* (1995) 185 CLR 307. Similarly, the courts have maintained a strict hold on the degree of subjective fault (or 'conscious maladministration') needed to make out a claim for misfeasance in public office: *Pyrenees Shire Council v Day* (1998) 192 CLR 330, 375 [124], and have declined to provide a civil remedy in connection with breach of constitutional norms: *James v Commonwealth* (1939) 62 CLR 339. For further discussion, see Ellen Rock and Greg Weeks, 'Monetary Awards for Public Law Wrongs: Australia's Resistant Legal Landscape' (2018) 41(4) *University of New South Wales Law Journal* 1159.

differ from case to case (e.g. which set of proceedings has been commenced first in time and the plaintiff's motives in commencing the claim, amongst other matters). In Mr Taylor's case, we can see that, while the causes of action were pursued independently, there are a number of ways in which they interacted with one another. As a starting point, we can see that the two causes of action functioned in a *staged* manner. The initial judicial review proceedings were commenced with a view to challenging the legality of the visa cancellation decisions which had served as the impetus for Mr Taylor's detention. Following resolution of those proceedings, Mr Taylor then commenced his claim in tort, building on the orders made in the judicial review case in order to make out one of the elements of the tort claim (i.e. that the detention lacked legal authority).

This staging process between these causes of action was not compulsory, however. Mr Taylor could instead have elected to challenge the underlying administrative decisions collaterally, by questioning their validity in his false imprisonment claim. As noted in Chapter 10, collateral attack offers an example of an *interdependent* relationship dynamic, whereby one cause of action is used in an indirect manner to achieve a result that could have been achieved directly via another.[82] In this sense, successful collateral attack of the underlying administrative order in tort proceedings could be used to resolve a question that could have been raised directly in judicial review proceedings. There might have been some benefit to adopting this approach (namely, reduction of legal costs and saving of court time). However, it was ultimately to Mr Taylor's benefit that he elected not to pursue this course. As was noted in Chapter 8, Mr Taylor succeeded in establishing that the decisions to cancel his visas had been invalidly made, either because the relevant statutory power did not apply to a person in Mr Taylor's situation, or because relevant jurisdictional requirements had not been complied with. It was also accepted that these visa cancellation decisions formed the foundation for Mr Taylor's detention; without these decisions, immigration officials could not have formed a reasonable suspicion that Mr Taylor was an unlawful non-citizen. Accordingly, the quashing of these visa cancellation decisions in judicial review proceedings removed the source of authority for the detention and gave effect to Mr Taylor's release. It is less certain whether this same result would have been achieved collaterally. As a starting point, we should note that the civil

---

[82] As a matter of practice, the validity point would be an aspect of the defence: see burden of proof as discussed in Section 8.3.2.4(ii) in Chapter 8.

trial for false imprisonment would have proved more costly and time consuming to pursue than judicial review proceedings, meaning that any result would have taken longer to achieve. It is also unclear how the majority of the High Court would have approached a collateral challenge to the visa cancellation decisions. As noted in Chapter 8, the majority judgment was not concerned with the causal role of the visa cancellation decisions in giving effect to the imprisonment, but was instead almost exclusively concerned with statutory interpretation of the provision which authorised immigration officials to detain Mr Taylor. This provision was found to have authorised Mr Taylor's detention irrespective of the invalidity of the cancellation decisions, and was therefore a complete answer to the false imprisonment claim. Accordingly, Mr Taylor was in a better position having elected to frame his causes of action in a staged, rather than interdependent relationship.

The *Taylor* litigation also offers an example of a potentially *mutually exclusive* dynamic between judicial review and false imprisonment proceedings. The government defendants in the false imprisonment claim sought to argue that Mr Taylor ought to be estopped from suing for damages in tort because he had not raised the matter in the judicial review proceedings. This argument depended on the *Anshun* doctrine, which obliges a party to bring forward their entire case to be dealt with in a single set of proceedings.[83] The *Anshun* doctrine can be thought of as a species of the court's inherent power to stay proceedings that constitute an abuse of process,[84] and may arise where 'the matter relied upon as a defence in [the] second action was so relevant to the subject matter of the first action that it would have been unreasonable not to rely on it'.[85] The court in *Taylor* summarily dismissed the application of the doctrine in that case.[86] Most emphatic was Meagher JA in the NSW Court of Appeal:

> An overall requirement of an *Anshun* estoppel is reasonableness. It does not arise unless it was unreasonable of the party sought to be estopped not to plead the cause of action in question. I cannot see how it would be unreasonable for Mr Taylor to refrain from mentioning to the High Court that he wished to sue the appellants in damages for wrongful

---

[83] JD Heydon, *Cross on Evidence* (11th ed., LexisNexis, 2017) 271.

[84] Justice KR Handley, '*Anshun* Today' (1997) 71 *Australian Law Journal* 934, 940.

[85] *Port of Melbourne Authority v Anshun Pty Ltd* (1981) 147 CLR 589, 602.

[86] *Ruddock v Taylor* (2003) 58 NSWLR 269, 278–79 [42]–[44] (Spigelman J), 285 [82] (Meagher JA); *Ruddock v Taylor* (2005) 222 CLR 612, 647 [131] (Kirby J).

imprisonment, particularly as there was not the slightest chance that the High Court would have done anything about it if he had.[87]

Accordingly, the doctrine of estoppel did not operate to create a *mutually exclusive* dynamic in the circumstances of the case.

Finally, it is interesting to consider the element of *reciprocity* in Mr Taylor's case, within the framework of the court hierarchy. As noted in Chapter 10, the reciprocity dynamic arises where one mechanism operates as a check on the exercise of power by another. There are clear limits to the operation of this dynamic within the legal system; many judicial rules and doctrines (e.g. *res judicata* and *stare decisis*) are designed specifically to prevent an earlier determination by the courts from being called into question in later decisions. It would not be open, for example, for the court in Mr Taylor's false imprisonment claim to second-guess the earlier determinations of the invalidity of the visa cancellation decisions which had been made in his judicial review proceedings. One area of the legal system in which reciprocity does play a role is in the appellate process, though this is somewhat limited by the nature of the questions (i.e. law or fact) which can be reconsidered by the reviewing court. Mr Taylor's false imprisonment case was determined in his favour by a judge of the NSW District Court. The government defendants had the opportunity to request that this decision be reviewed by the NSW Court of Appeal, and then by the High Court, which ultimately found in their favour. The ability for appellate courts to review the legality of judicial decisions operates as a check on power, producing the benefits of accountability and legitimacy discussed in Chapter 10.[88]

It is worth noting the operation of three other mechanisms in this saga, by way of postscript. First, as was documented in Chapter 8, the High Court revisited its decision in *Re Taylor* only two years later, holding in *Shaw* that the visa cancellation power which had been relied on in Mr Taylor's case could indeed be used in relation to long-term Australian residents born in England.[89] Accordingly, one of the bases on which Mr Taylor succeeded in having the cancellation decision quashed would not have been available to him at a later time (though that did not alter the outcome in his own case). This demonstrates again evidence of reciprocity within the legal system, as the apex court within the Australian

---

[87] *Ruddock v Taylor* (2003) 58 NSWLR 269, 285 [82] (Meagher JA).
[88] See discussion in Section 10.6.
[89] *Shaw v Minister for Immigration and Multicultural Affairs* (2003) 218 CLR 28.

hierarchy was able to overturn its own earlier decision in a manner that altered the scope of judicial review in similar cases going forward.

A second point to note is that the exercise of these deportation powers in relation to long-term residents has remained controversial since *Re Taylor* and *Shaw* were decided.[90] In 2006, shortly after Mr Taylor's failed civil proceedings, the Ombudsman completed an own-motion investigation into the use of s 501 to cancel the visas of long-term residents.[91] The Ombudsman made a number of recommendations about the manner in which the Department of Immigration managed such cases, including in connection with the provision of procedural fairness (which had been a factor in Mr Taylor's case). The Department accepted most of these recommendations, and outlined steps it intended to take to improve its procedures going forward.[92] Accordingly, when we adopt a systemic view, we might regard this intervention by the Ombudsman as going some way towards ameliorating the potential accountability deficit identified in the lack of deterrent-focused structures in Mr Taylor's case. While the Ombudsman was not empowered to review the conduct of ministers (itself raising the spectre of potential accountability deficit), the fact that many ministerial decisions are informed by departmental advice undercuts this limitation to a degree.[93]

Finally, it is worth noting the mechanisms that eventually supported Mr Taylor to make a successful application for Australian citizenship in 2012. His application was initially refused by the decision-maker on the basis that he was not of 'good character'.[94] Mr Taylor sought review of that decision by the Administrative Appeals Tribunal (AAT). The Tribunal is empowered to review a matter afresh, or to 'stand in the shoes' of the original decision-maker.[95] In this case, the Tribunal determined that in light of the available evidence, Mr Taylor was to now be regarded as a

[90] See Michelle Foster, 'An "Alien" by the Barest of Threads – The Legality of the Deportation of Long-Term Residents from Australia' (2009) 33(2) *Melbourne University Law Review* 483.

[91] Commonwealth Ombudsman, *Department of Immigration and Multicultural Affairs: Administration of s 501 of the Migration Act 1958 as it Applies to Long-Term Residents* (Report No 1, February 2006).

[92] Ibid 6–8.

[93] This was noted by the Ombudsman: ibid 1.

[94] This being one of the requirements for citizenship: *Australian Citizenship Act 2007* (Cth) s 21(2).

[95] *Re Taylor and Minister for Immigration and Citizenship* (2012) 129 ALD 311, 314 [12].

person of good character, and remitted the matter for reconsideration in light of that finding.[96]

11.2.3   Summary

Mr Taylor's litigation history reinforces the conclusion that accountability rationales are better served by a range of mechanisms operating in concert, rather than by a single mechanism operating in isolation. Chapter 8 raised some concerns about potential accountability deficits and overloads arising through the use of judicial review and tort proceedings to hold the government accountable for detaining Mr Taylor following the unlawful cancellation of his visa. This chapter has demonstrated that our concerns on this front would likely be ameliorated by a more nuanced understanding of the operation of these two causes of action, as well as other mechanisms that were subsequently brought to bear.

11.3   Ombudsmen and Administrative Compensation Regimes

The final scenario considered in Chapter 8 related to the Australian Apprenticeships Incentives Program, and in particular, the harm suffered by individuals who relied on misleading advice provided by private contractors acting on behalf of a government department. The two mechanisms that were considered in this context were investigation by the Commonwealth Ombudsman, and access to the Scheme for Compensation for Detriment caused by Defective Administration (CDDA Scheme), a discretionary compensation scheme designed to address detriment caused by defective administration.

11.3.1   Features of the System

Both the Ombudsman and CDDA Scheme operate in a relatively flexible and responsive manner, lacking the rigid formality and procedures utilised by the legal mechanisms deployed in the earlier scenarios. Looking first at the Ombudsman, we would describe this mechanism as highly *accessible, cost-effective, flexible* and *autonomous*. As identified in Chapter 8, there are no standing limitations that restrict access, with a party's interests in the subject matter of the action being relevant only if

---

[96] Ibid 321 [51].

the Ombudsman wishes to decline to investigate. Accordingly, public interest matters which might fall foul of standing rules in the context of a judicial review claim can validly be brought before the Ombudsman for investigation. Further, the Ombudsman is able to investigate even in absence of a complaint being made, with the ability to commence an own-motion investigation making the office highly autonomous. We would likely also regard this mechanism as very cost-effective. There are no fees associated with raising a complaint, and a complainant need not invest time or resources in generating evidence or advocating their case. Further, the Ombudsman is allowed a significant degree of flexibility in managing its investigations, with the governing legislation specifically providing that investigations may be conducted 'in such manner as the Ombudsman thinks fit'.[97]

We would likely also be satisfied that the Ombudsman enjoys a significant degree of *independence* in the performance of accountability functions. On a strict institutional interpretation, the Ombudsman falls within the executive branch of government,[98] which might give us some pause in classifying this mechanism as an independent means to challenge decisions and conduct of actors within that branch. Executive control over resourcing and appointments might also impact our assessment of independence.[99] Likewise, the statutory status of the office means that its functions are inherently subject to curtailment over time, perhaps affecting our assessment of the *permanence* of the office. Despite these structural concerns, ombudsmen are generally regarded as enjoying a significant degree of independence. Indeed, this is one of the core defining features of the office, as specified by the Members of the Australian and New Zealand Ombudsman Association. A policy statement published by the Association cites a range of factors as contributing to this independence, including the manner in which the office is established, security of tenure, lack of any requirement to follow directions from another person or body, and the unconditional

---

[97] *Ombudsman Act 1976* (Cth) s 8(2).
[98] As noted above, some would argue that agencies such as the Ombudsman might be treated as forming a fourth 'integrity' branch: see n 18.
[99] See, e.g., Brogan Elliot, 'The Hidden Influences That Limit Governmental Independence: Controlling the Ombudsman's Apparent Independence' (2013) 21 *Australian Journal of Administrative Law* 27, 33–34. For an argument regarding the use of parliamentary oversight, see Anita Stuhmcke, 'Australian Ombudsmen: Drafting a Blueprint for Reform' (2014) 24 *Australian Journal of Administrative Law* 1, 54–58.

right to publish reports and findings, amongst others.[100] Even though we might not place the Ombudsman in the same league as the courts in terms of independence, we would likely be satisfied that the office is highly regarded as an independent mechanism for the support of executive accountability in Australia.

While the Ombudsman might rate highly in terms of these other factors, we would regard the Ombudsman as an inherently *non-coercive* mechanism. The investigatory powers of the office are backed with threats of sanctions for non-compliance; however, the ultimate products of an investigation – the Ombudsman's opinions and recommendations – are not. An agency can elect not to adopt any recommendation made by the Ombudsman, with the only consequences being a threat of reporting 'up the chain' and attendant publicity if the Ombudsman elects to publish its investigation report. The combination of this range of factors, particularly the lack of coercive powers, might at first give us reason to query the utility of the Ombudsman when measured against the hypothetical benchmark of accountability. However, these features of the mechanism might be better understood as producing the opposite effect:

> [S]uccessful ombudsmen … depend on values of informality and trust which allow them to have ready access to officials and to be seen as reasonable and relatively unthreatening investigators of individual complaints. By keeping clear of major policy, they avoid embroiling officials in damaging political controversy. Lacking power to enforce, they can invoke a more open and cooperative response.[101]

In the context of the Incentives Program, we see evidence of this in the Department's acceptance of recommendations made by the Ombudsman. While the Ombudsman lacked power to force the Department to make structural changes in its management of the program, the co-operative approach adopted by the Ombudsman in fact resulted in the Department agreeing to most of the recommended changes. Further, the publication of the Ombudsman's report facilitated public awareness

---

[100] Australian and New Zealand Ombudsman Association, *Essential Criteria for Describing a Body as an Ombudsman: Policy Statement Endorsed by the Members of the ANZOA* (February 2010) <http://www.anzoa.com.au/assets/anzoa-policy-statement_ombudsman_essential-criteria.pdf> accessed 10 January 2019.

[101] Richard Mulgan, *Holding Power to Account: Accountability in Modern Democracies* (Palgrave Macmillan, 2003) 97.

of the one recommendation that the Department declined to adopt – creating access to compensation in cases such as these – which has opened the path to discussion of this shortfall at a whole of government level. As noted in Chapter 8, these types of outcomes are strongly aligned with the deterrence rationale for accountability.

Turning to the CDDA Scheme, there are again a number of noteworthy features of this mechanism. As for the Ombudsman, we would regard this mechanism as highly *accessible* and *cost-effective*, as there are no standing limitations or fees associated with making a request. Given the significant degree of discretion afforded to decision-makers under the Scheme, we would also regard this as a *flexible* mechanism. However, there are a number of features of the mechanism that potentially limit its accountability function. First, the same discretion that produces flexibility also reduces the *coerciveness* of the mechanism. There is no obligation on a decision-maker to award compensation, even if a case appears to fall within the criteria outlined in the guidelines. We would also regard this as an *impermanent* mechanism. Established pursuant to executive authority, the Scheme is subject to alteration and dismantlement. We would also say that the compensation mechanism established pursuant to the CDDA Scheme would not rate highly in terms of its *independence*. The decision-maker for the purpose of the CDDA Scheme is the relevant portfolio minister (or their delegate),[102] meaning that the political head of the agency responsible for the impugned decision or conduct is charged with deciding whether or not to compensate a victim. This lack of independence might raise concerns about the legitimacy of the Scheme as an accountability mechanism if it were a complainant's only option for redress.

Returning to the points made in Chapter 9, it is clear that these two accountability mechanisms differ in terms of some of their defining features, both as between each other, but most clearly by comparison to the more coercive legal mechanisms considered above. These differences in features should not, however, be immediately classed as limits on accountability. As noted above, many of the perceived limitations of the Ombudsman regime (i.e. lack of coercive power and position within the executive branch) in fact assist that mechanism in performing its accountability role. Further, it would be a mistake to point to any

---

[102] Department of Finance (Cth), *Scheme for Compensation for Detriment Caused by Defective Administration* (Resource Management Guide No 409, November 2018) [7] 'CDDA Scheme'.

potential limitations without considering the complementary role played by other mechanisms within the system, to which we now turn.

11.3.2 System Dynamics

In the scenario considered here, the Ombudsman and CDDA Scheme played quite different accountability roles. Neither mechanism was considered to satisfy the full expectations of the transparency, redress and deterrence rationales. The Ombudsman made its most prominent contribution to the deterrence rationale for accountability, while the CDDA Scheme was (at least in theory) directed towards the redress rationale. It was further noted that the CDDA Scheme failed to satisfy the redress rationale in the circumstances of this case, given its inapplicability to private contractors. This final section considers the relationship dynamics between these two mechanisms. As a starting point, these two mechanisms are capable of operating entirely *independently*. A matter may be investigated by the Ombudsman, and also be the subject of compensation pursuant to the CDDA Scheme. However, these two mechanisms are also capable of operating in a number of other ways.

First, the two mechanisms may operate in a *staged* fashion. An individual who suffers loss as a result of government maladministration may complain to the Ombudsman, who may investigate the matter and reach a view that the complainant ought to be offered compensation. The relevant decision-maker within the agency might then take steps to consider providing compensation pursuant to the CDDA Scheme. That sequence of events could be regarded as staged, with the latter taking effect once the former is finalised. Alternatively, we might cast the relationship between the Ombudsman and CDDA Scheme as *interdependent*. An interdependent relationship is one in which two mechanisms interact at various points without overtaking one another. Where the Ombudsman makes recommendations for the provision of compensation during the course of an investigation, there is a degree of symbiosis between those two mechanisms, with both providing contributions to the final result.

We might also note that there is an element of *reciprocity* in the relationship between these two mechanisms, as a person who is dissatisfied with an agency's decision in respect of the CDDA Scheme is able to complain to the Ombudsman, allowing them to review the decision and make recommendations. As with other aspects of the Ombudsman's powers, these recommendations are non-coercive. However, the applicable guidelines in relation to the CDDA Scheme provide that an agency 'must consider' those recommendations.[103] Because the Scheme lacks statutory backing, options for judicial review of decisions under the Scheme are limited,[104] and therefore an Ombudsman review plays an important role of securing reciprocal accountability.

Looking more widely at other potentially available mechanisms within this system, we can see clear evidence of *mutually exclusive* dynamics. Both the CDDA Scheme and (to perhaps a lesser extent) the Ombudsman are intended to play residual or gap-filling roles in the context of the wider accountability system. For the Ombudsman, this is evident in the discretion to decline to investigate matters in which other mechanisms could be brought to bear. The Ombudsman may refuse to investigate matters that are more squarely legal issues that have, or could be, litigated in a court or tribunal.[105] The Ombudsman may also decline to investigate a matter that could be the subject of internal review, or review by other accountability mechanisms such as an Industry Ombudsman, the Public Service Commissioner, the Parliamentary Service Commissioner, the Integrity Commissioner and the AFP Commissioner, amongst others.[106] Where the Ombudsman exercises this discretion, we would regard this as creating a relationship of mutual exclusivity between these mechanisms by subjugating the Ombudsman to a residual position. The dynamic is even more clearly evident in respect of the CDDA Scheme. The applicable guidelines indicate that the Scheme cannot apply before 'other avenues' that might remedy the loss.[107] Similarly, the Scheme does not apply if a matter could be litigated, as it is 'not to be used in relation to ... claims in which it is reasonable to conclude that the Commonwealth would be found liable, if the matter were litigated'.[108] These restrictions on the operation of the Scheme again confine it to a residual or gap-filling role, which is a feature of the mutually exclusive dynamic.

---

[103] Ibid [91].

[104] CDDA Scheme decisions are not made 'under an enactment' for the purpose of the *Administrative Decisions (Judicial Review) Act 1977* (Cth). Judicial review is potentially available under s 75(v) of the Constitution, and s 39B of the *Judiciary Act 1903* (Cth). For further discussion see Greg Weeks, *Soft Law and Public Authorities: Remedies and Reform* (Hart Publishing, 2016) 260–61.

[105] *Ombudsman Act 1976* (Cth) s 6(2)–(3).

[106] Ibid s 6.

[107] Department of Finance (Cth), *CDDA Scheme* (n 102) [19].

[108] Ibid [23].

Finally, it is important to note that the identified shortcomings of the Ombudsman and CDDA Scheme in restoring Mr A and Ms M may not present a full picture of the outcomes in this case, as further investigations reveal that the complainants may have had access to an alternative form of discretionary compensation. Act of grace payments are a form of discretionary payment provided for by the *Public Governance, Performance and Accountability Act 2013* (Cth), which allows the Finance Minister to authorise payments in 'special circumstances'.[109] Like the CDDA Scheme, act of grace payments are inherently discretionary, and no guidance is offered on the meaning of the 'special circumstances' in which a payment might be available.[110] This mechanism is intended to perform a purely residual role, as matters arising out of 'defective administration' are ordinarily to be dealt with pursuant to the CDDA Scheme.[111] In the present case, the inapplicability of the CDDA Scheme to private contractors raised the possibility of an act of grace payment, and correspondence obtained from the relevant government departments indicates that Mr A and Ms M were invited to make such an application.[112] The outcomes of any such applications have not been made public. This again reminds us that in the diagnosis of accountability deficits and overloads, it is necessary to have regard to the array of available mechanisms, and the relationships between them. The act of grace mechanism is a further reflection of the mutually exclusive dynamic, playing a gap-filling or residual role behind the more prescriptive CDDA Scheme, and offering the possibility of redress in a case that might otherwise have been classed as representing an accountability deficit.

11.3.3   Summary

Again, this section has demonstrated that it is critical that we adopt a systemic view of accountability mechanisms in order to make sense of claims of accountability deficit and overload. The Ombudsman and

---

[109] *Public Governance, Performance and Accountability Act 2013* (Cth) s 65.

[110] Department of Finance (Cth), *Requests for Discretionary Financial Assistance under the Public Governance, Performance and Accountability Act 2013* (Resource Management Guide No 401, April 2018) [7]–[10].

[111] Department of Finance (Cth), *CDDA Scheme* (n 102) [27].

[112] Correspondence obtained pursuant to a freedom of information application: copy on file with author.

CDDA Scheme cannot be treated as mechanisms operating in isolation. Rather, they play very defined failsafe roles within the wider accountability system, allowing an option for review of cases that do not fall within the ambit of other more coercive mechanisms. In our search for accountability deficits and overloads, the nuances of these roles must be borne in mind.

~

Conclusion

If accountability is indeed a 'golden concept that no one can be against',[1] and that operates to support the legitimacy of government, it is of little surprise that the identification of accountability deficits has proved to be such a perennially popular topic. And if increases in accountability are thought capable of influencing government conduct to the extent envisaged by those on the hunt for accountability deficits, it is little wonder that calls for increased accountability have given rise to a new breed of concerns about accountability overloads. However, there remains much work to be done in giving shape to these concepts if they can be meaningful beyond a rhetorical call for change. If the concept of accountability is contested and contestable, the task of articulating shortfalls and excesses in that concept is even more so.

This book outlines the two core areas in which we must invest our efforts in order to take the concepts of accountability deficit and overload out of the realm of rhetoric. First, it would be necessary to define a 'benchmark' of accountability. This benchmark would articulate, for the first time, what an 'ideal amount' of accountability would look like. On so doing, it would be theoretically possible to utilise that benchmark to measure a given mechanism and to identify areas in which it falls short of expectations (giving rise to a potential accountability deficit), and areas in which it overperforms against expectations (giving rise to a potential accountability overload). In order to formulate a benchmark, it would be necessary to transform the mechanistic description of accountability (i.e. who is accountable to whom, for what and how?) into a normative one (i.e. who *ought* to be accountable to whom, for what and how?). This would require us not only to come to a landing on the underlying rationale(s) for accountability, which may encompass transparency, control, redress, desert and deterrence, but also to consider the best means to

---

[1] Mark Bovens, 'Analysing and Assessing Accountability: A Conceptual Framework' (2007) 13 *European Law Journal* 447, 448.

achieve those ends. As outlined in Part II of this book, there are serious questions as to whether this is an achievable feat, as it raises many complex questions around the proper conception of government and what it means to hold that government to account. And if we admit that accountability may encompass a number of rationales, the shape of the benchmark thereby produced would be, at best, complex, and at worst, unworkable.

Assuming that it were possible to define a benchmark with the necessary degree of specificity, we might then be able to utilise that benchmark to assess the performance of a given mechanism in a particular case. This, however, leads to the second core area requiring attention; mapping out accountability mechanisms as a system. Part III of this book outlines the variety of characteristic features and relationship dynamics that may be encompassed within accountability systems. It is possible to view accountability mechanisms as forming a delicate balance in terms of their degree of accessibility, cost, flexibility, coerciveness, autonomy, independence and permanence. It would be a mistake to focus on one of these areas as producing an accountability deficit (e.g. that the ombudsman lacks coercive powers), without appreciating that this limitation may be balanced out by a concomitant feature of another mechanism (e.g. the coercive powers of the courts). Further, it is necessary to appreciate the nature of the relationships between mechanisms in order to make a claim of accountability deficit or overload. So, for instance, it would be a mistake to focus on the fact that ex gratia compensation is available only pursuant to a highly discretionary and opaque regime without appreciating that this mechanism plays only a residual role within the accountability system. Likewise, it would be a mistake to point to the fact that an individual is subject to numerous accountability mechanisms as a potential accountability overload (e.g. the same conduct may be the subject of a parliamentary enquiry, investigation by an ombudsman and tort proceedings) without appreciating the extent to which these mechanisms are staged, or are mutually exclusive of one another.

In order to demonstrate the utility of investing further time and energy in pursuit of these two goals (namely, articulating an accountability benchmark and mapping out the dynamics of an accountability system), this book includes two chapters which take the theoretical discussion of deficits and overloads into the real world. Chapter 8 adopted a hypothetical benchmark of accountability, which provided assumed answers to each of the accountability questions across the various rationales of transparency, control, redress, desert and deterrence. It then deployed that hypothetical benchmark in the context of three scenarios, in the attempt to identify potential accountability deficits and overloads in the context of government corruption, unlawful detention and loss caused by misleading government advice. Chapter 11 then took this analysis a step further, by outlining the features of, and relationships between, the mechanisms that were brought to bear in these scenarios. This hypothetical analysis provided a foundation to draw a number of tentative conclusions about the task of identifying accountability deficits and overloads.

First, the hypothetical reinforced the primary point made in Part II of this book, namely, the degree of difficulty involved in crafting a benchmark of accountability. The hypothetical benchmark purported to offer answers to each of the various questions of *who* should be accountable *to whom* and so on for the purposes of the various rationales of accountability. The assumptions adopted for this purpose demonstrate the inherent complexity, and perhaps impossibility, of defining such a benchmark. This is evident, for example, in the choice to adopt the application of 'weak sanctions' to 'soft targets' as a requirement for the purposes of the deterrence rationale. Taking this position denies any role for punitive sanctions as a deterrence measure, which is a view that many would disagree with. Further, the hypothetical benchmark was framed in deliberately general terms, for example indicating that the control rationale was relevant to contain the 'unlawful' exercise of public power, and the redress rationale was relevant to repair 'harm'. However, in order to apply this benchmark in practice, it would be necessary to drill further into these high-level labels and to specify the content of unlawfulness, harm and so on. Unless we can describe a benchmark of accountability in sufficiently detailed terms, its application for the purposes of identifying potential accountability deficits and overloads produces more questions than it offers answers. A further difficulty of framing an accountability benchmark which became evident was that, in a number of areas, the failure of a mechanism to 'bite' in the required manner was not necessarily attributable to a failing in the structure of the mechanism, but was due to external choices which limited its sphere of operation. So, for instance, Mr Taylor's failure to obtain redress in his false imprisonment claim might be better viewed as a reflection of the choice made by the Australian Commonwealth Parliament to confer wide-ranging powers of detention on immigration officials, rather than as an accountability shortfall in the structure of the false imprisonment tort.

Secondly, this book has demonstrated that if we adopt a variety of (potentially competing) rationales for accountability, we must in turn accept that accountability must be supported via a range of mechanisms. If we insist on multiple accountability functions being served by a single mechanism, we will find that our mechanism is internally conflicted, failing to perform any function to the degree anticipated by the benchmark. A number of examples of this have been highlighted in this book, including between the transparency and deterrence rationales (i.e. opening all ombudsman investigations to public scrutiny might negatively impact agencies' inclination to co-operate in respect of recommendations for reform), and between the desert and deterrence rationales (i.e. decreasing the punitive character of criminal sanctions with a view to bringing criminal prosecutions in line with the expectations of the deterrence rationale would potentially remove the core condemnatory feature implicit in the desert rationale). Rather than expecting a mechanism to pull in opposite directions at the same time, a better approach would be to allow multiple mechanisms to serve the various functions of accountability. As demonstrated in Chapter 8, most mechanisms aligned well with one or two rationales for accountability, but fell short of meeting the expectations of others.

Thirdly, any conclusions drawn in the analysis of a single mechanism can only ever stand as a tentative conclusion as to the potential presence of accountability deficits and overloads. For instance, potential accountability deficits were identified in looking at the operation of the New South Wales Independent Commission Against Corruption (ICAC) in Mr Obeid's corruption investigation, as that mechanism failed to deliver on the condemnatory requirements of the desert rationale. However, it was not possible to reach a firm view about whether this was an accountability deficit without appreciating how this mechanism fits into the wider accountability system. As this scenario demonstrated, the desert requirements were delivered by Mr Obeid's criminal prosecution for the offence of misconduct in public office, meaning that no deficit arose in that case. It is only after we look at all applicable mechanisms in a holistic manner that we can identify areas of the benchmark that remain unfulfilled (potential deficit), and areas that are addressed in an excessive manner (potential overload).

Finally, it is not possible to appreciate whether potential gaps and overlaps identified in the system are accountability deficits and overloads without engaging in a critical analysis of the manner in which the system works together as a whole. Chapter 11 demonstrated that some of the potential sources of concern arising in Chapter 8 were ameliorated when approached on a systemic level. Rather than representing a multiplicity of accountability sources operating at random, a more nuanced analysis revealed varying features and relationship dynamics between them.

Notwithstanding the rhetorical appeal of the concept of accountability and claims of accountability deficit and overload, much work remains to be done if we wish to give these ideas a firm foundation. The core problem highlighted in this book is that in order to make good a claim of either not enough, or too much, accountability, we need to be more prescriptive about what 'enough accountability' looks like. This draws us into complex normative territory and unresolved legal and philosophical debates about the nature of government and what we demand of it. These large questions are not of a kind that readily admits answers, but if there remains merit in searching for an ideal accountability balance, we must be willing to confront these issues head on.

BIBLIOGRAPHY

Ackerman, Bruce, 'The New Separation of Powers' (2000) 113 *Harvard Law Review* 633

Alder, John, 'Misconduct in Public Office: Modernising the Law' [2014] *Public Law* 369

Alexander, Larry, Kimberly Kessler Ferzan and Stephen Morse, *Crime and Culpability: A Theory of Criminal Law* (Cambridge University Press, 2009)

Allan, Alfred, 'Functional Apologies in Law' (2008) 15 *Psychiatry, Psychology and Law* 369

Allison, JWF (ed.), *The Oxford Edition of Dicey* (Volume 1, Oxford University Press, 2013)

Appleby, Gabrielle, Alexander Reilly and Laura Grenfell, *Australian Public Law* (3rd ed., Oxford University Press, 2019)

Aronson, Mark, 'Jurisdictional Error without the Tears' in Matthew Groves and HP Lee (eds.), *Australian Administrative Law: Fundamentals, Principles and Doctrines* (Cambridge University Press, 2007) 330

  'Public Law Values in the Common Law' in Mark Elliott and David Feldman (eds.), *The Cambridge Companion to Public Law* (Cambridge University Press, 2015) 134

Aronson, Mark, Matthew Groves and Greg Weeks, *Judicial Review of Administrative Action and Government Liability* (6th ed., Thomson Reuters, 2017)

Australian Law Reform Commission, *Managing Justice: A Review of the Federal Civil Justice System* (Report No 89, 2000)

Australian and New Zealand Ombudsman Association, *Essential Criteria for Describing a Body as an Ombudsman: Policy Statement Endorsed by the Members of the ANZOA* (February 2010) <http://www.anzoa.com.au/assets/anzoa-policy-statement_ombudsman_essential-criteria.pdf> accessed 10 January 2019

Baer, Miriam H, 'Choosing Punishment' (2012) 92 *Boston University Law Review* 577

Barendrecht, Maurits, 'Rule of Law, Measuring and Accountability: Problems to Be Solved Bottom Up' (2011) 3 *Hague Journal on the Rule of Law* 281

Barker, Kit et al, *The Law of Torts in Australia* (5th ed., Oxford University Press, 2012)

Barnard, Frederick, *Democratic Legitimacy: Plural Values and Political Power* (McGill-Queen's University Press, 2001)

Beaton-Wells, Caron, 'Judicial Review of Migration Decisions: Life after *S157*' (2005) 33 *Federal Law Review* 141

Behn, Robert D, *Rethinking Democratic Accountability* (Brookings Institution Press, 2001)

Bittner, Thomas, 'Punishment for Criminal Attempts: A Legal Perspective on the Problem of Moral Luck' (2008) 38 *Canadian Journal of Philosophy* 51

Black, Julia, 'Constructing and Contesting Legitimacy and Accountability in Polycentric Regulatory Regimes' (2008) 2 *Regulation and Governance* 137

Blackstone, William, *Commentaries on the Laws of England* (Clarendon Press, 1765–69)

Boughey, Janina, 'Re-evaluating the Doctrine of Deference in Australian Administrative Law' (2017) 45(4) *Federal Law Review* 597

Boughey, Janina, Ellen Rock and Greg Weeks, *Government Liability: Principles and Remedies* (LexisNexis, 2019)

Boughey, Janina and Greg Weeks, '"Officers of the Commonwealth" in the Private Sector: Can the High Court Review Outsourced Exercises of Power?' (2013) 36 *University of New South Wales Law Journal* 316

'Government Accountability as a "Constitutional Value"' in Rosalind Dixon (ed.), *Australian Constitutional Values* (Hart Publishing, 2017) 99

Boughey, Janina and Lisa Burton Crawford, 'Reconsidering *R (on the application of Cart) v Upper Tribunal* and the Rationale for Jurisdictional Error' [2017] *Public Law* 592

Bovens, Mark, *The Quest for Responsibility: Accountability and Citizenship in Complex Organisations* (Cambridge University Press, 1998)

'Public Accountability' in Ewan Ferlie, Laurence Lynn Jr and Christopher Pollitt (eds.), *The Oxford Handbook of Public Management* (Oxford University Press, 2005) 182

'Analysing and Assessing Accountability: A Conceptual Framework' (2007) 13 *European Law Journal* 447

'Two Concepts of Accountability: Accountability as a Virtue and as a Mechanism' (2010) 33 *West European Politics* 946

Bovens, Mark, Deirdre Curtin and Paul 't Hart, 'Studying the Real World of EU Accountability: Framework and Design' in Mark Bovens, Deirdre Curtin and Paul 't Hart (eds.), *The Real World of EU Accountability: What Deficit?* (Oxford University Press, 2010) 31

(eds.), *The Real World of EU Accountability: What Deficit?* (Oxford University Press, 2010)

Bovens, Mark and Thomas Schillemans, 'Meaningful Accountability' in Mark Bovens, Robert E Goodin and Thomas Schillemans (eds.), *The Oxford Handbook of Public Accountability* (Oxford University Press, 2014) 673

Bovens, Mark, Thomas Schillemans and Paul 't Hart, 'Does Public Accountability Work? An Assessment Tool' (2008) 86 *Public Administration* 225

Braithwaite, John, 'On Speaking Softly and Carrying Big Sticks: Neglected Dimensions of a Republican Separation of Powers' (1997) 47 *University of Toronto Law Journal* 305

'Accountability and Responsibility through Restorative Justice' in Michael Dowdle (ed.), *Public Accountability: Designs, Dilemmas and Experiences* (Cambridge University Press, 2006) 33

'Responsive Regulation and Developing Economies' (2006) 34 *World Development* 884

Brand-Ballard, Jeffrey, 'Moral Emotions and Culpability for Resultant Harm' (2011) 42 *Rutgers Law Journal* 315

Brandsma, Gijs Jan and Thomas Schillemans, 'The Accountability Cube: Measuring Accountability' (2013) 23 *Journal of Public Administration Research and Theory* 953

Brehm, Jack Williams, *A Theory of Psychological Reactance* (Academic Press, 1966)

Brennan, H Geoffrey et al, *Explaining Norms* (Oxford University Press, 2013)

Brooks, Thom, *Punishment* (Routledge, 2012)

Brown, AJ, 'Putting Administrative Law Back into Integrity and Putting Integrity Back into Administrative Law' (2006) 53 *AIAL Forum* 32

'The Integrity Branch: A "System", an "Industry", or a Sensible Emerging Fourth Arm of Government?' in Matthew Groves (ed.), *Modern Administrative Law in Australia: Concepts and Context* (Cambridge University Press, 2014) 301

Brown, L Neville and John Bell, *French Administrative Law* (5th ed., Oxford University Press, 1998)

Campbell, Enid, 'Private Claims on Public Funds' (1969) 3 *University of Tasmania Law Review* 138

'Enforcement of Public Duties Which Are Impossible to Perform' (2003) 10 *Australian Journal of Administrative Law* 201

Cane, Peter, 'Standing Up for the Public' [1995] *Public Law* 276

An Anatomy of Tort Law (Hart Publishing, 1997)

'Damages in Public Law' (1999) 9 *Otago Law Review* 489

'Mens Rea in Tort Law' (2000) 20 *Oxford Journal of Legal Studies* 533

Responsibility in Law and Morality (Hart Publishing, 2002)

Administrative Tribunals and Adjudication (Hart Publishing, 2009)

'Tort Law and Public Functions' in John Oberdiek (ed.), *Philosophical Foundations of the Law of Torts* (Oxford University Press, 2014) 148

Cane, Peter, Leighton McDonald and Kristen Rundle, *Principles of Administrative Law* (3rd ed., Oxford University Press, 2018)

Commonwealth Ombudsman, *To Compensate or Not to Compensate* (September 1999)

Department of Immigration and Multicultural Affairs: Administration of s 501 of the Migration Act 1958 as It Applies to Long-Term Residents (Report No 1, February 2006)

Making Things Right: Department of Education and Training, Compensation for Errors Made by Contracted Service Providers (Report No 1, March 2015)

Annual Report 2014–15 (October 2015)

Annual Report 2017–18 (October 2018)

Considine, Mark, 'The End of the Line? Accountable Governance in the Age of Networks, Partnerships, and Joined-up Services' (2002) 15(1) *Governance* 21

Craig, Paul, 'Compensation in Public Law' (1980) 96 *Law Quarterly Review* 413

Creyke, Robin, 'An "Integrity" Branch' (2012) 70 *AIAL Forum* 33

Cugueró-Escofet, Natàlia, Marion Fortin and Miguel-Angel Canela, 'Righting the Wrong for Third Parties: How Monetary Compensation, Procedure Changes and Apologies Can Restore Justice for Observers of Injustice' (2014) 122 *Journal of Business Ethics* 253

Dahl, Robert, 'The Concept of Power' (1957) 2 *Behavioral Science* 201

de Bruijn, Hans, 'Performance Measurement in the Public Sector: Strategies to Cope with the Risks of Performance Measurement' (2002) 15 *International Journal of Public Sector Management* 578

Department of Finance (Cth), *Requests for Discretionary Financial Assistance under the Public Governance, Performance and Accountability Act 2013* (Resource Management Guide No 401, April 2018)

Scheme for Compensation for Detriment Caused by Defective Administration (Resource Management Guide No 409, November 2018)

Dewees, Donald, David Duff and Michael Trebilcock, *Exploring the Domain of Accident Law: Taking the Facts Seriously* (Oxford University Press, 1996)

Dolinko, David, 'Punishment' in John Deigh and David Dolinko (eds.), *The Oxford Handbook of Philosophy of Criminal Law* (Oxford University Press, 2011) 403

Douglas, Roger, 'Standing' in Matthew Groves and HP Lee (eds.), *Australian Administrative Law: Fundamentals, Principles and Doctrines* (Cambridge University Press, 2007) 158

Dubnick, Melvin J, *Seeking Salvation for Accountability* (Annual Meeting of the American Political Science Association, Boston, 29 August–1 September 2002)

'Accountability and Ethics: Reconsidering the Relationships' (2003) 6 *International Journal of Organization Theory and Behavior* 405

'Accountability and the Promise of Performance: In Search of the Mechanisms' (2005) 28 *Public Performance and Management Review* 376

'Accountability as a Cultural Keyword' in Mark Bovens, Robert Goodin and Thomas Schillemans (eds.), *The Oxford Handbook of Public Accountability* (Oxford University Press, 2014) 23

Dyzenhaus, David and Michael Taggart, 'Reasoned Decisions and Legal Theory' in Douglas Edlin (ed.), *Common Law Theory* (Cambridge University Press, 2007) 134

Edelman, Justice James, Jason NE Varuhas and Simon Colton, *McGregor on Damages* (20th ed., Thomson Reuters, 2017)

Elliot, Brogan, 'The Hidden Influences That Limit Governmental Independence: Controlling the Ombudsman's Apparent Independence' (2013) 21 *Australian Journal of Administrative Law* 27

Elliott, Mark, 'Ombudsmen, Tribunals, Inquiries: Re-fashioning Accountability Beyond the Courts' in Nicholas Bamforth and Peter Leyland (eds.), *Accountability in the Contemporary Constitution* (Oxford University Press, 2013) 233

Fairgrieve, Duncan, *State Liability in Tort: A Comparative Study* (Oxford University Press, 2003)

Feinberg, Joel, 'The Expressive Function of Punishment' (1965) 49 *The Monist* 397
'Equal Punishment for Failed Attempts: Some Bad but Instructive Arguments Against It' (1995) 37(1) *Arizona Law Review* 117

Feldthusen, Bruce, 'Punitive Damages: Hard Choices and High Stakes' [1998] *New Zealand Law Review* 741

Finer, Herman, 'Better Government Personnel' (1936) 51 *Political Science Quarterly* 569

Finn, Paul, 'Official Misconduct' (1978) 2 *Criminal Law Journal* 307

Fisher, Elizabeth, 'The European Union in the Age of Accountability' (2004) 24 *Oxford Journal of Legal Studies* 495

Fisher, Elizabeth and Jeremy Kirk, 'Still Standing: An Argument for Open Standing in Australia and England' (1997) 71 *Australian Law Journal* 370

Fletcher, George, *A Crime of Self-Defense: Bernhard Goetz and the Law on Trial* (University of Chicago Press, 1988)

Flinders, Matthew, 'The Future and Relevance of Accountability Studies' in Mark Bovens, Robert Goodin and Thomas Schillemans (eds.), *The Oxford Handbook of Public Accountability* (Oxford University Press, 2014) 661

Foster, Michelle, 'An "Alien" by the Barest of Threads – The Legality of the Deportation of Long-Term Residents from Australia' (2009) 33(2) *Melbourne University Law Review* 483

French, Chief Justice Robert, 'Administrative Law in Australia: Themes and Values Revisited' in Matthew Groves (ed.), *Modern Administrative Law in Australia: Concepts and Context* (Cambridge University Press, 2014)

Friedrich, Carl, *Problems of the American Public Service* (McGraw-Hill, 1935)

Gillies, Peter, *Criminal Law* (4th ed., LBC, 1997)

Grant, Ruth and Robert Keohane, 'Accountability and Abuses of Power in World Politics' (2005) 99(1) *American Political Science Review* 29

Groves, Matthew, 'Outsourcing and Non-delegable Duties' (2005) 16 *Public Law Review* 265

'Outsourcing and s 75(v) of the Constitution' (2011) 22 *Public Law Review* 3

Groves, Matthew and Greg Weeks, 'Substantive (Procedural) Review in Australia' in Hanna Wilberg and Mark Elliott (eds.), *The Scope and Intensity of Substantive Review: Traversing Taggart's Rainbow* (Hart Publishing, 2015) 133

Halachmi, Arie, 'Accountability Overloads' in Mark Bovens, Robert Goodin and Thomas Schillemans (eds.), *The Oxford Handbook of Public Accountability* (Oxford University Press, 2014) 560

Halliday, Simon and Colin Scott, 'Administrative Justice' in Peter Cane and Herbert Kritzer (eds.), *The Oxford Handbook of Empirical Legal Research* (Oxford University Press, 2010)

Handley, Justice KR, '*Anshun* Today' (1997) 71 *Australian Law Journal* 934

Harlow, Carol, *Accountability in the European Union* (Oxford University Press, 2002)

'Public Law and Popular Justice' (2002) 65 *Modern Law Review* 1

State Liability: Tort Law and Beyond (Oxford University Press, 2004)

Understanding Tort Law (3rd ed., Sweet and Maxwell, 2005)

'A Punitive Role for Tort Law?' in Linda Pearson, Carol Harlow and Michael Taggart (eds.), *Administrative Law in a Changing State: Essays in Honour of Mark Aronson* (Hart Publishing, 2008) 247

'Accountability as a Value in Global Governance and for Global Administrative Law' in Gordon Anthony et al (eds.), *Values in Global Administrative Law* (Hart Publishing, 2011) 173

'Accountability and Constitutional Law' in Mark Bovens, Robert Goodin and Thomas Schillemans (eds.), *The Oxford Handbook of Public Accountability* (Oxford University Press, 2014) 195

Harlow, Carol and Richard Rawlings, 'Promoting Accountability in Multilevel Governance: A Network Approach' (2007) 13 *European Law Journal* 542

Hart, HLA, *The Concept of Law* (Clarendon Press, 1961)

Punishment and Responsibility: Essays in the Philosophy of Law (2nd ed., Oxford University Press, 2008)

Hart, HLA and Tony Honoré, *Causation in the Law* (2nd ed., Oxford University Press, 1985)

Heydon, JD, *Cross on Evidence* (11th ed., LexisNexis, 2017)

Hogg, Peter, Patrick Monahan and Wade Wright, *Liability of the Crown* (4th ed., Carswell, 2011)

Honoré, Tony, *Responsibility and Fault* (Hart Publishing, 1999)

Horder, Jeremy, *Criminal Misconduct in Office: Law and Politics* (Oxford University Press, 2018)

Hume, David, 'Of the Independency of Parliament' in Eugene F Miller (ed.), *Essays, Moral, Political, and Literary* (Liberty Fund, 1987) 42

Jackson, Michael, 'Responsibility versus Accountability in the Friedrich-Finer Debate' (2009) 15 *Journal of Management History* 66

Jaffe, Louis, 'Standing to Secure Judicial Review: Public Actions' (1961) 74 *Harvard Law Review* 1265

Jenke, Libby and Scott A Huettel, 'Issues or Identity? Cognitive Foundations of Voter Choice' (2016) 20(11) *Trends in Cognitive Sciences* 794

Kadish, Sanford, 'Foreword: The Criminal Law and the Luck of the Draw' (1994) 84 *Journal of Criminal Law and Criminology* 679

Kelly, Janet, 'The Accountability Trap' (2007) 96(3) *National Civic Review* 46

King, Jeff, 'The Instrumental Value of Legal Accountability' in Nicholas Bamforth and Peter Leyland (eds.), *Accountability in the Contemporary Constitution* (Oxford University Press, 2013) 124

Kirby, Justice Michael, 'Judicial Accountability in Australia' (2003) 6 *Legal Ethics* 41

Kirchengast, Tyrone, *The Victim in Criminal Law and Justice* (Palgrave Macmillan, 2006)

Koppell, Jonathan, 'Pathologies of Accountability: ICANN and the Challenge of "Multiple Accountabilities Disorder"' (2005) 65 *Public Administration Review* 94

Latham, The Hon Megan, 'Statement Regarding the Independent Commission Against Corruption Amendment Bill 2016' (15 November 2016)

Lau, Richard R, Mona S Kleinberg and Tessa M Ditonto, 'Measuring Voter Decision Strategies in Political Behavior and Public Opinion Research' (2018) 82(1) *Public Opinion Quarterly* 911

Lee, HP and Enid Campbell, *The Australian Judiciary* (2nd ed., Cambridge University Press, 2012)

Leeming, Mark, 'Standing to Seek Injunctions against Officers of the Commonwealth' (2006) 1 *Journal of Equity* 3

Lewis, David, 'The Punishment That Leaves Something to Chance' (1989) 18 *Philosophy and Public Affairs* 53

Linden, Allen, 'Tort Law as Ombudsman' (1973) 51 *Canadian Bar Review* 155

Lusty, David, 'Revival of the Common Law Offence of Misconduct in Public Office' (2014) 38 *Criminal Law Journal* 337

Mashaw, Jerry, 'Accountability and Institutional Design: Some Thoughts on the Grammar of Governance' in Michael Dowdle (ed.), *Public Accountability: Designs, Dilemmas and Experiences* (Cambridge University Press, 2006) 115

McLean, Janet, *Searching for the State in British Legal Thought: Competing Conceptions of the Public Sphere* (Cambridge University Press, 2012)

McMillan, John, 'Re-thinking the Separation of Powers' (2010) 38 *Federal Law Review* 423

Mercurio, Bryan and George Williams, 'Australian Electoral Law: "Free and Fair"?' (2004) 32 *Federal Law Review* 365

Mill, John Stuart, *On Liberty* (Cambridge University Press, 1989)

Moore, Michael, *Placing Blame: A General Theory of the Criminal Law* (Clarendon Press, 1997)

Causation and Responsibility: An Essay in Law, Morals, and Metaphysics (Oxford University Press, 2009)

Moore, Michael and Heidi Hurd, 'Punishing the Awkward, the Stupid, the Weak, and the Selfish: The Culpability of Negligence' (2011) 5 *Criminal Law and Philosophy* 147

Mosher, Frederick C, 'The Changing Responsibilities and Tactics of the Federal Government' (1980) 40 *Public Administration Review* 541

Mulgan, Richard, '"Accountability": An Ever-Expanding Concept?' (2000) 78 *Public Administration* 555

Holding Power to Account: Accountability in Modern Democracies (Palgrave Macmillan, 2003)

'One Cheer for Hierarchy – Accountability in Disjointed Governance' (2003) 55(2) *Political Science* 6

'Government Accountability for Outsourced Services' (2006) 65(2) *Australian Journal of Public Administration* 48

'Accountability Deficits' in Mark Bovens, Robert Goodin and Thomas Schillemans (eds.), *The Oxford Handbook of Public Accountability* (Oxford University Press, 2014) 545

Making Open Government Work (Palgrave Macmillan, 2014)

Mulgan, Richard and John Uhr, 'Accountability and Governance' in Glyn Davis and Patrick Weller (eds.), *Are You Being Served? State, Citizens and Governance* (Allen and Unwin, 2001) 152

Nagel, Thomas, *Mortal Questions* (Cambridge University Press, 1979)

New South Wales, *Parliamentary Debates*, Legislative Assembly, 26 May 1988 (Nicholas Greiner, Premier, Treasurer and Minister for Ethnic Affairs)

Parliamentary Debates, Legislative Assembly, 15 November 2016 (Paul Lynch, Member for Liverpool)

NSW Independent Commission Against Corruption, *Investigation into the Conduct of Ian Macdonald, Edward Obeid Senior, Moses Obeid and Others* (July 2013)

Reducing the Opportunities and Incentives for Corruption in the State's Management of Coal Resources (October 2013)

Operation Cyrus: Investigation into the Conduct of The Hon Edward Obeid MLC and Others Concerning Circular Quay Retail Lease Policy (June 2014)

Annual Report: 2014–15 (October 2015)

Annual Report: 2015–16 (October 2016)

Annual Report: 2016–17 (October 2017)

Public Inquiry Procedural Guidelines (February 2018)

O'Connell, Lenahan, 'Program Accountability as an Emergent Property: The Role of Stakeholders in a Program's Field' (2005) 65 *Public Administration Review* 85

Oliver, Dawn, *Government in the United Kingdom: The Search for Accountability, Effectiveness, and Citizenship* (Open University Press, 1991)

'Standards of Conduct in Public Life – What Standards?' [1995] *Public Law* 497

O'Malley, Pat, *The Currency of Justice: Fines and Damages in Consumer Societies* (Routledge-Cavendish, 2009)

'Theorizing Fines' (2009) 11 *Punishment and Society* 67

O'Neill, Onora, *A Question of Trust* (Cambridge University Press, 2002)

Panetta, Rossana, 'Damages for Wrongful Administrative Decisions' (1999) 6 *Australian Journal of Administrative Law* 163

Pannam, Clifford, 'Felonious Tort Rule' (1965) 39 *Australian Law Journal* 164

Parliamentary Privilege and Ethics Committee, Legislative Assembly (NSW), *Inquiry into matters arising from the ICAC report entitled "Reducing the opportunities and incentives for corruption in the State's management of coal resources"* (July 2014)

Review of the Code of Conduct for Members (June 2018)

Philp, Mark, 'Delimiting Democratic Accountability' (2009) 57 *Political Studies* 28

Plant, Jeremy, 'Carl J Friedrich on Responsibility and Authority' (2011) 71 *Public Administration Review* 471

Pollitt, Christopher, *The Essential Public Manager* (Open University Press, 2003)

Privileges Committee, Legislative Council (NSW), *Recommendations of the ICAC regarding aspects of the Code of Conduct for Members, the interest disclosure regime and a parliamentary investigator* (June 2014)

Review of the Members' Code of Conduct 2018 (November 2018)

Rock, Ellen, 'Accountability: A Core Public Law Value?' (2017) 24 *Australian Journal of Administrative Law* 189

'Fault and Accountability in Public Law' in Mark Elliott, Jason NE Varuhas and Shona Wilson Stark (eds.), *The Unity of Public Law? Doctrinal, Theoretical and Comparative Perspectives* (Hart Publishing, 2018) 171

'Misfeasance in Public Office: A Tort in Tension' (2019) 43(1) *Melbourne University Law Review* 337

'Resolving Conflicts at the Interface of Public and Private Law' (2020) 94 *Australian Law Journal* 381

Rock, Ellen and Greg Weeks, 'Monetary Awards for Public Law Wrongs: Australia's Resistant Legal Landscape' (2018) 41(4) *University of New South Wales Law Journal* 1159

Roughley, Fiona, 'Royal Commissions and Contempt of Court: The Effect of Curial Proceedings' (2015) 38 *University of New South Wales Law Journal* 1123

Schedler, Andreas, 'Conceptualizing Accountability' in Andreas Schedler, Larry Diamond and Marc F Plattner (eds.), *The Self-Restraining State: Power and Accountability in New Democracies* (Lynne Rienner Publishers, 1999) 13

Schuck, Peter H, *Suing Government: Citizen Remedies for Official Wrongs* (Yale University Press, 1983)

Scott, Colin, 'Accountability in the Regulatory State' (2000) 27 *Journal of Law and Society* 38

Sinclair, Amanda, 'The Chameleon of Accountability: Forms and Discourses' (1995) 20 *Accounting, Organizations and Society* 219

Spigelman, Justice JJ, 'The Integrity Branch of Government' (2004) 78 *Australian Law Journal* 724

Stapleton, Jane, 'Law, Causation and Common Sense' (1988) 8 *Oxford Journal of Legal Studies* 111

'Duty of Care: Peripheral Parties and Alternative Opportunities for Deterrence' (1995) 111 *Law Quarterly Review* 301

'Civil Prosecutions Part 1: Double Jeopardy and Abuse of Process' (1999) 7 *Torts Law Journal* 244

'Civil Prosecutions Part 2: Civil Claims for Killing or Rape' (2000) 8 *Torts Law Journal* 15

'Perspectives on Causation' in Jeremy Horder (ed.), *Oxford Essays in Jurisprudence (Fourth Series)* (Open University Press, 2000) 61

'Choosing What We Mean by "Causation" in the Law' (2008) 73 *Missouri Law Review* 433

Stephen, James Fitzjames, *A History of the Criminal Law of England* (Macmillan, 1883)

Stone, Bruce, 'Administrative Accountability in the "Westminster" Democracies: Towards a New Conceptual Framework' (1995) 8 *Governance* 505

Stone's Justices Manual (40th ed., 1908)

Strom, Kaare, 'Parliamentary Democracy and Delegation' in Kaare Strom, Wolfgang Muller and Torbjorn Bergman (eds.), *Delegation and Accountability in Parliamentary Democracies* (Oxford University Press, 2003) 55

Stuhmcke, Anita, 'Australian Ombudsmen: Drafting a Blueprint for Reform' (2014) 24 *Australian Journal of Administrative Law* 1

'Ombuds Can, Ombuds Can't, Ombuds Should, Ombuds Shan't: A Call to Improve Evaluation of the Ombudsman Institution' in Marc Hertogh and Richard Kirkham (eds.), *Research Handbook on the Ombudsman* (Edward Elgar Publishing, 2018) 415

Taggart, Michael, 'The Province of Administrative Law Determined' in Michael Taggart (ed.), *The Province of Administrative Law* (Hart Publishing, 1997) 1

Turpin, Colin, *British Government and the Constitution: Text, Cases and Materials* (Weidenfeld and Nicolson, 1990)

Uhr, John, *Terms of Trust: Arguments over Ethics in Australian Government* (UNSW Press, 2005)

Varuhas, Jason NE, *Damages and Human Rights* (Hart Publishing, 2016)
'The Development of the Damages Remedy under the New Zealand Bill of Rights Act 1990: From Torts to Administrative Law' [2016] *New Zealand Law Review* 213

Vesely, Arnost, 'Accountability in Central and Eastern Europe: Concept and Reality' (2013) 79 *International Review of Administrative Sciences* 310

Victorian Ombudsman, *Apologies* (April 2017)

Vines, Prue, 'Apologising to Avoid Liability: Cynical Civility or Practical Morality?' (2005) 27 *Sydney Law Review* 483

Walen, Alec, 'Proof Beyond a Reasonable Doubt: A Balanced Retributive Account' (2015) 76 *Louisiana Law Review* 355

Weeks, Greg, *Soft Law and Public Authorities: Remedies and Reform* (Hart Publishing, 2016)

Wille, Anchrit, 'The European Commission's Accountability Paradox' in Mark Bovens, Deirdre Curtin and Paul 't Hart (eds.), *The Real World of EU Accountability: What Deficit?* (Oxford University Press, 2010) 63

Wright, Richard, 'Causation, Responsibility, Risk, Probability, Naked Statistics, and Proof: Pruning the Bramble Bush by Clarifying the Concepts' (1988) 73 *Iowa Law Review* 1001

Zaibert, Leo, *Punishment and Retribution* (Ashgate Publishing, 2006)

Zellick, G, 'Bribery of Members of Parliament and the Criminal Law' [1979] *Public Law* 31

INDEX

Printed by Printforce, United Kingdom